The Canterbury and York Society

GENERAL EDITOR: DR P. HOSKIN

ISSN 0262–995X

DIOCESE OF COVENTRY AND LICHFIELD

CANTERBURY AND YORK SOCIETY VOL. XCVII

The Register of

Walter Langton

BISHOP OF COVENTRY AND LICHFIELD

1296–1321

VOLUME II

EDITED BY

J. B. HUGHES

The Canterbury and York Society

The Boydell Press

2007

First published 2007

A Canterbury and York Society publication
published by The Boydell Press
an imprint of Boydell & Brewer Ltd
PO Box 9, Woodbridge, Suffolk IP12 3DF, UK
and of Boydell & Brewer Inc.
668 Mt Hope Avenue, Rochester, NY 14620, USA
website: www.boydellandbrewer.com

ISBN 0 907239 67 6
ISBN 978 0 907239 67 3

A CIP catalogue record for this book is available
from the British Library

Details of previous volumes are available from Boydell & Brewer Ltd

This publication is printed on acid-free paper

Typeset by Pru Harrison, Hacheston, Suffolk
Printed in Great Britain by
Antony Rowe Ltd, Chippenham

CONTENTS

ACKNOWLEDGEMENTS

The register is published by the kind permission of the Diocesan Registrar at Lichfield. In addition to the thanks expressed in Volume I, I wish to thank Dr Philippa Hoskin for her helpful comments and for expertly guiding this volume to publication. I also wish to thank Professor Jeffrey Denton for his great help in resolving place-name queries.

BIBLIOGRAPHICAL ABBREVIATIONS

Beardwood, *Records*	*Records of the trial of Walter Langeton, bishop of Coventry and Lichfield, 1307–1312*, ed. A. Beardwood (Camden, 4th series, 6, 1969).
Beardwood, 'Trial'	A. Beardwood, 'The trial of Walter Langton, bishop of Lichfield, 1307–1312, *Transactions of the American Philosophical Society*, 54, part 3 (1964), 5–45.
BIHR	Borthwick Institute of Historical Research.
BL	British Library.
BRUC	A.B. Emden, *A biographical register of the university of Cambridge to A.D. 1500* (Cambridge, 1963).
BRUO	A.B. Emden, *A biographical register of the university of Oxford to A.D. 1500* (Oxford, 1957–9).
CCR	*Calendar of Close Rolls.*
CChR	*Calendar of Charter Rolls.*
CChW	*Calendar of Chancery Warrants.*
CDRS	*Calendar of documents relating to Scotland*, i–iv, ed. J.S. Bain (Edinburgh, 1881–8).
CFR	*Calendar of Fine Rolls.*
Churchill, *Canterbury administration*	I.J. Churchill, *Canterbury administration: the administrative machinery of the archbishopric of Canterbury illustrated from original records* (London, 1933).
Councils and synods	*Councils and synods, with other documents relating to the English church*, ed. F.M. Powicke, C.R. Cheney (Oxford, 1964), II, i, *1205–65*; II, ii, *1265–1313*.
CPL	*Calendar of Papal Letters.*
CPR	*Calendar of Patent Rolls.*
CYS	Publications of the Canterbury and York Society.
Denton, *Winchelsey*	J.H. Denton, *Robert Winchelsey and the crown 1294–1313* (Cambridge, 1980).
DNB	*Dictionary of national biography* (1885–1901).
Fasti	J. Le Neve, *Fasti ecclesiae Anglicanae 1300–1541* (London, 1962–7).
Foedera	*Foedera, conventiones, litterae et acta publica*, ed. T. Rymer, 4 vols. (Record Commission, 1816–69).
Foss, *Judges*	E. Foss, *The judges of England* (London, 1848–64), iii.
Foulds, *Thurgarton Cartulary*	*The Thurgarton Cartulary*, ed. T. Foulds (Stamford, 1994).
HBC	*Handbook of British chronology*, 3rd edn., ed. E.B. Fryde, D.E. Greenway, S. Porter, I. Roy (Royal Historical Society, 1986).

Hughes, 'Account roll'	Jill B. Hughes, 'A 1301 sequestrator-general's account roll for the diocese of Coventry and Lichfield', *Chronology, conquest and conflict in medieval England* (Camden, 5th series, 10, 1997), 105–39.
Hughes, 'Clergy list'	Jill B. Hughes, 'A 1319 clergy list of the Tamworth and Tutbury deanery in the diocese of Coventry and Lichfield', *Staffordshire Studies*, 6 (1994), 1–25.
Hughes, 'Episcopate'	Jill B. Hughes, 'The episcopate of Walter Langton, bishop of Coventry and Lichfield, 1296–1321, with a calendar of his register' (University of Nottingham unpublished Ph.D. thesis, 3 vols., 1992).
Hughes, 'Family'	Jill B. Hughes, 'Walter Langton, bishop of Coventry and Lichfield, 1296–1321: his family background', *Nottingham Medieval Studies*, 35 (1991), 70–6.
Hughes, 'Register'	Jill B. Hughes, 'Walter Langton, bishop of Coventry and Lichfield, 1296–1321, and his register', *Staffordshire Studies*, 9 (1997), 1–8.
JEH	*Journal of Ecclesiastical History*
LJRO	Lichfield Joint Record Office
Lunt, *Financial relations*	W.E. Lunt, *Financial relations of the papacy with England to 1327* (Cambridge, Mass., 1939).
Matthew, *Monasteries*	D. Matthew, *The Norman monasteries and their English possessions* (Oxford, 1962).
MRA	*The great register of Lichfield cathedral known as Magnum Registrum Album*, ed. H.E. Savage (William Salt Archaeological Society, 1924).
NA	National Archives. *Formerly* Public Record Office (PRO).
Parl. Writs	*Parliamentary writs and writs of military summons*, ed. F. Palgrave, 2 vols. (Recond Commission, 1827–34).
Reg. Cobham	*The register of Thomas de Cobham, bishop of Worcester, 1317–1327*, ed. E.H. Pearce (Worcerstershire Historical Society, 40, 1930).
Reg. Gandavo	*Registrum Simonis de Gandavo, diocesis Saresberiensis, A.D. 1297–1315*, ed, C.R.T, Flower, M.C.B. Dawes (CYS, 40, 41, 1934).
Reg. Greenfield	*The register of William Greenfield, lord archbishop of York, 1306–1315*, ed. W. Brown & A. Hamilton Thompson (Surtees Society, 145, 149, 151, 152, 153, 1931–1940).
Reg. Halton	*The register of John de Halton, bishop of Carlisle A.D. 1292–1324*, ed. W.N. Thompson (CYS, 12, 13, 1906–13).
Reg. Martival	*The register of Roger Martival, bishop of Salisbury, 1315–30*, i, ed. K. Edwards, ii, ed. C.R. Elrington, iii, ed. S. Reynolds, iv. ed. D.M. Owen (CYS, 55–9, 68, 1959–75).
Reg. Romeyn	*The register of John le Romeyn, lord archbishop of York, 1286–1296*, ed. W. Brown (Surtees Society, 123, 128, 1913–17).
Reg. Sutton	*The rolls and register of Bishop Oliver Sutton, 1280–1299*, ed. R.M.T. Hill (Lincoln Record Society, 39, 43, 52, 60, 64, 69, 76, 1948–86).

Reg. Winchelsey	*Registrum Roberti Winchelsey Cantuariensis archiepiscopi*, ed. R. Graham (CYS, 51, 52, 1952–6).
Robinson, *Hand list*	D. Robinson, *Staffordshire Record Office cumulative hand list, part 1, Lichfield Joint Record Office: diocesan, probate and church commissioners' records*, 2nd edn. (Staffordshire County Council, 1978).
Smith, *Guide*	David M. Smith, *Guide to Bishops' Registers of England and Wales* (London, Royal Historical Society, 1981).
Storey, *Diocesan administration (1959), (1972)*	R.L. Storey, *Diocesan administration in fifteenth century England* (St. Anthony's Press, York, 1959; 2nd edn. 1972).
TRHS	*Transactions of the Royal Historical Society*
VCH	*Victoria County History*
Worcester Sede Vacante Reg.	*The register of the diocese of Worcester during the vacancy of the see, usually called "Registrum Sede Vacante", 1301–1435*, ed. J.W. Willis Bund (Worcestershire Historical Society, 1897), i.

EDITORIAL METHOD FOR
THE ORDINATION LISTS AND INDEX

In the manuscript multiple presentations of ordinands by the same patron are often bracketed together and the patron is listed once only. Similarly, multiple ordinands from named religious and mendicant houses or orders have those houses and orders bracketed to their names. The calendar thus records such persons linearly and gives the patron, house or order once. The addition of '[patron]' has been inserted in the index if it is otherwise unclear that that person was a patron or an ordinand. The addition of 'A', 'S', 'D' and 'P' to the serial numbers allocated to the ordination lists indicates the orders of acolyte, subdeacon, deacon and priest respectively. When more than one canon, monk or friar from the same house has been ordained to the same minor or holy order at the same service, a numeral in round brackets indicates the number of ordinands. When place-names occur more than once in an ordination list that number too is indicated in round brackets. Canons, monks and friars are entitled *fratres* in the ordination lists. 'Fr.' is not given in the calendar to ordinands from named monastic houses or mendicant orders; the latter are signified by the following abbreviations:

OCarm.	Carmelite Order
OCist.	Cistercian Order
OFM	Franciscan Order
OP	Dominican Order
OSA	Augustinian Order

OTHER ABBREVIATIONS

abp.	archbishop		hosp.	hospital
archd.	archdeacon		jnr.	junior
Aug.	Augustinian		kt.	knight
Ben.	Benedictine		M.	Master
bp.	bishop		port.	portioner of
B.V.M.	Blessed Virgin Mary		preb.	prebendary of
Carm.	Carmelite		prebs.	prebendaries of
cath.	cathedral		Prem.	Premonstratensian
ch.	church		pres.	presented
Cist.	Cistercian		r.	rector of
col., cols.	column, columns		s.	son of
coll.	collegiate		snr.	senior
conv.	convent		t.	title
dioc.	diocese		t. pat.	title of patrimony
dim.	letters dimissory		v.	vicar of
fn.	footnote		vol.	volume
fo., fos.	folio, folios		vols.	volumes

THE REGISTER OF WALTER LANGTON

1285 [Fo. 92] [1]NOMINA ORDINATORUM APUD EKINTON IN VIGILIA TRINITATIS ANNO DOMINI .M^o.CCC^{mo}.[1] [4 June 1300].

[Col. 1] *Subdeacons*

Henry de Leyteford
John de Dodington
Robert de Langeton
William de Stanton, r. Haughton
Richard de Blaby
[2]Rector of Grendon
Rector of Whitnash, [3]in the gift of the chancellor[3]
[M.] Alexander, r. Biddulph[2]
[4]Ralph de Hellesby
William de Holford
John de Egerton[4]
John de Dunbelton, John de Aumesbur', [canons] of Ranton
Thomas de Herberbur', [monk of] Combermere
Adam de Kokeraym, [canon of] Burscough
Adam de Derset, John de Burbache, John de Sutham, [canons] of Arbury
Thomas de Deping, Hugh de Willugby, Robert de Welinghovere, OP
John de Longedon, [monk] of Burton upon Trent
Roger de Assheby, John de Shepesheved, [monks] of [5]Croxd[5]en
Robert de Bello Capite, [canon of] Beauchief[6]
William de Bruers, Nicholas de Snypston, [monks] of Dieulacres[7]
Gilbert de Roucestr', [canon] of Rocester
Fr. Robert de la Dale
Fr. John de Wyly

[Col. 2] *Deacons*

John de Wintringham, [8]he has nothing[8]
Thomas de Appelby, [8]he has nothing[8]
Robert de Coventr'
Richard de Melburn'
Oliver de Trusseley, t. pat.[9]
Robert de Weston
Ralph de Dunchurche
John de Manecestr'
William de Prestebur'
William de Dersett
Philip de Hilkesdon

Simon de Sutton, [8]he does not have the letter but it is being sealed[8]
Simon de Longeyton
John de Sparham
William de Bredeford
Robert de Wolrichton
John de Checkelee
Adam de Sutton
Henry de Bromlee
Ralph de Tunstal
William de Rokeby
Roger de Codinton
Robert de Torleston
Henry de Checkelee
John de Ichinton
William de Wich'
Gilbert de Bardingmor'
Robert, son of Thomas de Medio[10] Wyco
Nicholas de Leges
Henry de Alleslegh'
Richard de Alleslegh
William de Litul Ore
Roger de Roucestr'
William de Halughton
Adam de Shusstok
Richard de Pollesworth
Richard de Hokes

[Col. 3] *Priests*

Henry de Kirkeby, [8]he has the letter[8]
Ralph de Wolveye, [8]he has the letter[8]
Richard de Morton, he has
Henry de Brinkelowe
John de Kirkeby
Robert the vintner of Coventry
William de Prevesthorp, [8]he does not have the letter but it is being sealed[8]
John de Willugby, [8]the letter is being sealed[8]
M. William de Billeslee, v. St. Michael's, Coventry, [8]he has the letter[8]
Walter de Coventr'
William de Elmedon, [8]he has the letter [11]and the chancellor[11] gave it to prior of Coventry's nuncio[8]
Thomas de Coleshull
Alexander de Coleshull
Walter de Horlegh
Robert Trusseley
John de Langeton, r. Finmere, [12]dim. of J[ohn Dalderby],[13] the elect of Lincoln[12]
Roger de Ilkeston
John de Eton
Richard de Lillington, [8]he has and S. de C...[14] received the letter[8]

John de Langeleye
William de Houve
Roger Reynaud
Adam de Seggesleye
Alan de Assheburn
William de Longeyton
Geoffrey de Shulton
Robert de Midilton
William de Tamworth, [8]he has the letter[8]
William de Lillington, [8]the chancellor has given [?the letter] to the subprior of Stone[8]
Robert de Longedon
Nicholas de Kenilleworth
Thomas de Bromelee, [8]he has nothing and [the order] was conferred at the request of prior of Ranton[8]
Thomas de Colleshull
Richard de Southam
John de Norton
Nicholas de Bredford, [8]the chancellor has given two ...[15] at Rant[on][8]

[Fo. 92v col. 1 blank.]

[Col. 2] *Deacons*

Richard de Hereford, r. Pinxton
Simon de Hegham, r. Barton Blount
Thomas de Charneles, port. Condover, [8]he has[8]
Henry de Thurlaston
Philip de Coleshull
Henry Pyn of Biddulph
William de la More of[16] Birmingham
Peter de Cobynton
William de Edihale
M. William de Lancastr', r. Eccleston
   [The rest of col. 2 is blank.]

[Col. 3] *Priests*

John de Cobynton
Simon de Ostchurch
Hugh de Wychenovere
Henry de Staunton
Thomas de Luton
Thomas de Upwell
Richard de Rolleston
Hugh de Eccleshale
Richard de Estlymynton, [8]he has[8]
Roger de Okebrok'
John le Dekene of Burton upon Trent, [8]he has[8]

Stephen de Worthfeld, [2]he has[2]
Nicholas de Overe
Roger de Dunchurch
Richard, son of Clement de Wy[3]manbay
William de Stanlowe
Richard Noreys
Roger de Byrmingham
Rector of Wilmslow
Rector of Middleton
Richard, r. Berrington
Nicholas de Aillesbur', r. Pattingham
Roger, v. Wombourn
Alexander, r. Duffield
John de Weverham
Robert de Morton
William de Gretewych
Andrew Ulkeyl
Adam Giffard
Roger de Aldelime
Thomas de Hutesdon
Thomas de Cesterfeld
Hugh de Hulton
Henry de Whalleye
John de Neuton
William de Wylne
Adam de Morton
Thomas de Billneye

[Fo. 93 cols. 1 and 2 blank.]

[Col. 3] *Priests*

Robert de Boelton
Robert Fychet of Field
Richard de Kirkeby
John Scutard, William de Claverlee, [2]the chancellor gave the letters at Solihull from two bundles[2]
Robert de Kirtlington
John de Dovere
Henry de Derb', OP
Thomas de Staunton
Thomas de Singelton
John de Merton
Nicholas de Ostlaston
William de Makeneye

[1–1] Across cols. 1 and 2 below the col. headings.
[2–2] Written by a second contemporary hand in different ink. This hand also wrote the lists on fos. 92v and 93.
[3–3] Interlined later by a third contemporary hand.

4–4 Written by a fourth contemporary hand in different ink. Followed by *Rogerus* on the line below, now partially erased.
5–5 Interlined.
6 Interlined.
7 Interlined.
8–8 All added later by the third hand.
9 An interlineation above this name, possibly *li iiij*
10 Interlined.
11–11 Interlined.
12–12 Interlined.
13 Interlined over the interlineation.
14 Abraded.
15 Abraded, two words illegible.
16 Interlined.]

1286 [Fo. 93v] [1]NOMINA ORDINATORUM IN ECCLESIA CONVENTUALI DE BURTON SUPER TRENTAM DIE SABBATI QUATUOR TEMPORUM PROXIMO POST FESTUM SANCTE LUCIE VIRGINIS .ANNO DOMINI .M°.CCC^mo. ET CONSECRACIONIS EPISCOPI QUARTO[1] [17 December 1300].

[Col. 1] *Subdeacons*

Richard de Abberbur', r. Rodington
William Wasprey of Barham
John de Brentingham, port. Darley
John le Barber of Lichfield, t. Lichfield ch.
Hugh de Repindon, pres. by the prior of the same [Repton]
William de Pulesdon, r. Gratwich
Robert de Chaundys, r. Radbourne
John de Dumor of Kempsford, dim. dioc. Worcester
[2]William de Sutton[2]
Fr. Thomas de Birton
Fr. Robert de Rypoun
Fr. Thomas de Warmynton
Fr. Thomas de Wythebrok'
Fr. John de Shirleye
Fr. John de Bircheles
Fr. Richard[3] de Drayton
Thomas [canon] of Beauchief
John de Wyneslee, Adam de Besselowe, Laurence de Bettecote, William de Aston, monks of Shrewsbury
John de Burhale, William de Wodecote, Adam de Burton, monks of Combermere

[Col. 2] *Deacons*

M. Richard de Colleshull, r. Shustoke
Simon de Wykeford, preb. Tamworth [Wilnecote]
John de Donnington, dim. of J[ohn Dalderby], the elect of Lincoln
Thomas de Wisshawe, t. pat.
Richard de Rokeby, t. pat.
Robert de Filungleye, t. pat.

William de Betton, t. pat.
Peter de Longenolre, t. pat.
Richard de Wappenbur', t. pat.
Peter de Langeley, t. pat.
William de Longedon, t. pat.
Peter de Cobinton, t. pat.
William de Wotton, t. pat.
William Kyng of Lichfield, t. pat.
Walter de Yevelegh, t. pat.
John de Henore, t. pat.
Thomas de Smythesley, t. pat.
Peter de Bromcote, t. pat.
Simon de Rolleston, t. pat.
Henry de Staperton, t. pat.
Geoffrey de Cesterton, t. pat.
Richard le Cursoun, t. pat.
William de Braylesford, t. pat.
John del Estowe
Walter le Comber of Coventry
Walter le Mey of Birmingham
John de Greneburgh
John de Walsale
Nigel de Derset
Adam de Stretton
John de Sutham
Ralph de Camera
William de Erdeley
Thomas de Ambaston
Richard de Leycestr'

[Col. 3] *Priests*

Ralph de Tunstal, t. pat.
John de la Bourn of Lichfield
John de Sutton, t. pat.
Richard de Melburn', t. pat.
William de Wolrichston, t. pat.
Henry de Lullington, t. pat.
Robert de Wolrichton, t. pat.
Adam de Rokeby, t. pat.
Stephen de Morton, t. pat.
Roger de Ambaston, t. pat.
William de Middelton, t. pat.
William de Knyghtecote, t. pat.
William de Wulscote, t. pat.
Robert de Thurleston, t. pat.
William de Rokeby, t. pat.
Adam de Nouport
Ralph de Dunchurche

William de Hodynet
Henry de Lodbrok'
Henry de Bromley Abbatis
Henry de Assheburn
John de Sodbury
John de Assheburn
Henry de Thurlaston
William de Derset
William de Heywode
Philip de Colleshull
Roger de Roucestr'
Hugh Wilchar of Lichfield
Adam de Sarnshulf
Geoffrey de Othelaston
Henry de Otherton
Henry de Spondon called Godselan, t. pat.
Roger de Osmundeston
Richard de Yelgrave
Roger de Broughton
M. Walter de Thorp'
Richard de Blaby

[Fo. 94 col. 1] *Subdeacons*

William Curcoun, Roger de Louseby, OP Derby
William de Canele, monk of Stoneleigh
Ellis de Barling, canon of Dale
Nicholas de Longenolre, canon of Haughmond
Thomas de Wodecroft, canon of Newstead, dim. dioc. York
Robert de Eccleshale, Thomas de Nassinton, canons of Ranton
Fr. William de Repindon
Robert de Longedon, Robert de Kynalton, Henry de Yoxhale, monks of Burton
upon Trent Fr. Nicholas de Bromley
[4]Fr. William de ...[4]
   [The rest of the col. is blank.]

[Col. 2] *Deacons*

Fr. Henry de Coventr'
Fr. Robert de Holm
Fr. Thomas de Stafford
Fr. Robert de Beuchef
Fr. William de Brugg'
William de Sondon, Thomas de Coleshull, monks of Combermere
Thomas Deping, Hugh de Wyluby, Robert de Wellingovere, OP Derby
Robert de Wynchecumbe, monk of Stoneleigh
Roger de Esseby, John de Shepesheved, monks of Croxden
John de Breydeston, canon of Dale
John de Caumpedene, canon of Haughmond

John de Notingham, William de Dymgeley, canons of Newstead, dim. dioc. York
John de Dumbelton, canon of Ranton
Adam de Cokerham, canon of Burscough
John de Longedon, monk of Burton upon Trent
John de St. Albans, monk of Tutbury
John de Kenilleworth
Roger de Milverton

[Col. 3] *Priests*

Henry de Childeswell
William de Horsley
John de Sparham
Simon de Fennycompton
William de Thurmenton
John de Weston super Trentham
William Symple of Birmingham
William de More of Birmingham
Philip de Ilkesdon
Henry de Spondon
Nicholas de Foston
John de Ambaston
William Wilchar
Nicholas de Hintes
Richard de Pollesworth
Gilbert de Kynesbur'
John de Clifton
Adam de Sutton
Roger de Colleshull
John de Dunstapel, Ralph de Kirkeby, v. Lichfield cath.
John de capella
Henry de Checkelegh
Richard de Tamworth
William Luffe of Wellesbourne, dim. dioc. Worcester
John de Walton, dim. of the same
Roger de Keteleston
William de Repindon
Roger de Pollesworth
Robert de Trentham
M. William de Swepeston, r. Grendon
Thomas de Prestecote, v. Acton
Hugh de Peppelawe, v. Moreton Corbet
Thomas de Charnes, r. moiety of Condover

[Fo. 94v col. 1] *Acolytes*

William de Colleshull
William de Shepeye
Gregory called Haralt of Sutton Coldfield

Thomas de Hattelberg
Henry de Aston
Gregory Wyne
William de Astbury
Richard de Adbaston
Michael de Oclegh
John de Swynnerton
William de Staundon
Henry de Shenston
Richard de Shirley
Robert de Garshale
Peter de Trentam
Richard de Trentam
Walter de Derhull of Lichfield
William de Cruddeworth
William de Wynelesley
William de Bulley of Birmingham
Richard de Spondon
John Lutemay of Stone
William de Pacwode
Henry de Broughton
William de Morton
Richard de Wolvey
William de Wappenbur'
Henry de Longa Eyton
William de Elleford
Thomas de Legh'
Richard de Lodbrok'
John de Kirkeby
Henry de Tigeswell
Thomas de Spondon
Robert de Beleen
Richard de Hampton
William de Nouport
Adam de Mere
William de Brumaston
Henry de Coventr'
William Hughe of Melbourne
Henry de Ilkeston
John de Trafford
Geoffrey de Sandiacr'
Adam de Burton
Ralph de Rysley

[Col. 2] *Acolytes*

William de Staunton
Nicholas de Etewell
Robert de Lullington

Simon de Rydeware
Robert le Peleter
Ingram de Lych'
Robert Coket of Astbury
Robert de Coleshull
John de Breydeston
Robert le Turnour
William de Stretton
Adam le Keu of Coleshill
Robert de Dodynton
Simon de Duddeley
Geoffrey le Trotter
William de Kenylleworth
William de Appelby of Repton
John de Kyrkeby
Robert de Lalleford
John de Markeuton
John le Palmer' of Tamworth
Thomas de Monte of Tamworth
Robert de Marchumleye
John de Carlenton
William de Merston
Robert de Kyngesley
Robert de Sallowe
Richard de Filungley
Robert Asty of 'Eyton'
John de Edenesover
John de Lungassh
Philip de Cosseby
Henry de Napton
John Bele of 'Dassett'
Hugh Sterre
John de Pakenton
John Stevene of 'Dassett'
William Pype
John Danyel of Melbourne
Hugh de Eyton
John Edrych of Melbourne
William Talbot
John le Gardiner
John Chayn of 'Bromley'
Nicholas de Apeston
Walter de Etwell
Siward de Bretford

[Col. 3] *Priests*

Fr. Robert de Clive
Fr. William de Radeclive

Fr. William de Cumberton
Thomas de Berewyk, Philip de Dodinton, monks of Shrewsbury
Fr. Henry de Smalrys
William de Lodelowe, OP Derby
William de Hillington, monk of Stoneleigh
William de Normanton, canon of Dale
Geoffrey de Bovey, OSA Warrington
Richard de Gnousale, canon of Wombridge
John de Sutham, Adam de Derset, John de Burbache, canons of Arbury
Fulk, canon of Norton
Fr. Henry de Mamcestr'
Fr. Robert de Levere
Fr. William de Repindon
Fr. Nicholas de Burton
Fr. Richard de Repindon
John de Arireleye
Reginald de Longedon
Richard de Sutton
    [The rest of the fo. is blank.]

[Fo. 95 col. 1] *Acolytes*

Thomas de Eyton
Adam de '...[5]tamput'
John de Wappenbur'
Richard de Lucy
Peter de Repindon
David de Tuttebur'
Thomas le Cutiler
Thomas de Greveleye
Robert le Archer
William de Sutton
Ellis de Barwe
Henry de Maperlegh
Nicholas Paleys
Peter de Engelby
Ralph Bacun of 'Wych'
Adam Fayles
Richard de Leghes
John de Leghes
John de Wisshaghe
Henry de Kirkeby
Philip de Astbur'
Henry de Brewode
Benedict de Astbur'
William de Coventr'
Stephen de Eyton
Richard Chele of Astbury
Ralph de Astbur'

Richard de Aston
John the goldsmith of Coventry
John Waydour of the same
Henry de Ridware
Roger Matheu
Nicholas de Cressington
Simon de Sekindon
Thomas de Thronlegh
John le Espenser
Alan de Richeleye
Robert de Mere
Henry de Derhull
Stephen de Bidulf
William de Milionus
Robert de Greseleye
Gilbert de Checkeley
Robert de Hunnesworth

[Col. 2] *Acolytes*

Robert de Hunnesworth[6]
Ralph de Bromlegh
Henry de Bauquell
William Penk'
Nicholas de Tamworth
Fr. John de Cestr'
Fr. John de Parco
Richard Novi Castri, monk of Hulton
Hugh de Westbur, [canon][7] of Kenilworth
Thomas de Banbur', monk of Dieulacres
Hamond de Wenlok, Adam de Cleoburs, monks of Shrewsbury
Geoffrey de Byninton, William de Byninton, monks of Combermere
Ralph de Eginton, OP Derby
Robert de Weston, monk of Stoneleigh
John de Stone, monk of Croxden
Ralph de Staunford, OSA Warrington
Robert de Sheperton, canon of Ranton
Thomas de Assheburn, monk of Burton upon Trent
      [The rest of the col. is blank.]

[Col. 3]

Note that Geoffrey de Caldecote, priest, has shown himself to have been canonically ordained to all holy orders by L[lywelyn de Bromfield], bishop of St. Asaph.[8]
      [The rest of the recto is blank.
      1–1 Across the full width of the fo.
      2–2 Written by another contemporary hand in different ink.
      3 Repeated and cancelled by underdotting.

4–4 Entry partially erased.
5 The first letter has been altered and is unclear.
6 ?Listed twice.
7 MS. *monachus*
8 *HBC*, 295.]

1287 [Fo. 95v] [1]NOMINA ORDINATORUM IN ECCLESIA OMNIUM SANCTORUM DERB' DIE SABBATI QUATUOR TEMPORUM PROXIMO ANTE FESTUM NATALIS DOMINI ANNO EJUSDEM .Mº.CCCº. PRIMO ET CONSE-CRACIONIS EPISCOPI [SEXTO][2] PER VENERABILEM PATREM DOMINUM .J[OHANNEM]. CARLIOLN' EPISCOPUM DE LICENCIA .T[HOME]. DE ABBUR-BURIA VICARII[1] [23 December 1301].

[Col. 1] *Subdeacons*

Hugh de Hotot, r. Berrington
Thomas de Assheburn, monk of Burton upon Trent
Roger de Eginton, canon of Repton
Nicholas Spigurnel, Hugh Oky, monks of Coventry
Thomas Gery of Derby, t. pat.
M. William de Notingham, v. and sacrist of Lichfield ch.
Peter le Blund, pres. by R[obert de Redeswell], archd. of Chester
John de Valeys, pres. by E[llis de Napton], archd. of Derby
William de Fornwerk, pres. by the prior of Repton
Robert, son of Simon the cook, pres. by same
Reginald de Porteroye, pres. by same
Ellis, son of Richard de Thorp in Brampton, dim. dioc. Lincoln mentioning t.
Thomas de Wytherdele, monk of Merevale
Godfrey de Shathewell, canon of Rocester
Richard de Engelby, [pres.] by bp. of Carlisle by permission of M. Simon, without t.
John, son of Hugh, in like manner
Hugh de Merston, Richard de Hacton, canons of Haughmond
Richard upeþe Grenehull', t. pat.
John de Stone, monk of Croxden
Hugh Sterre, t. pat.

Deacons

Robert de Kenalton, Robert de Longedon, Henry de Yoxale, monks of Burton upon Trent
Fr. Nicholas de Bromeleye
William de Kegworth, canon of Repton
John called le Porter, v. Lichfield cath.
Hugh le Tannur of Repton, pres. by the prior and conv. of Repton
Fr. Robert de Wynchecumbe
William de Canele, monk of Stoneleigh

[Col. 2] *Deacons*

Nicholas de Longenovere, canon of Haughmond
Robert de Shepirton, canon of Ranton
Reginald de Moyad, monk of Tutbury
Ingram Rag' of Wolston, t. pat.
Adam de Morton, t. pat. by which he received the order of subd. at Burton upon Trent[3]
John de Wyke, canon of Darley
Peter de Athelastr', t. pat.

Priests

John de Foresta, r. Longford
Robert de Everdon, dim. dioc. Lincoln mentioning t.
William, son of Gerard, v. Alspath
Thomas le Bretun, r. Church Lawford
Peter de Langleye, t. pat. by which he was ordained at Burton upon Trent[4]
John Dun of Walsall, t. pat. by which he was ordained at Burton upon Trent[5]
John de Longedon, Henry de Hulton, monks of Burton upon Trent
Alan le Taverner of Derby, t. pat.
M. Ralph de Kyrkeby
John de Dunstaple, v. Lichfield [cath.]
Walter, son of Ralph de Hyklyng, t. pat.
William de Edyhale, t. pat.
John de Lich', t. pat.
Gilbert de Longeleye, canon of Rocester
Adam Hod of Rugeley, t. pat.
William de Edrichesleye, r. Grendon

[Col. 3] *Priests*

John de Haughmon, canon of the same [Haughmond]
John de Sutham, [pres.] by M. S. in Pericks...[6]
William le Kyng of Lichfield, t. pat.
William de Halughton, t. pat. by which he was ordained at Eckington[7]
Thomas de Nassington, Robert de Ecclesale, canons of Ranton
John de St. Albans, monk of Tutbury
Walter le Devener, dim. dioc. Norwich mentioning t.
Simon de Derlee, dim. dioc. Carlisle
John de Dyrkesworth, canon of Darley
    [The rest of the fo. is blank.
    [1-1] Across the full width of the fo.
    [2] Blank space.
    [3] Not listed at this service, see **1286**.
    [4] Ordained deacon 17 Dec. 1300, see **1286**.
    [5] Ordained deacon 17 Dec. 1300 as John de Walsale, see **1286**.
    [6] The end of this name is concealed by the binding.
    [7] Ordained deacon 4 June 1300, see **1285**.]

1288 [Fo. 96] ¹NOMINA ORDINATORUM IN ECCLESIA OMNIUM SANCTORUM DERB'² DIE SABBATI QUATUOR TEMPORUM POST EXALTATIONEM SANCTE CRUCIS ANNO DOMINI .M°.CCC°. SECUNDO PER DOMINUM .J[OHANNEM]. KARL' EPISCOPUM PER³ COMMISSIONEM ADMINISTRATORUM COVENTR' ET LICH' EPISCOPATUS¹ [22 September 1302].

[Col. 1] *Subdeacons*

William de Crast of Wolston, t. Sir Richard de Turvyle
William Bannok, pres. by the prior of Canwell
Richard de Ambaston, t. pat. approved
John Syward, t. pat. approved
William le Lyndraper of Derby, t. pat. approved
Henry de Wyco, t. pat. approved
Thomas de Okebrok', t. pat. approved
Simon Waryn of Aston upon Trent, t. pat. approved
Richard Matheu of Nantwich, t. pat. approved
Nicholas Tibbot, t. pat. approved
Henry de Stretton of Shrewsbury, t. pat. approved
William Norman, t. pat. approved
Henry de Hertindon, t. pat. approved
Roger de Rokeby, t. pat. approved
Henry de Lodbrok', t. pat. approved
Peter the clerk of St. Alkmund's, t. pat. approved
William, r. of Rugby
William de Neuton Sulneye, t. pat. approved
Henry de Furnerlegh, t. pat. approved
Adam Stuffyn of Shirebrook, t. pat. approved
John de Parco, [canon of] Lilleshall
William de Greseleye, pres. by the prior of the same [Church Gresley]
Walter de Lutterworth, Henry de Ichinton, Ralph de Minsterton, William de Coventr', [monks of] Combe
Geoffrey Spignel, [canon of] Rocester
William de Herdeburwe, John de Weston, [monks of] Merevale
Robert de Pedemor, John de Staff', [canons of] St. Thomas's, [Baswich by] Stafford
William de Stretton, t. pat.
Richard de Novo Castro, John de Staff', monks of Hulton
Richard de Asselakby, [monk of] Croxden
John de Pipe, canon of Kenilworth
Simon de Rideware, t. pat.
William de Bedeford, OP
William Deyncourt, pres. by J[ohn] Deyncourt
Richard Moysey, t. pat.
Richard de Bradewell, pres. by the abbot of Darley
Robert de Sutham, pres. by M. S[imon] de Shirlegh who supports him and the burden of his promotion

[Col. 2] *Deacons*[3]

Nicholas Toly of[3] Tamworth, t. pat. approved
Richard upon le Grene[3]hull', t. pat. approved
Richard de Engelby,[3] t. pat. approved
John de Clinton,[3] t. pat. approved
Alan de Wynesesle,[3] t. pat. approved
John de Cundulme, t. pat. approved
William de Notingham, sacrist of Lichfield
Richard de Drayton, canon of Lilleshall
Thomas Gery of Derby
Nicholas de Bannebury, John de Birchale, John de Stone, monks of Croxden
Peter le Blund
John de Valeys
Thomas de Assheburn, monk of Burton upon Trent
Henry de Bromley, t. pat.
William de Brotherton, OP
M. Richard de Birchelis, r. Chipping Campden, dim. dioc. Worcester
John de Melburn', t. pat.
Roger, canon of Repton
John de Wyrkesworth, canon of Darley
Henry Wychard, t. pat.
John de Borugh, t. pat.
Thomas de Lich', t. pat.
Robert de Chaundeys, r. Radbourne
John de Dunchirche, t. pat.
Thomas, canon of Beauchief

Priests

Robert de Ruton, t. pat.
Robert de Filungeleye, t. pat.
Oliver de Trusseleye, t. pat.
Robert de Greneberwe, t. pat.
Walter le Mey of Birmingham, t. pat.
Richard le Cursun of Streethay, t. pat.
Richard Laurence of Rugby, t. pat.
William le Waleys, t. pat.
John de Staunton, t. pat.
Robert de Olghton, t. pat.
Thomas de Ambaston, t. pat.
William de Wennebury, t. pat.

[Col. 3] *Priests*

Walter le Pynour of Coventry, t. pat.
William de Betton, v. St. Chad's ch., Shrewsbury
Thomas de Wysshawe, t. pat.
Richard de Wappinbur', t. pat.

John de Ichinton, t. pat.
Roger de Draycote, t. pat.
Henry de Allesle, t. pat.
John de Greneberwe, t. pat.
Adam de Morton, t. pat.
William de Sutham, t. pat.
John de Draycote, t. pat.
Robert, [canon of] Beauchief
John de Pollesworth, v. Lichfield [cath.]
Thomas de Staff', canon of Lilleshall
Nicholas de Canokbur'
Henry de Neuton, t. pat.
Richard de Froddesham, t. pat.
Ralph de Longedon, t. pat.
Richard le Estryveyn of Stone, t. pat.
William de Desselawe, t. pat.
Richard de Allesle, t. pat.
Hugh de Merston, Richard de Actun, canons of Haughmond
William de Brugg', monk of Hulton
Roger de Assheby, John de Shepisheved, Richard del Okea, monks of Croxden
Walter de Wrokwortheyn, t. pat.
Robert de Bechinton, monk of Birkenhead
Robert de Elmehirst, t. pat.
Robert de Longedon, Robert de Kynalton, Henry de Yoxhale, monks of Burton upon Trent
[Fr.] Nicholas de Bromley
Gilbert de Bekyngham, John de Neuton, canons of Shelford, dim. dioc. York
William de Erdele, t. pat.
Ingram de Woleston, t. pat.
Reginald de Moyad, monk of Tutbury
Robert Tyffun, t. pat.
Henry de Knyveton, t. pat.
Alan de Melewych, pres. by the prior and conv. of Stoneleigh

[Fo. 96v col. 1] *Priests*

William de Prestbur', t. pat.
John de Besing' of 'Draycott', t. pat.
Richard Swaby of Baginton, t. pat.
Peter de Condovere, t. pat.
Henry de Sheyle, t. pat.
John de Overe, t. pat.
Hugh Basset of Findern, t. pat.
Richard de Dounham, v. Bowdon
Henry de Coventr', monk of Evesham
Geoffrey de Kayngton, t. pat.
Henry de Bedworth, t. pat.
  [1–1 Across the full width of the fo.
  2, 3–3 A contemporary stitched tear extends some 5cm. down from these points in the

heading and into col. 2 where that heading and the first five names have been written around it.]

1289 [1]NOMINA ORDINATORUM IN ECCLESIA CATHEDRALI LICH' DIE SABBATI QUATUOR TEMPORUM MENSIS SEPTEMBRIS PER DOMINUM W[ALTERUM] COVENTR' EPISCOPUM ANNO DOMINI .MILLESIMO .CCC^mo. TERCIO ET CONSECARACIONIS EJUSDEM ANNO SEPTIMO[1] [21 September 1303].

Subdeacons

Adam de Longeford, t. pat. approved
William de Hughtisdon, v. Lichfield cath.
Thomas le Beel, t. pat. approved
John de Stokes, t. pat. approved
William Leger, t. pat. approved
Richard Simon of Nantwich, t. pat. approved
Ralph de Athelaxtre, t. pat. approved
Ralph de Mactlisfeld, t. pat. approved
John de Langeford, t. pat. approved
Richard de Lich', t. pat. approved
Richard de Wolseye, t. pat. approved
Andrew de Coventr', t. pat. approved
William de Beriwl', t. pat. approved
Henry de Langeford, t. pat. approved
Henry de Derhull, t. pat. approved
John Athelard of Withybrook, t. pat. approved
Walter Bacun of Coventry, t. pat. approved
Geoffrey de Wythibrok' of the same, t. pat. approved

[Col b.] [2]*Subdeacons*

Henry de Broughton
John de Hull'
Richard de Filungleye
William atte Chircheyerd of 'Itchington', t. pat.
Ranulph de Helesby, t. pat.
John de Kerkeby, t. pat.
William Kelle of Coventry, t. pat.[2]
William de Peondemer, t. pat.
Reginald de Eton, t. pat.
Adam Kayly of Lichfield, t. pat.
Henry de Wysshawe, t. pat.
John de Cancia of Shrewsbury, t. pat.
Henry de Tatenhale, t. pat.
Thomas Tillot of 'Newton', t. pat.
John de Lemyngton, t. pat.
Ralph de Kynnesbur', t. pat.
Thomas de Coleshull, t. pat.

Nicholas de Pakynton, t. pat.
Richard de Adbaston, t. pat.
William de Stretton, t. pat.
Walter de Neuport, t. pat.
William de Bradele of Seckington, t. pat.
William de Wylye, t. pat.
Henry Osan of 'Stretton', t. pat.
John de Birangul, t. pat.
William de Swynford, t. pat.
William Elys of Melbourne, t. pat.
Richard de Peverwych, t. abbot of Combermere, approved
Thomas, son of Richard de Novo Castro, t. pat.
Richard de Wykene, t. pat.
Roger de Hope of Bakewell, t. pat.
William de Sandiacre, t. pat.
William de Neuton Regis, t. pat.
Richard de Spondon, t. pat.
Robert de Northwych, t. pat.
John de Thurmorton, t. pat.
John de Oselaston, t. pat.
William de Appelby, t. pat.
Simon Spark of Melbourne, t. pat.
Ralph de Wolrichston, t. pat.
William de Shepey of Tamworth, pres. by M. Robert de Pytcheford and Roger de Clungeford, prebs. Tamworth

[Col. 3] *Subdeacons*

John de Ingham, dim. dioc. Bath and Wells
Henry de Aston super Trentham, t. prior of Church Gresley which we have
Richard de Davenham, t. M. Robert de Reddeswell which we have
John, son of Nicholas Roket, Philip de Astbur, t. the said M. Robert
John de Prevesthorp, t. pat.
John de Meysham, t. pat.
Richard de la Coppe of Solihull, t. pat.
Thomas de Longenore, t. pat.
William ad Spinam of Tamworth, t. pat.
William le Rous of Longdon, t. pat.
Roger de Beuriper, t. archd. of Chester, approved
Roger de Tatenhale, t. pat.
Philip de Hales, t. John de Cherleton, which we have
Richard de Wrokworthyn, t. pat.
Ralph de Wedinton, t. pat.
Henry Bon Enfaunt of Scropton, t. pat.
John de Edesovere, t. Sir Richard de Herchull, approved
Hugh de Ingestre, t. pat.
John de Moccliston, t. pat.
Richard Massi, t. pat.
John Ulkel, t. pat.

Gilbert de Bourton, t. pat.
Thomas de Hellesby, t. pat.
Roger de Weston of Bakewell, t. pat.
Robert de Sudbur', t. pat.
Robert de Aylwaston, t. pat.
Richard Yire of Melbourne, t. pat.
Henry de Wychenovere, t. pat.
Adam de Longa Ichinton, t. pat.
William de Staunton, t. pat.
Ralph de Adgarisleye, t. pat.
John de Kynnesbur', t. prioress and conv. of Holy Trinity of the Wood, near Markyate, which we have
Robert de Ekynton, t. pat.
John Herbert of 'Marston', t. pat.
Gregory de Sutham, t. pat.
John de Hotton, t. pat.
Nicholas le Mareschal of Nantwich, t. pat.
Richard Payn of Chester, t. pat.
Thomas de Radeweye, t. pat.

[Fo. 97 col. 1] *Subdeacons*

Thomas de Welton, t. pat.
William de Assheburn, t. pat.
Robert de Terven, t. pat.
Richard de Woderoue, t. pat.
Adam de Bettelegh, t. pat.
William Fox of 'Sutton', t. pat.
Roger de Eyton, t. pat.
Henry de Alewaston, t. pat.
Robert Ber of 'Draycott', t. pat.
Henry de Solihull, t. pat.
Walter Drake of Draycott, t. pat.
William Chubbok of Coventry, t. pat.
Richard the smith of Nantwich, t. pat.
Hamond de Merston, t. pat.
Adam de Gnousale, t. pat.
Roger le Koksmyth of Newport, t. pat.
William de Tibesale, t. pat.
Richard de Gnousale, t. pat.
Henry de Sutton, t. pat.
William de Warmynton, t. pat.
John de Derset, t. pat.
Thomas de Kattesby, t. pat.
Thomas de Herberbur', t. pat.
Roger de Ecclesale, t. pat.
William de Coventr', t. pat.
William de Farnburn, t. pat.
Hugh de Ecclesale, t. pat.

Robert de Couleye, t. pat.
William de Breydesale, t. prior of conv. of the new hospital of St. Mary without Bishopsgate which we have
Adam de Stretton, t. pat.
William Freman, t. pat.
William, son of Osbert, t. pat.
William Amyz of Tunstall, t. pat.
John de Seynpere, t. pat.
Robert de Coventr', canon of Darley
Ralph de Paylinton, t. pat.
Walter de Radeweye, t. pat.
William Cripst of Amerton, t. pat.
John Giboun of 'Sutton', t. pat.
Thomas de Boudon, r. Baxterley
Franco[3] Tyes, t. pat. approved, dim. dioc. Norwich

[Col. 2] *Subdeacons*

Stephen de Cumpton Murdak, t. pat. approved
John de Berkeswell, Robert de Persore, canons of Kenilworth
Hugh de Morthwayt, [monk of] Northampton Priory
Peter de Condovere, t. pat.
William de Brocholes of Abbots Bromley, t. pat.
James Knybbe of Newport, t. pat.
Hugh de Assheburn, t. pat.
John Lelly, t. pat.
Thomas, son of Ranulph de Drenketon, t. pat.
Thomas de Berdemore, t. pat.
Thomas de la Crane, t. pat.
Peter de Olughton, t. pat.
John de Chaddlishunte, t. pat.
William le Mazoun of Little Stretton, t. pat.
Thomas de Sutham, t. pat.
John atte Ok' of Abbots Bromley, t. pat.
William de Wytemor', t. pat.
Richard de Etewelle, t. pat.
Ralph de Horlegh, t. pat.
John, son of William le Sergaunt [4]of Egginton,[4] t. pat.
Roger del Bothes, t. pat.
Thomas de Wytherdele, monk of Merevale
Richard de Hampton, t. pat.
Robert de Stansted, monk of Whalley
John Popyn, t. pat.
William de Hulle, t. pat.
William de Prestwelle, t. pat.
John le Despenser of Lichfield, t. pat.
John de Kynefare, t. pat.
Henry de Hatfeld, t. pat.
John de Radeweye, t. pat.

Henry de Rodburn, t. pat.
Nicholas de Bracinton, t. pat.
Roger de Clifton, t. pat.
Robert de Mackworth, t. pat.
Alan de Ruggel', t. pat.
Henry de Astansfeld, t. pat.

[Col. 3] *Subdeacons*

William de Pakwode, t. pat.
Simon de Roctelegh, t. pat.
Richard Chaumberleyn of Lilleshall, t. pat.
Geoffrey le Trottere of Tamworth, t. pat.
William, son of Alexander de Crudeworth, t. pat.
John, son of Robert, t. pat.
Thomas de Stonlee, t. pat.
Robert de Eton, t. pat.
Peter de Dunchirche, t. pat.
Hugh de Horlegh, t. pat.
William Grym of Derby, t. pat.
Walter le Tannour of Derby, t. pat.
William de Eyton, t. pat.
John de Lusseby, t. pat.
Thomas de Hotcumbe, t. pat.
Robert de Melewych, t. pat.
William de Wetton, t. pat.
Roger Symenel of 'Walton', t. pat.
Adam de Neuport, t. house of Combermere
John de Boruyate, t. pat.
William de Herdeborough, t. pat.
Roger de la More of Birmingham, t. pat.
Roger [*recte* Ralph] de Whytemor', t. pat.
Bartholomew de Patingham, t. pat.
Henry le Bonere of Bishopton, t. pat.
Robert de Hambury, t. pat.
William de Chedle, t. pat.
Henry Sauvage, t. pat.
William de Deresborough, t. pat.
William de Sefeld, OP
Roger de Bedeworth, t. pat.
Robert de Parva Barre, t. pat.
John de Wrokwordyn, t. pat.
Ralph de Greseley, t. pat.
Simon de Moeles, r. Thurstaston
Robert de Bruera, r. Pulford

[Fo. 97v col. 1] *Deacons*

Richard the fishmonger of 'Newcastle', t. pat.
Richard de Astbur', t. pat.
William de Stretton, t. pat.
Thomas de Okebrok', t. pat.
John Syward of Arbury, t. pat.
Henry de Hertindon, t. pat.
Roger de Rokeby, t. pat.
Henry Wych', t. pat.
Simon Waryn of Aston upon Trent parish, t. pat.
William le Lyndraper, t. pat.
Walter le Plumer, t. pat.
Roger Matheu of Nantwich, t. pat.
John de Curborough, t. pat.
Hugh de Saimllesbury, t. pat.
William de Yelgreve, t. pat.
John de Tideswelle, t. pat.
Henry de Lodbrok', t. pat.
Walter de Filungley, t. pat.
John de Barewe, t. pat.
William de Kynnesbury, t. pat.
Roger de Blemenhull, t. pat.
Roger de Arleye, t. pat.
John de Whytinton, t. pat.
Henry de Rideware, t. pat.
Robert de Repindon, t. pat.
Robert de Wetherham, t. pat.
John Swetman of Penkridge, t. pat.
Peter de Derb', t. pat.
William de Lalleford, t. pat.
William de Lene of Newport, t. pat.
Richard de Amabaston, t. pat.
[Adam] [5]Stuffynch, t. pat.
Reginald Porteroie, t. pat.
Richard de Fyndirne, t. pat.
William le Teynterer of Birmingham, t. pat.
Jordan de Werynton, t. pat.
William de Neuport, t. pat.
William de Coteriage, t. pat.
William de Repindon, t. pat.
Henry de Furnerlegh, t. pat.
William de Crast of Wolston, t. pat.
William de Duston, t. pat.

[Col. 2] *Deacons*

Adam Salweye, t. pat. approved
William Bannock, t. prior and conv. of Canwell

Richard de Weford, t. pat.
Robert de Hodenhull, t. pat.
Henry de Coppe of Solihull, t. pat.
Walter de Rodeford, t. pat.
John de Breudemor, t. pat.
Robert Colcestr', t. pat.
Adam de Ambrighton, t. pat.
Henry Ramayl, t. pat.
Adam de Clydelowe, t. pat.
Henry de Drayton, bound to the Benedictine order at Canwell monastery and he was accepted at their presentation
Walter de Muddel', t. pat.
William de Tatton, t. pat.
Geoffrey de Bolde, t. pat.
Nicholas de Honylegh, t. pat.
Hugh Rose, t. pat.
William de Rodburn, t. pat.
Richard de Bykenhull, t. pat.
William de Chirchelalleford, t. pat.
John de Knyghtecote, t. M. E[llis de Napton], archd. of Derby
William de Greselegh, pres. by same
Geoffrey de Brugg'
Fr. Roger de Hogcumbe of the order of St. J[ohn]
John de Gloucestr', William de Eccleston, John de Elton, monks of Whalley
Geoffrey, canon of Rocester
Robert de Weston, Thomas de Wotton, Thomas de Geydynton, [monks][6] of Stoneleigh
Benedict de Surston, Henry de Salop', monks of Shrewsbury
Robert de Locryngton, canon of Kenilworth
William de Preston, OFM
Alan de Calverhale, OFM
Thomas Banastre, OFM

[Col. 3] *Deacons*

Roger de Clungenford, preb. Tamworth
Richard de Bradewell, v. Bolsover
Richard de Bletcheley, r. Tilston
William de Bynynton, Geoffrey de Bynynton, William de Preston, [monks of] Combermere
Thomas de Aston, monk of Buildwas
John de Staff', Richard de Novo Castro, monks of Hulton
William de Herdeborugh, John de Weston, monks of Merevale
Richard de Longerigg', Robert de Pennesby, monks of Chester
Robert de Bartona, canon of Dale

Priests

John de Maklesfeld, t. pat. approved
Nicholas Tibbot of Tamworth, t. pat.
Henry Sampson of Coventry, t. pat.
Alan de Wynelesle, t. pat.
Simon de Ridware Mauveysyn, t. pat.
William de Wyco, t. pat.
Hugh Sterre of Lichfield, t. pat. approved
Henry de Ronton, t. pat. approved
John de Spondon, t. pat. approved
Stephen de Fynnesheved, t. abbot of Owston[7]
Peter de Cobynton, t. pat.
Robert de Draycote, t. pat.
Roger de Kenilleworth, t. pat.
Nicholas de Leyes, t. pat.
John de Burgo, t. pat.
Roger de Ambrighton, t. pat.
William de Wotton, t. pat.
Thomas de Lich', t. pat.
John de Cundulme, t. pat.
Adam de Stratton, t. pat.
Richard de Aston of Frodsham, t. pat.
Henry Coket of Tamworth, t. pat.
William de Morton, t. pat.

[Fo. 98 col. 1] *Priests*

Roger de Codynton, t. pat.
John de Dunchirche, t. pat.
Richard de Engelby, t. pat.
John, son of Hugh de Melburn', t. pat.
Simon de Heygham, r. Barton Blount
William de Leone, r. Rugby
Henry de Bromley, t. pat.
Peter de Aldulstre, t. pat.
Robert de Ecclesale, t. pat.
Richard de Hereford, r. Pinxton
Robert de Chaundoys, r. Radbourne
Henry de Walsale, t. pat.
John de Kenilleworth, t. pat.
John de Elynton of Coventry, t. pat.
Robert de Bisshebury, t. pat.
Peter de Bromcote, t. pat.
Hugh de Hertingdon, t. pat.
Ralph de Camera of 'Newcastle', t. pat.
Robert de Weston super Trent', t. pat.
Thomas Gery of Derby, t. pat.
John de Solihull, t. pat.

Richard de Kenilleworth, t. pat.
Henry Pyn of Biddulph, t. pat.
Richard de Brunton, t. pat.
Hugh de Repindon, t. pat.
Thomas, son of Ralph de Novo Castro, t. pat.
William de Solihull, t. pat.
William de Meysham, t. pat.
Geoffrey de Pipe, t. pat.
William de Wetton, t. pat.
John de Leyecros, t. pat.
William de Braylesford, t. pat.
Thomas, son of Robert de Chakculue, t. pat.
Simon de Monyassh, t. pat.
Robert de Mortiona, t. pat.
Robert de Bollesovere, t. pat.
John de Penne, t. pat.
William de Parva Overe, t. pat.
John de Wynesleye, Laurence de Bettecote, William de Wlston, [monks] of Shrewsbury
John de Parco, canon of Lilleshall Thomas de Assheburn, monk of Burton upon Trent

[Col. 2] *Priests*

Adam de Greston, Robert de Tappehull, Geoffrey de Brikehull, Robert de Driffeld, [monks of] Whalley
Robert de Bentile, monk of Hulton
Adam de Burton, William de Wodecote, John de Bourchale, [monks of] Combermere
John de Wylye, John de Wyrkesworth, [canons of] Darley
Fr. Provincialus de Eton
Thomas de Alferton, Walter de Whyteleye, canons of Beauchief
> [1–1 In col. 1.
> 2–2 Written around a contemporary stitched tear which extends some 5cm. down.
> 3 *Sic*
> 4–4 Interlined.
> 5 Abraded, see the index of persons and places.
> 6 MS. *canonici*
> 7 Interlined.]

1290   [1]NOMINA ORDINATORUM IN ECCLESIA CONVENTUALI DE LILLESHULL IN VIGILIA PASCHE ANNO DOMINI .M°.CCC^mo. QUARTO PER DOMINUM .W[ALTERUM]. COVENTR' ET LICH' EPISCOPUM[1] [28 March 1304].

Acolytes

Simon de Dringgeworth
John de Birmyngham of St. Thomas [the Martyr's] hospital, Birmingham
John de Bruges, canon of Haughmond
Osbert de Wysshawe, canon of Stone

Robert de Horsle
Philip de Berewyk

Subdeacons

William de Wodestok', OSA Shrewsbury
Robert de Ideshale, Henry de Stok', canons of Lilleshall
Richard de Essheburn, Robert de Brugg', Ranulph de Caldon, Adam de Uttoxhather, monks of Dieulacres
Richard de Cestr', monk of Chester
Fr. Richard de Eton
Robert de Doffeld, canon of Darley
Hugh Mascy, r. Wallasey
Roger de Malpas
Thomas de la Sousche, OFM Nottingham
Richard de Repinghale, OFM Nottingham

[Col. 3]

M. Andrew de Essheburn, canon and preb. Gnosall
Richard de Tywe, canon of Stone
Thomas de Acton Burnelle, t. pat.
Richard le Poygvur of Wroxeter, t. pat.
M. John Hurel, t. pat.
Thomas de Harlee, t. pat.

Deacons

Thomas le Waleys, r. Acton
William de Thorpwatervile
Simon de Molis, r. Thurstaston
Thomas de Braylesford, r. Brailsford
Thomas le Hunte, r. Madeley[2]
William Elys of Melbourne
Simon Spark of the same
Thomas Tyllot of the same
Richard, son of Ivon of the same
William, son of John of the same
Walter Bacun of Coventry
William Deyncourt, r. Morton
Robert de Couleye
Richard Wodero
Ranulph de Cestr', monk of Chester
Richard de Aslakeby, monk of Croxden
William de Huctghtisdon, v. Lichfield [cath.]
Ralph de Benteleye, canon of Church Gresley
Roger, r. Kemberton
William de Estl...,[3] canon of Haughmond
Walter Balle of Newport

[4]William de Sheldon, OFM Coventry
Edmund de Lodbrok', of the same order and ...[4]

[Fo. 98v col. 1] *Deacons*

Robert de Wyco, canon of Stone
William de Berihull, t. pat.
John de Horton, t. pat.
John de Thurmeton
Roger de Bothes
Roger de Tetenhale
Thomas Meverel
Adam de Gnousale
Robert de Norwyco
Henry le Sauvage, r. Hartshorne
Adam, parson of Lilleshall
Thomas de la Hoo

Priests

Robert de Cliderhou, r. Wigan
Richard de Novo Castro, John de Staff', monks of Hulton
Madoc de Bedewas, OP Shrewsbury
John de Hales, OP Newcastle under Lyme
Richard de Longerich, Robert de Pennisby, monks of Chester
Godfrey, canon of Rocester
John de Stone, monk of Croxden
Roger de Hoccumbe, of Holy Trinity hospital, Bridgnorth
Nicholas de Baunford, OFM Coventry
Hamond de Wenlok, monk of Shrewsbury
Robert de Sheperton, canon of Ranton
[5]John de Whytinton, t. pat.
Richard de Davenham, t. pat.
William de Neubold
Thomas de Aston, monk of Buildwas[5]

[Col. 2] *Priests*

William de Greseleye, [6]pres. by the prior and conv. of Church Gresley[6]
Walter de Mudle
Adam de Cliderhou

    [The rest of the fo. is blank.
    [1-1] In col. 2.
    [2] Interlined.
    [3] MS. stained.
    [4-4] Written around a contemporary stitched tear which extends some 5cm., and the
MS. is abraded.
    [5-5] Written around the same stitched tear.
    [6-6] Added by another contemporary hand.]

[Fo. 99r blank.
This fo. measures approximately 20cm. by 16cm.]

1291   [Fo. 99v Copy of] the charter of W[alter], bishop of Coventry and
Lichfield, son and heir of Simon Peverel, giving, granting and confirming to the
abbot and convent of Selby and their successors a toft and 20 acres of land with its
appurtenances in Adlingfleet, together with the advowson of the church of the
same town with all its rights and appurtenances. To have and to hold to the same
abbot and convent and their successors freely, quietly, peacefully and wholly in
pure and everlasting alms. The bishop, his heirs and assigns will warrant, acquit
[and] defend[1] the aforesaid toft of land with its appurtenances, and also the
advowson of the said church with all its rights and appurtenances, to the aforesaid
abbot and convent and their successors against all men forever. In witness of which
the bishop has affixed his seal to this charter. These being witnesses etc. [1305].[2]
  [1 Interlined.
  2 Unfinished. The king's mortmain licence was granted 9 May 1305, *CPR 1301–7*, 342.]

1292   All the faithful of Christ are to know that W[alter] de Langeton, bishop of
Coventry and Lichfield, son and heir of Simon Peverel, has remitted and entirely
quitclaimed for himself, his heirs and assigns to the abbot and convent of Selby and
their successors all the right and claim he has had or might have in future in a toft
and 20 acres of land with its appurtenances in Adlingfleet and in the advowson of
the church of the same town, with all its rights and appurtenances; so that neither
he, his heirs or assigns, nor other persons in his name, might henceforth demand
any right or lay [any] claim in the aforesaid toft, land and advowson, rights or
appurtenances. In witness [etc. 1305].

1293   All are to know that W[alter] de Langeton, bishop of Coventry and
Lichfield, has assigned Richard Oisel [1]and Richard[1] de Celario, or either of them,
to deliver and hand over in his name full seisin to the abbot and convent of Selby of
a toft and 20 acres of land with its appurtenances in Adlingfleet, and the advowson
of the church of the same town with all its rights and appurtenances, having
authorised the same Richard and Richard, or either of them, to act for him in the
foregoing. In witness of which the bishop has caused these his letters patent to be
sealed with his seal. Given etc. [1305].
  [1–1 Interlined.]

1294   [Fo. 100] [1]NOMINA ORDINATORUM IN ECCLESIA CONVENTUALI DE
KENILLEWORTH DIE SAB[B]ATI QUATUOR TEMPORUM MENSIS DECEMBRIS
PER VENERABILEM PATREM DOMINUM .W[ALTERUM]. DIE GRACIA COVENTR'
ET LICH' EPISCOPUM RITE ORDINES CELEBRANTEM ANNO DOMINI .MILLESIMO
CCC^mo. QUARTO[1] [19 December 1304].

[Col. 1] *Subdeacons*

Simon de Rocteleg', t. pat.
Thomas de Westhalum, t. pat.
Henry le Mareschal of Coventry, t. pat.
Robert de Rocteleg', t. pat.

Richard de Ansteleg', t. pat.
Stephen de Thornestoft, r. Eversholt [dioc. Lincoln]
Robert, son of Henry de Melbourn, t. pat.
John Wylimot of Monks Kirby, t. pat.
Oliver de Wythibrok', t. pat.
William, son of Reginald de Norton, t. pat.
John de Ichinton, t. pat.
Richard de Coleshul', t. pat.
Richard de Stanes, t. pat.
William de Prestewell, t. pat.
John de Brok', pres. by the nuns outside Stamford
Richard de Ruton, t. pat.
John de Flaumvill', t. pat.
Roger de Clifton, t. pat.
Roger de Neu²bold, t. pat.
Henry de Bramcote, t. pat.
Peter de Engelby, t. pat.
William de Wappenbur', t. pat.
Richard de Rugele, t. pat.
Alexander de Fekkenho, t. pat.
Nicholas de Morton, t. pat.
William de Bulkinton, t. pat.
William de Wyssawe, t. Thomas de Boydyn³
⁴Thomas de Casteldonynton, dim. dioc. Lincoln⁴
Richard de Dendeston, t. pat.
Henry de Shulton, t. pat.
Robert de Braylesford, t. pat.
John Broun of Hillmorton, t. pat.
Henry de Twyford, t. pat.
Simon de Wylmeleghton, t. pat.
Ranulph de Burton super Trentham, t. pat.
William de Henyngham, t. pat.
John Marchet of Newbold, t. pat.
William de Onderwode, t. pat.
Robert de Bretteby, t. pat.
Robert Harewy of Church Lawford, t. pat.
John de Huxton, t. pat.

[Col. 2] *Subdeacons*

Henry Andreu of Tideswell, t. pat.
Adam de Salebrugg', t. pat.
Adam de Perton, t. pat.
Henry de Sutham, t. pat.
Robert de Dunchirch, t. pat.
William the baker of Coventry, t. pat.
Robert de Ansti, t. pat.
John de Roucestr', t. pat.
William de Mershton, t. pat.

Adam de Kyngleg', t. pat.
Walter de Stretton, t. pat.
William de Herbury, t. pat.
Robert the scribe of Lichfield, t. pat.
Thomas de Filungle, t. pat.
William de Hauneton, t. pat.
William de Napton, t. pat.
Robert de Farndon, r. Great Harborough
John, son of William de Chadeshunt, t. pat.
William de Longedon, t. pat.
Robert de Stonystanton, t. pat.
Ralph de Stonistanton, t. pat.
Roger Kentrix of Tamworth, t. pat.
Thomas de Sutham, t. pat.
John Lotemay, t. pat.
Henry de Merston Prioris, t. pat.
Robert de Wabberleye, t. pat.
Andrew de Matherfeld, t. pat.
William de Rodeȝeth, t. pat.
John de Shavynton, t. pat.
Thomas de Shulton, t. pat.
Robert de Notingham, t. Bradley ch.[5]
William, son of Robert de Melbourn, t. pat.
John Pym of Shrewsbury, t. pat.
Andrew de Welton, t. pat.
John de Bonington, t. pat.
Robert de Ethorp, t. pat.
Robert de Sutham, t. pat.
Nicholas de Kenilleworth, t. Darley ch.[6]
Roger de Beulton, t. pat.
Philip de Bretford, t. pat.
Ancellus le Seler of Coventry, t. pat.
Roger de Wyco, t. pat.
Richard de Bromwych, t. pat.

[Col. 3] *Deacons*

John atte Ok' of Abbots Bromley, t. pat.
John Athelard of Withybrook, t. pat.
Richard de Wolseye, t. pat.
Geoffrey Ceret of Withybrook, t. pat.
John, son of Godde de Oslaston, t. pat.
John de Longeford, t. pat.
William, son of William Kelle of Coventry, t. pat.
Henry de Bourton, pres. by the prior and conv. of Launde
Adam de Longeford, t. pat.
Philip de Astebury, John Rouket of Davenham, pres. by archd. of Chester
Philip, son of Richard de Estlemynton
Henry, son of Henry de Derehull

Henry de Bilston
Richard de Etewell
William de Appelby
Gregory Harald of Sutton Coldfield
Nicholas de Bracynton
John de Kynefare, t. pat.
Henry de Aklaston, t. pat.
Richard, son of Richard Massey, clerk, t. pat.
Henry, son of Geoffrey de Whissawe, t. pat.
Henry de Aston, pres. by the prior and conv. of Church Gresley
William de Swynford, t. pat.
Adam de Euledon, t. pat.
William Fox of 'Sutton', t. pat.
Adam de Neuport, pres. by the religious of Combermere
Thomas de Longenolre
Ralph, son of Walter de Salop'
Robert de Hambury
John de Mukkliston
Andrew de Coventr'
Nicholas de Pakinton Parva
Richard de Morton, pres. by R[obert de Redeswell], archd. of Chester
Thomas, son of Ranulph de Drengeton
William de Ichinton, clerk
William de Chedle
John de Meisham
Ingram de Lich'

[Fo. 100v col. 1] *Deacons*

Thomas, son of John the smith of Harbury, t. pat.
Richard de Wykene, t. pat.
Ralph de Maklesfeld, t. pat.
Roger de Beurepeyr, t. pat.
John de Ulkel, t. pat.
Ralph de Stretton, t. pat.
John de Berangre, pres. by the abbot and conv. of Leicester
Reginald de Eton, t. pat.
Richard de Filongeleg' of Ryton, t. pat.
Richard de la Coppe of Solihull, t. pat.
Richard de Lich', t. pat.
M. John Hurel, t. pat.
M. John Pupard, r. Plemstall
Henry de Solihul, clerk, t. pat.
Stephen de Compton Mordak, t. pat.
John de Kyrkeby, clerk, t. pat.
Peter, son of Henry Juet, t. pat.
Hugh de Horleye, t. pat.
John Giboun of 'Sutton', t. pat.
William le Mazon of Little Stretton, t. pat.

Richard de Pacwode, pres. by the prior and conv. of the Holy Sepulchre, Warwick
Ralph, son of William de Whytakre, t. pat.
William de Esshebourn, t. pat.
Henry de Longeford, t. pat.
John de Stok', t. pat.
Roger ad Crucem of 'Eyton'
Ralph de Whytemor', t. pat.
John, son of William le Spenser, t. pat.
Henry de Whychenovere, t. pat.
William, son of John Freman of Ash
Roger de Twyford, clerk, t. pat.
William le Rous of Longdon, t. pat.
Thomas Adjuet of Melbourne, t. pat.
Robert de Sudbury of 'Aston', t. pat.
Adam de Birthingburi, t. pat.
Ralph de Horleye, t. pat.
Henry de Sutton, t. pat.
Thomas de Berdemor, t. pat.
John de Derset, t. pat.
Thomas, son of William the baker of Southam, t. pat.
Henry de Tetenhale, t. pat.
James Knibbe of Newport, t. pat.
William de Wytemor', t. pat.

[Col. 2] *Deacons*

Robert de Melewych, t. pat.
William de Ruton, t. pat.
Richard de Malopassu, t. pat.
Richard Mandut, t. pat.
John Lely of Derby, t. pat.
John de Ednesovere, t. pat.
William de Hulle, t. pat.
Richard de Gnousale, t. pat.
Robert de Terven, t. pat.
Ralph de Kynesbury, t. pat.
Ralph de Albarston of Longford, t. pat.
John de Notingham, r. Whittingham, dim. dean and chapter of York, *sede vacante*
Gilbert de Bourton, t. pat.
Roger de Birmingham, pres. by the prior and conv. of Wolston
William ad Spinam, t. pat.
Richard Prudhome, t. pat. of Henry, minister of Thelsford of the Trinitarian order
Thomas de la Grave, t. pat.
John Hert of 'Marston', t. pat.
John de Kynesbury, pres. by the prioress and nuns of Markyate
Robert de Eginton, t. pat.
Ralph de Wolricheston, pres. by Sir Richard de Turvill', kt.
John de Pevesthorp, t. pat.
Richard le Wodere of Bishopton, t. pat.

Geoffrey le Trotter of Tamworth, t. pat.
Hugh de Neuton, canon of Norton
John de Berkeswell, monk of Stoneleigh
Geoffrey de la Dale, canon of the same [Dale]
Richard de Esheborn, Robert de Brugg', monks of Dieulacres
Robert de Barre, pres. by John, v. Baschurch

[Col. 3] *Priests*

Richard Peverwych, pres. by the abbot and conv. of Combermere
William de Burihull, t. pat.
Adam Stuffyn of Shirebrook, t. pat.
Henry de Lodebrok', t. pat.
William de Crast of Wolston, t. pat.
Adam de Ambrighton, t. pat.
Thomas Tillot, t. pat.
William, son of John, t. pat.
William Elys, t. pat.
William de Hughtesdon, t. pat.
Robert de Coule, t. pat.
Robert de Repyndon, t. pat.
John de Thurmeton, t. pat.
Adam Salewy of Cannock, t. pat.
John de Horton, t. pat.
Adam de Gnousale, t. pat.
Stephen de Brewode, t. Tibshelf ch.[7]
Richard de Bissopeston, t. pat.
Adam de Bondon, r. Blendworth [dim. dioc. Winchester][8]
William de Rodbourn, t. pat.
William de Yelegreve, t. pat.
Henry de Hertindon, t. pat.
Roger de Shepeye, t. pat.
Richard de Gnousale, t. pat.
Geoffrey de Brugg', t. pat.
Richard de Sanbag', t. pat.
Thomas Meverel, t. pat.
John de Kent, t. pat.
Henry de Wyco, t. pat.
Robert de Rokeby, t. pat.
Henry Savage, r. Hartshorne
Roger de Bissopeston, t. Kemberton ch.[9]
Walter Balle, t. pat.
Richard, son of Ivon, t. pat.
M. Andrew de Essheborn
John de Sancto Petro, r. Bunbury
William de Kynnesbury, t. pat.

[1–1] Across the full width of the fo.
[2] *u* interlined.
[3] Interlined.

4–4 Added by another contemporary hand in the space between cols. 1 and 2.
5 Instituted 23 Jan. 1305, see **264**.
6 Port. Darley, instituted 11 Nov. 1304, see **263**.
7 Rector of Tibshelf, instituted 6 Feb. 1304, see **256**.
8 Admitted 30 Jan. 1303, see *Registrum Johannis de Pontissara, episcopi Wintoniensis, A.D. MCCLXXXII–MCCCIV*, ed. C. Deedes (CYS, 19, 30, 1915–24), i.161.
9 Rector of Kemberton, collated 26 Jan. 1304, see **339**.]

1295 [Fo. 101] ¹NOMINA ORDINATORUM IN ECCLESIA PAROCHIALI DE COLEWYCH DIE SAB[B]ATI QUATUOR TEMPORUM MENSIS DECEMBRIS ANNO DOMINI .Mᵒ.CCCᵐᵒ. QUINTO A DOMINO DEI GRACIA CANDIDE CASE, DOMINI .W[ALTERI]. COVENTR' ET LICH' EPISCOPI SUFFRAGANEO ORDINES TUNC IBIDEM CELEBRANTE¹ [18 December 1305].

[Col. 1] *Subdeacons*

Thomas de Spondon, t. pat.
Robert de Whichenovere, pres. by the prior and conv. of Canwell
Thomas de Lauton, William de Croxhale, pres. by R[obert de Redeswell], archd. of Chester
John de Fiskerton, t. pat.
John de Dersete, t. pat.
William Hewe of 'Kyngesneuton', t. pat.
John le Gardiner, t. pat.
William de Terven, t. pat.
Richard de Leyes, t. pat.
Richard, r. Eaton Constantine chapel, t. pat.
Richard, son of Edmund le Chaloner, t. pat.
Philip de Clinton, r. Ratley
Adam de Oulesberwe, r. King's Stanley,² dim. of the vicar-general, dioc. Worcester
Richard le Corzon, r. Breadsall
William de Blithefeld, t. pat.
John Boket of Shrewsbury, t. pat.
John de Tibinton, t. pat.
William de Griseleye, t. pat.
John de Sekkindon, t. pat.
John de Breres, t. pat.
John de Greseleye, pres. by the prior of the same [Church Gresley]
John de Herewelle, pres. by the abbot of Beauchief
Guy de Neuton, t. pat.
Richard le Demor of Trentham, t. pat.
M. William l'Archer, r. Baddesley Clinton
Thomas de Scrapetoft, Richard de Coventr', monks of Coventry
Andrew de Corleye, monk of Stoneleigh
Peter de Opton, monk of Coventry
Griffin de Mether, OP Warwick
Alexander de Atherton, OFM Chester
John de Donyngton, canon of Burscough
Hugh, monk of Birkenhead
John de Burton, monk of Chester

[Col. 2 *Subdeacons*]

William de Cestr', Robert de Castro, OP Newcastle under Lyme
Thomas de Clifton, OSA
William de Oddeston, monk of Dieulacres
Robert de Stapenhull, William de Tutteburi, monks of Burton upon Trent
Ralph de Duram, William de Audelym, Robert de Stone, canons of Hulton
Fr. William de Whitacr'
Fr. Walter de Eyton
Robert de Wyshawe, canon of Stone
John de Staunford, canon of Beauchief

Deacons

John de Hulle, t. pat.
William de Pacwode, t. pat.
John de Chadleshunte, t. pat.
William de Whiteleye, t. pat.
Alexander de Flekkenho, t. pat.
Simon de Wylmeleghton, t. pat.
Robert de Braylesford, t. pat.
Henry de Twyford, t. pat.
William de Napton, t. pat.
William de Wyleys, t. pat.
William de Prestewell, t. pat.
Robert de Rocteleye, t. pat.
M. Ralph de la Bolde, r. Edgmond
William de Roules of 'Stretton', t. pat.
Walter Drake of Draycott, t. pat.
Richard de Stone, t. pat.
Robert de Ethorp, t. pat.
Robert de Makworth, t. pat.
Walter, son of Nicholas the hunter, t. pat.
Robert, son of Henry de Melebourn
John Lytemay
John Wylimot of Monks Kirby
John de Hugtesdon
John, son of Thomas le Taillour of[3] Castle Donington, dim. dioc. Lincoln

[Col. 3] *Deacons*

Richard de Bromwych, t. pat.
William de Hopton, pres. by Richard de Draicote, kt.
M. Andrew, r. Forton
Hugh, r. Bushbury
Richard le Poyvour of Wroxeter
M. John de Burton, r. West Felton
John de Chadleshunt, t. pat.
Richard de Abberburi, r. Rodington

John Pyn of Shrewsbury, t. pat.
Thomas de Shulton, t. pat.
Richard Payn of Chester, t. pat.
Roger le Hare of Northwich, t. pat.
Robert de Staunton, t. pat.
Ralph de Staunton, t. pat.
William de Donynton, t. pat.
Andrew de Welton, t. pat.
William de Holond, t. pat.
William Grym of Derby, t. pat.
Nicholas de Morton, t. pat.
Simon de Franketon, Simon de Leycestr', Richard de Lodbrok', monks of Coventry
Richard de Neubold, monk of Combe
Richard de Buterbon, OP Warwick
Thomas de Coventr', OFM Chester
Richard Gest, Henry de Stok', canons of Lilleshall
Richard de Cestr', monk of the same [Chester]
John de Spalding, Henry de Bredon, William de Rotteford, William de Bollesovere, [canons] of Welbeck, dim. dean and chapter of York, *sede vacante*
Richard Harald, Richard de Chedle, John, OP Newcastle under Lyme
William de Werington, OSA
Ranulph de Caldon, Adam de Percy, monks of Dieulacres
Richard de Saxilbi, monk of Burton upon Trent

[Fo. 101v col. 1] *Deacons*

Richard de Trentham, canon of the same [Trentham]
Richard de Twe, canon of Stone
Thomas de Sallowe, canon of Beauchief
John de Haghmon', canon of the same [Haughmond]
John de Luceby, Thomas de Radeweye, canons of St. Mary's, Shrewsbury

Priests

Henry de Burton, pres. by the prior and conv. of Launde
Reginald Porteroye of Repton, t. pat.
Thomas de Longenolre, t. pat.
Philip de Estlemynton, t. pat.
Philip de Astbury, Richard de Morton, pres. by archd. of Chester
Robert le Sergeant of Egginton, t. pat.
Robert de Norwyco, t. pat.
Ralph, son of Walter de Salop', t. pat.
Ralph de Wolricheston, pres. by Sir Richard de Turvill', kt.
Richard de Wolseye, t. pat.
John le Spenser of Lichfield, t. pat.
William de Appelby, t. pat.
Richard de la Coppe of Solihull, t. pat.
Nicholas de Bracinton, t. pat.

Adam de Eweldon, t. pat.
John de Ednesovere, t. pat.
Henry, son of Henry de Derhull, t. pat.
John de Knyghtecote, John de Dersete, pres. by archd. of Derby
Stephen de Compton Mordak, t. pat.
Richard de Macy, t. pat.
Roger ad Crucem of 'Eyton', t. pat.
Robert de Terven, t. pat.
Henry de Sutham, t. Th[omas] de Sutham
Hugh de Hurleye, t. pat.
John de Kirkeby, t. pat.
John de Kynnesbury, pres. by the prioress and conv. of Markyate
Reginald de Eton
Nicholas de Parva Pakynton
William de Brum3erd, r. Plemstall

[Col. 2] *Priests*

M. John Hurel, r. Thurstaston
William Bannok, pres. by the prior of Canwell
Walter le Plumber of Lichfield, pres. by M. Luke de Ely, chancellor of Lichfield
Geoffrey le Trotter of Tamworth, t. pat.
Richard de Filongel' of Ryton, t. pat.
Jordan de Werynton, t. pat.
Henry de Sotton, pres. by archd. of Derby
John Ulkel, t. pat.
William Lyndraper of Derby, t. pat.
Henry de Longeford, t. pat.
Roger de Twyford, t. pat.
Gregory Harald of Sutton Coldfield, t. pat.
William de Ruton, pres. by M. Richard de Norhampton
John Athelard of Withybrook, t. pat.
Ingram de Lich', t. pat.
Robert de Halsop, v. St. Peter's ch., Derby
Nicholas de Kenilleworth, r. Darley
Thomas de Berdesmor, pres. by archd. of Derby
Henry de Aston, pres. by the prior of Church Gresley
Richard de Albaston, t. pat.
Robert de Barre, t. pat.
Thomas, son of Ranulph de Drengeton, t. pat.
Richard de Ambeldeston, t. pat.
William Veycy, t. pat.
John del Breudemor, t. pat.
Ralph de Maklesfeld, t. pat.
Hugh Rose of Stone, t. pat.
Walter, son of Jordan de Yevele, pres. by the master of the hospital [of St. John] of Jerusalem in England
Peter de Derby, t. pat.
Ralph de Hurleye, t. pat.

Richard de Gnousale, pres. by Henry de Leycestr', on pain of 100 marks
Bartholomew de Patingham, t. pat.
Adam de Neuport, pres. by the abbot of Combermere
Robert de Sudbury, t. pat.

[Col. 3] *Priests*

Roger Matheu, t. pat.
Henry de Tetenhale, t. pat.
Robert Modi, t. pat.
Ralph de Fynderne, t. pat.
Robert de Melewych, t. pat.
William Fox, t. pat.
William de Whitenton, John Godde of Osleston, John Lely, Henry de Sudbury, Henry de Aston, William de Kel of Coventry, Robert de Sudbury, Ralph de Kynnesbury, Nicholas de Honyleye, Robert de Walton super Trent', t. pat., by command of the suffragan
John de Berkeswell, monk of Stoneleigh
Simon de Bathkynton, Henry de Ichinton, Robert de Bathkynton, Ralph de Minsterton, William de Coventr', monks of Combe
Richard de Lodbrok', John de Leycestr', Robert de Sotherton, OP Warwick
Henry de Kanewell, monk of the same [Canwell]
Edmund de Lodbrok', OFM Chester
Henry de Salop', canon of Lilleshall
Ranulph Cestr', monk of the same [Chester]
John of St. Thomas the Martyr's hospital, Birmingham
Richard de Marchan, canon of Norton
David de Com', OP Newcastle under Lyme
Richard de Hopton, Robert de Brugg', monks of Dieulacres
Richard Morice, canon of St. Thomas's, [Baswich by] Stafford
John, of the house of St. [Thomas the Martyr], [4] Birmingham

    [1–1] Across the full width of the fo. below the col. headings.
    [2] *The Register of Walter Reynolds, Bishop of Worcester, 1308–1313*, ed. R.A. Wilson (Dugdale Society, 9, 1928), 85. Listed there as Adam de Holeberg.
    [3] An 8mm. natural hole is at this point.
    [4] MS. *John*]

1296 [Fo. 102] [1]NOMINA ORDINATORUM IN ECCLESIA FRATRUM PREDICA-TORUM DERBEYE DIE SAB[B]ATI QUATUOR TEMPORUM QUA CANTATUR OFFICIUM SCICIENTES ANNO DOMINI .MILLESIMO .CCC^mo. QUINTO. A VENERABILI PATRE DOMINO DEI GRACIA CANDIDE CASE EPISCOPO DOMINI .W[ALTERI]. EADEM GRACIA COVENTR' EPISCOPI SUFFRAGANEO IBIDEM ORDINES CELEBRANTE[1] [19 March 1306].

[Col. 1] *Subdeacons*

Robert, son of Adam the marshal of Brewood, pres. by Sir William Tromwyne, kt.
John de Baledeyn, t. pat.
Nicholas Trusseloue, t. pat.

Richard de Riseleye, pres. by Roger de Brymesleye and Alan de Hemunton
John Michel of Breaston, pres. by Simon Pouger
Henry de Wyrkesworth, pres. by Nicholas de Hungerford
John Opy of Sawley, pres. by Sir Henry de Braylesford
Hugh de Hanle, t. pat.
Osbert de Folesbourn, v. St. Mary's collegiate ch., Stafford
William de Yoxhale, v. of the same
William, son of Robert de Pipe, pres. by William de Norton, clerk
Richard de Biricote, pres. by Sir Richard de Turvill', kt.
William de Dunham, clerk of the bishop of Whithorn, pres. by the same
John de Petton, r. Petton
John de Stok, r. Blore
Henry de Ibole, pres. by M. W[illiam] de Swepston
Ralph de Sutton, pres. by John de Sheuche
Thomas de Manecestr', pres. by Sir Richard de Hulton, kt.
Richard de Hales, canon of Ranton
John de Tamworth, monk of Stoneleigh
Adam de Hunsterton, OP
John de Haghman', canon of the same [Haughmond]
John de Bradeford, OSA Shrewsbury
    [The rest of the col. is blank.]

[Col. 2] *Deacons*

William the baker of Coventry, pres. by William Rivel of Newbold Revel
Richard le Corson, r. Breadsall
Hugh de Warr', pres. by Sir Thomas de Sandbache
Richard, son of Roger de Wyco, t. pat.
Walter de Marketon, t. pat.
William, son of William de Sandiacr', t. pat.
William Huwe, t. pat.
John de Longassh, pres. by Anketill de Insula
Richard, r. Eaton Constantine
Roger de Weston of Bakewell, t. pat.
Roger called le parson of Bakewell, t. pat.
Robert de Ansty, t. pat.
William de Terven, pres. by John de Oudel'
Nicholas le Mareschal of Nantwich, t. pat.
William de Farnberwe, t. pat.
William de Neuton Sulney, pres. by Philip de Daleby
John de Ichinton, t. pat.
William Leger, pres. by William de Brikhull
Richard le Deymour of Trentham, t. pat.
M. Richard le Bray, r. Clopton, dim. dioc. Ely
John de Kynardeseye, r. Tatenhill
William de Burdeleys, r. Shenley, dim. dioc. Lincoln
William atte Chirchethorn of 'Itchington', pres. by the minister of house of Thelsford
Peter de Donchirch, pres. by the dean of Marton

William de Wilye, pres. by Robert the baker of Coventry
John de Greseleg', pres. by the prior and conv. of Church Gresley
Anketel le Teler of Coventry, pres. by William de Wilesleg', v. St. Michael's [Coventry]
Roger Wylemyn of 'Bulton', pres. by Robert de Verdon
Richard de Ruton, pres. by the dean of the Christianity of Coventry and William de Penle
Thomas, son of John le Sergeant of Southam, pres. by Thomas de Sutham

[Col. 3] *Deacons*

Robert, son of Robert de Shirleye of Southam, pres. by Thomas de Sutham
Richard le Chamberleyn of Lilleshall, pres. by the abbot and conv. of the same
Thomas de Castesby, pres. by William Ruis
Thomas de Hotcombe, pres. by the prior of St. John's hospital, Bridgnorth
John Beged of Shrewsbury, pres. by William Gillot of Shrewsbury
William de Herdesbour', pres. by Thomas de Boydon
John le Gardiner, t. pat.
Stephen de Chelaston, pres. by William de Chelaston
Walter de Eschebourn, pres. by Robert le Warde of Mackworth
Richard de Hampton in Ardena, pres. by John Pecche, kt.
Richard de Ansedeleye, pres. by Ralph de Hybern'
Robert de Eton, t. pat.
Henry de Dumeville, t. pat.
William, son of Ralph de Chelaston, pres. by William, lord of the same [Chellaston]
Peter de Holueton, pres. by John de Waleton
Roger le Locsmyth of Newport, pres. by Sir Ralph le Botiller, lord of Norbury
Thomas de Donynton, dim. dioc. Lincoln
Philip de Bredford, t. pat.
Thomas de Scesteford, pres. by Sir John de Harecourt, kt.
Nicholas de Morton, pres. by Richard de Harle, kt.
Andrew de Matherfeld, pres. by Herbert de Norbury
Ranulph de Rokeby, t. pat.
Thomas de Radewey, pres. by John de Chadleshunt
Walter le Tannour of Derby, pres. by Ranulph de Halsope
John de Egynton, pres. by Robert de Claw[2]...
Hugh de Ingetre, t. pat.

[Fo. 102v col. 1] *Deacons*

William de Tixhale, pres. by Richard Basset of 'Weldon', kt.
Peter de Hengelbi, pres. by Robert de Staunton
John de Roucestr', pres. by Robert de Akovere, lord of Denstone
William de Haunton, t. pat.
William Amys of Tamworth, pres. by W[illiam], prior of Alvecote
Gregory Wyne of Tamworth, pres. by Sir Alexander de Frevill', kt.
William de Sutton, pres. by William de Baillol
William Sweyn of Blithfield, pres. by Richard, lord of the same

John de Seckyndon, pres. by Richard de Whitacr'
Robert de Whychenovere, pres. by the prior and conv. of Canwell
Henry Boneinfant, pres. by Walter de Waltshef
Robert the scribe of Lichfield, t. pat.
John de Hertewelle, pres. by the abbot and conv. of Beauchief
Henry de Austanefeld, pres. by Adam, lord of 'Wyrslowe'
John de Fiskerton, pres. by John Proudfoot
William de Croxhale, pres. by the lord of Croxall
John de Wyleby, t. pat.
 [The rest of the col. is blank.]

[Col. 2] *Priests*

Adam de Lilleshul, pres. by the abbot and conv. of the same [Lilleshall]
Nicholas, son of Nicholas le Mercer of Bridgnorth, pres. by the abbot and conv. of
Lilleshall
Adam de Longeford, t. pat.
Richard Foliot of Etwall, pres. by Ralph de Rolleston
Andrew de Coventr', pres. by Robert de Stok'
Walter Drake of Draycott, pres. by the master and Fr. S. of St. Helen's hospital,
Derby
Robert de Roctele, pres. by Nicholas de Gyldeford, r. Chesterton
John de Longeford, t. pat.
William de Staunton, t. pat.
William de Ichinton, pres. by John Hug' of Chadshunt
John de Hulle, Gilbert de Bourton, pres. by Sir Thomas de Garshale, kt.
Ralph de Whitemor', t. pat.
Adam de Burthyngbury, pres. by Sir Robert de Verdon, kt.
Henry de Alewaston, pres. by William de Chelardeston
Henry de Wyshawe, t. pat.
Henry de Twyford, t. pat.
William, son of John Freman, pres. by the prior of St. James' [hospital], Derby
William de Hopton, pres. by Richard de Draycote, kt.
Geoffrey de Geydon, t. pat.
William, son of Robert de Melbourn, t. pat.
Walter de Radeford, pres. by Richard de Corzon of Breadsall
Andrew de Welton, t. pat.
John Colebeyn, t. pat.
Ralph de Stretton, t. pat.
Hugh, r. Bushbury
John de Chadleshunt, t. pat.
Richard de Wykene, pres. by Robert Pykerel of Stivichall
Thomas, son of John the smith of Harbury, pres. by John de Lodebrok', kt.
William de Fornwerk, t. Repton monastery
John Gybtun, Walter de Radewey, pres. by John Pecche
Richard the paver of Wroxeter, t. pat.
Richard de Shustok', pres. by Richard de Whytacr'

[Col. 3] *Priests*

Simon de Aston, pres. by John de Dalby
John de Chadleshunt, pres. by Jordan, lord of Farnborough
Richard de Trentham, canon of the same [Trentham]
William de Salop', OSA
Geoffrey de Benynton, William of the same, monks of Combermere
John de Benager, OP
Richard Harald, OP
Richard de Chedle, OP
Henry of St. John's, Stafford
John de Haghman, canon of the same [Haughmond]
William, canon of Repton
Robert de Doffeld, Robert de Coventr', canons of Darley
Richard de Aselakeby, monk of Croxden
    [The rest of the fo. is blank.
    1-1 Across the full width of the fo. below the col. headings.
    2 w interlined; MS. stained.]

1297 [Fo. 103] ¹NOMINA ORDINATORUM APUT² STAFFORD' IN ECCLESIA FRATRUM MINORUM³ DIE SAB[B]ATI QUATUOR TEMPORUM MENSIS DECEMBRIS ANNO DOMINI MILLESIMO .CCC^mo. SEXTO. A VENERABILI PATRE DOMINO .T[HOME]. CANDIDE CASE EPISCOPO, DOMINI .W[ALTERI]. DEI GRACIA COVENTR' ET LICH' EPISCOPI SUFFRAGANEO RITE ORDINES CELEBRANTE¹ [17 December 1306].

[Col. 1] *Subdeacons*

Richard de Waleys, r. Walton upon Trent
Roger de Norhampton, v. Lichfield [cath.]
William de Stanton of Solihull, pres. by John de Brocton
Walter de Wysshawe, pres. by Alice de Bereford
Thomas de Honle, pres. by Thomas de Titteleye
Ralph Coldwyne of 'Itchington', pres. by John de Lodebrok'
Richard de Kanewelle, t. pat.
Henry de Heywode, t. pat.

Deacons

John de Petton, r. Petton
M. Geoffrey Moelis, r. Coddington
Robert de Bretteby, pres. by William de Inguardby
Thomas de Lauton, pres. by archd. of Chester
Simon de Sutham, t. pat.
Roger de Albriston, t. pat.

Priests

John Lutebmay, pres. by the baron of Stafford
John Touk', r. Blore

John de Sheynton, r. of the same [Sheinton]
Richard, r. Eaton Constantine
John Beket of Shrewsbury, t. pat.
Richard de Annesdeleye, pres. by Thomas de Nevill'
William de Croxhale, pres. by archd. of Chester
John de Fiskerton, pres. by J. de Segrave
William de Swynesford, pres. by Sir J[ohn] de Somery
John Beget, pres. by Isabella Berry
John de Sekynton, pres. by J[ohn] de Petton
Thomas de Morton, pres. by M. Richard de Coleshull
Henry de Rideware, pres. by Richard de Teyethorp

[Col. 2] *Priests*

William Sweyn of Blithfield, pres. by the lord of Blithfield
James de Novo Burgo, pres. by Ralph Botiller
Henry Ostheleye, t. pat.
Roger de Northkyte, t. pat.
William de Neuport, William de Onderwode, pres. by bp. of Whithorn
    [¹⁻¹ Across the full width of the fo. below the col. headings.
    ² *Sic*
    ³ Interlined over *predicatorum* deleted.]

1298   ¹NOMINA ORDINATORUM DIE SABBATI QUATUOR TEMPORUM MENSIS
DECEMBRIS ANNO DOMINI .Mᵒ.CCCᵐᵒ. SEPTIMO IN ECCLESIA FRATRUM
PREDICATORUM DERB' A VENERABILI PATRE DOMINO ,J[OHANNE]. DEI GRACIA
CARLIOL' EPISCOPO, DOMINI W[ALTERI]. EADEM GRACIA COVENTR' ET LICH'
EPISCOPI SUFFRAGANEO¹ [23 December 1307].

Subdeacons

Nicholas, r. Wishaw
Henry de la Lee, r. Halsall
Thomas, r. moiety of Walton, dim. dioc. Lincoln
Matthew de Novo Castro super Tynam, dim. dioc. Durham
Roger de Erdynton, t. pat.
Ancellus de Sutton, t. pat.
John de Weston, t. pat.
William de Astbury, t. pat. and pres. by R[obert de Redeswell], archd. of Chester
Henry de Novo Castro, t. Freeford hospital
Robert de Norton, t. R. de Aston, dim. dioc. Lincoln
Gilbert de Brockeleye, t. pat.
William de Barr', pres. by Robert de Barre Maugni
Nicholas de Pollesworth, pres. by Sir John de Pollesworth
Robert del Wode of Longdon, t. pat.
Henry le Savage of Brewood, pres. by Brewood Black Ladies

[Col. 3] *Subdeacons*

John de Elmhurst, Peter de Sperham, pres. by archd. of Chester
Robert de Codeshalle, t. pat.
Richard le Spicer of Lichfield, t. pat.
Richard Abovethewey, t. pat.
John Broun of Lichfield, t. pat.
Robert de Halseye, t. pat.
Robert de Yoxhale, t. pat.
Roger de Worthfeld, pres. by Sir H. de Con...[2]
Robert de Byscheton, t. pat.
Richard[3] de Polesworth, pres. by Sir Nicholas of the same
John Lok', dim. dioc. Lincoln, pres. by the prior of Kenilworth
Richard le Sergeant of Egginton, t. pat.
Robert de Hodinet, pres. by Sir Philip de Say
John Wylimot, pres. by Richard de Blithefelt
Robert de Buldewas, t. pat.
Siward de Bretford, pres. by Sir Thomas de Gershale, kt.
John de Frodesham, pres. by the prior of Burscough
William called the clerk of Astbury, t. pat.
Geoffrey Craunage, t. pat.[4]
Adam de Cruddeworth, pres. by the prior and conv. of Canwell
Reginald de Billawe, pres. by the prioress of King's Mead by Derby
John Elys of Melbourne, t. the hermitage of Handsacre
Nicholas de Kersinton, at the request and presentation of the cardinal's proctor
Peter le Graunt of Derby, pres. by J[ohn] Beck
William de Wyco, t. pat.
Robert de Gardino of Solihull, pres. by John le Grey, kt.
John de Elyves, t. pat.
William le Claver of Repton, t. pat.
William the cook of the same, t. pat.
John le Parker of Heathcote, t. pat.
Moyses de Forton, t. pat.
John de Elleford, pres. by r. of the same [Elford]
Robert de Croxhale, t. pat.
Roger de Hulle of 'Sutton', t. pat.
Robert the archer of 'Bromley', t. pat.

[Fo. 103v col. 1] *Subdeacons*

William, son of Alan de Bromleg', t. pat.
Alexander de Sutton, t. pat.
Robert de Overe, pres. by the abbot of Croxden
William de Overe, pres. by John de Chaundeys
Ralph de Bromleg', pres. by the abbot and conv. of Burton upon Trent
Robert Dodeyn' of Derby, pres. by W. de Codinton
Richard Frere of 'Burton', pres. by Matthew Virers
William de Longedon, pres. by J. de 'Miners'
William le Oyler of Derby, t. pat.

Ralph del Wodehous, t. pat.
Robert, son of Geoffrey de Okele, pres. by Richard de Okele
Pagan, son of Simon de Derby, t. pat.
John de Honigham, t. pat.
Richard, son of Robert de Grendon, t. pat.
Roger de Horleye, t. pat.
Geoffrey de Amynton, t. pat.
Nicholas de Tressecote, t. pat.
Richard de Clifton, t. pat.
Thomas de Bobenhull, t. pat.
Henry de Greneberg', pres. by Henry de Brauneston
Henry de Parva Halum, t. pat.
William de Bonleye, t. pat.
Henry de Herdewyk, t. pat.
John de Wylmyncote, t. pat.
Reginald Dymnok, t. pat.
William, son of Ralph de Melbourn, t. pat.
John, son of John de Wygan, t. pat.
Richard, son of William de Onderwode, t. pat.
John called the smith of 'Aston', pres. by Richard le Corzon, lord of Breadsall
Richard de Twyford, pres. by the prior of Church Gresley
William, son of Gregory, t. pat.
Robert, son of John, son of Hugh, t. pat.
John de Ekynton, t. pat.
Walter, son of Ellis de Melebourn, t. pat.
John de Spondon, t. pat.
William Baroun, t. pat.
John le Maceon of 'Weston', t. pat.

[Col. 2] *Deacons*

Thomas de Lega, r. Blithfield
Henry de Berleston, port. Darley
Thomas de Poule, r. Newton Regis
Roger de Norhampton, v. Lichfield [cath.]
Henry de Bromcote, t. pat.
William de Bromcote, pres. by John de Coventr'
Thomas de Westhalum, t. pat.
John de Hull', t. pat.
William de Brokhole, t. pat.
Alan de Tydeswelle, pres. by Henry, perpetual v. Childwall
John called Borȝate of 'Sutton', pres. by Richard, r. 'Sutton'
Ralph Coldwyne of Mollington, pres. by John de Lodebrok', kt.
Walter de Derhul, t. pat.
Robert de Brewode, pres. by Ralph Basset, kt.
Henry de Heywode, t. pat.
Roger Martyn of 'Newbold', t. pat.
William de Wappenbury, t. pat.
John March' of Newbold, t. pat.

Richard, son of Edmund le Chaloner of Birmingham, t. pat.
Robert le Ber, t. St. Helen's hospital, Derby
Alan de Tonge, t. pat.
William de Notbrek' of Berkswell, pres. by the prior and brethren of the hospital of St. John of Jerusalem
Henry de Unkeswrth, pres. by Nicholas de Loungerford
Henry de Ibole, pres. by Robert de Ibole
Hugh de Haneleye, t. pat. and pres. by Sir William de Mere, kt.
Robert Hathewy of Church Lawford, pres. by John de Oddingeseles
William de Merchton, pres. by Robert Baldewyne
Roger de Buddeworth, pres. by Hugh de Sutton
John de Spondon, pres. by Richard Daniel
William de Dersbury, t. pat.
Roger de Clifton, t. pat.
Nicholas de Wyrkesworth, t. pat.

[Col. 3] *Deacons*

Henry called Mastlins of Lilleshall, pres. by the religious of the same
Henry de Haddefeld, pres. by Sir[5] W[illiam] Staff'
Richard, son of Simon de Wy3', t. pat.
John Michel of Breaston, t. pat.
Richard de Ulinton, t. pat.
Richard de Riseleye, pres. by Roger de Wodehall
Henry the marshal of Coventry, t. pat.
John Opy, pres. by Thomas Power
Richard de Cavereswelle, pres. by the prior and conv. of St. Thomas by Stafford
Richard de Donynton, pres. by Alan de Colneye, dim. dioc. Lincoln
Thomas called Chapmon of 'Dassett', t. pat.
Thomas Chaunceler of Davenham, t. pat.
Ralph de Coleshull, pres. by r. Boylestone
Adam de Stretton, t. pat.
John Popyn of 'Morton', pres. by R. de Cunenby
William de Bradeleye of Seckington, t. pat. and pres. by Henry de Caunvill'
Richard de Leyes, pres. by the baron of Stafford
Henry de Shulton, pres. by Sir W[alter] de Charnel'
Thomas, son of Robert de Spondon, t. pat.
Robert Dunchirch, t. pat.
Adam de Kyngesleye, t. pat.
William de la Lane of Hunningham
Richard de Byrcot, pres. by Richard de Turvill'
William de Stanton of Solihull, pres. by William of the same
Roger de le Bechthorp, dim. dioc. Lincoln, pres. by the house of Canterbury
Walter de Wyshawe, t. pat.
William, son of William Corzon, t. pat.
Osbert de Foulbourn, William de Yoxhale, pres. by the dean of St. Mary's church, Stafford
John de Breres, pres. by the prior of St. James' [hospital], Derby
William de Barre, pres. by Ralph Botiller

John de Chaunton, t. pat.
William, son of Richard de Cosinton, t. pat.
Roger de Alriston, t. pat.

[Fo. 104 col. 1] *Priests*

M. Geoffrey de Mewles, r. Coddington
Richard, r. Rodington
William, r. Lawton
Robert, perpetual v. Leighton
Richard, r. Breadsall
Thomas de Lauton, pres. by archd. of Chester
John called de la Lowe of 'Huytesdon', t. pat.
Roger de Weston of Bakewell, pres. by M. Thomas de Ristberwe
Henry de Sutton, pres. by H[enry] Mauveysyn
William de Norton, t. pat.
William de Hulle, t. pat.
William le Rous of Longdon, t. pat.
Robert the scribe of Lichfield, t. pat.
Richard le Wowere, pres. by P[hilip] de Chetewynd
Peter Blount, v. Lichfield [cath.]
William de Hordeborugh, pres. by T[homas] Boydyn
Thomas de Sutham, pres. by Robert de Napton, kt.
Gregory le Wyne, pres. by Richard Vernoun
John Kynefare, t. pat.
Roger Power, pres. by Mabel de Rokeby
William le Deyster of Birmingham, pres. by William of the same, kt.
Richard de Stowa, pres. by Richard Basset, kt.
Thomas de Hocumbe, pres. by the prior of Bridgnorth hospital
William de Cokenage, pres. by Sir Robert de Staundon, kt.
William de Haunton, t. pat.
Simon de Wylmeleghton, t. pat.
John le Gardiner, t. pat.
Roger de Neuport, pres. by Ralph le Botiller
John de Muccleston, Richard le Chamberleyn, pres. by the abbot of Lilleshall
William de Neuton Soli, pres. by the prior of Church Gresley
Robert de Loudam, dim. dioc. York
Richard Payn of Chester, t. pat.
John de Roucestr', t. pat.
Robert de Sutham, t. pat.
Thomas de Sutham, t. pat.
William de Whitemor', t. pat.
John de Stoke, t. pat.
William Leger, t. pat.
Nicholas le Mareschal, t. pat.
John de Flaumvill' of Willoughby, pres. by William, his father

[Col. 2] *Priests*

Peter de Olughton, pres. by J. de Walton
Alexander de Trengeton, dim. dioc. Lincoln
Walter le Tannor of Derby, t. pat.
Thomas de la Lee, pres. by the religious of Markyate
John, son of Thomas le Tailler of Castle Donington, [dim. dioc. Lincoln], t. pat.
Simon de Wyshawe, t. pat.
Richard de Trentham, pres. by the religious of Trentham
Richard Crast, pres. by J[ohn] Comyn, lord of Newbold Comyn
Richard, son of Roger the smith of Nantwich, t. pat.
William de Donham, pres. by the abbot and conv. of Chester
Philip de Bretford, pres. by Richard Blaby
Ranulph de Rokeby, t. pat. and pres. by the dean of Marton
William de Notyngham, dim. dioc. York
William de Ichinton, pres. by the prior and brethren of Thelsford
Walter Bacoun, t. pat.
Roger called Mendyng', t. pat.
Simon de Sutham, t. pat.
William Macwode of Birmingham, t. pat.
Robert de Mackeworth, t. pat.
Roger de la More of Birmingham, t. pat.
Robert de Whiteleye, pres. by Sir John de Makestoke
Richard Roul of Hampton in Arden, pres. by Sir Geoffrey de Hereys
Robert de Eton, pres. by the lord of 'Chireford'
Peter, son of Roger de Engelby, pres. by Robert de Standon and t. pat.
Peter de Donchirch, pres. by Robert de Verdon and t. pat.
Robert de Whichenovere, pres. by Sir Edmund de Somervill'
Roger Wylemyn of 'Belton', pres. by Sir Robert de Verdon, kt.
Thomas de Okebrok', pres. by Robert Sauntcheverel, lord of 'Bolton'
Stephen de Chelardeston, t. pat.
John de Franketon, pres. by Sir J[ohn] de Suleye
Thomas de Catesby, pres. by William Rivel
Anketel le Teler of Coventry, pres. by W[illiam], v. St. Michael's [Coventry]
Henry de la Coppe of Solihull, t. pat.
William Grym of Thorpe, t. pat.

[Col. 3] *Priests*

Simon de Rocteleye, pres. by archd. of Derby
Roger, parson of Bakewell, t. pat.
Walter de la Slade of Fillongley, pres. by William de la Slade
William de Wylie, pres. by Robert the bailiff of Coventry
John de Barewe, t. pat.
Robert de Anesti, pres. by Sir Geoffrey le Hyreys
William Amys of Tunstall, pres. by the religious of Canwell
William, son of William de Sandiacr', t. pat.
Robert de Bretteby, t. pat.
John de Greseleye, pres. by the religious of the same [Church Gresley]

William, son of Hugh de Kyngesneuton, t. pat.
John Syward of Chilvers Coton, t. pat.
Richard de Ruton, pres. by Sir Thomas de Garsale, kt.
John de Ichinton, pres. by Sir J[ohn] de Sudleye
Robert de Hambury, t. pat.
Andrew de Maclesfeld, t. pat.
William, son of Roger de Ichinton, pres. by archd. of Derby
Hugh de Ingestre, pres. by Sir R. de Sandbach, kt.
William Freman of 'Willey', t. pat.
Robert de Hodinhull, t. pat.
William de Prestwelle, t. pat.
William de Faneberg', t. pat.
Peter de Hodynhull, t. pat.
William de Sutton, t. pat.
Robert de Braylesford, pres. by Henry of the same
John Wylimot of Monks Kirby, t. pat.
Thomas, son of Richard de Novo Castro, t. pat.
Robert de Ethorp, pres. by Sir T[homas] de Garsale, kt.
Robert le Flecher of Melbourne, t. pat.
Robert de Stanton, t. pat.
John de Hertwell, pres. by the abbot of Beauchief
William de Napton, pres. by Richard de Napton
Thomas de Cefford, pres. by Sir J[ohn] de Harecourt
Richard de Elmedon, pres. by W. Corbyson
Ralph de Stonistanton, t. pat.
      [The rest of the col. is blank.
      1–1 In col. 2.
      2 MS. stained.
      3 Added later in different ink.
      4 Marked with a cross at the left-hand side.
      5 Interlined.]

1299 [Fo. 104v] ¹NOMINA ORDINATORUM APUD BERKESWELL DIE SAB[B]ATI IN VIGILIA SANCTE TRINITATIS .ANNO DOMINI .Mº.CCCᵐº. OCTAVO A VENERABILI PATRE DOMINO .G[ILBERTO]. DEI GRACIA ENAGDUNENS' EPISCOPO AUCTORITATE ET COMMISSIONE MAGISTRI .R[ADULPHI]. DE REDESWELL ARCHIDIACONI CESTR' DOMINI COVENTR' ET LICH' EPISCOPI EO EXTRA DIOCESIM SUAM AGENTE VICARII¹ [8 June 1308].

[Col. 1] *Subdeacons*

Roger Illari, r. Aldridge
Richard de Solihull, t. pat. and pres. by v. St. Michael's, Coventry
John de Bedenhale, pres. by Sir Robert de Bures
      [The rest of the col. is blank.]

[Col. 2] *Deacons*

Matthew de Novo Castro, dim. dioc. Durham
Henry de Novo Castro, pres. by St. Leonard's hospital, Freeford

Robert de Norton, dim. dioc. Lincoln
John de Weston, t. pat.
Roger atte Grene of Erdington, t. pat.
Robert de Codeshale, t. pat.
Gilbert de Brockeleye, t. pat.
John de Wylmyndecote, t. pat.
Ancellus de Sotton, t. pat.
Henry Savage of Brewood, pres. by Brewood Black Ladies
John Broun, t. pat.
William Claver, t. pat.
William Cocus of Repton, t. pat.
John de Elueford, pres. by Sir John de Ardern, kt.
William de Barre, pres. by Robert de Barre Magna
Roger de Hulle, t. pat.
Richard the baker of Lichfield, t. pat.
Henry de Pipa, t. pat.
Richard de Twyford, pres. by the prior of Church Gresley
    [The rest of the col. is blank.]

[Col. 3] *Priests*

John de Leycestr', canon of Lichfield
William de Astbury, pres. by archd. of Chester
Roger de Norhampton, v. Lichfield [cath.]
Robert de Yoxhale
John called Champyon of 'Dassett'
William de Staunton
Walter de Derhul
Robert de Brewode, pres. by R[alph] Basset of Sapcote, kt.
William de Brochole, t. pat.
John Broun of Hillmorton
John de Buryate, t. pat.
William de Pipe, t. pat.
Henry de Warewyke, dim. dioc. Worcester
    [The rest of the fo. is blank.
    [1-1] Across the full width of the fo. below the col. headings.]

1300 [Fo. 105] [1]NOMINA ORDINATORUM APUD CESTR' DIE SAB[B]ATI IN FESTO SANCTI MATHEI .ANNO DOMINI .MILLESIMO .CCC^mo. OCTAVO A VENERABILI PATRE DOMINO .G[ILBERTO]. DEI GRACIA ENAGDUNEN' EPISCOPO AUCTORITATE ET COMMISSIONE MAGISTRI .R[ADULPHI]. DE REDESWELL ARCHIDIACONI CESTRIE DOMINI COVENTR' ET LICH' EPISCOPI EO EXTRA DIOCESIM SUAM AGENTE VICARII[1] [21 September 1308].

[Col. 1] *Subdeacons*

Adam de Donecastr', dim. dioc. Norwich
Simon de Swelle, t. pat.
Simon Lynet, t. pat.

William Kyng, t. pat.
Richard the baker, t. pat.
William de Ocleston, t. pat.
Gilbert de Lalleford, pres. by John Heroun, lord of the same [Church Lawford]
William de Milverton, t. pat. and pres. by John Comyn of Newbold Comyn
John de Wolriston, pres. by Sir Richard de Turville, kt.
John de Weston subtus Brewode, t. pat.
Richard de Elleford, pres. by J[ohn] de Ardern
Henry de Egynton, pres. by the religious of Dale
John de Barton, t. pat. and pres. by Sir John Bakeputz, kt.
Ellis de Mere, pres. by Robert Dotton
William de Brynygton, t. pat.
William de Staunton, pres. by Vivian of the same
Matthew de Coventr', t. pat.
William de Medio Wyco, t. pat.
Roger de Norwyco, t. pat.
Richard le Coupere of Ashbourne, pres. by v. of the same
Thomas de Bolton, pres. by the abbot of Whalley
Hugh le Spenser, t. pat.
Richard Wyther, pres. by William de Brikhull
Richard de Mefford, t. pat.
Roger de Lemynton, pres. by Sir J[ohn] de Oddingeseles, kt.
William de Standich, pres. by r. of the same [Standish]
Richard de Adbaston, t. pat.
Simon de Shepeye, pres. by the prior of Canwell
Richard de Wyderesleye, pres. by Thomas de la Lee
William, son of John de Dene
William s. Silvester de Kyrkeby
Thomas Wolveye, pres. by Thomas of the same
Thomas de Bromleye, pres. by v. Leek

[Col. 2] *Subdeacons*

Thomas de Weston, pres. by the abbot of Dieulacres
Thomas de Stretton, t. pat.
Roger de Maklesfeld, t. pat.
Robert de Cestr', t. pat.
Robert de Astebury, t. pat.
Richard de Bradeborne, pres. by Sir Roger of the same [Bradbourne]
William de Whitewyk, t. pat.
John Hulbek' of 'Kyrkeby', t. pat.
John, son of William de Wyco Malbano, t. pat.
Reginald de Norton in Halys, t. pat.
Alan Lanerek', t. pat.
Henry de Chedle, pres. by Roger of the same, kt.
Robert le Roter, pres. by the religious of Norton
William de Werynton, pres. by the abbot and conv. of Chester
Henry, son of Ivon de Weston, Henry, son of Henry de Crosto, pres. by Sir Robert
de Bures

Robert de Spondon, t. pat.
Richard de Tydrinton, t. pat.
Philip de la Lee, pres. by John de la Lande
Richard de Cotes, pres. by the nuns of Nuneaton
William Matheu, t. pat.
Richard de Sondbache, t. pat.
Nicholas de Frodesham, t. pat.
Ralph de Novo Castro, pres. by the abbot and conv. of Chester
William de Lauton, pres. by Richard de Wolston
Adam de Melver', pres. by Adam, r.[2] Great Mitton
Thomas de Dutton, pres. by William de Dutton
Robert de E[3]gelton, pres. by the religious of Haughmond, dim. dioc. Lincoln
Thomas Hert of Tabley, t. pat.
John de Tunstal, t. pat.
Henry de Clifton, t. pat.
Adam de Byrlebrok', t. pat.
William de Hyda, pres. by Sir Thomas de Burgo
John le Valeys, pres. by Robert le Valeys, v. Longdon
John de Herteford, pres. by the prior of Norton and t. pat.
William de Byrleye, pres. by William de Standisch
Adam de Dalylee, t. pat.

[Col. 3] *Subdeacons*

Roland de Staunton, pres. by Robert de Staunton
Robert de Whytele, t. pat.
Bertram de Torporleg', t. pat.
John Poydras, t. pat.
Ralph Tolone, pres. by Richard de Vernoun, kt.
Nicholas, son of Richard de Frodesham, t. pat.
Richard de Wroctesleg', t. pat.
Thurstan de Wygan, pres. by William de Brikhull
Robert de Furnoys,[4] pres. by Roger de Pyl[5]kynton'[5]
William Ster, t. pat.
John Pecok, t. pat.
Walter, son of William, son of Magote, t. pat.
Andrew de Bemhurst, t. pat.
Richard de Boterdon, t. pat.
Robert de Lullington, pres. by Sir Peter de Greseleg', kt.
William Michel of Ladbroke, pres. by Sir John de Lodbrok', kt.
Thomas de Knotton, t. pat.
Henry de Corleye, t. pat.
Gilbert de Honygham, t. pat.
Richard de Gnousale, t. pat.
William de Ambaldeston, t. pat.
Richard ad Fontem of Newcastle under Lyme, t. pat.
Alan Cox, t. pat.
Henry de Honyngham, pres. by Sir Thomas de Garsale, kt.
Thomas de Thurleston, t. pat.

Henry de Estlemynton, t. pat.
Henry le Folour of Tamworth, t. pat.
Robert de Medio Wyco, t. pat.[6]
John de Waleshale, t. pat.
Adam Juwet of Ashow, t. pat.
William, son of Robert le Botiller of Lichfield, t. pat.
Nicholas, son of William the miller, t. pat.
Richard de Hondesacr', t. pat.
John the marshal of Derby, t. pat.
Giles de Cloune, t. pat.
William the carpenter, t. pat.
Adam de Blakeborn, t. pat.
John Falghes, t. pat.

[Fo. 105v col. 1] *Subdeacons*

[7]Roger de Duffeud, t. pat.[7]
Adam, son of John de Ashesho, pres. by Thomas de Pype
Roger Broun of Church Lawford, pres. by Lady Annabel de Mondevill'
Roger Blondel of Chesterfield, pres. by ...[8] de Theworth, kt.
William Cok' of Bednall, pres. by the baroness of Stafford
Thomas de Waverton, t. pat.
William de Cobeleye, t. pat.
Walter de Rockeleye, pres. by Sir Nicholas dicti[9] de Eton, lord of Ratley
Simon de Aruwe, pres. by Henry de Caumvill'
Alexander de Cobbeleye, t. pat.
Thomas de Eyton, t. pat.
William de Thorp, t. pat.
Robert, son of Robert de Wych, t. pat.[10]
William de Ervefen, pres. by Sir Roger de Swynnerton
Adam de Ervefen, pres. by Ralph Basset
Geoffrey the carpenter, pres. by Margaret, baroness of Stafford
Henry Adam of 'Walton', pres. by Sir Robert Mohaut
Robert Pecok of Abbots Bromley, t. pat.
Walter de Frodesham, t. pat.
Richard, son of Alexander le Ferour, t. pat.
William Westdewy of Lichfield, t. pat.
Robert de Teynton, t. pat.
William, son of William Salewy del Cannok', t. pat.
Alexander de Plumbleg', t. pat.
Peter Swannesswer' of Darley, t. pat.
Nicholas de Brewode, t. pat.
Thomas de Gumpeʒate, t. pat.
Nicholas Bisshop of Lichfield, t. pat.
Roger de Repyndon, t. pat.
Richard de Wolaston, t. pat.
Robert de Terven, t. pat.
Roger, son of Roger de Thurleston, t. pat.
Roger de Venables, t. pat.

Simon Clippelok', t. pat.
Roger de Bradeleye, pres. by Sir Richard, lord of Kniveton
Robert, son of Roger de Baquell, pres. by Thomas de Folgeambe
John de Ronton, t. pat.
Richard de Estham, t. pat.
Thomas called Miles of Chester, t. pat.

[Col. 2] *Subdeacons*

Robert de Stone, pres. by Sir Hugh Meygnyl
Nicholas de Calden, t. pat.
Nicholas de Eccleshale, t. pat.
Richard de Egbaston, Walter de Egbaston, Adam de Egbaston, pres. by the dean of Lichfield
Robert de Burton, t. pat.
Adam Aylrych of Ashow, t. pat.
Nicholas Fremont of Newport, pres. by the prior and conv. of Wombridge
Roger de Elton, pres. by Adam de Kelsale, r. Thornton le Moors
Walter Hubert of Cooks' Lane, t. pat.
Hugh de Acton, t. pat.
Roger called Elyot, pres. by the prior of St. John's [hospital], Shrewsbury
Nicholas de Snocton, pres. by Sir Robert de Bromleg', kt.
Thomas de Essheborne, t. pat.
John de Mamcestr', t. pat.

Deacons

Nicholas de Blaston, v. Tarvin
Roger Ilary, r. Aldridge
Hugh de Aldeleye, r. Blore
Roger Gerard, r. 'Mablethorpe' [dim. dioc. Lincoln]
John de Tybynton, t. pat.
Nicholas de Pollesworth, pres. by Sir John of the same
Richard de Pollesworth, pres. by Nicholas of the same
Robert the archer of 'Bromley', t. pat.
Richard Aboveþewe, t. pat.
Walter de Stretton, t. pat.
Reginald Dymmok, t. pat.
Geoffrey de Amynton, t. pat.
Robert de Byssheton, pres. by John de Colewych
Nicholas Wyȝh', t. pat.
Robert de Croxhale, t. pat.
Robert de Ocleye, t. pat.
Siward de Bretford, pres. by Sir Thomas de Gersale, kt.
Robert de Gardino of Solihull, pres. by Sir John de Grey, kt.
John le Parker of Ascote, t. pat.
William called the clerk of Astbury, t. pat.
Richard de Solyhul, pres. by M. William de Billesleye, v. St. Michael's, Coventry

[Col. 3] *Deacons*

John de Egynton, t. pat.
Richard le Serjeant of Egginton, t. pat.
John de Stonleye, t. pat.
Adam Pye of Lichfield, t. pat.
John de Norton, t. pat.
John Lok', pres. by the religious of Kenilworth, dim. dioc. Lincoln
Roger de Wortfeld, pres. by same[11]
William de Farewell, t. pat.
Thomas de Bobenhull, t. pat.
John the smith of 'Aston', pres. by Richard de Corzon
Geoffrey de Craunage, t. pat.[12]
John de Bedenhal, pres. by Sir Robert de Bures, kt.
John de Tervyn, pres. by Sir Robert de Henynton[13]
Richard de Clyderowe, t. pat.
William le Oyler, t. pat. and pres. by the prior of St. James' [hospital], Derby
Roger de Horleye, t. pat.
William Da of Nantwich, t. pat.
John Wylymot, pres. by Richard de Wolseleye
Robert de Kedelyngton, pres. by the religious of Haughmond, dim. dioc. Lincoln
Hugh de Eccleshale, pres. by archd. of Derby
Pagan de Derby, t. pat.
John de Frodesham, t. pat.
[14]William de Dunhod, t. pat.
John Elys of Melbourne, t. pat.[14]
John de Spondon, t. pat.
Adam de Cruddeworth, t. pat.
Geoffrey de Erleston, t. pat.
Hugh de Fossebrok', t. pat.
William Gregori of Ticknall, t. pat.
Robert, son of John de Meleborn, t. pat.[15]
John de Honyngham, t. pat.
Adam de Bokkeleg', t. pat.
Nicholas de Trescote, t. pat.
Robert Dodeyn of Derby, t. pat.
Moyses de Hampton, t. pat.
William de Overe, pres. by Sir John Chandoys
John, son of John de Toft of Egginton, t. pat.
Richard Frere of 'Burton', pres. by the prior of Tutbury
Henry de Parva Halum, t. pat.
Nicholas de Kersynton, pres. by Henry de Hopton

[Fo. 106 col. 1] *Deacons*

Peter le Grant of Derby, pres. by Nicholas de Marchynton
Henry de Herdewych, t. pat.
John, son of Robert de Spondon, t. pat.
Ralph de Bromleg', pres. by the abbot of Burton upon Trent

Simon, son of Stephen Cestr', t. pat.
Alexander, son of Henry the miller of 'Stockton', t. pat.
Richard le Spycer of Lichfield, t. pat.
Richard de Preston, t. pat.
Thomas de Honle, t. pat.
William de Poleye, t. pat.
Richard de Pollesworth, t. pat.
Adam Wysbryd, t. pat.
Thomas de Stretton, t. pat.
William Pope of Kemberton, pres. by the religious of Lilleshall
William, son of Alan de Bromleg', t. pat.

Priests

Thomas de Polee, r. Newton Regis
Henry de la Lee, r. Halsall
Thomas de Pyctesleye, dim. dioc. Lincoln
Richard, v. Caverswall
Mathew de Novo Castro super Tyn, pres. by M. Robert de Redd[eswell], archd. of Chester, dim. dioc. Durham
Henry de Novo Castro, pres. by the master and brethren of St. Leonard's hospital, Freeford
Adam de Stretton, t. pat., he is commanded, on pain of excommunication, he shall have cure of souls of a parish within two years
Richard de Donyngton, pres. by Alan de Colney, dim. dioc. Lincoln
Thomas de Spondon, t. pat.
Henry de Bromcote, t. pat.
William de Bromcote, t. pat.
William de Merxston, pres. by Robert Baldewyne
William de Notebrok', pres. by the prior of the hospital of St. John of Jerusalem
William de Wappenbury, t. pat.
William de Bradeleye of Seckington, t. pat.
William de Honyngham, t. pat.
Ralph Goldwyne, t. pat.
Henry de Shulton, pres. by Sir W[alter] de Charnel', kt.
Robert le Bier of 'Draycott', t. pat.
Richard le Chaloner, t. pat.
John de Cotes of 'Kynton', t. pat., dim. dioc. Lincoln
John Broun of Lichfield, t. pat.
Thomas de Shulton, t. pat.
Alan Tonge, t. pat.
Richard de Thwyford, pres. by the prior of Church Gresley
Hugh de Haneleg', t. pat. and pres. by W[illiam] de Mere, kt.[16]

[Col. 2] *Priests*

Henry Savage, pres. by Brewood Black Ladies
John de Egynton, t. pat.
Robert de Codeshale, t. pat.

John de Elleford, pres. by John de Ardern', kt.
William le Claver of Repton, t. pat.
Henry de Wyrkeworth, pres. by Sir Nicholas Hon[17]gerford
Henry de Ibole, pres. by Sir Thomas Folgeambe, kt.
John de Breres, pres. by Sir Ralph de Rolleston, kt.
Ralph de Coleshull, pres. by John, lord of Boylestone
Henry de Solyhull, t. pat. and pres. by Sir John de Grey, kt.
Roger de Erdynton, t. pat.
John Opy of Sawley, pres. by Thomas Power
Ancellus de Sotton, t. pat.
Thomas the clerk of Davenham, t. pat.
Henry de Pypa of Lichfield, t. pat.
William de Yoxhale, pres. by Sir Richard Ymmer
John de Spondon, pres. by Sir Richard Daniel, kt.
Walter de Wysshawe, pres. by Thomas, his brother
Gilbert de Brockeleg', t. pat.
Nicholas de Wyrkesworth, t. pat.
John de Wylmyndecote, t. pat.
Henry de Heywode, t. pat.
William the cook of Repton, t. pat.
Robert de Norton, dim. dioc. Lincoln
[18]John de Weston, t. pat.
Thomas de Westhalum, t. pat.
Roger de Alvereston, t. pat.
Roger de Sutton, t. pat.[18]
Roger de Beddeworth, pres. by William de Dotton
Alan de Childewell, pres. by v. of the same [Childwall]
William de Ware, pres. by Ralph le Botiller,[19] kt.
Richard Symon of Nantwich, t. pat.
Osbert de Folbourn, v. Stafford
Richard de Lies, pres. by Edmund, bar[19]on of Stafford
Richard de Ryseleye, pres. by Roger[19] del Wodehalle
John de Schavynton, t.[19] pat.
Adam de Kyngesleye, t.[19] pat.
Ralph de Bunnesbury, pres. by Sir John de Bracebrigg'
John Maresch' of Newbold, t. pat.; [20]let there be a letter[20]
William, son of William Corzon of Croxall, t. pat.
Richard de Byrycote, pres. by Sir Richard Turvill', kt.
Robert de Hathewey, t. pat.
John Popyn, pres. by Henry de Lich'
William the baker, pres. by William Rivel
William de Barre, pres. by Robert de Magna Barr'

[Fo. 106v col. 1] *Priests*

Roger de Lobesthorp, pres. by the prior of Chacombe, dim.
Roger de Hulle, t. pat.
William de Deresbury, t. pat.
William de Tervyn, t. pat.

Robert Hodynet, t. pat.
Henry de Alstansfeld, t. pat.
Henry de Hadefeld, pres. by William de Stafford
Richard Wodenover, pres. by the prior of Wombridge
Henry called Mastlyng, pres. by the religious of Lilleshall
    [Followed by four blank lines.
    [1–1] Across the full width of the fo. below the col. headings.
    [2] Interlined.
    [3] One letter erased.
    [4] Marked with .G. at the left-hand side.
    [5–5] Continued on the line below.
    [6] Marked with a cross at the left-hand side.
    [7–7] Added at the top of the list by another contemporary hand.
    [8] MS. stained.
    [9] *Sic*
    [10] Marked with a cross at the left-hand side.
    [11] Marked with a cross within a circle with four dots around it at the left-hand side.
    [12] Marked with a cross at the left-hand side.
    [13] Marked with a cross at the left-hand side.
    [14–14] Marked with .G. at the right-hand side.
    [15] Marked with a cross at the left-hand side.
    [16] Interlined.
    [17] A 7mm. natural hole is at this point and the name is written around it.
    [18–18] Two natural holes of 8mm. and 5mm. are at the right-hand side of these names.
    [19–19] A contemporary stitched tear extends some 8.5cm. diagonally to the right of the two holes and the following names have been written around it at these points.
    [20–20] Added later.]

1301 [1]NOMINA ORDINATORUM APUD COLEWYCH DIE SAB[B]ATI QUATUOR TEMPORUM MENSIS SEPTEMBRIS ANNO DOMINI MILLESIMO .CCC[mo]. NONO A VENERABILI PATRE FRATRE .G[ILBERTO]. DEI GRACIA ENAGDUNENS' EPISCOPO VICE ET AUCTORITATE DOMINI .W[ALTERI]. EADEM GRACIA COVENTR' ET LICH' EPISCOPI RITE ORDINES CELEBRANTE[1] [20 September 1309].

Subdeacons

Herbert Pouger, t. pat., he has sworn himself satisfied
Robert de Hyb[ernia] of Shustoke, pres. by John le Botiller, as above
Pagan Swyft of Derby, t. pat., as above
Thomas de Okebrok', pres. by the religious of Leeds, as above
Robert Ynge, pres. by the religious of Tutbury
John de Kyrkeby, pres. by Nicholas, lord of Willey
Robert de Swynnerton, pres. by Sir Roger of the same, kt.
Gilbert de Wythybrok', pres. by Sir George de[2] Castro, kt.
Richard[2] de Cokkeslene, pres. by John de Cotes
William de[2] Stretton, pres. by the prior of St. John's hospital, Shrewsbury
Robert de Lemynton, pres. by John Comyn
Thomas de Croukhul, pres. by St. Giles' hospital, Shrewsbury
Thomas Mudle, pres. by Sir John Strange, kt.

Thomas Kytewyld of Southam, pres. by r. of the same
William de Madleye, warden of Holy Sepulchre hospital, Radford
Henry de Shelden, pres. by Nicholas, lord of the same

[Col. 2]

Roger Cosyn, t. pat.
John Shyrlok, John Knystecote, son of Henry of the same, Philip de Warmynton,
Richard of the same, Roger, s. Richard de Eccleshale, Geoffrey, s. Robert le
Staleworth of Stoneleigh, William de Blees of Radway, Jordan le Mareschal of
Farnborough, pres. by archd. of Derby
William le Boner of Atherstone, pres. by r. of the same
Richard de Aspes, pres. by Henry de Brandeston
Adam de Okebrok', pres. by William Freman of the same [Ockbrook]
Henry called the smith of Coventry, t. pat.
John de Asthul, pres. by Henry le Bret
Walter, son of Ralph Giffard of Chillington, pres. by the abbot and conv. of
Lilleshall
John, son of Ranulph de Boughton, pres. by the master of house of St. Giles of the
same [Boughton, Chester]
Andrew de Brandon, pres. by Thomas de Garsale
Henry de Okebrok', pres. by Simon Pouger of 'Draycott'
Hugh de Okebrok', pres. by William de Alwaston
Roger Lambeday of Church Lawford, pres. by John Heron, lord of the same
John de Borthyngbury, pres. by Robert de Verdon
Henry Wibbot of Ockbrook, pres. by Robert de Muscham of 'Stanton'
John le Fermente of Ockbrook, pres. by Hugh Bordet of Kirk Hallam
John de Sutham, t. pat.
Roger de Horseleg', pres. by William de 'Salni', lord of Stanton
John Seþane, pres. by William Rivel
William de Spondon, pres. by Hugh Bordet, lord of Kirk Hallam
Richard de Pylkynton, pres. by the prior of Tut³bury³
William Talbot, pres. by the prior and conv. of Church Gresley
William de Overa, pres. by the abbot of Hulton
Thomas de Elleford of Eccleshall, pres. by Sir John de Ardern, kt.
John de Stonle, pres. by John Pecche, kt.
William, son of William Pynnor of 'Stockton', pres. by Sir Edmund de Somervill'
Thomas Morice of Derby, pres. by r. Weston upon Trent
John de Fylongeleg', pres. by Henry le Charnels, kt., lord of Bedworth

[Fo. 107 col. 1] *Subdeacons*

M. Ralph de Derby, r. Litton, dim. dioc. Bath and Wells
Henry Suet, pres. by John Suet of 'Aston'
William, son of Richard de Keleborn, pres. by William Rosel, lord of Denby
Richard de Wolfecote, pres. by the master of Freeford hospital
William de Waverton, pres. by v. Polesworth
William, son of Roger de Norton, t. pat.
Roger de Olvesmore, t. pat.

Richard de Lucy, t. pat.
Richard de Bromwych, t. pat.
Robert Paramour, pres. by William de Weston
William le Spenser of Mickleover, pres. by Sir W[illiam] de la Warde
Richard de Kent, pres. by John de Kent of Shrewsbury
John Gery of Clive, pres. by Sir Thomas Corbet
Walter Doune of Eccleshall, pres. by Sir Roger de Bradeborn, kt.
John de Hulle, pres. by Sir William de Hastyng'
John de Brynkelowe, pres. by Thomas Boydyn
Richard de Bascote, pres. by Sir Peter de Lymmerse
John de Parva Overa, pres. by M. Nicholas de Over'[4]
Henry Lilkok of Bakewell, t. pat.
George de Wythibrok', pres. by Richard Boot of the same [Withybrook]
Thomas de Burthyngburi, pres. by Laurence de Preston
Adam Warner of Long Itchington, pres. by Sir John de Oddyngeseles
Adam de Lamputtes, pres. by Sir Philip de Baryngton
Philip de Thamworth, pres. by William de Walton
Richard de Over', pres. by Robert le Fuyrbraz of Willington
John de Bobenhull, pres. by Sir Robert s. Guy, kt.
William de Opton, pres. by W., v. Eccleshall
John de Wolrenhampton, pres. by John de Trysel
Henry le Broune of Rolleston, pres. by Ralph of the same, kt.
Simon de Meysham, pres. by William de Inguarby
Robert de Byrchesleg', pres. by Robert Ball of Coventry
Robert de Staveleye, Adam le Warner, pres. by St. John's hospital, Yeaveley
John Cryspyn of 'Barrow', pres. by Fr. William de Toton
Roger de Kyngesleye, pres. by Richard, lord of Blithfield
John Quenyld of Egginton, pres. by William Tymmor
Robert Portegeoye, pres. by William de Neuton
John de Herberbury, pres. by John de Lodbrok'
Thomas Drake of Coleshill, pres. by M. Richard of the same
Ralph Dandy, Robert de Stapelford, William de Morton, Richard de Albryston,
pres. by Sir Richard de Chadesden'
Reginald de Pakynton, pres. by Sir Geoffrey Hereys

[Col. 2] *Subdeacons*[5]

Nicholas Corzon of Breadsall, pres. by Richard Corzon
William, son of Swain de Blythefeld, Richard de Kenerdale, pres. by Richard, lord
of the same [Blithfield]
Hugh de Northmondesleg', pres. by v. Milwich
Henry de Bromleg', t. pat.
John de la Lawe, pres. by Geoffrey de Kenerdale
Adam de Mere, pres. by Sir Robert Toke
Simon de Brokes, pres. by John,[6] r. Lawton
John de Spondon, pres. by Richard le Grey, kt.
Richard de Brynkelowe, pres. by Thomas de Reddeswell
Richard de Swerkeston, pres. by the prior of Bread[7]sall
Walter de Ponte of Frodsham, t. pat.

[8]Henry de Perton, t. pat.
Nicholas de Scropton, t. pat.[8]
William de Reyndon, pres. by Richard de[7] Stredleye
Ralph de Derset, t. pat. and pres. by William[7] de Derset
John de Shepey, pres. by the abbot and conv. of[7] Burton upon Trent
John ad Fontem of 'Aston', pres. by Henry[7] Fitzherbert, lord of Norbury
Richard de Tatenhul, pres. by Sir Robert[7] of the same
Thomas de Bylney, pres. by Robert de Stoke
John de Botebby, pres. by Sir William Tromwyne
Reginald de Stonleye, t. pat.
Richard, son of William de Norton, t. pat.
Thomas, son of Andrew de Byrmyngham, t. pat.
Stephen de Ednesovere, pres. by the abbot of Rocester
Robert, son of Reginald de Brugg', t. pat.
Peter de Maclesfeld, t. pat.
William de Mere, t. pat.
Richard de Catton, pres. by W[illiam] de Freford
Robert de Attelberug', pres. by v. Nuneaton
Adam de Newenham, pres. by Thomas de Garsale
John de Waverton, t. pat.
Robert de Borthyngbury, t. pat.
Robert de Shyppele, t. pat.
John de Pollesworth, t. pat.
Andrew de Herberbury, t. pat.
William de Dalbury, t. pat.
Andrew de Bemhurst, t. pat.
Stephen de Stonleye, t. pat.
Thomas Rossel of 'Over', t. pat.
John, s. Nicholas de Leycestr', t. pat.

[Fo. 107v col. 1]

Henry de[9] Hatherdon, pres. by Sir William Tromwyne
William de Sutham, pres. by John[9] de Sutham
William Sharpmor of 'Bromwich',[9] pres. by Thomas of the same
William le Spenser, pres. by William de Hugeford
Hugh de Morton, pres. by Sir Thomas de Garsale
Henry de Wavere, pres. by William de Freford
William de Congulton, Roger de Standys, William de Mancestr', John de Stapelford, t. pat. by J. de Hottot
Roger Ju[10]wet, pres. by Philip de Somervill'
Roger[10] Burnel, t. pat.
Alan le Murager of Chester, t. pat.
Henry de Cobynton, pres. by Sir John Pecche, kt.
Henry de Steyveston, pres. by John de Rougate
Walter[11] Abel of Tamworth, pres. by Thomas de Wyssawe
William[11] de Brynkelowe, t. pat.
Thomas[11] Freman of Coleshill, t. pat.

Hugh de Halum, Richard, s.[11] Nicholas de Waleshale, John de Ey[11]ton, Richard de[11] Eyton, Laurence de[11] Eyton, Thomas de[11] Eyton, t. pat. by J[ohn] de Hottot
William de Breydeston, Thomas de Stanton, Gilbert de Spondon, Richard de Fynham, t. pat. by J[ohn] de Hottot
Thomas de Montesorell, pres. by the prior of Sandwell
Adam le Mouner of 'Burton', t. pat.
Thomas de Ambaston, t. pat.
Simon de Clyve, pres. by John de Bracebrygg'
Alan Chyeu of Chesterfield, t. pat.
William de Wystwyck, t. pat.
Henry de Edalveston, t. pat.
William de Ashover', t. pat.
Bartholomew de Wappenbur', [Bertram][12] le Wodeward, pres. by William de Stok'
Nicholas de Waverton, pres. by r. Drayton Bassett
William Percy, pres. by r. Blithfield
Adam de Fetherston, pres. by Robert Champyon
Robert Broun of 'Haywood', t. pat.
Ralph de Haneyate, t. pat.
Hugh de Wybbenbury, t. pat.
William Portegeoye, pres. by William Wyldegoos
Robert de Warylowe, Richard de Cokkeslene, pres. by John de Cotes

[Col. 2] *Subdeacons*

John s. William del Stowestrete of Lichfield, t. pat.
John Randolf of Stareton, William de Ruton, Reginald de Edulston, John Auneys, t. pat. by J[ohn] de Hottot
Richard de Stretton, Richard Bygge, Roger de Braylesford, Laurence de Knottesford, t. pat. by J[ohn] de Hottot
Richard the deacon of Gaydon, pres. by M. Richard de Norhampton
Peter de Wybetoft, t. pat.
Roger de Kenewaston, t. pat.
John de Otherton, t. pat.
John de Kyngeston, t. pat.
John de Boudon, t. pat.
Nicholas de Stanle, t. pat.
John de Hore of Fradswell, t. pat.
Jordan de Hampton, t. pat.
John de Kyngeston, pres. by r. Chesterton
Nicholas de Stanle, pres. by the master of the hospital of St. John of Jerusalem
Richard Warmeyte, t. pat.
Thomas de Clyve, t. pat.
Robert de Bromleye, t. pat.
Nicholas Musard, r. of Staveley chapel
Gilbert de Wratting, r. 'Newton', dim. dioc. Norwich
Ranulph Torold of Birkenhead, pres. by the prior of the same
John, son of Andrew de Byrmyngham, John brother of the said John, pres. by John de Bentleye
Geoffrey the clerk of Wolverhampton, t. pat.

Henry de Weston, t. pat.
Henry de Croft, t. pat.
Richard de Weston, pres. by r. of the same
Thomas de Bannebury, pres. by Adam de Berle
Richard de Huton, pres. by the prior of Birkenhead
John de Whytinton, t. pat.
John de Barwe, Robert Leonard, Thomas s. Robert, William Leonard, t. pat. by
Sir R. de Hoyland
   [The rest of the fo. is blank.]

[Fo. 108 col. 1] *Deacons*

William s. Silvester de Kyrkeby, t. pat.
William Bere, t. pat.
Richard de Clifton, t. pat.
Richard de Egbaston, t. pat.
Alan Cox, t. pat.
Robert Pecok of Abbots Bromley, t. pat.
Adam s. John de Ashesho, pres. by Thomas de Pype
Ranulph de Burton, t. pat.
Henry le Folour of Tamworth, t. pat.
Richard de Mefford, t. pat.
Robert de Bosco of Longdon, t. pat.
Giles de Cloune, t. pat.
Adam Aylrych of Ashow, t. pat.
William the carpenter of Tamworth, t. pat.
Robert de Halsey of Longdon, t. pat.
Ellis de Mere, t. pat.
Richard de Elleford, pres. by Sir John de Ardern
William de Ervefen, pres. by Sir Roger de Swynnerton
William de Standon, pres. by Vivian, lord of the same
Adam de Ervefen, pres. by Roger de Swynnerton
William de Ambaldeston, t. pat.
John de Barton, t. pat.
William de Molverton, t. pat.
Roger Broun of Church Lawford, t. pat.
Gilbert de Chirchelalleford, t. pat.
Walter Elys of Melbourne, t. pat.
Robert s. Roger de Baquelle, pres. by Sir Thomas de Follegeambe
Adam Juwet of Ashow, t. pat.
William de Thorp, t. pat.
Thomas de Thurleston, t. pat.
Peter Swannesswer' of Derby, t. pat.
Simon de Shepey, pres. by the prior of Canwell
Alexander de Cobeleye, t. pat.
Thomas de Gompeʒate, t. pat.
William de Cobeleye, t. pat.
Alexander de Plumleye, t. pat.
Henry de Egynton, pres. by the abbot of Dale

Simon de Arwe, t. pat.
Thomas de Bolton, t. pat.
Henry de Lemynton, t. pat.
Oliver de Wythibrok', t. pat.
Simon de Swelle, t. pat.
William called the king, of Lichfield, t. pat.
William le Bolter of Lichfield, pres. by William de Brikhull
William s. William Salewy del Cannok, t. pat.
Simon Lynet of Lichfield, t. pat.
William Baroun, t. pat.
Thomas de Waverton, t. pat.
Richard de Bosco, t. pat.
John de Ronton, t. pat.
Nicholas Bisshop of Lichfield, pres. by Sir Thomas de Nevill'

[Col. 2] *Deacons*

Walter de Roctele, t. pat.
John de Luceby, dim. dioc. Durham
John de Holing', t. pat.
Nicholas de Frodesham, t. pat.
Roger de Clyfton, pres. by Sir John de Lodbrok'
Henry de Greneberg', pres. by Henry de Brandeston
Nicholas Fremond', pres. by the prior of Wombridge
Richard de Bradeborn, t. pat.
Robert le Teyntour of Coventry, t. pat.
Walter de Cockeslene, t. pat.
John de Wolrichiston, pres. by Sir Richard Turvill'
Richard de Wolaston, t. pat.
Robert de Lollington, t. pat.
Thomas de Mamcestr', t. pat.
Andrew de Bemhurst, t. pat.
Henry de Corleye, t. pat.
Thomas de Bromleg', t. pat.
Henry Adam of 'Walton', pres. by Robert de Montalt
Richard de Boterton, t. pat.
John de Weston, t. pat.
Hugh le Spenser of Davenham, t. pat.
John de Hertford, t. pat.
Robert de Medio Wyco, t. pat.
William de Herberbury, t. pat.
William de Medio Wyco, t. pat.
John Poydras, t. pat.
Roger de Heleg', t. pat.
Robert Coket, t. pat.
Richard le Coupier of Ashbourne, t. pat.
Adam de Bylrebrok', t. pat.
Roger de Wytteney, pres. by Sir John de Oddingeseles
Thomas de Asheborn, t. pat.

Robert de Spondon, t. pat.
Robert de Blakeborn, t. pat.
Richard de Wedresleg', t. pat.
Henry de Chedle, t. pat.
John de Falges, t. pat.
Adam de Blakeborn, t. pat.
William de Weryngton of Ashbourne, pres. by the prior of Tutbury
William de Brynigton, t. pat.
Richard de Tyderington, t. pat.
William de Caldecote, t. pat.
William de Dene, t. pat.
John Holbok, t. pat.
Thomas de Eyton, pres. by Thomas de Horseleg'
Roland de Stanton, t. pat.
Henry de Honyngham, t. pat.

[Fo. 108v col. 1] *Deacons*

Roger de Repydon, t. pat.
Ralph Tolone, t. pat.
Gilbert de Honyngham, t. pat.
William Michel of Ladbroke, t. pat.
Adam de Egbaston, t. pat.
Ralph de Cotes, pres. by the nuns of Nuneaton
John, son of John de Wygan, t. pat.
Robert Frere, t. pat.
William de Longesdon, t. pat.
Richard de Hondesacr', t. pat.
John de Waleshale, t. pat.
Richard de Ambaston, t. pat.
Roger Elyot, t. pat.
William de Longedon, t. pat.
Richard the baker of Lichfield, t. pat.
Reginald de Norton in Halys, t. pat.
Ralph del Wodehous, t. pat.
Simon de[13] Chyppenol, t. pat.
John de Elmhurst, t. pat.
Nicholas de Snoxton', t. pat.
Richard de Sondbache, t. pat.
Robert de Stone, pres. by the prior of the same
William de Standon, t. pat.
Roger de Venables, t. pat.
Thomas de Wolveye, t. pat.
Walter, son of Richard de Frodesham, t. pat.
Richard de Gnousale, t. pat.
John de Weston, t. pat.
Stephen de Gnousale, t. pat.
Richard ad Fontem of Newcastle under Lyme, t. pat.
Nicholas, son of Richard de Frodesham, t. pat.

William Cok of Bednall, t. pat.
Thomas de Dotton, t. pat.
Henry de Clifton, t. pat.
William de Okleston, t. pat.
Nicholas de Brewode, t. pat.
Geoffrey de Castro juxta Stafford', t. pat.
Thomas Hert of Tabley, t. pat.
Thomas Miles of Chester, t. pat.
Robert Preco of Nantwich, t. pat.
William Matheu of the same, t. pat.
John de Mamcestr', t. pat.
Robert de Forneys, t. pat.
Robert le Rotier, t. pat.
Roger, son of Stephen de Norwyco, t. pat.

[Col. 2] *Deacons*

William, son of Oliver de Wystwych, dim. dean of Tettenhall
Thomas, son of Roger de Thurleston, t. pat.
Thurstan de Wygan, t. pat.
Robert the clerk of Tarvin, t. pat.
Richard de Estham, t. pat.
Robert de Cestr', t. pat.
Roger de Elton, t. pat.
Walter de Cubbele of Edgbaston, t. pat.
Robert de Burton super Trentham, t. pat.
Roger de Duffeld, t. pat.
Hugh de Acton, t. pat.
Bertram de Torpurle, t. pat.
Nicholas de Calton, t. pat.
William de Lauton, t. pat.
Robert de Whetele, t. pat.
Walter Maggot, t. pat.
Richard Wythier, t. pat.
John Pecok, t. pat.
William Ster, t. pat.
Ralph del Wodehouse, t. pat.
Philip de la Lee, t. pat.
Thomas de Stretton, t. pat.
Richard le Ferour of Shipton, t. pat.
William de Wolvardele, r. Quatt
    [The rest of the col. is blank.]

[Col. 3] *Priests*

Roger de Clifton, t. pat.
Reginald Dymmok of Shrewsbury, t. pat.
Richard Frere of 'Burton', t. pat.
John de Bedenhale, t. pat.

Robert le Ster of 'Bromley', t. pat.
Robert, son of John de Maleton, t. pat.
William Gregori, t. pat.
Robert Dodeyn of Derby, t. pat.
John de Spondon, t. pat.
John de Tybynton, t. pat.
Alexander de Fleckenho, t. pat.
Robert de Gardino, t. pat.
Richard de Solyhull, t. pat.
John Elys of Melbourne, t. pat.
Siward de Bretford, t. pat.
Peter le Grant of Derby, t. pat.
William le Oylier, t. pat.
Richard de Pollesworth, t. pat.
Richard del Hul of Lichfield, t. pat.
Ralph de Bromleye, t. pat.
Richard de Olughton, t. pat.
Roger Martyn of 'Newbold', t. pat.
William de Poleye, t. pat.
Richard le Fysher of 'Newcastle', t. pat.
Robert de Donechurch, t. pat.
Roger de Hurleg', t. pat.
Nicholas de Pollesworth, t. pat.
Geoffrey de Erleston, t. pat.
Benedict de Rushton, t. pat.
John de Stonle, t. pat.
William, son of Richard de Cosynton, t. pat.
John Wylymot, t. pat.
Henry le Mareschal of Coventry, t. pat.
Henry de Parva Halum, t. pat.
William Da[14] of Nantwich, t. pat.
Pagan Woriegoot, t. pat.
Roger de Worfeld, t. pat.
William Alani of 'Bromley', t. pat.
Robert de Redlyngton, dim. dioc. Lincoln
Robert de Egenton, t. pat.
Adam Pye of Lichfield, t. pat.
Geoffrey de Craunage, t. pat.[15]
Nicholas Wych of Lichfield, t. pat.
John de Honyngham, t. pat.
Henry Bonenfant, t. pat.
Nicholas de Kersynton, t. pat.
John de Egynton, t. pat.
John de Shepeye, dim. dioc. Lincoln

[Fo. 109 col. 1] *Priests*

John de Aston, pres. by Richard Corzon
Richard de Grendon, t. pat.

Walter de Stretton, t. pat.
Adam de Molvere, t. pat.
John le Mazon of 'Weston', t. pat.
Henry de Norton Greseleye, dim. dioc. Lincoln
Adam de Betteleye, t. pat.
Richard de Bromwych, t. pat.
Moyses de Wolrenhampton, t. pat.
Adam de Cruddeworth, t. pat.
John de Curborugh, t. pat.
Robert de Croxhale, t. pat.
Robert de Ockle, t. pat.
Nicholas de Trescote, t. pat.
William Drinhod of Rudheath, t. pat.
Roger de Froddesleye, t. pat.
William, son of Richard de Longedon, t. pat.
Simon de Coton, t. pat.
John de Toft of Egginton, t. pat.
John de Norton, t. pat.
Richard le Sergeant of Egginton, t. pat.
John de Hethcote, t. pat.
Richard de Barwe, dim. dioc. Lincoln, pres. by the religious of Selby
John, son of Reginald de Terven, t. pat.
Robert de Byssopeston, t. pat.
William de Astebury, t. pat.
Richard de Staunton super Hynheth, t. pat.
Roger Illary, r. Aldridge
William de Qwatford, t. pat.
Thomas de Stretton, t. pat.
Richard de Preston, t. pat.
Hugh Gunne of Eccleshall, t. pat.
Adam Wysebryd, t. pat.
Geoffrey de Amynton, t. pat.
Robert de Rectote, t. pat.
Alexander de Supton, t. pat.
Nicholas Wych of Lichfield, t. pat.
Thomas de Honlee, t. pat.
Hugh de Audele, r. Blore
Robert de Inguarby, r. Kingsley

[The rest of the recto is blank.

[1-1] In col. 1.
[2-2] The following names have been written around the same stitched tear at these points.
[3-3] Interlined.
[4] Marked at the left-hand side with a cross with a dot in each segment.
[5] A contemporary stitched tear extends some 6cm. below the col. heading to the first name.
[6] Written around an 8cm. hole at this point.
[7-7] A contemporary stitched tear extends some 5cm. from this point and this name and the four following have been written around it.
[8-8] A small drawing, possibly of an animal, is at the right-hand side of both names.

9–9 Written around the stitched tear mentioned in n.5 at these points.
10–10 Written around the 8cm. hole at these points.
11–11 Written around the stitched tear mentioned in n.7 at these points.
12 MS. *Bartholom'*
13 Interlined.
14 Interlined.
15 Marked with a cross at the left-hand side.]

1302 [Fo. 109v] [1]NOMINA ORDINATORUM IN ECCLESIA CONVENTUALI DE RONTON DIE SAB[B]ATI QUATUOR TEMPORUM MENSIS DECEMBRIS ANNO DOMINI MILLESIMO .CCC[mo]. NONO PER DOMINUM .W[ALTERUM]. DIE GRACIA COVENTR' ET LICH' EPISCOPUM CONSECRACIONIS EJUSDEM ANNO TERCIODECIMO[1] [20 December 1309].

[Col. 1] *Acolytes*

William de Dutton, presented to Tatsfield ch., dioc. Winchester
Fr. Gregory de Salop'
Fr. John de Lememstre

Subdeacons

William de Nevill', r. Sudbury
Robert called Scot of 'Langton', dim. dioc. Lincoln, pres. by the prior and conv. of Ranton
Hugh de Shustok', pres. by the prior and conv. of Ranton

[Col. 2] *Deacons*

Henry de Walmesford, r. Kirkheaton, dim. dioc. York
Richard de Modburle, r. Mobberley
Herbert Pouger, presented to Horsley vicarage[2]

[Col. 3] *Priests*

William del Stonhalle, r. Little Blakenham, dim. dioc. Norwich,
William de Wolvardele, r. Quatt
   [1–1 Across the full width of the fo. below the col. headings.
   2 Instituted 15 March 1310, see **1035**.]

1303 [1]NOMINA ORDINATORUM IN ECCLESIA COLLEGIATA DE TAMWORTH DIE SABBATI QUATUOR TEMPORUM PROXIMA POST DIEM CINERUM ANNO DOMINI MILLESIMO TRESCENTESIMO NONO PER DOMINUM WALTERUM DEI GRACIA COVENTR' ET LICH' EPISCOPUM CONSECRACIONIS EJUSDEM QUARTODECIMO[1] [14 March 1310].

[Col. 1] *Subdeacons*

William de Dacre, r. Prescot
Thomas de Wolveye, pres. by Thomas, lord of the same [Wolvey]

John Prince of Bonsall, pres. by Robert Dethek
Richard le Vilers, t. pat.
Richard de Kanneleye, t. pat.
Robert de Plumton, v. Lichfield [cath.]
William de Maclesfeld, t. pat.
Adam de Covene, t. pat.
Nicholas de Eyton, t. pat.
William de Longeleye, t. pat.
Adam de Cuve, t. pat.
Robert de Draycote, pres. by the prioress of Nuneaton
Robert de Halum, pres. by Nicholas, son of John de Breydeston
Richard de Chadleshunte, t. pat.
Walter Elys of Melbourne, t. pat.
Richard de Aston, pres. by William de Freford
William de Westhalum, pres. by the prior of Breadsall
John Orm of Burnaston, pres. by John de Bersingcote

[Col. 2] *Subdeacons*

John del Hert of Baginton, pres. by Sir Richard de Herthull
Roger de Repyndon, pres. by the prior of Church Gresley
William de Lokhay, pres. by the prior of St. James' [hospital], Derby
Nicholas de Bromleye, t. pat.
Henry de Compton, t. pat.
Thomas de Letton, t. pat.
Thomas in le Dale, pres. by [Peter][2] de Lymeseye
Richard de Maperleye, pres. by the abbot and conv. of Dale
John, son of Adam de Rodbourne, pres. by Sir John de Chandos
Richard de Preston, t. pat.
Robert de Comberbache, t. pat.
Adam Bonde of Chesterfield, t. pat.
Robert de Whabberleye, t. pat.
Thomas de Spondon, t. pat.
Thomas Hemery, t. pat.
Robert de Croxhale, pres. by William de Corzon
Thomas de Wolricheston, pres. by Sir Thomas de Garshale

[Col. 3] *Subdeacons*

Henry le Ropere of Tamworth, t. pat.
Geoffrey de Berchynton, t. pat.
William de Cestrefeld, t. pat.
Jordan de Waverton, t. pat.
William de Shippeleye, pres. by Robert de Strelleye
John de Hatton in Hynehet', pres. by Thomas Corbet
Ralph de Franketon, t. pat.
John de Acton, t. pat.
John de Stapelford, t. pat.
John de Radeford of Coventry, pres. by Robert de Chilton

Nicholas de Beahrepeyr, pres. by Henry de Hopton
Robert de Dulverne, pres. by Sir Ralph Basset
John de Byrtton, pres. by John del Lee
John, son of William de Stretton, pres. by the prior of Canwell, dim. dioc. Lincoln
William Alibon of Burton upon Trent, pres. by the abbot of Burton upon Trent
Hugh de Chadleshunt, t. pat.
Henry de Merston, pres. by William de Aula of the same
William de Wappyngbury, pres. by Sir Robert de Napton

[Fo. 110 col. 1] *Subdeacons*

John de Workesleye, t. pat.
Walter de Coleshull, pres. by v. of the same [Coleshill]
William de Borewes, pres. by Henry de Braylesford
Richard de Melborne, t. pat.
Richard de Barton, t. pat.
Thomas de Staundon, t. pat.
William Balehevede of Rolleston, t. pat.
John Kerdyf of Egginton, pres. by William de Eginton
Thomas de Godlesdon, t. pat.
Andrew de Bromleye, pres. by John Bagot, lord of the same [Bromley Bagot]
William Talebot, pres. by the prior of Church Gresley
Nicholas de Makeney, pres. by William, lord of 'Burley'
John de Bracebrigge, t. pat.
John de Broughton of Longdon, t. pat.
David de Spondon, pres. by the master of the hospital of St. Lazarus in England
Richard de Haliwalle, t. pat.
Thomas de Barewe, t. pat.
Ralph de Ronchorn, t. pat.
Richard de Blakenhale, t. pat.
Hugh de Barewe, t. pat.
John de Burton, t. pat.
Robert de Radeclyve, t. pat.
William de Haselovre, pres. by Geoffrey Salveyn
John de Sutton, t. pat.
Adam Selet of Youlgreave, t. pat.
Richard called le Taillour of 'Eyton', t. pat.
Robert de Alderdemor, pres. by Richard Pype
Thomas de Bolton, pres. by Richard, lord of the same
Richard de Herlaston, pres. by Richard de Vernoun
John de Swynesheved, pres. by Vivian de Staundon
John de Neuton, pres. by Henry de Neuton, r. Arrowe
Richard de Breydeshale, pres. by the lord of the same [Breadsall]
Nicholas de Honesworth, pres. by John, lord of Great Barr
Geoffrey de Tixhale, pres. by Geoffrey le Wasteneys
Jordan de Lymme, t. pat.
Ralph de Neuton, t. pat.
William de Walton, t. pat.
William de Cotes, pres. by Robert de Cotes

Richard de Bromwych, pres. by the prior of Sandwell
John le Hunte of Tamworth, t. pat.
John de Slepe, t. pat.
William de Poleye, t. pat.
John de Aston, t. pat.
Adam de Kyngesleye, t. pat.
Ranulph de Crosseby, t. pat.

[Col. 2] *Subdeacons*

Peter le Bedel of Lichfield
William de Wyrkesworth, t. pat.
Nicholas de Sekkyndon, t. pat.
William le Parker of Doveridge, t. pat.
Robert Russel of Coventry, t. pat.
John de la Bruere, t. pat.
Adam Heregrym of Rugeley, t. pat.
Silvester de Alrewas, pres. by Sir Edmund de Somervill'
William le Bykere, pres. by the same E[dmund]
William de Pollesworth, pres. by the prior of the Holy Sepulchre, Warwick
John de Yolegreve, pres. by William de Grafton
Robert de Walford, pres. by Vivian de Staundon
Thomas de Tydeswelle, pres. by Philip de Somervill'
Thomas de Huxton, pres. by William de Breydeshale
Robert de Chilinton, pres. by John Giffard
Richard de Boudon, t. pat.
Roger Wylde of Stoke Dry, t. pat.
John Lyme of Coleshill, t. pat.
Adam Matheu of Curdworth, t. pat.
John de Stonleye, t. pat.
Geoffrey de Wytegreve, t. pat.
Robert de Drengeton, pres. by M. Robert de Bromleye
Ralph de Drayton Basset, t. pat.
Hugh le Rede of Derby, t. pat.
Nicholas de Shustoc', t. pat.
Roger de Ruyhull, pres. by Sir Ralph Basset
Richard Eysil of Shustoke, pres. by Sir Robert Marmeon
William de Sowe, pres. by Robert le Harpour of 'Chesterton'
Geoffrey Harald of Lillington, t. pat.
Thomas Textor of Tamworth, t. pat.
Hugh de Waverton, t. pat.
Adam de Fysherwyk, t. pat.
John de Burton, t. pat.
Thomas de Whychenovere, t. pat.
Adam, son of William de Stodley, pres. by Sir William de Byrmyngham
John de Staunford, dim. dioc. York, t. pat.
William de Sallowe of Lichfield, pres. by M. Hugh de la Dale
William Heer of Tamworth, t. pat.
Ivon de Assho, t. pat.

John le Couper of Eckington, t. pat.
William Coleman, t. pat.
Robert de Morleye, pres. by the prior of Breadsall
William Herbert, pres. by William de Euovere
John de Baschirche, pres. by the prior of Wombridge

[Col. 3] *Subdeacons*

Richard de Twyford, t. pat.
William de Herberbury, t. pat.
William de Clypston, t. pat.
Thomas de Ernesford, t. pat.
William le Bret of Bilton, t. pat.
John de Bromleye, pres. by Sir Henry Mauveysyn
John de Offeleye, pres. by Roger, lord of Leamington Hastings
John de Eton, pres. by v. Nuneaton
Geoffrey Peowale of 'Harborough', t. pat.
Simon de Munesworth, pres. by Walter de Wynterton

Deacons

Robert Scot of 'Langton', pres. by the prior and conv. of Ranton, dim. dioc. Lincoln
Thomas de Staunton, pres. by Robert de Muscham
Richard de Aspes of 'Beulton', pres. by Henry de Braundeston
John de Kyrkeby, pres. by Nicholas de Wylie
Stephen de Ednyngshore, pres. by the abbot of Rocester
William Talbot of 'Willey', pres. by the prior and conv. of Church Gresley
Gilbert de Wythibrok', pres. by the religious of Kenilworth
Hugh de Okebrok', pres. by William de Aylwaston
Robert de Stapelford, pres. by the religious of Norton
Thomas de Eccleshale, pres. by Sir John de Ardena
John Cryspyn, pres. by the master of the hospital [of St. John] of Jerusalem
Walter Abel, t. pat.
John de Waverton, t. pat.
John de Whytinton, t. pat.
John de Pollesworth, t. pat.
Roger Cosyn of Newbold on Avon, t. pat.
Robert de Byrchesleye, pres. by the prior of Coventry
William de Waverton, pres. by John de Longedon
John de Barwe, pres. by the master of Yeaveley hospital
William le Sweyn of Blithfield, pres. by the lord of the same
Richard de Pylkynton, pres. by the prior of Tutbury
Robert de Hyb' of Shustoke, pres. by John le Botiller
John Gery, pres. by Sir John le Strange
Roger de Osolveston, dim. dioc. Lincoln, t. Owston
Robert de Lemynton, pres. by John Comyn of Newbold Comyn
Richard de Fynham, t. pat.
Roger Blundel of Chesterfield, t. pat.

Nicholas de Waverton, t. pat.
Richard de Eyton, pres. by John de Eyton

[Fo. 110v col. 1] *Deacons*

Thomas de Clyve, pres. by Richard Burnel
Richard, son of Nicholas de Waleshale, t. pat.
John de Eyton, t. pat.
Ralph de Hanyate, t. pat.
Hugh de Parva Halum, t. pat.
William de Opton, pres. by John de Opton
Nicholas de Staneleye, pres. by Yeaveley hospital
Roger de Olvesmor'', t. pat.
William de Reyndon, t. pat.
Walter, son of Ralph Giffard, pres. by the religious of Lilleshall
Roger de Lambeday, pres. by John Heroun, lord of Church Lawford; [3]let there be
a letter[3]
John ad Fontem of 'Aston', pres. by Sir Henry Fitzherbert; let there be a letter
Henry Wibbot of Ockbrook, pres. by Robert de Muscham of 'Stanton'; let there be
a letter
John Seþane, pres. by Sir Geoffrey le Ireys; let there be a letter
Richard de Bromwych, t. pat.; let there be a letter
Richard de Catton, t. pat.
William Shappmor of 'Bromwich', t. pat.; let there be a letter
Adam de Mere, t. pat.
William de Ashovere, pres. by Sir Robert Dymok; let there be a letter
Walter Doune of Etwall, pres. by Roger de Bradeborn
Henry de Shelden, pres. by Sir Nicholas de Shel[4]don[4]; let there be a letter
William Boner of Atherstone, pres. by John de Herle, r. Mancetter; let there be a
letter
Richard de Wolfecote, t. pat.
Henry the smith of Coventry, t. pat.; let there be a letter
Peter de Maxfeld, t. pat.
John de Shepeye, t. pat.
Bertram le Wodeward, pres. by William de Stok'; let there be a letter
Thomas de Billeye, pres. by Sir T[homas] de Garsale; let there be a letter
Andrew de Braundon, pres. by same
Richard Pygot, t. pat., let there be a letter
Richard de Kente, t. pat.
Thomas de Blymenhull, t. pat., let there be a letter
Geoffrey de Stonleye, t. pat.
Adam de Burton, t. pat.
Walter, son of Robert de Ponte of Frodsham, t. pat.
William de Kylbourne, pres. by the abbot of Dale; let there be a letter
Thomas de Okebrok', pres. by the prior of Leeds
Philip de Warmynton, Richard de Warmynton, Roger, son of Richard de
Eccleshale, John Shirlok of Warmington, pres. by archd. of Derby
Simon de Clyve, t. pat.
Roger de Ambaldeston, pres. by M. Adam de Aumundestham

Roger de Kyngesleye, pres. by Richard, lord of Blithfield

[Col. 2] *Deacons*

Thomas de Croukhul, pres. by the master of St. Giles' hospital, Shrewsbury
Andrew de Bemhurst, pres. by John de Flamstede
Henry Broun of Rolleston, pres. by Thomas, son of Ralph de Rolleston; let there
be a letter
Richard de Bascote, pres. by Sir Peter de Lymesy; let there be a letter
Adam de Ichynton, pres. by Sir John de Oddingesheles; let there be a letter
Richard de Lucy, t. pat.; let there be a letter
Thomas de Colleshull, t. pat.
Henry de Bromleye, t. pat.
Henry de Overa, t. pat.; let there be a letter
Robert de Warylowe, pres. by Henry Oweyn; let there be a letter
Richard de Weston, pres. by William de Weston; let there be a letter
John de Bobenhull, pres. by Sir Robert, son of Guy; let there be a letter
John de Hull', pres. by Henry de Erdynton
John de Boughton, pres. by St. Giles' hospital [Boughton], Chester; let there be a
letter
William Leonard, t. pat.
Nicholas le Corzon, pres. by Richard le Corzon
John de Stonleye, pres. by Sir John Pecch'
John Quenyld of Egginton, pres. by William de Tymmor
Adam le Warner of Long Itchington, pres. by Sir John de Oddingsheles; let there
be a letter
Adam de Newenham, pres. by Sir Thomas de Garshale
Roger de Horseleye, pres. by William de Salny; let there be a letter
Robert Paramour, t. pat.; let there be a letter
Thomas Kytewylde of Rugby, t. pat.
Robert de Bourton, pres. by Sir Robert de Verdon; let there be a letter
Andrew de Alveton, pres. by M. Henry de Bray
Richard de Tatenhulle, pres. by Sir Robert Tok'
Pagan Swyft, t. pat.
Richard de Huyton, t. pat.
William de Brynkelowe, t. pat.
Laurence de Eyton, pres. by William Brayn
Henry de Steyveston, pres. by John, lord of Reigate
John de Brynkelowe, pres. by Thomas de Boyden
William de Burley, pres. by William de Standysh; let there be a letter
William de Wystwyk, t. pat.
Richard Warmete, t. pat.
Adam de Faþreston, t. pat.; let there be a letter

[Col. 3] *Deacons*

Thomas de Munserel, dim. dioc. Lincoln, pres. by the religious of Sandwell
Robert de Shipley, pres. by Geoffrey de Cadacre; let there be a letter
Adam de Okebrok', pres. by William Freman of the same [Ockbrook]

Henry de Okebrok', pres. by Simon Pougyl
John de Okebrok', t. pat.
M. John de Sutham, t. pat.
Richard de Albriston, pres. by Richard de Chaddesden'
Robert de Swynnerton, pres. by Sir Roger of the same
William le Spenser of Mickleover, pres. by Sir William de la Warde
Henry de Perton, pres. by Sir William de Wrottesleye
William de Sutham, t. pat.
Henry Lylkoc of Bakewell, t. pat.
Nicholas the miller of Lichfield, t. pat.
Thomas Achard of 'Hampton', pres. by Sir John Peche
Thomas Morice of Derby, pres. by r. Weston upon Trent
William, son of Roger de Norton, t. pat.
Gervase de Hassop, t. pat., let there be a letter
John, son of Andrew de Byrmyngham, pres. by Sir William de Byrmyngham; let
there be a letter
Jordan de Wolrenhampton, t. pat.
Gilbert de Spondon, t. pat.; let there be a letter
Henry de Geydon, t. pat.
William, son of William de Norton, t. pat.
William Portegeoye, pres. by Sir John de Bakepuz; let there be a letter
John Reynald of Packington, t. pat.
John de Butteby, t. pat.; let there be a letter
William Ludkyn of Madeley, t. Holy Sepulchre, Radford by Stafford
John de Kyngeston, pres. by Nicholas de Guldeford
John the smith of Fillongley, pres. by Sir Peter de Lymesy
Thomas de Houre, pres. by William de Shirle
Robert de Attelberge, pres. by John de Hynkele
Hugh de Normonesleye, pres. by Philip de Draycote
Simon de Brokes, pres. by r. Haughton
William de Spondon, pres. by Hugh Bordet
Ralph de Derset, t. pat.
Richard de Swerkeston, t. pat.
John de Spondon, t. pat.
John de Byrþenbury, t. pat.
Thomas de Knotton, t. pat.
Thomas de Ambaston, t. pat., let there be a letter
Henry de Haþerdon, t. pat.
John de Fylongeleye, t. pat.
Robert de Brugg', pres. by the prior of Holy Trinity, Bridgnorth; let there be a
letter
Nicholas de Scropton, pres. by the prior of Breadsall
Thomas de Eyton, pres. by Sir Hugh Meynyl
Thomas de Mudle, pres. by Sir John le Strange; let there be a letter
Geoffrey de Wolrenhampton, t. pat.
William de Chaddesden, t. pat.

[Fo. 111 col. 1] *Deacons*

John de la Lawe, pres. by Geoffrey de Kenerdal'
William de Blees, t. pat.
Stephen de Stanlowe, t. pat.
Alan Chu, pres. by Sir Thomas de Cheworth; let there be a letter
Robert Broun of 'Haywood', pres. by Geoffrey de Wasteneys
Richard de Geydon, t. pat.; let there be a letter
Laurence de Knudesford, t. pat.
Richard de Kenerdale, pres. by G[eoffrey] de Kenerdale
Henry de Edleston, pres. by Serle Mongeoye; let there be a letter
Richard de Kokeslene, by command of the bishop
Nicholas de Hopton, pres. by Robert de Knisteleye; let there be a letter
Robert de Burthenbury, pres. by Sir John Paynel; let there be a letter
Adam de Style, t. pat.
Thomas, son of Robert de Meleborne, t. pat.
Roger de Bradeleye, t. pat.
Robert Portegeoye, pres. by William de Neuton by order of the bishop; let there be
a letter
John de Asthul, pres. by Henry Charnels
Robert Leonard of Melbourne, pres. by William Bas'
Roger de Edleston, pres. by Henry Herbert, kt.; let there be a letter
John Rossel of 'Itchington', t. pat.; let there be a letter
Ralph Sandi, t. pat.
Henry de Wavere, t. pat.
John de Tonstal, t. pat.
Alan Murager, t. pat.
Thomas Drake of 'Gudleston', pres. by M. Richard de Coleshull
John le Valeys, pres. by Robert de Valeys
John ad Moram of Wolverhampton, t. pat.
Richard de Brynkelowe, t. pat.; let there be a letter
George de Wythybrok', pres. by Richard Bot', let there be a letter
John de Frodeswell, t. pat.
    [The rest of the col. is blank.]

[Col. 2] *Priests*

Alexander de Plumleye, pres. by Sir Hugh de Dotton
Giles de Cloune, t. pat.
Thomas de Gumpeyate, t. pat.
William Bere, t. pat.
Alan Cox, t. pat.
Richard de Bradeborn, pres. by Sir Roger de Bradeborn; let there be a letter
Henry le Folour, t. pat.
Adam Juwet of Ashow, t. pat.
Henry de Egynton, t. pat.
Ellis de Mere, pres. by Sir Robert de Dotton
Ralph Tolone, t. pat.
Thurstan de Wygan, t. pat.
Richard de Boterton, t. pat.

Stephen de Gnoushale, t. pat.
William Cok' of Bednall, t. pat.
William de Staundon, t. pat.
Henry de Grenebergh, t. pat.
Alan, son of John de Asheshoo, pres. by Thomas de Pype
Robert de Stone, t. pat.
William de Ambal⁵de⁵ston, t. pat.; let there be a letter
John de Walsale, t. pat.
Philip de la Lee, t. pat.; let there be a letter
Thomas de Thurleston, t. pat.
Simon de Arewe, pres. by Henry Canvill'
Robert de Bradebourne, t. pat.
William de Dene, t. pat.
Henry de Corleye, t. pat.
Thomas de Waverton, t. pat.
William de Okleston, t. pat.
Robert de Bromleye, t. pat.
John de Falwes, t. pat.; let there be a letter
Walter, son of Ellis de Melborn, t. pat.
Adam Aylrych of Ashow, t. pat.
Thomas de Asheborne, t. pat.; let there be a letter
Richard de Wolaston, t. pat.
William s. Silvester de Kirkeby, t. pat.
Robert de Spondon, t. pat.
Thomas Hert of Tabley, t. pat.
Richard de Bosco, t. pat.
George de Wythibrok', t. pat.
Robert, son of Roger de Baquell, t. pat.
Geoffrey the carpenter, t. pat.
Andrew de Bemhurst, t. pat.; let there be a letter
William de Ervefeld, t. pat.
Thomas de Bolton, t. pat.
Adam de Ervefen, t. pat.
Richard de Elleford, t. pat.
Oliver de Wythibrok', t. pat.; let there be a letter

[Col. 3]

William the carpenter, t. pat.
John de Lillingston, t. pat.
Roger de Wytteney, dim. dioc. Lincoln, t. pat.
Richard le Ferour of 'Sutton', t. pat.
Thomas de Stretton, t. pat.
Roger de Doffeld, t. pat.
William de Thorp, t. pat.
Robert le Rotier, t. pat.
Richard de Mefford, t. pat.
Thomas de Bobenhull, t. pat.; let there be a letter
Richard de Egbaston, t. pat.

Thomas de Eyton, t. pat.
William de Overe, t. pat.
John de Luceby, dim. dioc. Lincoln, t. pat.
Richard de Gnousale, t. pat.
Richard de Ambaldeston, t. pat.; let there be a letter
John de Weston subtus Brewode, t. pat.
Thomas de Turleston, t. pat.; let there be a letter
Robert de Whiteleye, t. pat.
Henry de Honyngham, t. pat.
John de Wolricheston, t. pat.
Richard de Clifton, t. pat.
William de Standysh, t. pat.
Robert Frere, t. pat.
William Oliver of Whitwick, t. pat.
William de Milverton, t. pat.
Simon de Chyppeknol, t. pat.
Nicholas de Froddesham, t. pat.
Roger de Elton, t. pat.
William de Langesdon, t. pat.
Nicholas Fremond of Newport, t. pat.
William Salewy, t. pat.
Richard de Wytheresleye, t. pat.
Gilbert de Honyngham, t. pat.
John de Hertford, t. pat.
Richard de Estham, t. pat.
William de Caldecote, t. pat.[6]
Robert de Halsey, t. pat.
Thomas de Mamcestr', t. pat.; let there be a letter
Nicholas, son of Richard de Frodesham, t. pat.
William de Herberbury, t. pat.; let there be a letter
John de Holyngs, t. pat.; let there be a letter
Gilbert de Lalleford, t. pat.; let there be a letter
Adam de Bylrebrok', t. pat.
William Matheu of Nantwich, t. pat.
Thomas de Bromleye, t. pat.
Henry de Clifton, t. pat.; let there be a letter
Robert de Lullington, t. pat.
Alexander de Cobeleye, t. pat.
Thomas de Dotton, t. pat.; let there be a letter
William Baron, t. pat.
Henry Adam of 'Walton', t. pat.

[Fo. 111v col. 1] *Priests*

Simon Lynet, t. pat.
Henry, son of Ivon de Weston, t. pat.
Henry super Croftum of 'Weston', t. pat.
Roland de Staunton, t. pat.
Henry de Estlemynton, t. pat.

John, son of John de Wystham, t. pat.
Simon de Swelle, t. pat.
John Hubbok', t. pat.
Roger Broun of Church Lawford, t. pat.
Richard Peverey, t. pat.
Richard de Tydrinton, t. pat.
Richard le Coupere of Ashbourne; let there be a letter
John de Weston
Roger de Helsbie
Hugh le Deppenser
Ralph de Cotes
Walter de Cokeslene
Nicholas de Snoxton
Richard ad Fontem of Newcastle under Lyme
Robert de Furneys
William de Brymyngton
Roger de Norwyco
William de Cobbeleye
John de Elmhurst, pres. by archd. of Chester
Nicholas de Caldon; let there be a letter
Roger de Repyndon; let there be a letter
Richard Wyther; let there be a letter
Walter Magot; let there be a letter
John Pecok; let there be a letter
John de Ronton
Thomas de Wolvey
Robert de Burton
Adam de Egbaston
Roger Elyot
Walter, son of Richard de Frodesham
Walter de Egbaston
Walter de Rocteleye
William de Wyco
Herbert Pouger, v. Horsley
    [The rest of the col. is blank.
    ^{1–1} Across the full width at the centre of the fo.
    ² MS. *prioris*
    ^{3–3} All *sit littera* in this list added later.
    ^{4–4} Interlined.
    ^{5–5} Interlined.
    ⁶ A line is drawn to the right-hand side of this name.]

1304 [1]NOMINA ORDINATORUM DIE SABBATI QUATUOR TEMPORUM IN VIGILIA TRINITATIS ANNO DOMINI .MILLESIMO .CCC^{mo}. DECIMO. IN ECCLESIA CONVENTUALI COVENTR' PER VENERABILEM PATREM DOMINUM W[ALTERUM]. DEI GRACIA COVENTR' ET LYCH' EPISCOPUM[1] [13 June 1310].

[Col. 2] *Subdeacons*

Roger le Fonu, pres. by Richard le Fonu

Walter de Perton, r. Stirchley
Hamond de la More, r. Isombridge chapel
Thomas de Weston, r. Weston under Lizard
John, son of Geoffrey Pygon of Milverton, t. pat.
William Cornet, t. pat.
[Followed by two blank lines.]

Deacons

Hugh le Rede of Derby, t. pat.
Robert de Plumpton, v. Lichfield cath.
John, son of William de Stretton, dim. dioc. Lincoln, pres. by the prior of Canwell
Roger le Wylde of Stoke Dry, dim. dioc. Lincoln, pres. by the hospital of St. John of Jerusalem in England
William de Sallowe of Lichfield, t. pat.
Peter de Wybetot, t. pat.
Robert de Wabberleye, t. pat.
[The rest of the col. is blank.]

[Col. 3] *Priests*

M. John de Sutham, t. pat.
William de Preez, r. Childs Ercall
John de Pollesworth, t. pat.
Nicholas Broun of 'Langton', dim. dioc. Lincoln, pres. by the abbot of Owston
Robert Scot of 'Langton', dim. dioc. Lincoln, pres. by the prior of Ranton
Roger de Oseldeston, dim. dioc. Lincoln, pres. by the house of Owston
Robert de Ashton, r. Ashton on Mersey
Henry de Sheldon, pres. by Sir Nicholas de Sheldon, kt.
William de Overe, t. pat.
Thomas de Coleshull, t. pat.
Nicholas de Staneley, pres. by the master of the hospital of St. John of Jerusalem in England
John le Valeys of Lichfield, pres. by v. Longdon
Richard de Albriston, t. pat.
[The rest of the fo. is blank.
[1-1] Across cols. 2 and 3 at the head of the fo. above the col. headings.]

1305 [Fo. 112] [1]NOMINA ORDINATORUM IN ECCLESIA PREBENDALI DE ICHINTON DIE SABBATI QUATUOR TEMPORUM MENSIS SEPTEMBRIS ANNO DOMINI .M^o.CCC^{mo}. DECIMO PER W[ALTERUM]. COVENTR' ET LYCH' EPISCOPUM[1] [19 September 1310].

[Col. 1] *Subdeacons*

William de Loges of 'Chesterton', t. pat.
John de Stocton, pres. by Sir W[illiam] de Hondesacr', dim. dioc. Durham
Thomas de Gatewyk, t. pat.

William de Stretton, dim. dioc. Lincoln
Richard Abbot of Coventry, t. pat.
Roger de Rodbourn, t. pat.
[The rest of the col. is blank.]

[Col. 2] *Deacons*

William de Olughton, t. pat.
Richard de Meleborne, t. pat.
Walter Elys of Melbourne, t. pat.
Thomas de Wolsey, pres. by Sir Thomas de Wolseye, kt.
Roger de Clifford, r. Kirkby Thore,[2] dim. dioc. Carlisle
Ranulph Thorald, pres. by the prior of Birkenhead
Hamond de Mere, r. Isombridge
Nicholas, son of Ralph de Beaurepeyr, pres. by Henry de Hopton
William Herbert, pres. by John de la Cornere of Derby
Hugh de Shustok', pres. by the prior of Ranton
William Cornet, t. pat.
John Herbert, t. pat.
Geoffrey de Tyxhale, t. pat.
[The rest of the col. is blank.]

[Col. 3] *Priests*

Roger Cosul of Newbold on Avon, t. pat.
Gilbert de Wythibrok', t. pat.
Robert de Leminton, t. pat.
Richard de Fynham, t. pat.
John de Kingeston, t. pat.
Richard de Pilkinton, t. pat.
William Talbot, t. pat.
Thomas, son of Robert de Meleborn, t. pat.
John Leonard of Kingesneuton, t. pat.
John, son of William de Stretton, t. pat.
Roger, son of Robert de Suthcroxton, t. pat.
Adam de Donecastr', r. Kessingland, [dim.] dioc. Norwich
John de Verny, of house of Nuneaton
Ralph de Haneyate, t. pat.
Thomas de Bilneye, t. pat.
Hugh le Rede of Derby, t. pat.
Thomas de Okebrok', t. pat.
William de Madeley, warden of Holy Sepulchre [hospital] outside Stafford
Robert de Hybn' of Shustoke, t. pat.
Robert de Attelberge, t. pat.
Roger Wilde of Stoke Dry, dim. dioc. Lincoln, t. pat.
Henry de Bauquelle
William Chandoys
Roger de Clifton
Richard le Spicer of Lichfield

Richard, son of Nicholas de Waleshale
> [The rest of the recto is blank.
> 1–1 Across the full width of the fo. above the col. headings.
> 2 *Reg. Halton*, 301, 308.]

1306 [Fo. 112v] [1]NOMINA ORDINATORUM IN ECCLESIA PREBENDALI DE COLEWYCH DIE SABBATI QUATUOR TEMPORUM MENSIS DECEMBRIS ANNO DOMINI .MILLESIMO .CCC[mo]. DECIMO. PER DOMINUM .W[ALTERUM]. DEI GRACIA COVENTR' ET LYCH' EPISCOPUM[1] [19 December 1310].

[Col. 1] *Subdeacons*

M. William de Bourton, r. Frome Whitfield,[2] dim. dioc. Salisbury
Robert de Dutton, r. Eccleston
William de Ilkeston, pres. by Sir William de Roos
Geoffrey de Villar', pres. by the abbot of Merevale, dim. archbishop of Rouen
Hugh de Vernoun, t. pat.
William de Filongeleye, t. pat.
Simon de Wygan, t. pat.
Richard de Kemeseye, t. pat.
Robert, son of Thomas de Whitinton, pres. by William, lord of 'Torvenhorn'
William de Muneworth, r. moiety of Kingsbury
John de Leycestr', r. Foston, dim. dioc. Lincoln
William Davy, r. moiety of Mugginton
Nicholas de Brademere, pres. by Sir Thomas Garshale
Peter de Stok', pres. by Robert, r. Sibson, dim. dioc. Lincoln
John de Caldecote, t. pat.
Thomas de Colnham, t. pat.
M. Adam Byron, r. ['Donington'],[3] dim. dioc. Lincoln
Roger de Wygan, pres. by the prior of Burscough
Thomas, r. West Felton
William de Dunton, r. Tatsfield,[4] dim. dioc. Winchester
John de Staunton, pres. by Robert de Stanton
Thomas de Whalleye, t. pat.
John de Stretton, t. pat.
Robert de Chebbeseye, t. pat.
Simon de Walton, t. pat.
Richard de Ekynton, pres. by the master and brethren of Yeaveley hospital
William de Walton, r. Stoke Dry, dim. dioc. Lincoln
Ralph de Hanewell, Thomas de Teu, pres. by archd. of Chester
Abel de Eton, t. pat.

[Col. 2] *Deacons*

William de Morton, t. pat.
John de Stapelford, t. pat.
Thomas de Staundon, t. pat.
Henry Suet of 'Aston', pres. by John Suet of 'Aston'
Thomas de St. Neots, pres. by Thomas de Chaddesden, dim. dioc. Lincoln

John de Hareworth, pres. by the lord of Swinfen, dim. dioc. York
William de Haselovere, pres. by Geoffrey Salveyn
Richard Coleth of Harlaston, pres. by Richard de Vernon, lord of Haddon
Richard de Weford, t. pat.
John de Slepe, t. pat.
M. Robert de Overe, pres. by the religious of Croxden
William de Walton, t. pat.
John Prince, pres. by Sir Robert de Devesque, kt.
Simon de Muneworth, pres. by Walter de Wynton'
Adam Heregrym of Rugeley, pres. by Richard de Wolseleye
Ralph de Ronchorn, t. pat.
Nicholas de Eyton, t. pat.
Hugh de Chadleshunte, t. pat.
Jordan de Waverton, t. pat.
Robert Russel of Coventry, t. pat.
William de Stretton, dim. dioc. Lincoln
Nicholas de Shustok', t. pat.
Richard Eysil of Shustoke, t. pat.
William de Fylongele, pres. by John de Ruyton
Robert de Chilinton, pres. by John Giffard
William Lochay, pres. by the prior of Kenilworth
Ranulph de Crosseby, t. pat.
Nicholas de Bromle, t. pat.
Peter, son of Reginald de Lich', t. pat.
Robert de Bostok, pres. by W[illiam] de Brikhull
Adam de Stepelton, pres. by the prior of Kenilworth
John Inge, pres. by the prior of Tutbury
Richard the forester of 'Overe', pres. by Nicholas de Fynderne
John de Stocton, pres. by Sir William de Hondesacr', dim. dioc. Durham
William de Stretton, t. pat.
John, son of Nicholas de Leicestr', t. pat.
John de Brocton of Longdon, t. pat.
Simon de Meysham, t. pat.
John de Hatton, t. pat.
Richard le Taillour of Penkridge, t. pat.
William de Borewes, pres. by Nicholas de Longeford

[Fo. 113 col. 1] *Deacons*

Robert de Morleye, t. pat.
William de Coleshull, t. pat.
William de Mere, t. pat.
Adam de Cuve, t. pat.
John de Barton, pres. by Henry de Canvill'
Thomas de la Dale, pres. by Sir Peter de Lymeseye
William de Maklesfeld, Roger Morice of Repton, William Coleman, [pres.] by archd. of Chester

Priests

Thomas de Rakedale, dim. dioc. Lincoln, t. prior of Launde
Robert de Whabberle, t. pat.
Thomas de Monte Sorell, t. house of Sandwell, dim. dioc. Lincoln
Thomas de Staunton, pres. by Robert de Muscham
William Ster, Robert le Somenour, Bertram de Torpurle, Ralph Dandi, Richard de Lucy, t. pat. by W[illiam] de Brikhull
Adam called le Warner, pres. by Sir John de Oddingeseles
William Boner of Atherstone, pres. by r. Mancetter
Thomas de Blymenhull, pres. by r. Avon Dassett
John de la Lawe, t. pat.
Walter, son of Ralph Giffard, pres. by the abbot of Lilleshall
John Saþene of Long Lawford, t. pat.
Thomas de Overe, pres. by John de la Cornere of Derby
Roger Lambeday, pres. by John Heroun
William Herbert, pres. by John de la Cornere of Derby
Geoffrey de Tyxhale, pres. by Geoffrey de Wasteneys
William Cornet, t. pat.
Philip de Warmynton, pres. by archd. of Derby
Robert de Staveleye, pres. by the prior of St. John of Jerusalem in England
Andrew de Brandon, pres. by Sir Thomas de Garshale
Roger de Horseleye, pres. by the prior of Breadsall
Robert Broun of 'Haywood', pres. by Henry de[5] Park' Heywode
William de Sallowe, pres. by M. Hugh Cencar'
Hugh de Normoneslegh, pres. by Philip de Draicote

[Col. 2] *Priests*

John de Staunton, pres. by Robert de Stanton
Henry de Okebrok', t. pat.
Richard Kent of Shrewsbury, pres. by John Kent
Ranulph Thorald, v. Bowdon
William de Waverton, pres. by v. Polesworth
William, son of Roger de Norton, t. pat.
John[6] Andrew of Birmingham, t. pat.
Thomas de Croukhull, pres. by the abbot of Lilleshall
Richard Deen of Gaydon, t. pat.
Richard the baker of Lichfield, t. pat.
John de Baschirch, pres. by the religious of Wombridge
Peter de Wybetot, t. pat.
Ralph de Burton, t. pat.
Roger de Braylesford, t. pat.
John de Frodeswell, t. pat.
Robert de Teynton, t. pat.
Richard Aboveþewey, t. pat.
Adam de Sharngshulf, pres. by Sir William Tromwyne
Henry de Hatherdon, t. pat.
Adam de Blakeborne, t. pat.

Hugh de Boveye, t. pat.

Thomas de Eccleshale, t. pat.

Henry de Herdewyk, pres. by Sir R[oger] Trumwyne

John del Stowestrete, t. pat.

Thomas Legat of Leicester, [7]dim. dioc. Lincoln[7], t. pat.

Henry de Bromleye, t. pat.

Robert de Swynnerton, pres. by the prior of Tutbury

Richard de Warmynton, John de Warminton, Philip de Warmynton, pres. by archd. of Derby

Nicholas the clerk of Boylestone, t. pat.

Robert de Warilowe, pres. by Henry Oweyn

Robert Portegeoye, pres. by William Burdeleys

John de Stonle, pres. by Sir John Pecche, kt.

William de Burleye, pres. by William de Standysh

John de Wytinton, t. pat.

Walter Doune of Etwall, t. pat.

Robert de Leicestr', t. pat.

Richard de Tatenhull, t. pat.

William, son of Swain de Blithefeld, pres. by Richard de ...[8]

Roger de Clifford, r. Kirkby Thore, dim. dioc. Carlisle

[Fo. 113v col. 1] *Priests*

Richard de Catton, t. pat.

Richard de Sondbach, t. pat.

Henry de Rolleston, t. pat.

William Portegeoye, pres. by William le Mortimer, lord of 'Sutton'

Adam de la Fale of Birmingham, pres. by Sir W[illiam] de Birm[ingham]

John de Burton, t. pat.

Richard de Cokeslene, t. pat.

John de Botteby, t. pat.

Henry de Edeleston, pres. by Roger de Bradeborne

Roger de Edeleston, t. pat.

William de Werinton, t. pat.

Adam de Longa Ichinton, pres. by Sir John de Odding[9]geseles[9]

Richard Pygot, Thomas de Rokeby, Robert Coket of Astbury, John de Tonstal, pres. by archd. of Chester

[The rest of the fo. is blank.

[1–1] Across the full width of the fo. above the col. headings.

[2] *Reg. Gandavo*, 891.

[3] MS. *Wynton'*, but see **1307D**.

[4] *Registrum Henrici Woodlock, diocesis Wintoniensis, A.D. 1305–1316*, ed. A.W. Goodman (CYS, 43, 44, 1940–1), 547, 831.

[5] Followed by *Heywode* interlined and partially erased.

[6] Interlined.

[7–7] Interlined.

[8] MS. stained.

[9–9] Interlined to leave room for a second col. which was, nevertheless, left blank.]

1307 [Fo. 114] [1]NOMINA ORDINATORUM DIE SABBATI QUATUOR TEMPORUM PROXIMO POST DIEM CINERUM .ANNO DOMINI .Mº.CCCᵐᵒ. DECIMO IN ECCLESIA PREBENDALI DE ECCLESHALE PER DOMINUM W[ALTERUM]. COVENTR' ET LICH' EPISCOPUM[1] [6 March 1311].

[Col. 1] *Subdeacons*

Richard de Radeclive, r. Radcliffe
Thomas Barri, r. 'St. Ishmael', dim. dioc. St. David's
Henry de Peverwych, pres. by r. 'St. Ishmael'
Thomas de Brimpton, r. Church Eaton
Richard de Poliley, r. Oldbury, dim. dioc. Hereford

Deacons

Geoffrey de Vilers, dioc. Rouen, pres. by the religious of Merevale
Roger de Stevenasche, pres. by the prior of Wymondley, dim. dioc. Lincoln
John de Heth of Baginton, pres. by Sir Richard de Herchull
John de Okleye, pres. by the abbot of Biddlesden, dim. dioc. Lincoln
William de Rolleston, t. pat.
John, son of William de Wyco Malbano, t. pat.
Robert de Croxhale, pres. by William, lord of Croxall
Andrew de Herberbury, pres. by Sir John de Lodbroc'
William de Cotes, pres. by Sir Robert de Cotes
Robert de Halum, pres. by Nicholas, son of John de Breideston
Richard de Blakenhale, pres. by Sir John de Grey
Richard de Breydeshale, pres. by Richard de Corson
Richard de Kemeseye, t. pat.
Henry le Roper, t. pat.
Abel de Eton, t. pat.
Thomas Hemery, t. pat.
William de Langeleye, t. pat.
Thomas de Gatewych, t. pat.
Richard Abbot of Coventry, t. pat.
John de Herberbury, pres. by John de Lodbrok'
William de Wappenbur', pres. by Sir Robert de Napton
Henry de Mershton, pres. by William de Mershton
William Here, t. pat.
John de Aston, t. pat.
William de Ildeston, t. pat.
David de Spondon, t. pat.
Thomas de Spondon, t. pat.

[Col. 2] *Deacons*

John de Stretton, t. pat.
Ivon de Ashesho, t. pat.
Thomas de Capella, t. pat.
Robert de Dulverne, pres. by Sir Ralph Basset

Nicholas de Brademere, pres. by Sir Thomas de Grshale
Henry de Knotton, t. pat.
Nicholas de Makeneye, t. pat.
Robert de Waleford of Eccleshall, pres. by E[llis] de Napton[2]
Reginald Boner, pres. by the prior of Church Gresley
John de Offeley, pres. by Roger de Lethinton
John de Swynesheved, pres. by Vivian de Staundon
William de Poleye, t. pat.
John de Milverton, t. pat.
Thomas the dyer, t. pat.
Adam Sele of Youlgreave, t. pat.
Thomas de Burthingbury, pres. by the religious of Canons Ashby
Nicholas de Honesworth, pres. by John de Barre
John de Stonle, t. pat.
John de Sutton, t. pat.
Richard de Cestrefeld, t. pat.
John de Burton, t. pat.
Ralph de Franketon, pres. by Sir Thomas de Garshale
Robert de Whitynton, pres. by William de Freford
Richard de Bromwych, pres. by M. Richard de Coleshul'
William Pynmor of 'Stockton', Silvester de Alrewas, William Bykere of Wichnor, pres. by Sir E[dmund] de Somervill'
Simon de Wygan, pres. by Robert de Hurlton
William le Parker of Doveridge, t. pat.
John de Radeford, t. pat.
Richard de Eginton, pres. by the master and brethren of Yeaveley hospital
Thomas de Stone, pres. by the religious of Stone
John de Rodborne, pres. by John Chaundoys
M. William de Bourton, r. Frome Whitfield, dim. dioc. Salisbury
M. Adam Byron, r. 'Donington', dim. dioc. Lincoln
Adam de Covene, t. pat.
William de Sowe, pres. by Robert le Harpour

[Fo. 114v] *Deacons*

Thomas de Boulton, pres. by the lord of 'Bolton'
Andrew de Bromleg, pres. by John Bagot
William de Fylongele, t. pat.
Roger de Ruyhull, pres. by Sir Ralph Basset
Thomas de Wolrichton, pres. by Thomas de Garsale
Roger de Freculton, pres. by Citharede, lady of Urmston
Richard Byg', pres. by John de Bek
Robert de Dutton, r. Eccleston
William de Ilkeston, pres. by Hugh Burdet
John de Parva Overa, pres. by Nicholas de Overa[3]
Richard de Chadleshunte, t. pat.
Robert de Drengeton, t. pat.
Robert de Radeclyve, t. pat.
John le Hunte, t. pat.

Roger de Aldredemor, pres. by Richard de Pype
John de Byriton, pres. by Alexander Mancestr'
Robert de Draycote, pres. by Robert de Bradewell
Richard de Vylers, t. pat.
Ralph de Neuton, t. pat.
Hugh de Waverton, t. pat.
William de Chippeleye, pres. by the abbot of Dale
John de Bracebrigg', t. pat.
Richard de Preston, t. pat.
Thomas de Wychenor, t. pat.
Reginald de Stonle, pres. by Ralph de Perham
William de Westhalum, pres. by the prior of Breadsall
Hugh de Barewe, pres. by Roger Spark
Jordan de Lyme, t. pat.
Nicholas de Seckyndon, t. pat.
William de Breideston, t. pat.
Adam de Kyngesleye, t. pat.
Adam Bonde, t. pat.
John Kerdyf, pres. by Sir Ralph de Rolleston
Thomas le Tyu, pres. by archd. of Chester
John de Brenaston, pres. by John de Brusingtot'
Thomas de Letton, t. pat.
Thomas de Olughton, t. pat.
Roger de Radborne, t. pat.
William le Bret of Bilton, t. pat.
Henry Pougier, pres. by Hugh Pouger of Risley

[Col. 2] *Deacons*

William de Munneworth, r. Kingsbury
Thomas de Barewe, t. pat.
Geoffrey de Wytegreve, t. pat.
Arnold de Ketlesbergh, pres. by the religious of Tickford
John de Boudon, t. pat.
William de Clifton, t. pat.
John de Acton, pres. by M. Adam Byrom
Richard de Kaneleye, t. pat.
Richard de Boudon, t. pat.
M. William l'Archier, t. pat.
Henry de Spondon, t. pat.
John de Workesleye, t. pat.
William de Dutton, r. Tatsfield, dim. dioc. Winchester
Thomas de Brewode, pres. by William de Brikhull

Priests

M. Robert de Overa, pres. by John de la Cornere
John de Hatton, pres. by Roger Corbet
Ranulph de Crosseby, t. pat.

Nicholas de Waverton, t. pat.
William Sharpermor of 'Bromwich', t. pat.
John de Boughton, t. pat.
William de Lauton, t. pat.
John Gery of Clive, pres. by Sir John le Strange
Thomas Morice, pres. by r. Weston upon Trent
Nicholas de Shustok', pres. by John le Botiller
Roger de Ambaston, pres. by Edmund Somervill'
Richard de Halywall', t. pat.
Henry de Overa, t. pat.
Thomas de Ambaston, t. pat.
Laurence de Knuttesford, t. pat.
William de Walton, t. pat.
John de Barewe, John Crispyn of 'Barrow', pres. by the prior of St. John of Jerusalem
Richard de Meleborne, t. pat.
Thomas Miles of Chester, t. pat.
Richard Warmet, pres. by Henry Hastang'
Henry de Chedle, pres. by Sir Roger de Chedle
Pagan Swyft of Derby, t. pat.
Peter, son of Reginald the Beadle of Lichfield, t. pat.
Richard, son of William de Norton, t. pat.
Richard de Wolfecote, t. pat.
John Poydras, t. pat.

[Fo. 115 col. 1] *Priests*

William de Lochay, pres. by the prior of St. James' [hospital], Derby
John de Brinkelowe, pres. by Thomas Boydyn
William de Chaddesden, t. pat.
Robert de Morleye, t. pat.
Roger Blundel of Chesterfield, t. pat.
Nicholas de Eyton, t. pat.
Andrew de Bemhurst, pres. by John de Flamstede
Richard the baker of Lichfield, pres. by the lord of Fisherwick
Richard de Swerkeston, pres. by the prior of Breadsall
John de Hull', pres. by John Hervill'
Laurence de Longa Eyton, pres. by William Brian
Henry de Wavere, t. pat.
Reginald de Norton in Halys, t. pat.
Richard de Brinkelowe, t. pat.
Hamond de la More, r. Isombridge chapel
Thomas de Longa Eyton, pres. by William Roseby
Stephen de Hungerford, v. Uttoxeter
William Olughton, t. pat.
William de Mere, t. pat.
William de Haselovere, Walter de Froddesham, pres. by W[illiam] de Brichull
Thomas de[4] Mudle, pres. by Sir Thomas de Hasting'
John Russel of 'Itchington', t. pat.

John de Kyrkeby, pres. by Nicholas de Wylie
Nicholas de Corson, pres. by Richard de Corzon
John de Bonteshale, t. pat.
Thomas de Wolvey, pres. by Sir Thomas de Wolvey
Bertram le Wodeward, pres. by Thomas de Wappenbur'
Gervase de Hassop, pres. by the dean of Lichfield
John Queneld of Egginton, pres. by William Tymor
Roger, son of Richard de Eccleshale, pres. by the archd. of Derby
Thomas de la Dale of Birmingham, pres. by Nicholas de la Dale
Richard de Bromwych, t. pat.
Ralph de Ronchorn, t. pat.
John de Waverton, t. pat.
Richard dc Wcford, t. pat.
William de Haselovere, pres. by Clement de la Forde
William de Opton, pres. by the lord of Upton
Hugh de Merton, pres. by Sir Thomas de Garshale
Robert de Birchesleye, pres. by Robert the baker of Coventry
William de Ruton of Fillongley, pres. by John, his brother
Henry de Cobynton, pres. by William de Cobinton
Henry de Okebroc', pres. by Simon Pougier
Adam de Burton, t. pat.
Peter Swanneswere, t. pat.
William de Reyndon, t. pat.

[Col. 2] *Priests*

Roger de Olvismor', t. pat.
John de Overton, t. pat.
William de Maclesfeld, t. pat.
Nicholas de Bromle, t. pat.
William Coleman, t. pat.
Richard the forester of 'Overe', pres. by Robert de Fyndirne
William de Gilborne, pres. by the abbot of Dale
Jordan de Waverton, t. pat.
Hugh de Chadleshunte, t. pat.
Hugh de Acton, t. pat.
John de Bobenhull, pres. by Sir Robert, son of Simon
Adam de Mere of 'Burton', pres. by Sir Robert Tok'
John Reynald of Packington, pres. by Sir Henry de Mort...[5]
John Lorimer of Long Eaton, t. pat.
Geoffrey de Stonle, t. pat.
Simon de Clyve of Kingsbury, t. pat.
Richard le Taillor of Penkridge, t. pat.
Stephen de Ednesovere, pres. by the religious of Rocester
Adam de Okebroc', pres. by William Freman of Ockbrook
William de Spondon
Robert Russel of Coventry
William de Hullmorton
Walter Abel of Amington

John the smith of Fillongley, pres. by Ralph de Arleye
John Agnes of Fillongley, pres. by William de Allespathe
Adam de Cuve, t. pat.
John de Hareworth, pres. by Philip de Swynefen, dim. dioc. York
John de Okebroc', pres. by the religious of Dale
Nicholas de Hopton, pres. by Sir Robert de Dotton
Hugh de Okebroc', pres. by Robert de Draicote
Simon de Munworth, pres. by Walter de Winterton
John Pope of Birdingbury, pres. by Sir Thomas de Garshale
Robert de Bourton, pres. by Sir Robert de Verdon
Peter de Maclesfeld, t. pat.
Walter, son of Robert de Ponte of Frodsham, t. pat.
William de Frollesworth, pres. by the religious of the Holy Sepulchre, Warwick, dim. dioc. Lincoln
Richard de Bascote, pres.[6] by Sir Peter de Lymese
John de Stocton, pres. by Sir William de Hondesacr', dim. dioc. Durham
Richard des Aspes of 'Bulton', pres. by Henry de Braudeston
Gilbert de Spondon, t. pat.
Walter Elys of Melbourne, t. pat.
Henry de Geydon, t. pat.
Robert Neuman of Bridgnorth, pres. by the prior and conv. of Bridgnorth

[Fo. 115v col. 1] *Priests*

Henry de Steyveston, pres. by Sir John de Reygate
Andrew de Alveton, pres. by M. Henry de Bray
John de Asthull, pres. by William d'Aubeney of 'Aston'
John de Barton, pres. by Henry de Canvill'
Richard de Huton, t. pat.
William de Blees of Radway, t. pat.
John de Slepe, t. pat.
Hugh de Parva Halum, t. pat.
Richard Wilimot of Long Eaton, pres. by T[homas] de Eyton
Robert de Medio Wyco, t. pat.
Alan le Muragier, t. pat.
Thomas de Clyve, t. pat.
William de Brinkelowe, t. pat.
Ralph de Derset, t. pat.
Robert de Burthingbury, t. pat.
Robert Paramour of Shardlow, pres. by Edmund del Hull' of 'Aston'
Robert de Chilington, pres. by John Giffard
Adam de Salebrugg', pres. by Robert de Langeleye
John de Mamcestr', t. pat.
Roger de Kyngesleye, t. pat.
    [The rest of the fo. is blank.
    [1-1] Across the full width of the fo. above the col. headings.
    [2] Interlined.
    [3] Marked at the right-hand side by a cross with a dot in each segment.
    [4] The name is written around a small hole at this point.

⁵ MS. stained.
⁶ Interlined.]

1308   [Fo. 116 A cancelled copy of **588–593**. See the introduction, *The Register of Walter Langton, Bishop of Coventry and Lichfield, 1296–1321* vol. I (CYS, 91, 2001), pp. xvii–xviii.]

ORDINES.

1309   TAMWORTH'.¹ ²ORDINES IN ECCLESIA PREDICTA CELEBRATI DIE SABBATI QUATUOR TEMPORUM MENSIS DECEMBRIS PER VENERABILEM PATREM: FRATREM .G[ILBERTUM]. DEI GRACIA ENAGDUN' EPISCOPUM PER COMMISSIONEM RADULPHI DE LEYCESTRIA VENERABILIS PATRIS DOMINI .W[ALTERI]. EADEM GRACIA COVENTR' ET LYCH' EPISCOPI IPSO IN REMOTIS AGENTE VICARII IN SPIRITUALIBUS GENERALIS ANNO DOMINI MILLESIMO .CCCᵐᵒ. DUODECIMO² [23 December 1312].

[Col. 1] *Acolytes*³

Robert de Schakeston, Henry de Derley, ⁴canons of Darley⁴
M. Roger de Appilby
Peter de Parva Cestria
William de Kaldewell
Henry de Spondon
Walter de Meysam
Alexander de Spondon
William de Trowelle
Robert de Weston
John de Yepstones
Gilbert, son of Roger de Pecco
John de Leyes
Roger de Pecco
John de Yeveley
William the dyer
Geoffrey de Staunton
John de Sadebury
Ranulph de Lullinton

[Col. 2] *Acolytes*⁵

Henry de Newton
Richard de Allrewas
Henry de Canoco
Nicholas Stordy
William, son of Reginald Budelli
Robert de Levedale
Thomas de Levedale
William de Schuttinton
Henry Broun of 'Haywood'

William de Honnesworth
Thomas de Swynesheved, Henry de Wasteneys, canons[6] of [Baswich by] Stafford[7]
William, son of Thomas de Brewede
Thomas de Frankevyle
Henry de Trentteham
William de Wichawe
Henry de Fylungley
Henry Aintelot'
John de Fylungeley

[Col. 3] *Subdeacons*[8]

Roger de Wythibrok', pres. by the abbot and conv. of Leicester
Robert de Sallowa, t. pat.
John de Twyford, t. pat.
William de Luttele, pres. by Sir Andrew de ...[9]
William, son of Peter, pres. by the prior of St. James' [hospital], Derby
Robert de Eppeley, t. pat.
Thomas de Tressecote, t. pat.
Henry de Felonglegh, t. pat.
Thomas de Hulston, pres. by W. de Leycestr', canon of Lichfield cath.
Robert de Brekeling, pres. by same W., dim. dioc. York
Thomas de Wolaston, t. pat.
Roger de Penne, t. pat.
William de Balyden, pres. by St. Helen's [hospital], Derby
William de Chilmerdon, pres. by the abbot and conv. of Merevale

[Fo. 116v col. 1] *Deacons*

Thomas de Pakynton, t. pat.
William de Dalbur', t. pat.
John le Couper of Eckington, t. pat.
Geoffrey Walraunde, t. pat.
John de Caldecote, t. pat.
William de Lyle, t. pat.
Henry de Stockton, t. pat.
Richard de Aston, t. pat.
Ralph de Breydeston, t. pat.
William de Wetton, t. pat.
Richard de Barton, t. pat.
John de Balyden, t. pat.
John de Staunton, t. pat.
    [Followed by a line drawn across the col.]

Priests[10]

Nicholas, son of Ralph de Beureper, t. pat.
William Leonard, t. pat.
Ralph de Beureper, t. pat.

Thomas de Getewike, t. pat.
John Pygon', t. pat.
Adam Heregrym of Rugeley, t. pat.
Henry de Spondon, t. pat.
John de Brunaldeston, t. pat.
Reginald de Stanleye, t. pat.
John de Acton, pres. by M. Adam Byrom
William Machoun of Breaston, t. pat.
Nicholas de Brewode, t. pat.
Simon de Meysam, t. pat.
William de Rolleston, t. pat.
William Here of Tamworth, t. pat.
Ralph de Neuton, t. pat.
Richard de Horlaston, t. pat.
Robert de Dulverne, t. pat.
Adam de Kyngesley, t. pat.
Richard de Weston, pres. by the prior and conv. of Church Gresley
William de Stretton, pres. by the prior of Canwell, dim. dioc. Lincoln
William, son of Hugh, pres. by same house, dim.
William Alybon, pres. by the prior and conv. of Tutbury
David de Spondon, t. pat.
Nicholas de Sekynton, t. pat.
William de Poley, t. pat.
Hugh de Waverton, t. pat.
William de Cotes, t. pat.
Robert de Waleford, t. pat.
Abel de Eton, t. pat.
Thomas de Brewode, t. pat.

[Col. 2] *Priests*

Henry Roper of Tamworth, t. pat.
Adam de Covene, t. pat.
Thomas Hemery, t. pat.
Thomas the dyer, t. pat.
John de Leycestr', t. pat.
John de Acton, t. pat.
Adam Cele of Youlgreave, t. pat.
Richard de Blakenhale, t. pat.
John ad Fontem of 'Aston', t. pat.
John de Kyngesford, pres. by Sir J. de Klynton
William de Schepel', pres. by the prior and conv. of Dale
Nicholas the miller of Lichfield, t. pat.
Thomas de Knocton, t. pat.
John Henge, pres. by the prior and conv. of Tutbury
Roger de Ruyhull, pres. by Roger Klingesforde, canon of Tamworth
Richard de Vilers, t. pat.
Thomas de Whychenor, t. pat.
William de Whitwikke, t. pat.

Henry de Perton, t. pat.
John de Mikynhull, t. pat.
Robert de Dreycote, t. pat.
Geoffrey de Wolverhamton, t. pat.
Jordan of the same, t. pat.
John de Offeley, t. pat.
John de Sutton, t. pat.
Richard Eysil, t. pat.
Richard de Swerkeston, t. pat.
Robert Barkols, pres. by the prior of the hospital of St. John of Jerusalem
William de Frodeley, t. pat.
Silvester de Allrewase, pres. by Sir Edmund de Somervile
Thomas de Stayneston, t. pat.
Nicholas de Hondesworth, pres. by J[ohn] de B[arre][11]
Robert de Croxale, pres. by Sir W[illiam] of the same [Croxall]
Robert de Whytinton, t. pat.
Henry Pouger, pres. by W[illiam] Pouger
Nicholas de Makeney, pres. by the lord of 'Bu[rley'][12]
John Folejambe, v. Tideswell
Walter de Coleshull, t. pat.
John de Workesley, t. pat.
William de Loskowe, pres. by Hugh Burd', lord of Kirk Hallam
Richard de Breydeshal, pres. by Richard de Cursoun, lord of Breadsall
John de Overa, pres. by Nicholas de Overa

[[1] In the left-hand margin.
[2]–[2] Across the full width of the centre of the fo.
[3] Underlined.
[4]–[4] At the top of col. 2.
[5] Underlined.
[6] In col. 3 and separated from the rest of that col. by a line.
[7] At the left-hand side of the name and separated from the rest of col. 1 by a line.
[8] Underlined.
[9] Abraded.
[10] Underlined.
[11] Abraded. See **1307**D.
[12] Abraded. See **1303**S.]

1310 [Fo. 117] [1]NOMINA ORDINATORUM IN ECCLESIA CATHEDRALI LICH'
DIE SABBATI QUATUOR TEMPORUM PROXIMO POST DIEM CINERUM ANNO
DOMINI MILLESIMO .CCC^mo.XIII. PER DOMINUM WALTERUM DEI GRACIA
COVENTR' ET LICH' EPISCOPUM[1] [2 March 1314].

[Col. 1] *Subdeacons*

Richard de Touecestr', r. Rugby
John de Leycestr', r. Harley
Roger le Brun, r. Loughton, dim. dioc. Lincoln
[Followed by three blank lines.]
William, son of Roger called Richer of Tutbury, pres. by the prior of the place
Henry de Kirketon, pres. by Sir Ralph de Vernoun, kt.

Walker de Ashmeresbrok', t. pat.
Richard de Clint of Cheadle, pres. by Sir Ralph Basset
John Wildegos of 'Aston', pres. by Sir William de Ferrar', kt.
William de Avletton, pres. by the abbot of Croxden
Geoffrey, son of William le Wodeward of Whitgreave, t. pat.
Henry de Astonesfeld, pres. by Adam de Hereford
John de Passeleye of Hasbury, pres. by Roger de Brade[2]burn[2]
William de Bilneye, pres. by Sir Thomas de Garshale
Richard, son of Roger Geoffrey of Aldridge, t. pat.
Stephen de Swyneriston, pres. by Sir Roger de Swyneriston
William de Pilcot, pres. by Roger de Okevere
Ralph, son of William de Grendon, pres. by Sir R[alph] de Grendon
Hugh de Vernoun, pres. by Ralph de Vernoun
William le Graunger of Derby, t. pat.
John de Snalrich, t. pat.
William de Marchinton, William de Bostok, pres. by archd. of Chester
John Onle of Derby, pres. by the prior of Breadsall
John de Upinton, pres. by Sir Thomas Hasting'
Roger de Meleburn, pres. by William Gilbert of Melbourne, receiver of Chester, t. pat.
Richard de Alkynton, pres. by Ralph Bakepeus
William de[3] Cardeil of Spondon, t. pat.
Thomas, son of Andrew Oteyn, t. pat.
John Bret of Polesworth, pres. by r. Barwell
Richard le Mazoun of Polesworth, t. pat.
Thomas de Neubold, pres. by Sir Edmund de Somervill'
William, son of William Mangepayn, t. pat.
Robert de le Keu of Ashbourne, pres. by v. Nosterfield
John de Hurleye, pres. by Sir R[alph] Basset of Drayton Bassett
John de Forewell, pres. by the prioress and conv. of same [Farewell]
[4]John le Lech', to adequate t.[4]

[Col. 2] *Subdeacons*[5]

Ralph de Cleve, t. pat.
Pagan de Langwath, t. pat.
William, son of Richard Yol of Birmingham, pres. by the lord of the town
Robert de Weston, t. pat.
William de Treston, pres. by Brewood Black Ladies
William de Coumpton, pres. by r. Whitnash
William le Sauvage of 'Newton', t.[6] pat.
Henry le Plomer of Youlgreave, pres. by Richard de Herchull
Henry de Merton, pres. by J[ohn, v. [7]], of the same [Marton]
William Raven of 'Ravuneclif', t. pat.
Richard, son of Robert de Sutham, pres. by Sir R[ichard] Turvill'
Robert de Lamputtes, t. pat.
Hugh de Bodesleye, pres. by Sir T[homas] de Charshale
William de Alspathe, pres. by T[homas] de Boydyn
Richard de Marketon, pres. by Philip de Somervill'

William, son of Robert de Okebrok', pres. by the prior of [8]St. James[8], Derby
Andrew, son of Nicholas atte Brugge, pres. by Robert Robert[9] de Beck of Upper Tean
William de Eccles, pres. by the prior and conv. of Birkenhead
John Power of Solihull, t. pat.
Richard de Kyrkeby, pres. by Walter, lord of Alspath
Thomas, son of Richard de Fitteleye, t. pat.
Robert, son of Richard atte Chyrcheyerd of Aldridge, pres. by John de Bentele
John, son of William de Rodene, t. pat.
Richard de Wyrkesworth, pres. by N[icholas] de Hungerford
John, son of Richard, servant of the mayor of Chester, pres. by W[illiam] de Brikhull'
Adam de Wythibrok', pres. by Henry de Appeford
Thomas de Swyneriston, pres. by Roger de Swyneriston
Robert de Weston super Trent', pres. by J. de de[10] Hinbole
Roger de Derewent, t. pat.
Henry, son of Richard Payn, pres. by Ranulph de Stanton
William de Felde of Breaston, pres. by Geoffrey de Sandiacr'
John de Okebrok', pres. by the abbot of Dale to all holy orders
Roger, son of William de Coten, t. pat.
John de Hale, t. pat.
Richard, son of Maurice de Lich', t. pat.
William de Wolricheston, pres. by J[ohn], lord of Frankton
John de Hildeston, pres. by W[illiam] de Praeris of 'Weston'
John, son of J. en le Quecches of Milwich, t. pat.

[Fo. 117v] *Subdeacons*[11]

William Drak' of Tamworth, t. pat.
Ralph de Leyghton of Nantwich
Henry Bussel, t. pat.
William Duncan, t. pat.
Henry, son of John Edith of Featherstone, t. pat.
Alan, son of William Brid', t. pat.
Thomas, son of Philip the goldsmith, pres. by Sir R[oger] de Swynerton
William, son of Henry de Wodeherugh, pres. by the master of St. Helen's [hospital], Derby
Roger de Aldustr', pres. by Gerard de Sekkyndon
Ralph de Welsele, pres. by N[icholas] de Ingwordeby
William de Camera, pres. by William de Camera
Walter de Bredon, t. pat., dim. dioc. Lincoln
Ellis de Magna Cuve, t. pat.
Roger called chapeleyn of Newbold on Avon, [12]t. pat.[12]
William de Smethewyk, pres. by Robert le Baytere of Coventry
John de la Bruere, t. pat.
John le Graund of 'Hopton', t. pat.
William Spaldyng of Sowe, pres. by J[ohn] Heyroun
Richard de Chaddesden of Coventry, t. pat.
William, son of Henry de Coventr', t. pat.

Robert called the cook, of 'Ekynton', t. pat.
Thomas de Buddeworth, t. pat.
Roger Daggescho of 'Newbold', t. pat.
William de Swell of Lichfield, t. pat.
Richard de Beulton, t. pat.
Thomas de Fulford, t. pat.
Nicholas Sturdy of Eckington, t. pat.
Geoffrey Curteys of Little Lawford, pres. by Geoffrey de Craster[13]
Adam de Derby, pres. by the prior of St. James' [hospital], Derby
Simon de Denhall, t. pat.
William Knyt of Wolstanton, t. pat.
Roger de la Dale, t. pat.
Richard Godefrey of Markeaton, t. pat.
Henry atte Brock' of Bishops Itchington, t. pat.
Henry Bret of Bilton, t. pat.
Robert de Eton, pres. by T[homas] de Garsal', kt.
John the baker of Atherstone, t. pat.
Thomas de Alespathe, pres. by T[homas] Boydyn
John de Birtyngbury, t. pat.
Walter de Messingham, t. pat.
Henry de Hopton, t. pat.
William de Brikunhull, t. pat.
Adam de Ichinton Episcopi, t. pat.

[Col. 2]

Nicholas de Wavere, t. pat.
Walter de Aespath, t. pat.
John de Felton, t. pat.
John de Ichinton, t. pat.
Henry de Wodeford, t. pat.
John de Bulkynton, pres. by Sir J[ohn] de Wyluby
J[ohn] de Honikot of Coventry, pres. by R[obert] de Chilterne
William Kyde of Coventry, t. pat.
Roger Russel of Nantwich
Robert James of Clifton, pres. by the prior of Luffield
Thomas, son of Adam de Wolstanton
John de Northerene of Coventry, t. pat.
William Greneberd, pres. by Sir J[ohn] Precche
Richard de Preston of Wildmore, t. pat.
Hugh de Smethewyk, pres. by J[ohn] le Waus, kt.
Hugh de Ireton, t. pat.
Nicholas de Ethewell, pres. by the prior of St. James' [hospital], Derby
Richard de Allespath, pres. by Walter de Morkot
Roger de Pulton, t. pat.
William de Overe, pres. by Osbert de Clinton
Richard de Cotington, t. pat.
J. de Bernewell of Meaford, pres. by H[enry] de Verdon
William de Grendon, t. pat.

Richard de Bromwych, pres. by H[enry] de Erdinton, kt.
Richard Thomas of Drointon, t. pat.
William de Crulefeld, t. pat.
Henry de Overe, pres. by N[icholas] de Overe
Thomas de Caldecot', pres. by the abbot of Merevale
J[ohn] de Fulcushull in Wolston, pres. by Sir Richard de Turvill', kt.
John le Blount of Lichfield, t. pat.
William, son of William de Sutton Duston in 'Stretton', pres. by Sir Robert de Verdon, kt.
Robert de Suthwynefeld, pres. by W[illiam] de Eston, lord of the same
Simon de Compton Murdack, pres. by Sir J[ohn] de Lodbrok'
Henry de Weston, pres. by H[enry] de Ofchirch in Wappenbury
William Curteys of Repton, t. pat.
William, son of H. de Sondon, t. pat.
William de Pristford, t. pat.
Walter de Bostok of Chester, t. pat.
William, son of Geoffrey de Beiyton, t. pat.
John de Cruddewych, t. pat.
J. de Sutton, t. pat.
Geoffrey de Mapurleye, pres. by the abbot of Dale
Roger de Kyrkeby, pres. by Thomas Boydyn
William de Clayton of Abbots Bromley, t. pat.
Richard de de[14] Cyancestr', pres. by J[ohn] Herle

[Fo. 118 col. 1]

William de Mancestr', pres. by Hugh de Mancestr'
John de Salford, pres. by John de Hulton
Robert, son of William called the reeve of Rugby, t. pat.
Richard Amite of Tutbury, pres. by Walter Curteys of Tutbury
Peter Pekoc, pres. by William de Neuton
John de Sondon, t. pat.
Peter de Selebrugg', t. pat.
William de la Lye of Pemberton, t. pat.
William Bacun of Rolleston, t. pat.
Richard, son of Adam de B[15]o[15]routon, pres. by Ellis de Borouton
Richard Wylot of Foxwist, pres. by Guy de Neuton
William de Saltford, t. pat.
Richard de Pynkylton, pres. by Roger de Pinkylton
William Richard of 'Newbold', t. pat.
William Manduth, pres. by N[icholas] de Sheldon, kt.
Philip de Cave, t. pat.
Thomas de Burweston, t. pat.
Thomas de Mikilhull, t. pat.
Simon de Ongres of Melbourne, pres. by Sir John Swynnerton, kt.
William, son of Andrew de Birmyngham, pres. by Nicholas de Sheldon
Gilbert, son of J. de Legh', t. pat.
Simon, son of Thomas Pynicok, t. pat.
J., son of William de le Heth, t. pat.

William de Shyrbrock, pres. by Sir Ralph de Vernoun
Robert de Alkemunton of Longford, pres. by Ralph de Bakepus
William, son of William Richard of 'Stretton' of the king's free chapel, dim. of the
dean's commissary, t. pat.
Richard de Whythybrock, pres. by J[ohn] de Bromleye
J[ohn] Raulyn of Macclesfield, pres. by Thomas de Whythynton
Nicholas le Mascy of Morley, pres. by the abbot and conv. of Dale
P[eter] de Teynton of Coventry, pres. by Henry de Irreys of Ansty
Robert Note of Sheldon, pres. by N[icholas] de Sheldon, kt.
Richard Grestel of Macclesfield, pres. by Edmund de le Donneys
Ralph Bonvalet of Nantwich, t. pat.
Richard de Acton Reymer, pres. by Richard Gery of same [Acton Reynold]
William de Prees, pres. by J[ohn] de Styvynton
Robert Walleys of Bakewell, t. pat.
William de Bondethorp, t. pat.
Richard, son of William de Aula in Derby, pres. by the abbot and conv. of Dale
Richard de Wamborme, t. pat.
Richard Thorn of Drointon, pres. by John de Swynnerton

[Col. 2]

Henry, son of Thomas de Heyford in Radbourne, pres. by the prior of ...[16]
Nicholas Pender of Bretford, pres. by Sir R[obert] de Napton
Reginald de Terven, t. pat.
Robert de Chershale, pres. by the prior and conv. of Wombridge
Walter Grym of 'Haywood', pres. by the prior of Tutbury
Richard, son of Henry de Barowe, pres. by the prior of St. John of Jerusalem in
England
Edmund de Rydeware, t. pat.
William called le Burgeys of Eccleshall, pres. by W. de Adbaston
Adam de Trentam, t. pat.
Walter Heyryng of 'Newton', t. pat.
John de Beumarreys, pres. by William de Brichull
Adam Aveyn of Chesterfield, t. pat.
John de Shotewyk, t. pat.
John de Arlerton, pres. by Sir Roger de Wymerston, kt.
John de Compton Murdak, pres. by T[homas] de Murdak
Thomas de Hakedon, pres. by Henry, lord of Wyverstone
William, son of Richard de Chylynton, pres. by Sir J[ohn] Giffard
William, son of Walter de Medio Wyco, t. pat.
Richard de Uttokeshatr', t. pat.
Peter de Albruhton, pres. by Roger Carles of Albrighton
John Payne of Sudbury, pres. by Sir William de Ferariis, kt.
Richard de Swerkeston, pres. by William Broun of Swarkeston
William de Derby, t. of Robert de Ibole, v. Ashbourne
Alan, son of le Clerk of 'Bradley', pres. by H. de Harcourt of Ludlow
Roger de Peverwych, t. pat.
Richard de Paginton, pres. by Sir J[ohn] Pech, kt.
Richard de Wasteneys, pres. by Geoffrey le Wasteneys

William de Wambourn, pres. by John de Tresel'
Thomas de Fynham, t. pat.
William de Lynton', pres. by Sir Richard de Horwod'
John de Revthestorne, pres. by W[illiam] de Modberlegh
John de Denston', t. pat.
Henry Pulpayn of 'Burton', t. pat.
Robert Olyver of Coventry, pres. by G[eoffrey] le Chaloner of Coventry
John de Thorp, pres. by Walter Wiȝer
Henry de Ronton, pres. by John de Cotes
Ralph de Ceilmardon, pres. by J[ohn] de Congesdon
Geoffrey de Bradele, pres. by the prioress and conv. of Brewood Black Ladies
John, son of John Ryot of Brewood, t. pat.
William le Rydere of 'Burton', t. pat.
John the miller of Lichfield, pres. by the prioress of Nuneaton
Ralph de Ravenescroft, t. pat.
Hugh de Asseby, t. pat.
Robert de Bobenhull, pres. by Sir Robert de Napton
Roger de Compton Mordak, pres. by Sir J[ohn] de Lodbrok'
John de Tene, pres. by Sir Richard de Draycote
Thomas de Prestebur', t. pat.
John le Bore of Solihull, t. pat.
Peter de Grenebergh, t. pat.
Thomas Otheyn of Solihull, t. pat.

[Fo. 118v col. 1] *Subdeacons*[17]

Thomas de Neuport, t. pat.
John de Spondon, pres. by Richard de la Dale
William de Ichinton, t. pat.
Henry de Spondon, t. pat.
Ellis de Brerton, pres. by Sir Roger de Chedle
Adam de Cannok, pres. by Sir William Tromwyn
John Pugier, t. pat.
Hugh de Wippenbury, pres. by John de Merton
Richard de Tunston, t. pat.
Thomas de Breydeston, pres. by Simon Pugier
Robert de Merston, t. pat.
Robert Picard of Melbourne, t. pat.
Simon de Roucestr', pres. by Richard, lord of Blithfield
William Shynnyng of Ockbrook, pres. by the religious of Dale
Hugh March' of 'Newbold', pres. by Sir Edmund de Somervill'
Thomas de Cimiterium of Long Eaton, pres. by William de Grenehull' of Long Eaton
Richard de Ruggele, pres. by Sir Ralph Basset
William de Brunaston, pres. by John Tullok
Walter de Norton, t. pat.
Thomas de Tydeswell, pres. by Sir T[homas] Folejambe
Richard de Rokeby, t. pat.
William, son of Nicholas de Foryate, t. pat.

John de Rokeby, t. pat.
Ralph the baker of Nantwich, t. pat.
Simon de Rokeby, pres. by J[ohn] de Lodbrok'
Adam de la Leegh', t. pat.
Thomas Hereward, pres. by Sir Roger de Swyneriston
Nicholas de Brugge, pres. by the abbot and conv. of Lilleshall
John James of 'Itchington', pres. by Sir J[ohn] de Oddinge[18]seles[18]
John de Woxcestr', pres. by W., lord of 'Eton'
Alan de Waverton, t. pat.
Nicholas de Misternon, t. pat.
Richard de Hoclowe, pres. by the religious of Lilleshall
William, son of Roger de Stocport, t. pat.
Richard de Colton, pres. by the prior of Breadsall
Richard de Pakynton, pres. by William de Inguarby
J[ohn] de Bertumlegh, pres. by William de la Bruere
Nicholas de Camera of Ladbroke, pres. by Sir J[ohn] de Lodbrok'
John de Cobynton, pres. by Nicholas Wyring
Thomas de Kenelwerth, t. pat.
William de Greneberge, t. pat.
Reginald de Berkeswell, pres. by Adam de Notebrok'

[Col. 2]

Robert le Corveyser of Stafford, pres. by W[illiam] de Brikhull
William de Hissop, t. pat.
Robert de Erdynton, pres. by Richard de Pype
Stephen Organ, pres. by Adam Organ
Roger de Kembriston, pres. by Sir W[alter] de Hungerford
William, son of Ralph de Aldelyme, t. pat.
Roger de Lodbrok', pres. by Henry de Lodbrok'
Thomas, son of Richard de Sutham, t. pat.
John de G[19]n[19]ousale, t. pat.
John de Amynton, t. pat.
Roger de Swerkeston, pres. by Richard de Swerkeston
Robert de Rokeby, t. pat.
William de Knistecote, t. pat.
Robert de Lalleford, pres. by J[ohn] Heroun, lord of Church Lawford
Walter de Lillyngton, pres. by the prior of the Holy Sepulchre, Warwick
Osbert de Wythibrok', pres. by Lady Alice Corbet
Richard de Somersale, pres. by Richard de Calewich
Simon de Condolme, t. pat.
Henry de Ichinton, pres. by Sir Adam de Walton
Roger Austyn of Leamington Spa, pres. by J[ohn] Comyn
William de Tamworth, pres. by R., v. Lichfield [cath.]
Henry de Oulghton, pres. by M. Thomas of house of St. Edmund, Bretford
William de Olughton, pres. by Thomas de Pype
Henry Coleman, pres. by Philip de Somervill'
Henry de Calke, t. pat.
Roger Asty of 'Eyton', pres. by Roger Hosse of the same

Robert de Weston, pres. by Sir Robert de Napton
William de Breydeshale, pres. by the religious of Dale
Simon de Rydeware, t. pat.
Walter de Compton, t. pat.
Richard de Betteleye, t. pat.

[The rest of the fo. is blank.
1–1 Across the full width of the fo. above the col. headings.
2–2 Interlined.
3 *Sic* see **1312**D.
4–4 Added at the foot of the col. by another contemporary hand.
5 Added by a later hand.
6 Interlined.
7 MS. *rectoris*
8–8 Interlined.
9 Repeated in error.
10 Repeated in error.
11 Added by a later hand.
12–12 Interlined.
13 Interlined.
14 Repeated in error.
15–15 Interlined.
16 MS. stained.
17 Added by a later hand.
18–18 Interlined.
19–19 Interlined.]

1311 [Fo. 119] ¹NOMINA ORDINATORUM DIE SABBATI QUATUOR TEMPORUM MENSIS DECEMBRIS IN ECCLESIA PREBENDALI DECCLESHALE .ANNO DOMINI MILLESIMO .CCCᵐᵒ.XIIIIᵒ· PER DOMINUM WALTERUM EPISCOPUM COVENTR' ET LICH'¹ [21 December 1314].

[Col. 1] *Subdeacons*

Hugh de Chernok', t. pat.
William de Fonte of 'Newcastle', pres. by Sir William de Mere
John the clerk of 'Burton', pres. by Sir Thomas de Garshale
M. Robert de Wakefeld, r. Heswall
Peter de Rothing', dim. dioc. London, pres. by Sir John de la Leg'
John, son of John Waleis of Chebsey, t. pat.
Hugh de Webenbur', t. pat.
John de Wolaston, pres. by William de Sondford
John de Breudemor, t. a perpetual pension granted to him by Walter called the clerk of Preston
William de Shelton, r. Baginton
John, r. Cranfield, dim. dioc. Lincoln
John de Warr' of Chester, t. pat.
Thomas, son of Henry de Kaverswell, pres. by Henry, his father
Robert, son of Henry de Caverswell, pres. by Henry, his father
John de Brademyr', t. pat.
Ralph de Brerton, r. Brereton chapel
Richard de Chebeseye, t. pat.

Thomas, son of Ranulph, pres. by Reginald de Charnes
John de Bromleye, t. pat.
Richard de Morthweyt, pres. by the prior of Birkenhead
Henry de Hanlegh, pres. by Thomas de Dounes
Robert, son of John del Hul of Lichfield, t. pat.
William Austyn of Albrighton, pres. by Roger de Brayles
John called the smith of 'Boulton', t. pat.
Robert Trip of 'Beulton', t. pat.
William de le Croft, t. pat.
Richard de Werynton, t. pat.
John de Aula of Derby, t. pat.
John, son of Thomas de Rodburn, pres. by the prioress of Nuneaton
Richard the baker of Nantwich, t. pat.
Henry de Chadleshunt, t. pat.
John de Warmynton, pres. by M. Richard, r. North Wingfield

[Col. 2]

Richard de Alrewych, pres. by the prior of Tutbury
John de Aldeport, t. pat.
Robert de Golda, t. pat.
Walter, son of John de Wrocworthyn, t. pat.
Nicholas de Salop', t. pat.
    [Followed by ten blank lines.]

Deacons

William de Cumpton, t. pat.
William de Womburn', t. pat.
Richard de Womburn', pres. by John de Tresel'
Thomas de Neubold, pres. by Sir Edmund de Somervile
Hugh March' of 'Newbold', pres. by same
Richard de Marketon, pres. by Philip de Somervile
John Qwecche of Milwich, t. pat.
William le Ridere of 'Burton', t. pat.
Pagan de Langwat', pres. by Sir Roger de Shelton
Peter de Wytinton, pres. by William de Freford
Roger de Cumpton Mordak, pres. by Sir Henry de Lodbrok'
John de Burthyngbur', pres. by Sir Robert de Napton
Richard s. [Robert][2] de Sutham, pres. by Sir Henry de Lodbrok'
Roger le Chapeleyn of Newbold on Avon, t. pat.
William Drake of Tamworth, t. pat.
Richard Moriz of Lichfield, t. pat.
Richard Allewene of 'Beulton', t. pat.
William Kyng of Wolstanton, pres. by the abbot of Hulton
John de Cumpton Mordak', pres. by Sir Thomas Murdak'
Simon de Cumpton Murdak', t. pat.

[Fo. 119v col. 1] *Deacons*[3]

Roger, r. Smethcott
John de Opinton, t. pat.
Richard de Acton, t. pat.
Gilbert de Lega, t. pat.
William de Presteford, t. pat.
Reginald de Terven, t. pat.
John de Braundon Forje, t. pat.
Adam de Ichinton, t. pat.
Simon de Roucestr', pres. by the lord of Blithfield
Richard Throstel, pres. by Sir Edmund de Dounes
John de Felton, pres. by Ranulph Paen
Ralph Bonvalet, t. pat.
William Hassop, t. pat.
Adam de Cannok, pres. by Sir Roger Tromwyn
William de Stretton, t. pat.
John de Derby, pres. by the prior of Breadsall
Thomas de Hakedon, pres. by Henry de Wyverston
Jordan de Farneborw, t. pat.
Thomas de Fulford, t. pat.
Walter Hyngham, t. pat.
William de Hampton, pres. by the prior of the hospital of St. John
Roger de Swerkeston, pres. by Richard de Swerkeston
[Geoffrey][4] de Bradelegh', pres. by the prioress of Brewood Black Ladies
Pagan de Languath,[5] t. pat.
William de Aldelime, t. pat.
Henry atte Brok' of Bishops Itchington, t. pat.
John de Ichinton
John, son of John Sellar' of Lichfield, t. pat.
William de Bromleg', t. pat.
Richard de Wastoneys, t. pat.
Robert de Merston, t. pat.
Robert de Merston,[6] t. pat.
Adam de Legh', t. pat.
Richard de Foxwyst, t. pat.
John, son of Richard Cestr', t. pat.
Thomas de Bruera, t. pat.
William de Olireston, t. pat.
Richard Tailour of Lichfield, t. pat.
Robert de Alrewych, pres. by John de Bentleye
Richard de Rokeby, pres. by John le Palmere
John de Rokeby, pres. by Thomas Garshale
John James of 'Itchington', pres. by Sir John de Oddin[7]gesles[7]

[Col. 2]

William de Ichinton, t. pat.
William de Prees, pres. by John de Stevynton

Peter de Albrighton, pres. by Roger Kareles
Geoffrey Curteys of Little Lawford, pres. by Geoffrey de Craster
Henry le Breet of Bilton, t. pat.
John de Bulkynton, t. pat.
Henry Paen of Standon, pres. by Ranulph de Staundon
William le Coylter of Lichfield, t. pat.
William de Knyhtecote
Richard de Eton, t. pat.
Robert de Weston, t. pat.
John the miller of Lichfield, t. pat.
William de Greneborow, t. pat.
Alan Bryd', t. pat.
William de Eccleshal', pres. by the prior of Birkenhead
Hugh de Vernoun, pres. by Sir Ralph de Vernoun
William de Shebbrok', pres. by Sir Ralph de Vernoun
Robert, son of William de Coton, t. pat.
Richard de Ruggelegh, pres. by Sir Ralph de Chedle
William de Tressecote, pres. by Brewood Black Ladies
John de Asteleye of Lichfield, t. pat.
Richard de Pakynton, pres. by Thomas de Irreys
Richard de Joneston, t. pat.
Richard de Wyrk', t. pat.
William Rycher of Tutbury, pres. by the prior of Tutbury
William Dunkan, t. pat.
Thomas de Rideware, t. pat.
William de Chilinton, pres. by Sir John Giffard
Thomas de Boruhston, t. pat.
William de Lych', t. pat.
Walter de Norton, t. pat.
Adam de Derby, pres. by the abbot of Dale
John de Chedle, t. pat.
    [The rest of the fo. is blank.]

[Fo. 120 col. 1] *Priests*

Thomas de Brewode, t. pat.
Adam de Bascote, pres. by Sir Peter de Lemiseye
William de Kynnesbur', t. pat.
Robert de Weston, t. pat.
Guy de Neuton, r. Coddington
Hugh de Preez, t. pat.
Roger de Derewent, pres. by William de Preez
Robert Natte of Melbourne, t. pat.
John Alvane, t. pat.
Henry de Kyrketon, pres. by Sir Ralph de Vernoun, junior
Thomas de Colnham, pres. by the prior and conv. of Wombridge
William Leges, t. pat.
William de Forʒate, t. pat.
Robert de Clyve, t. pat.

John de Yolgrave, t. pat.
John de Twyford, t. pat.
Robert de Chebeseye, pres. by Sir John de Hastang'
William Wodecok' of Birmingham, t. pat.
Robert de Sallowe, t. pat.
William de Cheylnerdon, pres. by the abbot and conv. of Merevale
William de Aula of Derby, t. pat.
Thomas de Olughton, pres. by Sir Robert de Thorp, kt.
Richard, son of William de Aula of Derby, pres. by the abbot and conv. of Dale
Robert Hykeling, pres. by the prior of Coventry
Geoffrey de Wytegreve, t. pat.
John de Asshovere, pres. by Sir William de Brykhull
William de Sowe, t. pat.
John de Draycote, t. pat.
John de Chadleshunte, pres. by Richard de Gaydon

    [The rest of the col. is blank.
    1-1 Across the full width of the fo. above the col. headings.
    2 MS. omitted.
    3 Added by a later hand.
    4 MS. *Gilbert.*
    5 ?Listed twice, see p. 106 Pagan de Langwat'.
    6 ?Listed twice.
    7-7 On the line below.]

1312 [Col. 2] NOMINA ORDINATORUM IN ECCLESIA PREBENDALI DE COLEWYCH DIE SABBATI QUATUOR TEMPORUM IN VIGILIA TRINITATIS ANNO DOMINI MILLESIMO .CCC^{mo}.XV. PER DOMINUM WALTERUM EPISCOPUM COVENTR' ET LICHEFELDEN' [17 May 1315].

Subdeacons

John, r. Carsington
Ralph de Brantingham, r. Bonsall
William, r. Boylestone
William, son of William Semon of Ely, dim. dioc. Ely, t. pat.
William, son of Robert de Neuton, t. pat.
Robert Sharp of Wilsthorpe, pres. by William de Breyd'
Jordan de Peninton, pres. by the lord of Stockport
William, son of Thomas de Sallowe, pres. by William Tebard of Draycott
Richard de Sanford, t. pat.
Thomas Ern, pres. by Roger de Totnesovere
Richard Alewyne of 'Norton', t. pat.
Ralph de Stanclyf, pres. by the abbot and conv. of Beauchief
William de Neusum, t. pat.
Robert de Falyngbrom, t. pat.
Gilbert, r. Whittington
Thomas de Clipston, dim. dioc. Lincoln, pres. by the house of Luffield
Robert de Trussele, t. pat.
William de Bernham of Gumley, dim. dioc. Lincoln, pres. by the house of Chacombe
Henry de Burywey, t. pat.

Ralph de Bakewelle, pres. by Thomas de Folejambe, kt., to all holy orders
Adam de Derby, pres. by John Paunel of Wilsthorpe
Richard de Hauekesok', t. pat.
Peter de Parva Cestr', pres. by St. Helen's [hospital], Derby
Henry de Restweyt, pres. by the house of Dale
William de Rode, r. Newport
Thomas Baldewyn, pres. by the dean and chapter of St. Mary de Castro, Leicester
William de Sottonton, pres. by John Amyot of 'Sutton'
Richard de Cruch, pres. by the abbot and conv. of Dale
Thomas le Gaunter of Tamworth, t. pat.
Richard le Marshal of Shrewsbury, t. pat.
Nicholas de Brugge, pres. by the prior of Holy Trinity hospital [Bridgnorth]
William de Hethull', pres. by the abbot of Lilleshall
Thomas de Bykedon, t. pat.
Thomas de Tyford, t. pat.

[Fo. 120v col. 1] *Subdeacons*

John de Gnoushale, pres. by William de Burgo
Roger de Halughton, t. pat.
William de Maclesfeld, t. pat.
William de Estlemynton, pres. by Sir John Oddingesles
Robert de le Graunges of Spondon, pres. by the religious of Dale
John de Ederinghale, t. pat.
Peter, son of William atte Nore of Chillington, pres. by Sir John Giffard
Henry Broun of 'Haywood', pres. by M. John de Shoteswell
Nicholas de Welde, t. pat.
Peter, son of Henry de Tuttebur', pres. by Sir Philip de Barinton
Hugh, son of Roger Maysemore, t. pat.
Roger de Appelby, pres. by Sir Richard de Herchull', dim. dioc. Lincoln
Adam, son of William the cook of Lichfield, pres. by William de Sparham
John de Yevele, t. pat.
William de Braylesford, pres. by Sir John de Twyford, kt.
William de Hinkele, pres. by Lady Matilda Burnel, dim. dioc. Lincoln
Geoffrey de Joneston, pres. by Sir Robert de Dutton
John, son of Henry de Fylungleye, t. pat.
Roger de Baggeleye, pres. by Sir Thomas de Garshal'
John de Shulton, t. pat.
Roger de Boulton, pres. by Robert, lord[1] of Bradshaw
John de Ruton, pres. by the prior and brethren of the Holy Sepulchre, Warwick
Robert de Keel, t. pat.
Alan de Thurmenton, pres. by William de Breydeston
Simon de Magna Derset, pres. by Sir Thomas de Garshal'
Walter de Lillyngston, pres. by the prior of Luffield, dim. dioc. Lincoln, to all [orders]
Richard Wych', t. pat.
      [The rest of the col. is blank.]

[Col. 2] *Deacons*

William de Tamworth, pres. by v. Lichfield [cath.]
Roger de Peverwych, t. pat.
Simon, son of Thomas Pynikok, t. pat.
John, son of William de Roden, t. pat.
Adam Albeyn of Chesterfield, pres. by Ralph, lord of Brailsford
Simon de Denhale, t. pat.
William Manduyt, pres. by Sir Nicholas de Sheldon
Richard de Alrewych, pres. by the prior and conv. of Tutbury
John Bryht, pres. by John, r. Barwell
Richard de Preston, t. pat.
William de Dorandesthorp, t. pat.
Andrew, son of Nicholas atte Bruggeende, pres. by Robert de Beck
William de Brunaston, pres. by Robert Ferbraz
Richard de Wythibrok', pres. by John de Bromleg', lord of Hapsford
John de Warmynton, pres. by Richard of the same [Warmington], r. North Wingfield
Richard le Maceon of Polesworth, t. pat.
John de Passelegh', pres. by Sir Roger de Bradebourn
Robert le Keu of Ashbourne, pres. by Sir Robert Tookey
Richard Osmond of Wilnecote, t. pat.
William de Crulefeld, t. pat.
John Pouger, t. pat.
William de Campo of Breaston, t. pat.
Thomas de Breydeston, pres. by Simon Pouger
Richard de Pylkynton, pres. by Sir Roger de Pylkynton
John Poer of Solihull, t. pat.
Henry de Weston, pres. by Henry de Ofchirche
Ralph de Clyve, t. pat.
Robert de Walleye, t. pat.
Alan de Waverton, t. pat.
Roger Austin, pres. by John Comyn
Richard de Morthawyth, pres. by the house of Birkenhead
Henry Oliver of Marton, t. pat.
Thomas de Aula of 'Walton', t. pat.
William Sauvage of 'Newton', t. pat.
Thomas de Flittelegh, t. pat.
John de Thorp, pres. by Walter Wyther
John de Hyldreston, pres. by William de Praers
Walter Eyring of 'Newton', t. pat.
Richard de Colton, pres. by William, lord of Colton
Henry de Spondon, t. pat.
Peter de Salbrigge, pres. by Robert de Langle
William Yol of Birmingham, pres. by Sir William de Bermyngham
William Shymnyng of Ockbrook, pres. by the abbot of Dale

[Fo. 121 col. 1] *Deacons*

Henry de Olughton, t. pat.
William, son of Richard de Neubold, t. pat.
Nicholas de Brugge, William de Pylcote, pres. by the abbot and conv. of Lilleshall
Thomas, son of Philip the goldsmith of Stafford, pres. by Sir Roger de Swynnerton
John, son of Thomas de Rodbourn, pres. by the nuns of Nuneaton
Henry de Hopton, t. pat.
John le Graund of Hopton, t. pat.
Ralph de Welesleye, pres. by Nicholas de Inguarby
Hugh de Chernok', pres. by Adam, lord of Charnock
Henry de Rodbourn, t. pat.
Richard de Codinton, t. pat.
Henry de Ichinton, pres. by Adam de Walton, kt.
John Brangwayn of Birmingham, t. pat.
Richard de Kyrkeby, pres. by the lord of Alspath
John Pryne, pres. by Sir Walter de Montgomery
John de Hale, t. pat.
Robert, son of John del Hull', t. pat.
Walter de Compton, t. pat.
Nicholas de Wavere, t. pat.
Richard de Bromwych, pres. by Sir Henry de Erdinton
Henry le Plomer of Youlgreave, pres. by Henry de Herchull
Roger de Lodbrok', pres. by Sir Henry of the same [Ladbroke]
Adam de Harpelegh, t. pat.
William de Acton, t. pat.
Nicholas de Salop', t. pat.
Richard de Bectelegh, pres. by Robert de Preers
Henry Polpayn of 'Burton', t. pat.
Hugh de Smethewyk, pres. by the succentor of Lichfield
Walter Bostok' of Chester, t. pat.
Philip de Cave, t. pat.
William Andreu of Birmingham, pres. by Sir Nicholas de Sheldon
John de Breudemor, t. pat.
Nicholas Sturdy of Eckington, t. pat.
Osbert de Wythibrok', pres. by the lady of Withybrook
Philip Beumareys, pres. by Sir William de Brykhull'
Robert le Corviser of Stafford, t. pat.
Thomas Astyn of 'Dassett', t. pat.
Stephen Organ of Edingale, t. pat.
Robert Oliver of Coventry, pres. by Geoffrey le Chaloner
Walker de Esmerebrok', t. pat.
Walter Grym of 'Haywood', t. pat.

[Col. 2] *Deacons*

John de Wolaston, pres. by William de Saunford
Thomas Otheyn of Solihull, t. pat.
Robert Pycard of Melbourne, t. pat.

William de Alveton, pres. by the abbot and conv. of Croxden
John de Blourton, pres. by Sir Roger de Swynnerton
Robert de Lamputtes, t. pat.
William Spalding of Sowe, pres. by John, lord of Church Lawford
Henry de Alstanesfeld, pres. by Adam de Bereford
William Mangepayn of Repton, t. pat.
Richard, son of Geoffrey de Alrewych, t. pat.
William de Wolricheston, pres. by John le Palmere
Robert de Rokeby, t. pat.
William Benet of Fillongley, t. pat.
John de Aula of Derby, pres. by William de Aula of Derby
Henry de Morton, pres. by Sir John de Hastang'
Robert de Erdinton, pres. by Richard de Pipe
Hugh de Baddelegh', pres. by Sir Thomas de Garshal'
Simon de Cundulme, t. pat.
Richard de Alkemunton, pres. by Ralph de Bakepuyz
Peter de Teinton of Coventry, pres. by Henry Hyreys
Roger de Melbourn, [2]pres. by William Gilbert[2]
John de Wroxcestr', pres. by Hugh, lord of Baslow
Peter de Rothing', [3]dim. dioc. London,[3] pres. by Sir John de la Legh', kt.
Thomas Hereward, pres. by Sir Roger de Swynnerton, kt.
William in le Legh' of 'Smethwick', t. pat.
Henry Sampson of Weeford, pres. by Ralph, lord of Tykke...[4]
Robert James of Clifton, pres. by the house of Luffield
Thomas, son of Andrew Othyn, t. pat.
William de Bylneye, pres. by Sir Thomas de Garshal'
Richard de Ottokeshather, t. pat.
Thomas ad Cimiterium of Long Eaton, pres. by William de Grenehull'
Henry de Chadleshunte, pres. by the prior of the Holy Sepulchre, Warwick
Ralph the baker of Nantwich, t. pat.
William de Grendon, pres. by Sir Thomas de Garshal'
Nicholas de Camera of Ladbroke, pres. by Sir Henry de Lodbrok'
John de Elaston, pres. by Ralph de Stanton
Richard de Somershal', pres. by Richard de Colewych
Peter de Grenebergh, t. pat.
Hugh de Wybenbury, t. pat.
Stephen de Swynnerton, pres. by Sir Roger de Swynnerton
William de Overa, pres. by the prior and conv. of Church Gresley

[Fo. 121v col. 1] *Deacons*

Thomas de Fynham, t. pat.
John de Honicote of Coventry, pres. by Robert de Chilterne
John de Smalrys, t. pat.
William de Okebrok', pres. by the abbot and conv. of Dale
Nicholas de Etewell, pres. by Robert Ferbraz
Richard de Barewe, pres. by the prior of St. John of Jerusalem
William Cardryl' of Spondon, t. house of Burton Lazars
Richard de Hokelowe, pres. by the house of Lilleshull

William de Fonte of 'Newcastle', pres. by Sir William de Mere
Richard de Pakinton, pres. by William de Inguardi
Richard de Allespath, pres. by Walter de Mopcote
Henry Andreu of Tideswell, t. pat.
Robert de Lalleford, pres. by John, lord of Church Lawford
William le Granger of Derby, t. pat.
John called le Northerne of Coventry, t. pat.
Richard Godefrey of Markeaton, t. pat.
John de Denston', t. pat.
Thomas de Tideswell, pres. by Sir Thomas Folegaumbe
John de Spondon, pres. by the abbot and conv. of Dale
John le Leche of Draycott, to an adequate t.
William de Smethewych, pres. by Robert the baker of Coventry
Thomas de Alspath, pres. by Thomas Boydyn
John de Tene, pres. by M. Adam Byron
Robert de Suthwynefeld, pres. by William, lord of 'Eston'
[John][5] Wyldegos of 'Aston', pres. by Sir William de Ferrar', kt., to all [orders]
William de Derby, pres. by Robert, v. Ashbourne
William, son of Geoffrey de Beghton, t. pat.
John de Folkeshull, pres. by Robert Tirvill'
Henry de Calke, t. pat.
William de Barkesford, t. pat.
Thomas de Prestebury, t. pat.
Richard de Swerkeston, pres. by William Broun of Swarkeston
Robert de Cavereswell, pres. by Henry de Cavereswell
Thomas de Cavereswell, pres. by Henry de Cavereswell
Henry Bussel of Otherton, t. pat.
Ralph de Locton', t. pat.
William de Linton', t. pat.
William de Sondon', t. pat.

[Col. 2]

John de Cruddeworth, t. pat.
John de Salford, t. pat.
Nicholas le Macy of Morley, pres. by the abbot and conv. of Dale
William, son of Henry de Coventr', t. pat.
Robert de Alkemonton, pres. by Ralph de Bakeputz
Richard de Cravene, canon of Penkridge
Richard de Pakynton, pres. by Thomas Hyrreys
Ralph de Ravenescroft, t. pat.
Robert de Weston, t. pat.
[6]Geoffrey de Bathekynton pres. by Richard de Herchull[6]
John de Bourton, pres. by Sir Thomas de Garshal'
Simon de Rydeware, t. pat.
Walter de Meysham, t. pat.
Robert Goldeyen, t. pat.
William de Camera of Marchington, pres. by Henry de Camera of Marchington
Henry de Hanele, t. pat.

Walter de Lockesford, dim. dioc. Exeter, pres. by Sir Nicholas de Audeley
Roger de Kembriston, pres. by Sir Walter de Hungeford
William Corteys, t. pat.
William de Leya, t. pat.
William Austyn, pres. by Roger Careles
Ellis de Brerdon, pres. by Richard, lord of Swettenham
Robert Trip of 'Beulton'
John Pek of 'Newton', pres. by the prior of Luffield
John de Gnoushale, t. pat.
Thomas de Wolstanton, t. pat.
Richard de Chaddesdene of Coventry, t. pat.
William Raven, t. pat.
William de Mauncestr', pres. by Hugh de Mauncestr'
William Bakun of Rolleston, t. pat.
Henry, son of Henry de Ronton, pres. by John de Cotes
Henry Colemon of Longdon, pres. by Philip de Somervill'
Reginald de Notebrok' of Berkswell, t. pat.
    [The rest of the fo. is blank.]

[Fo. 122 col. 1] *Priests*

John Hillar', r. Cranfield, dim. dioc. Lincoln
Thomas, r. Weston under Lizard
Roger, r. Smethcott
John de Bolkynton, pres. by John de Wylugbi
John de Horslegh, pres. by the house of Canwell
William Knyst of Wolstanton, pres. by the abbot of Hulton
Hugh de Vernoun, pres. by Sir Ralph de Vernoun
Thomas de Folford, t. pat.
William Richer of Tutbury, pres. by the prior and conv. of Tutbury
Walter de Norton, t. pat.
John de Atherston of Lichfield, t. pat.
Pagan de Langwayt', t. pat.
Richard de Rokeby, t. pat.
Adam de la Legh', t. pat.
Geoffrey de Berchinton, t. pat.
Geoffrey le Wodeward, t. pat.
Richard de Wombourne, t. pat.
John de Rokeby, pres. by Sir Thomas de Garshal'
Thomas de Neuport, t. pat.
Roger de Swerkeston, pres. by Richard de Swerkeston
William de Shilbrok', pres. by Sir Ralph de Vernon
William de Suthwynefeld, pres. by Sir John Heryz
John de Cestr', pres. by the prior and conv. of Birkenhead
Adam de Ichinton, t. pat.
John James of 'Itchington', pres. by Sir John de Oddingesles
Richard Thomas of Drointon, pres. by Sir John de Swynnerton
Geoffrey de Bathkynton, pres. by Sir Richard de Herchull
Richard Throstel of Macclesfield, t. pat.

Geoffrey Walrand of Lillington, t. pat.
Roger Chapeleyn of Newbold on Avon, t. pat.
William de Wombourn, pres. by John de Tresel'
Walter de Allespath, t. pat.
Robert, son of William de Coton, t. pat.
William de Ichinton, t. pat.
John de Ichinton, t. pat.
William de Eccleshal', pres. by the prior and conv. of Birkenhead
Simon le Maceon of Chesterfield, t. pat.
Richard de Spondon, pres. by the prior and conv. of Dale

[Col. 2]

Peter de Whytinton, pres. by William, lord of Freeford
Ellis de Magna Cuve, t. pat.
William Drake of Tamworth, t. pat.
John de Milverton, t. pat.
William de Knistecote, t. pat.
Richard de Maperlegh, pres. by the abbot and conv. of Dale
Richard de Sutham, pres. by Sir Henry de Lodbrok'
John the baker of Milverton, pres. by the house of the Holy Sepulchre, Warwick
Henry le Bret of Bilton, t. pat.
Geoffrey Corteys of Little Lawford, t. pat.
Henry de la Dale, pres. by Thomas de Piverwych
William de Grenebergh, t. pat.
Robert de Merston, t. pat.
Richard the tailor of Lichfield, t. pat.
Thomas de Neubold, pres. by Sir Edmund de Somervill'
Richard Moriz of Lichfield, t. pat.
John Lime of Coleshill, t. pat.
Richard de Coleshull, t. pat.
William Michel of Ladbroke, pres. by the lord of Ladbroke
John de Opinton, pres. by Sir Thomas de Hastang'
William de Cesterfeld, t. pat.
Walter Ingram, t. pat.
William de Olugton, t. pat.
Richard Wylot of Foxwist, pres. by Guy de Neuton
Thomas Fauk of 'Harborough', pres. by Geoffrey de Cras[ter][7]
Thomas de Mukelhull, t. pat.
Thomas de Whalleye, t. pat.
Thomas de Hakedon, pres. by the lord of Wyverstone
John de Burthingbur', pres. by Sir Robert de Napton
William le Coylter of Lichfield, t. pat.
William de Bromlegh, t. pat.
William de Hassop, t. pat.
William de Presteford, t. pat.
Robert Notte of Sheldon, pres. by Nicholas de Sheldon
Adam Cannok, pres. by Sir William Tromwyne
William Burgeys, t. pat.

William de Swelle, t. pat.
Reginald de Terven, t. pat.
Thomas de Bouluas, t. pat.
Simon de Brokes, pres. by John, r. Haughton
Henry de Ichinton, t. pat.
John called the miller, pres. by Adam de Ruggelegh'
John de Beverleye, t. pat.
Richard Alewyn of 'Beulton', t. pat.

[Fo. 122v col. 1] *Priests*

Thomas de Aldelmestre, t. pat.
Edmund de Rideware, t. pat.
Philip de Barnevill', t. pat.
John de Chedle, t. pat.
Thomas de Borweston, t. pat.
Peter de Albriston, pres. by Roger Carles
William de Stretton, t. pat.
Hugh March' of 'Newbold', pres. by Sir Edmund de Somervill'
Richard de Acton, t. pat.
Robert de Westun, t. pat.
John en le Quecches of Milwich, t. pat. [8]t. pat.[8]
William de Cumpton, pres. by Sir Henry de Cumpton
William, son of Richard de Chelinton, pres. by Sir John Giffard
William Pymmore of 'Stockton', pres. by Sir Edmund de Somervill'
Richard de Wasteneys, t. pat.
Geoffrey de Bradeleye, pres. by Brewood Black Ladies
Ralph Bonvalet of Nantwich, t. pat.
John Raulyn of Macclesfield, t. pat.
John de Hanewell, t. pat.
William de Trescote, pres. by Brewood Black Ladies
John de Astele, t. pat.
Richard de Grinston', t. pat.
John de Brademere, dim. dioc. York
Richard de Wyrkesworth, pres. by Nicholas de Hungerford
Gilbert de Lega, t. pat.
John de Brademere, pres. by the abbot and conv. of Dale
Robert de Bromlegh, pres. by Simon Scot
Henry de Staunton, pres. by Ranulph of the same
   [The rest of the fo. is blank.
   [1] Interlined.
   [2–2] Underlined.
   [3–3] Interlined.
   [4] Unclear.
   [5] MS. *Philippus*
   [6–6] Deleted and partially erased.
   [7] Abraded.
   [8–8] Interlined and partially erased.]

1313 [Fo. 123] [1]NOMINA ORDINATORUM IN ECCLESIA CONVENTUALI DE RONTON DIE SABBATI QUATUOR TEMPORUM MENSIS DECEMBRIS .ANNO DOMINI .MILLESIMO .CCC[mo]. QUINTODECIMO PER W[ALTERUM] EPISCOPUM COVENTR' ET LICH' UBI FUIT LATA SENTENCIA SUB HAC FORMA [20 DECEMBER 1315].

In the name of God, Amen. Walter by divine permission bishop of Coventry and Lichfield, celebrating [his] orders in Ranton conventual church on Saturday *quatuor temporum* [20] December 1315, warns and enjoins each and every person present, assembled because of the orders to be received from [him] that, firstly, secondly and thirdly, and in peril of [their] souls and also under pain of greater excommunication, no one shall enter such orders to be received unless he is examined and admitted by the examiners appointed for this; also no one from another diocese without letters dimissory of his bishop; also no one who is bigamous or married to a widow; [or] married; by omission of a degree of ordination; by simony; of illegitimate birth without having dispensation; of servile status; no one shall receive two holy orders or a single holy order and another minor order [this day]; [or be] a murderer; [2]ordained to holy orders[2] unless he has adequate title with which he considers himself satisfied for [the bishop's] discharge and that of [his] successors; from a royal chapel [in the bishop's] diocese without [his] special licence; [and] if anyone happens or audaciously ventures to contravene the foregoing [the bishop] wishes [him] to incur the aforesaid sentence of excommunication thereby.[1] [3]

[Col. 1] *Subdeacons*

William Letis of 'Newcastle', t. pat.
William Schyrrene of Ockbrook, pres. by the abbot and conv. of Dale
William de Bruggeston', t. pat.
Nicholas de Baxterle, pres. by the abbot of Merevale to all holy orders
Thomas de Stokyforth, t. pat.
William de Sutham, pres. by J[ohn] de Oddinges'
Robert de Whytemor', t. pat.
Roger de Bobenhull, pres. by W[illiam] de Willeby
Hugh Pruwlin of Whitmore, t. pat.
Thomas de Mapelton, pres. by J[ohn] de Mapelton
Robert de Tydeswell, pres. by Thomas Folejamb and t. pat.
William de Foston, pres. by R[alph], lord of Brailsford
William, son of Die of Tamworth, t. pat.
John de Halughton, pres. by Vivian de Staundon, junior
Adam de Fyndron, pres. by Robert de Fyndren
William Cole of Rugby, pres. by J[ohn] Revel
William de Wolseye, pres. by J[ohn] de Shireford
Simon de Barton, pres. by J[ohn] de Bakepuz
Richard de Stretton, t. pat.

[Col. 2] *Subdeacons*

Robert de Overe, pres. by J[ohn] Gery of Derby
William de Morton Say, t. pat.

Laurence Borrey, pres. by Owen de Montgomery
Richard de Pecham, t. pat.
John, son of Robert de Lound, pres. by the abbot of Croxden[4]
Robert de Whythorslegh, t. pat.[5]
William de Adingburgh, pres. by W. Dauns, dim. dioc. York
Richard Martin, pres. by Sir Adam de Bereford
William called Parent, pres. by the lord of 'Naudon'
William de Nesse, to t. of William de Posselowe
William de Hereward, pres. by John de Swynnerton
Roger de Aston, t. pat.
John Horn of Rugby, t. pat.
Thomas de Bradewell, pres. by J[ohn] de Hastang'
Robert de Frodesham, t. pat.
Richard Large of 'Lynhull', t. pat.
John de Toft, pres. by J[ohn] de Oddingesles
Peter de Melbourn, t. pat.
John de Audeford, t. the perpetual chantry of T[homas] de Welles
William de Norrton, pres. by R[ichard], lord of Blithfield

[Fo. 123v col. 1] *Subdeacons*

M. Henry de Kyrkeby, r. Wappenbury
M. Robert de Preston, r. Fitz
M. William de Pontesbur', r. Trusley
Simon de Womborn, v. Lichfield [cath.]
Thurstan, r. Hanbury
Robert de Blecchelegh, r. Tarporley
William de Praers, r. Barthomley
M. Nicholas de Guthmondelegh, r. Trimley St. Martin, dim. dioc. Norwich
John de Asteleye, t. pension from J., son of Adam de Asteleygh
Roger de Grendon, pres. by R[6]obert[6] de Verdon
Richard de Makstok', pres. by the lady of Maxstoke
Geoffrey de Merston, t. pat.
William de Carberton, dim. dioc. York, t. pat.
John de Cevene, t. pat.
Robert Cadas, pres. by Richard Folejamb
John atte Wall, pres. by Henry de Heywod
William de Bontesleye, pres. by the prior of Canwell
Richard called Nel of 'Harwood', pres. by Richard de Horwode, dim. dioc. Lincoln
Richard de Delverne, t. pat.
Adam Bagot, t. pat.
William Waleys, pres. by R[obert] Waleys of 'Eyton'
Thomas de Faston, pres. by William de Faston
Adam Wildy of 'Aston', pres. by John de Perton
William le Maceon of Repton, t. pat.
John called le Fox, t. 40 shillings
William del Ewode, t. pat.
Robert de Bilston', t. pat.

John de[7] Tresel', pres. by John de Tresel'
Henry de Stycheford, pres. by Thomas, lord of Little Bromwich
John de Overe, pres. by Henry de Corndone
Robert de Steyveston, pres. by Nicholas de Overa
Hugh de Yoxhale, t. pat.
Henry de Chetewynde, pres. by John de Chetewynde
John de Toft, pres. by Henry de Merinton
Thomas de Merston, t. pat.
Gilbert le Maceon, pres. by the prior of Church Gresley

[Col. 2] *Subdeacons*

Thomas de Burton, t. pat.
Richard de Sondbache, t. pat.
Fr. John de le Newe Toun
Fr. Simon de Peywyk
Robert de Schakeston, canon of Kenilworth
Fr. Henry de Aspunwale
Fr. Thomas de Rouclif
Fr. Arnold de Emsey
Fr. Richard de Wyco
William de Scharnebrok', OP
Fr. Peter de Asteleye
Fr. William de Havern
Fr. Thomas de Wodehous
Fr. Roger de Salop'
William de Doninton, pres. by Roger Carles
Nicholas de Albrygton, pres. by John de Byspeton
John Mervynne, pres. by Thomas de Garsal'
Thomas de Burgo, t. pat.
William Cosyn, t. pat.
Henry de Horsleye, t. pat.
Robert de Dodinton, pres. by William de Stafford
Richard de Wytonstal, t. pat.
Ralph de Rode, t. pat.
John de Ronton, pres. by John de Cotes
Thomas called the marshal of Lichfield, t. pat.
Henry de Ecles, pres. by the abbot of Combermere
William de Norton, t. pat.
Richard de Merston of Coventry, pres. by Sir Robert de Napton
Thomas le Taillour of Dudmaston, t. pat.
     [Followed by three blank lines.]
Note that William de Blythe was admitted to the order of subdeacon at the presentation of M. Richard de Coleshull, but he was not then ordained
     [The rest of the fo. is blank.]

[Fo. 124 col. 1] *Deacons*

Simon Pite, r. [moiety of] Belchford, dim. dioc. Lincoln

Richard de Radeclive, r. Radcliffe
Robert de Kel, pres. by Vivian de Staundon, senior
Jordan de Penynton, pres. by Nicholas de Eton, lord of Stockport
John de Fylungleye, t. pat.
John de Bruera, t. pat.
John de Bromleye, t. pat.
William le Gardener of Leamington Hastings, pres. by Sir John de Hastang'
Alan de Thurnton, pres. by Roger Husse
John the smith of 'Beulton', t. pat.
M. Roger de Appelby, t. pat.
Nicholas de Bretford t. Sir Robert de Napton
William de Sallowe, pres. by William Thebaut of Draycott
M. Thomas Ern, t. pat.
Robert Scharp of Sawley, pres. by William de Breydeston
Peter de Parva Cestr', t. pat.
John de Ʒeveleye, t. pat.
William de Stocford, t. pat.
Richard the marshal of Shrewsbury, t. pat.
Hugh de Malo passu, t. pat.
William, son of Robert de Neuton, t. pat.
Ralph de Cheylmardon, pres. by John de Congesdon
Roger de Halugton, t. pat.
Thomas de Kenelworth, t. pat.
Robert de Falingbrom, t. pat.
John de Bertumle, pres. by William de Bruer'
Thomas Baldwyne de 'Chesterton', pres. by John de Schyreford
Adam de Derby', pres. by John Faunel of Wilsthorpe
Richard Alewyne of 'Norton', t. pat.
William de Maclesfeld, t. pat.
William de Wodborow, pres. by St. Helen's [hospital], Derby

[Col. 2] *Deacons*

Roger de Bolougton, t. pat.
William de Salford, t. pat.
Robert de Grangus of Spondon, pres. by the abbot of Dale
John de Chebeseye, t. pat.
Adam de Trentham, t. pat.
Geoffrey de Joneston, pres. by Sir Robert de Dutton
Nicholas de Welde, pres. by the prior of Tutbury
Adam de Oselaston, pres. by Sir John de Montgomery
Thomas de D⁸ubbrugg', t. pat.
Ralph de Stanclyf', pres. by the abbot of Beauchief
Robert the cook of 'Egynton', t. pat.
Richard de Chebeseye, t. pat.
John de Ruyton, t. pat.
Thomas de Swynnerton, pres. by Sir Roger de Swynnerton
John de Cubynton, pres. by Nicholas Wyring of Austrey
Richard, son of Adam de Burton, pres. by Ellis de Burton

Robert de Trusseleye, t. pat.
William de Braylesford, pres. by Sir John de Twyford
Peter Hervy of Tutbury, pres. by Sir Philip de Barinton
William Thurkel, pres. by Roger de Montgomery
Simon de Rokeby, pres. by Sir Ralph de Lodbrok'
Henry de Burywey of Lichfield, t. pat.
William de Schutinton, pres. by Roger Strech'
John de Etinghal', t. pat.
Geoffrey de Maperley, pres. by the abbot of Dale
John de Etewell, pres. by John de Schoteswell
[Richard]⁹ de Cruce, t. pat.
John Blount, pres. by John Blount, v. Lichfield [cath.]
Ralph de Baukwell, pres. by Sir Thomas Folejamb
Walter de Magna Lillington, dim. [dioc. Lincoln], t. house of Luffield
Roger de Kyrkeby, pres. by Thomas Boydin
Richard de Sondford, pres. by the lady of Sandford
Thomas de Buddesworth, t. pat.

[Fo. 124v col. 1] *Deacons*

Roger de Appelby, dim. dioc. Lincoln, t. pat.
William de Hethull', pres. by the abbot and conv. of Lilleshall
Richard de Routhestorn, t. pat.
John Moriz of Shrewsbury, t. pat.
Geoffrey de Joneston, t. pat.
Alexander de Bradelegh', pres. by Richard Bilinton
John de Atherston, t. pat.
Thomas the glove-maker of Tamworth, t. pat.
Roger de Aldelvestre, pres. by Gerard de Sekyndon
William de Duston, pres. by the prior of the Holy Sepulchre, Warwick
William de Bykenhull, t. pat.
Richard the baker of Nantwich, t. pat.
Robert de Weston, pres. by Robert de Napton
William de Breydeshale of Horsley, pres. by the abbot of Dale
Roger de Bagustho, t. pat.
John de Farewell, t. pat.
Henry Wych', t. pat.
Henry de Repyndon, t. pat.
Richard de Haukeshok', t. pat.
Simon de Magna Derset, pres. by Sir Thomas de Garsale
John de Chyldewell, t. pat.
Adam, son of William the cook of Lichfield, pres. by William de Sparham
Thomas de Sutham, t. pat.
Richard the marshal of Chester, t. pat.
John de Lodelowe in Shropshire, pres. by Roger de Walton, with which title he swore himself satisfied
Fr. John de Roucestr'
Fr. William de Loughteburg'
Fr. John de Tetenhale

Fr. William de Novo Castro
Fr. John de Donington
Fr. Simon de Barton
Fr. William de Caldewall
Fr. John de Bradebourn
Fr. Ralph de Derby
Fr. John de Tuttel'
Fr. Andrew de Belwod'
Fr. Andrew de Lodelowe
Peter, Roger, William, [monks] of Vale Royal
[10]Fr. Walter Broun
Fr. Roger Martin[10]

[Col. 2] *Priests*

Thomas ad Cimiterium of Long Eaton, t. pat.
William de Neusom, dim. dioc. York, t. pat.
John de Denston', t. pat.
Richard le Maceon of Polesworth, t. pat.
Richard de Hokelowe, pres. by the abbot of Lilleshall
John, son of William de Rodene, t. pat.
Thomas, son of Henry de Cavereswell, t. pat.
Robert, son of Henry de Cavereswell, t. pat.
Thomas de Tydeswell, pres. by Sir Thomas Folejamb
William Austin of Albrighton, pres. by Roger Carles
Hugh de Baddeslegh, pres. by Thomas Garsal'
William de Ovre, pres. by Nicholas de Overa
John de Thorp, pres. by Walter Wyther
John Bryght of Polesworth, pres. by John, r. Barwell
Henry de Ichinton, pres. by Sir Henry de Lodbrok'
Roger de Melbourn, [11]pres. by William Gilbert[11]
John de Tene, pres. by Adam Byrom
Hugh de Maisemor, t. pat.
Roger de Pulton, t. pat.
Thomas de Aula of 'Walton', t. pat.
John de Smalris, t. pat.
Robert de Southwynefeld, pres. by William de Ofton
William de Bruynaston, pres. by J. de Trussel
Thomas de Bykinton, pres. by Reginald de Rossale
Roger de Peverwych, t. pat.
Simon de Shepeye, pres. by the prior of Canwell
John de Warmynton, pres. by M. Richard de Warmynton
John de Wulrischton, pres. by Robert Turvill'
Robert de Rokeby, t. pat.
Nicholas le Mascy of Morley, pres. by the abbot and conv. of Dale
Walter de Meisham, t. pat.
Richard, son of Geoffrey de Alrewych, t. pat.
John de Hale, t. pat.
Richard de Beveleye, t. pat.

[Fo. 125 col. 1] *Priests*[12]

William de Alveton, pres. by the abbot of Croxden
Roger de Cumpton Murdak, t. pat.
William Yool de Byrmingham, pres. by Sir William de Birmyngham
Robert de Erdyngton, t. pat.
Henry Sampson of Weeford, t. pat.
John de Wolaston, pres. by William de Sondford
John de Compton Murdak, pres. by Sir T[homas] Murdak
Simon de Denhal, t. pat.
Andrew [13]s. Nicholas[13] ate Brigg', pres. by Robert de Leek
Henry de Astenefeld, pres. by Adam de Beresford
Robert Pykard of Melbourne, t. pat.
Thomas de Prestbury, t. pat.
William Raven, t. pat.
Henry del Wode of Ranton, t. pat.
Richard de Preston, t. pat.
Richard de Barewe, pres. by the prior of the hospital of St. John of Jerusalem
Simon de Compton Murdak, t. pat.
Richard de Bromwych, pres. by Sir John de Somery
Ellis de Brerton, pres. by Richard de Swetenham
William de Bylneye, pres. by Sir Thomas de Garshale
Robert James of Clifton, pres. by John Rivel
Richard de Somersale, pres. by Richard de Calewych
John de Elaston, pres. by Ralph de Stanton
William de Pylkot, pres. by Thomas de Pylkot
John de Cruddeworth, t. pat.
William le Rydere of 'Burton', t. pat.
Alan de Waverton, t. pat.
Roger de Lemynton, pres. by John Comyn of Newbold Comyn
Henry de Spondon, t. pat.
Richard de Uttoxhather, t. pat.

[Col. 2] *Priests*[14]

Henry de Morton, pres. by Sir John Paynel
Nicholas de Etewell, pres. by Robert Feerbraz
Thomas Hereward, pres. by Sir Roger de Swynerton
Stephen de Swynnerton, pres. by Sir Roger de Swynnerton
John Wyldegos of 'Aston', pres. by Sir William de Ferariis
Richard Osmund of Wilnecote, t. pat.
William de Smethewyk, pres. by Robert the baker of Coventry
John de Barton, pres. by Sir John de Bakepuys
Richard de Pakynton, pres. by William de Inguardeby
William Manduyt, pres. by Sir Nicholas de Scheldon
Thomas de Flitteleye, t. pat.
Henry Busschel, t. pat.
William Dunkan, pres. by William de Pylatenhal'
William de Acton, t. pat.

Simon de Roucestr', pres. by Richard, lord of Blithfield
Henry le Plummere of Youlgreave, pres. by Sir Richard de Herthull
Robert de Whalleye, t. pat.
William de Fonte of 'Newcastle', pres. by the abbot of Hulton
Nicholas Sturdy of Eckington, t. pat.Henry de Rodbourne, t. pat.
Robert, son of John del Hul of Lichfield, t. pat.
Robert Oliver, t. pat.
John Pouwer of Solihull, t. pat.
John de Hyldreston, pres. by William de Praers
Henry de Calk, t. pat.
Thomas Otheyn, t. pat.
Richard, son of Adam the smith of Colton, pres. by William Juvenis of Colton
Nicholas de Wavere, pres. by William de Wavere
William de Derby, pres. by Robert Ibol'
Roger Russel of Nantwich, t. pat.
William Cardyl, t. pat.
Richard de Alespath, pres. by Walter de Morcot'
Roger de Lodbrok', pres. by Sir Henry de Lodbrok'

[Fo. 125v col. 1] *Priests*[15]

John de Spondon, pres. by the abbot of Dale
William de Durandesthorp, t. pat.
John Brangwayn of Birmingham, pres. by Sir Nicholas de Scheldon
Robert de Cumberbache, t. pat.
Jordan de Farebarewe, t. pat.
Walter Eyring of 'Newton', t. pat.
Thomas, son of Andrew Othein, t. pat.
Nicholas de Lodbrok', pres. by Sir Henry de Lodbrok'
John, son of Henry de Fulkstan, dim. of lord [archbishop] of Canterbury, pres. by
the said lord of Canterbury
Peter de Grenbarwe, t. pat.
Robert de Weston super Trentam, t. pat.
Walter de Wyghtwyk, t. pat.
John de Blorton, pres. by Sir Roger de Swynnerton
William Sauvage of 'Newton', t. pat.
Ralph de Clive, t. pat.
Ralph de Welesleye, pres. by Nicholas de Inguardeby
John le Leche of 'Draycott', pres. by Robert of the same
Ranulph de Wyk', dim. dioc. Worcester, t. pat.
Hugh de Smethewyk, pres. by Sir John de Vallibus
William on la Lee of 'Smethwick', t. pat.
Richard de Chaddesden of Coventry, t. pat.
Richard de Kyrkeby, pres. by William de Allespath
Simon, son of Thomas Pynicok, pres. by Richard Tochet
Henry de Hovere of the county of Chester, t. pat.
Richard de Wythibrok', pres. by John de Bromleg'
William, son of Richard de Neubold Paunton, t. pat.
Thomas de Huggeston, t. pat.

William Schymming of Ockbrook, pres. by the abbot of Dale
Henry de Hanleye, t. pat.
William Bacoun of Rolleston, t. pat.
Robert de Alkmynton, pres. by John de Cressy
Simon de Coundene, t. pat.
Osbert de Wythibrok', pres. by Lady Alice, lady of the same [Withybrook]
John de Honicote, t. pat.
Nicholas de Mistretone, dim. dioc. York, t. pat.
John de Breudemor, t. pat.

[Col. 2] *Priests*[16]

Philip de Berewyk, t. pat.
Richard de Pylkinton, pres. by Sir Roger de Pilkinton
John de Salford, pres. by John de Hulton
Alexander de Alvreston, pres. by the abbot of Lilleshall
William, son of Henry de Horseleye, t. pat.
William de Grendon Stretton, pres. by Sir Thomas de Garsale
William de Aldelime, t. pat.
Henry de Olughton, t. pat.
William de Wolrishton, pres. by John le Palmere
Robert de Lalleford, t. pat.
John Pouger of Wilsthorpe, t. pat.
Roger de Kembryghton, pres. by Walter de Hugeford, kt.
Robert de Bobenhull, pres. by Sir Robert de Napton
Hugh, son of Richard de Cestr', t. pat.
William, son of Henry de Coventr', t. pat.
William Strange, Roger de Forneys, Thomas de Wyleby, OFM
Hugh de Westheved, OSA
Fr. Adam de Asteleye
Fr. John de Estby
Fr. William de Roucestr'
Fr. Robert Godmon
Fr. Roger de Cestria
Fr. Andrew de Staunford
Fr. Ralph de Litlebury
Fr. Henry de Boveye
Fr. John de Aston
Fr. Andrew de Barwe
Fr. Peter de Boulton
Robert de Esseby, William de Peppelowe, Richard de Rommesburi, canons of Lilleshall
Fr. Adam Gyu of Chester
Robert de Schakeston, Henry de Waverton, canons of Darley
William de Prez, pres. by John de Stivington
William de Marchinton, pres. by Henry de Camera
Philip Cave, t. pat.
Robert Oliver, pres. by Geoffrey le Chalener, burgess of Coventry
Adam de Happelegh, t. pat.

[¹⁻¹ Across the full width of the fo.
²⁻² Interlined.
³ See the introduction p. xxi.
⁴ On the line below and separated from the following name by a line drawn around it.
⁵ A later hand, possibly seventeenth-century, has interlined three numbers and four letters above this name which are unclear.
⁶⁻⁶ Interlined.
⁷ Interlined.
⁸ Over another letter and the entry has been marked at its left-hand side with a cross and a symbol resembling a figure 8.
⁹ MS. *Robertus*
¹⁰⁻¹⁰ At the right-hand side of the col. at the foot.
¹¹⁻¹¹ Underlined.
¹² Added by a later hand.
¹³⁻¹³ Interlined.
¹⁴ Added by a later hand.
¹⁵ Added by a later hand.
¹⁶ Added by a later hand.]

1314 [Fo. 126] ¹NOMINA ORDINATORUM IN ECCLESIA CONVENTUALI DE SONDWELL DIE SABBATI QUATUOR TEMPORUM PROXIMO POST DIEM CINERUM .ANNO DOMINI .MILLESIMO .CCCᵐᵒ. QUINTODECIMO. PER .W[ALTERUM]. COVENTR' ET LICH' EPISCOPUM¹ [6 March 1316].

[Col. 1] *Subdeacons*

Thomas Kyng of Lichfield, t. pat.
William Whytecok' of 'Willoughby', dim. dioc. York, t. pat.
Richard le Mareschal, pres. by Robert, his father

Deacons

M. Henry called² de Kyrkeby, r. Wappenbury³
John de Ronton, pres. by John de Cotes
Simon de Wombourn, v. Lichfield [cath.]
Thomas, son of John the tailor of Dudmaston, t. pat.
William de Carberton, dim. dioc. York which we have in our possession, t. pat.
William de Bernham of Gumley, dim. dioc. Lincoln, t. prior and conv. of Chacombe
Nicholas de Ambrighton, pres. by John de Aula of Bishton
Walter de Wrocwardyn, pres. by Sir Fulk le Strange
M. Nicholas de Guthmundelegh, r. Trimley St. Martin, dim. dioc. Norwich
William de Clinton, r. Ratley
Fr. Thomas de le Wodehous, Fr. Roger de Salop', pres. by the prior of Tutbury

Priests

M. Thomas de Clerleton', r. Walton on the Hill
M. Simon Pite, r. moiety of Belchford, dim. dioc. Lincoln
John de Sweltenham, r. Leire, dim. dioc. Lincoln
Richard de Twyford, r. chapel of St. Laurence, Isle of Wight, dim. dioc. Winchester

William de Wykleswolde, r. Boylestone

[Col. 2] *Priests*

Fr. William de Caldewell, Fr. John de Bradebourn, Fr. Ralph de Derby, Fr. John de Tuttebury, pres. by the prior of Tutbury
[The rest of the recto is blank.
[1-1] Across the full width of the fo. above the col. headings.
[2] *Sic*
[3] Interlined.]

1315 [Fo. 126v] [1]NOMINA ORDINATORUM IN ECCLESIA PAROCHIALI DE BROMLEYE ABBATIS DIE SABBATI IN VIGILIA TRINITATIS ANNO DOMINI .MILLESIMO .CCC^mo.XVI. PER .W[ALTERUM]. COVENTR' ET LICH' EPISCOPUM ET FUIT SENTENCIA QUE EST SUPRA IN ORDININBUS DE RONTON COMMINATA[1] [5 June 1316].

[Col. 1] *Subdeacons*

Robert de Holden', r. Rolleston
Ellis de Stapilton, r. Horsington, dim. dioc. Lincoln
Robert Fleming, r. Harrington, dim. [dioc. Lincoln]
M. John de Materfeld, pres. by Sir Roger de Okovere
Robert de Barton, pres. by Sir John Bakepuz
John de Horncastr', pres. by Edmund de Aston
Adam, son of Henry de Eyton, pres. by John de Brympton
Thomas de Cristelton, t. pat.
Richard de Stretton, t. pat.
Adam de Aula of Coventry, pres. by John de Rodeford
Henry de Merschton, pres. by the abbot and conv. of Tutbury
William de Newenham, t. pat.
Geoffrey de Salford, pres. by Roger de Fondefeld
Thomas le Wallere of Coventry, pres. by [2]Adam Kyng
Henry de Bromleye, t. pat.[2]
Philip de Wyginton, t. pat.
Fr. Robert[3] de Bruera
Fr. Thomas Baldewyn
Fr. Richard Tok'
Fr. John de Offenham
Fr. Walter le Waleys
Fr. Robert de Pulteneye
Thomas de Canteloue, John, William, [monks] [4]of Merevale[4]
Fr. Hugh de Assheburn
Walter de Watford, [5]canon of Wombridge[5]
William de Hulton, William Russel, Roger de Stanton, John de Sotton, David, [6]OFM[6]
Robert, [7]canon of Repton[7]
Thomas de Hoton, [8]OCarm.[8]
Simon de Middelton, [9]dim. dioc. Lincoln, t. house of Bruern[9]

[Col. 2] *Deacons*

Thurstan, r. Hanbury
Robert Burnel, r. Ruckley chapel
Roger de Aston, t. pat.
Geoffrey de Merschton, t. pat.
William de Sutham, pres. by Sir J[ohn] Oddingeseles
Richard de Dulvarum, t. pat.
William de Foston, pres. by Ralph de Brailesford
Thomas de Stokyford, t. pat.
Nicholas de Baxterleye, t. abbot and conv. of Merevale
William Cok' of Hinckley, dim. dioc. Lincoln, pres. by Robert de Turvyll'
Roger de Bobenhull, pres. by W[illiam] de Wilugby
Gilbert le Maceon of 'Sutton', t. pat.
William Cole of Rugby, pres. by John Rivel
Robert de Steyveston, pres. by J[ohn] Gery of Derby
John, son of Robert de Lound, pres. by the abbot and conv. of Croxden
Adam de Fyndirne, pres. by Robert de Findern
William, son of Robert de Ewode, t. pat.
William de Stokeport, t. pat.
William Waleys of 'Eyton', t. pat.
Robert de Frodesham, t. pat.
William de Bentelegh, pres. by the prior of Canwell
Richard de Stretton, t. pat.
Robert le Esquyer, t. pat.
Robert de Grendon, pres. by Robert Turvill'
John de Halughton, pres. by Vivian Staunton, junior
William de Wolvey, pres. by John de Schirford
Thomas de Burton, t. pat.
Roger de Baggelegh, pres. by Sir Thomas de Garsal'
John de Toft, pres. by Hugh de Mertton
Richard Neel of 'Harwood', dim. dioc. Lincoln, pres. by Sir Richard de Horwode

[Fo. 127 col. 1] *Deacons*

William de Hynkelegh, dim. dioc. Lincoln, pres. by John de Morton, v. High Ercall
Richard Cruych, pres. by the abbot and conv. of Dale
William le Maceoun of Repton, t. pat.
Thomas de Faston, pres. by William de Faston
Robert Cadas, pres. by Richard Folechambe
Thomas de Mapelton, pres. by Henry de Mapelton
William de Neuton, pres. by John de Weston
Thomas Kyng of Lichfield, t. pat.
Richard de Maxstok', pres. by Peter, r. of the same [Maxstoke]
Robert de Eton, pres. by Sir Thomas Garshal'
Hugh Prwlyn of Whitmore, t. pat.
Richard Martyn of Tideswell, pres. by Adam de Beverysford
Roger de la Dale, pres. by the abbot and conv. of Dale

John Fox of Lichfield, t. pat.
John de Toft, pres. by Ellis de Bourgton
Peter Pecok of Tutbury, pres. by William de Neuton
Simon de Barton, pres. by Robert Meynel
Robert de Tydeswell, t. pat.
Richard Large, t. pat.
William de Morton, t. pat.
William Hereward, pres. by John de Swynnerton
Richard de Pecham, t. pat.
Ralph de Rode, t. pat.
William Hurkel of Chester, t. pat.
William de Edyngburgh, dim. dioc. York, t. pat.
Adam Bagot, t. pat.
William Whitecok' of 'Willoughby', dim. dioc. York, t. pat.
Clement [10]or William[10] de Tideswell of York, dim. [dioc. York], t. pat.
Nicholas, son of Roger Speching' of Bridgnorth, t. prior and brethren of Holy Trinity hospital, Bridgnorth
John, son of Robert atte Wall of 'Haywood', pres. by Henry de Heywode
Robert de Wythereslegh, t. pat.
William, son of Robert de Norton, by command of the bishop

[Col. 2]

William de Tideswel, t. pat.
John Teler of 'Rising', [dim.] dioc. Norwich, t. pat.
Henry de Sticheford, pres. by Thomas de Bromwych
William Letice, t. pat.
Henry de Reystwyt, pres. by the abbot of Dale
John de Astelegh, t. pat.
Adam Wyldi of 'Aston', t. pat.
Richard Muchet of 'Marston', pres. by the prior of Tutbury
Robert de Whitemor', t. pat.
Fr. Nicholas de Weston
Fr. John de Chesterfeld
John, Simon, John, Stephen, John, William, [monks] of Merevale
John de Donigton, [monk] of Croxden
Fr. Ranulph de Rope
Richard,[11] [canon] of Repton
Fr. Nicholas de Weston
Fr. John de Chesterfeld
Fr. John de Harleye
Fr. Walter de Mursseleye
Walter de Huxsdon, dim. dioc. Lincoln, pres. by John Comyn of Newbold Comyn to all holy orders
M. William de Mees, r. Morton Bagot,[12] dim. dioc. Worcester
    [The rest of the col. is blank.]

[Fo. 127v col. 1] *Priests*

William de Clinton, r. Ratley
M. Henry de Kyrkeby, r. Wappenbury
Jordan de Peninton, pres. by Nicholas de Eton
William, son of Robert de Neuton, t. pat.
Simon de Wombourn, v. Lichfield [cath.], t. same church
Peter de Parva Cestr', pres. by the master of St. Helen's [hospital], Derby
John de Felton, t. pat.
Richard Godefrey, t. pat.
Henry de Buruwey, t. pat.
John Prine of Sudbury, pres. by Sir Walter de Montgomery
Thomas de Fynham, t. pat.
Richard de Marketon, pres. by Philip de Somervill'
John de Filungleye, t. pat.
William, son of Robert de Okebrok', pres. by the abbot of Dale
Philip de Bradeleye, t. pat.
Thomas de Breydeston, pres. by Simon Pouger
William, son of Thomas de Sallowe, pres. by William Tebaut of Draycott
John de Passeleye, pres. by Sir Roger de Bradebourn
John the smith of 'Beulton', t. pat.
Robert le Cu of Ashbourne, pres. by Sir Richard de Hethhull'
William Benet of Fillongley, t. pat.
William de Crulefeld, t. pat.
William, son of Geoffrey de Beghton, t. pat.
Adam de Trentham, t. pat.
William de Mamcestr', pres. by Hugh de Mamcestr'
Peter de Teinton, pres. by Henry Irreys, lord of Ansty
William de Spalding of Sowe, pres. by John Heron
Ralph de Stanclif, t. pat.
Thomas de Alspath, pres. by Thomas Boydene
Geoffrey de Joneston, pres. by Sir Robert de Dutton and t. pat.
Ralph the baker of Nantwich, t. pat.
Thomas de Casteldonigton, dim. dioc. Lincoln, t. pat.
Henry Pulpayn, t. pat.
John de Edeinghal', t. pat.
William de Braylesford, pres. by Sir John de Twyford
Thomas de Douvebrugg', pres. by Adam de Bereforde

[Col. 2]

Henry de Weston, pres. by M. John de Shoteswell
Thomas le Horsknave of Tideswell, pres. by Richard Broun, lord of Whitefield
Thomas de Swynnerton, pres. by Sir Roger de Swynnerton
Thomas Baldewyne of 'Chesterton', pres. by John de Shirford
Hugh de Malo passu, t. pat.
William de Bernham of Gumley, dim. dioc. Lincoln
Ralph de Cheylmardon, pres. by John de Conkesden
Ralph de Baukwell, pres. by Thomas de Beleye

Thomas the glove-maker of Tamworth, t. pat.
John de Beaumarsh of Chester, pres. by William de Brikhull
Nicholas le Mercer, who has been presented to other holy orders elsewhere and it
was made known by Tabellionus, pres. by the abbot and conv. of Lilleshall
Peter de Sparham, v. Lichfield [cath.]
Walter de Cumpton, r. Exton, dim. dioc. Bath and Wells
Richard de Alrewych, pres. by the prior and conv. of Tutbury
Simon de Ridware, t. pat.
Richard the marshal, t. pat.
M. Nicholas de Guthmundelegh, r. Trimley St. Martin, dim. dioc. Norwich
Robert de Trusselegh, t. pat.
William Thurkel, pres. by Roger de Montgomery
[Robert][13] Trippe, t. pat.
Roger de Boulton, t. pat.
Robert de Keel, pres. by Vivian de Staundon
Simon de Derset, pres. by Sir Thomas Garshal'
Robert de Falingburn
John de Atherston, t. pat.
William, son of Andrew, pres. by Sir Nicholas de Sheldon
Nicholas de Aula of Albrighton, t. pat.
Hugh de Assheby, t. pat.
William de Felde of Breaston, pres. by William Pouger

[Fo. 128 col. 1]

William de Burton, Walter, [canons] of Repton
William de Charnesbrok', Peter de Rodburn, John de Kyrkeby, John, [monks] of
Merevale
[14]M. William de Mees, r. Morton Bagot, dioc. Worcester[14]

> [Followed by three blank lines.
> [1-1] Across the full width of the fo. above the col. headings. See **1313**.
> [2-2] Added by another contemporary hand.
> [3] Interlined over *Willelmus* deleted.
> [4-4] Added by a third contemporary hand.
> [5-5] Added by the same third hand.
> [6-6] Added by the same third hand.
> [7-7] Added by the same third hand.
> [8-8] Added by the same third hand.
> [9-9] Added by the same third hand.
> [10-10] Interlined.
> [11] Followed by a 2cm. line drawn over an erasure.
> [12] *Worcester Sede Vacante Reg.*, 186.
> [13] MS. *Rogerus*
> [14-14] Entry duplicated see p. 130, and partially erased.]

1316 ¹NOMINA ORDINATORUM IN ECCLESIA PREBENDALI DE ICHINTON EPISCOPI DIE SABBATI QUATUOR TEMPORUM MENSIS DECEMBRIS ANNO DOMINI .MILLESIMO .CCCᵐᵒ. SEXTODECIMO ²PER .W[ALTERUM]. COVENTR' ET LICH' EPISCOPUM IN QUIBUS FUIT SENTENCIA QUE EST SUPRA IN ORDINIBUS DE RONTON PUBLICE LATA ET PRONUNCIATA¹ ² [18 December 1316].

Subdeacons

Thomas de Eyton, treasurer of Lichfield
Edmund Fytun, r. Gawsworth
M. Thomas de Merston, t. pat.
M. Robert Bernard, [t.] St. Peter's chantry, Lichfield [cath.]
Edmund de Mottrum, t. pat.
Roger de Lodbrok', pres. by the prior of Coventry for v. Offchurch
John Wildegos, pres. by the abbot of Dale
Robert de Clifton of Ashbourne, pres. by Nicholas de Marchinton
John le Mercer of Ashbourne, pres. by John Fitzherbert
John, son of John de Punfrett of 'Harborough', t. pat.
William Ernald of Brockhurst, pres. by John Wauteroun of Pailton
Henry de Ethorp, pres. by Thomas Wasingl'
Robert Barset of Ticknall, t. pat.
Robert de Spenne, pres. by Walter de Verdoyn
Nicholas de Crast, t. pat.
Thomas de Durandesthorp, pres. by the prior of Tutbury, dim. dioc. Lincoln
John de Evereslegh of Banbury, pres. by the abbot of Eynsham, dim. [dioc. Lincoln]

[Col. 2]

John le Parlour of Coventry, t. pat.
Richard de Assheburn, pres. by Sir Richard Herchull, kt.
John de Calewych, pres. by Sir³ Roger de Okovere
Richard de Yorton, t. pat.
Peter de Walton, t. pat.
Hugh de Walcote, t. pat.
William de Craunford, pres. by the abbot of Croxden
Henry de Fylungleye, t. pat.
Simon de Knyghtecote, t. pat.⁴
Richard de Ichinton Longa, pres. by Sir J[ohn] de Oddingesl'
Richard de Olughton, t. pat.
Walter de Beulton, t. pat.
John de Atthelastre, pres. by Philip de Stradel'
Thomas le Marchal' of Derby, pres. by the prior of St. James' [hospital], Derby
Thomas Basset, pres. by Richard Curson of Breadsall
Richard de Wyleby, pres. by Gerard de Alspath
William de Wotton, t. pat.
Thomas de Herdewyk, t. pat.
Hugh de Toucestr' of Coventry, t. pat.
Thomas de Morton, pres. by Thomas, lord of Morton

John de Roddislegh, pres. by Nicholas Selveyn of Rodsley
Roger de Cosford, t. pat.
William de Derbaston, t. pat.
William de Brocton, pres. by the prior of Tutbury
Ellis de Wotton, t. pat.
William de Merston Jabet, pres. by William de Stokyforth
William de Stretton, pres. by Richard de Stretton
Richard de Overe, pres. by the prior of St. James' [hospital], Derby
Philip de Bretford, pres. by Sir Robert de Verdeyn
John de Tresel', pres. by John de Perton
Robert de Drakenegge, t. pat.
Robert de Barwe, pres. by John Gery of Derby
Adam de Roudich of Derby, pres. by Philip de Somervill'

[Fo. 128v col. 1] *Subdeacons*

Geoffrey de Keteliston, pres. by Philip Somervill'
William de Herdwyk Prioris, t. pat.
Ralph le Fysher of Newbold on Avon, t. pat.
Ralph, son of Ralph de Rolleston, t. pat.
Roger, son of Robert de Mallisor', pres. by Robert de Verdoyn
William Redemon of 'Newbold', t. pat.
Henry atte Cros of Coventry, pres. by John, his father
Henry de Trentham, t. pat.
John de Greneber', pres. by Sir Thomas de Garshale
Richard de Derlaston, pres. by William, lord of 'Darlaston'
Alan de Wygynton, pres. by the abbot of Merevale
John de Burthingbur', pres. by Sir John Paynel
Philip de Dene, t. pat.
Roger de Acton, t. pat.
Alan Snel of Prees, pres. by Richard de Norton, v. Prees, t. pat.
Richard de Bourghton, t. pat.
Hugh Payn, t. pat.
William, son of Walter Rymbald, t. pat.
Henry Wareyn of Mayfield, pres. by Sir Roger de Okovere
Henry de Coventry of Derby, pres. by John de la Corner' of Derby
William Kempe of Southam, t. pat.
John Balraven of Southam, t. pat.
Fr. Roger de Breyles
Fr. William de Merston
Fr. Geoffrey de Belegrave
Fr. Andrew de Covenore
    [The rest of the col. is blank.]

[Col. 2] *Deacons*

Robert de Clipston, canon of Lichfield cath.
William de Praers, r. Barthomley

John de Tykenhal', r. Sutton Bonnington,[5] dim. dean and chapter of York, keepers of the spiritualities of the archbishopric of York, *sede vacante*
Philip de Wykynton, pres. by the prior of Wolston
John de Maderfeld, pres. by Sir Roger de Acton, kt.
William Parent, pres. by Robert de Cotes
Thomas de Cristelton, t. pat.
Ralph Elie of Killingworth, t. house of Selby, dim. dioc. Lincoln
Laurence Worrey, pres. by Alan Roshal'
John Mervyn of Dunchurch, pres. by Sir Thomas de Garshal', kt.
Adam de Wythibrok', pres. by Sir Thomas de Clinton
John de Tresul', pres. by John, lord of Trysull
Richard Mechet, pres. by the prior of Tutbury
Henry de Merston, pres. by the prior of Tutbury
William de Bruggeton, t. pat.
Robert de Barton, pres. by Sir John de Bakepuz, kt.
Peter de Melburne, t. pat.
Thomas le Waller' of Coventry, t. pat.
William Cosin of Rugby, t. pat.
Robert de Overa, pres. by John Gery of Derby
Thomas de Tyford, t. pat.
William Nesse, t. pat.
Robert de Willeston', t. pat.
Richard de Wytenasch, t. pat.
Simon de Middelton, [dim.] dioc. Lincoln, pres. by the house of Bruern
Richard Sondbach, t. pat.
M. William de Stonlegh, t. house of Kenilworth
Henry de Horseleye, t. pat.
Adam de Leye, pres. by Sir Richard de Draycote
Thomas de Merston, t. pat.
Henry de Chetewynde, pres. by Sir John de Chetewynde, kt.
John de Shulton, t. pat.

[Fo. 129 col. 1] *Deacons*

John de Horncastr', pres. by Edmund de Aston super Trentam
John Balraven, t. pat.
William Kempe, pres. by Sir Robert de Napton
William de Schulton, r. Baginton
William de Neunham, t. pat.
Fr. Robert de Pulteneye
Fr. William de Acton
Fr. Robert de Leye
Fr. William de Bisshopeston'
Fr. William de Ofnam

Priests

Richard de Haukesok', t. pat.
Robert Scharp of Wilsthorpe, pres. by William de Breydeston

Henry de Chadleshunte, t. pat.
William le Gardener of Leamington Hastings, pres. by John de Hastang, kt.
John de Halughton, pres. by John, lord of Bromley Bagot
Peter de Salbrugg', pres. by Robert de Langeleye, lord of Wolfhamcote
Thomas de Stokyforth, t. pat.
John de 3eveleye, t. pat.
Reginald de Berkeswell, t. pat.
John Hamund of 'Carleton', dim. dioc. Lincoln, t. pat.
Adam de Derby, pres. by John Paunel of Wilsthorpe
Robert de Wytemor', t. pat.
William de Neuton, pres. by Richard, lord of Blithfield
Simon de Barton, pres. by Sir John de Bakepuz
John de Lound, pres. by the abbot and conv. of Croxden
William de Stokeport, t. pat.
Adam Albeyn of Chesterfield, pres. by Ralph de Braylesford
William the smith of Hinckley, pres. by John de Aldenham, dim. dioc. Lincoln
William de Foston, pres. by Ralph de Braylesford
William de Bykenhull, t. pat.
William de Lemynton of Southam, pres. by Sir John de Oddingesles, kt.

[Col. 2]

Thomas, son of Richard de Sutham, t. pat.
Richard the marshal of Shrewsbury, t. pat.
Roger de Baggeleye, pres. by Sir Thomas de Garsale
Nicholas Spyching of Bridgnorth, pres. by Holy Trinity hospital, Bridgnorth
Richard de Delvern, pres. by Ralph Basset, lord of Sapcote
John Onwyn of Braunston, [dim.] dioc. Lincoln, t. [house of] Newstead by Stamford
William de Morton, t. pat.
John, son of Henry de Toft, pres. by Ellis de Burton
John de Toft, pres. by Hugh de Merinton
Robert de Longeleye, r. Ruckley chapel
John, son of Roger de Ruyton, t. a corrody and pension which he has from house of the Holy Sepulchre, Warwick
William le Graunger, t. pat.
Henry Andreu of Tideswell, t. pat.
William Cole of Rugby, pres. by John Rivel, lord of Newbold Revel
Simon Kytewylde of Rugby, pres. by Sir Henry de Lodbrok'
John de Bourton, pres. by Sir Thomas de Garsal'
Richard Geryn of Leicester, dim. dioc. Lincoln
William de Salford, t. pat.
John de Castelton, t. house of Southwark
Gilbert de Sutton, t. pat.
Geoffrey de Merston, pres. by Thomas Wythergeyn
William the tailor of Stockport, t. pat.
Robert Cadas, pres. by Richard de Folejambe
Richard de Swerkeston, pres. by William Broun
Thomas de Kenelworth, t. pat.
Roger de Aldrestre, pres. by Gerard de Sekyndon

William Letice of 'Newcastle', t. pat.
John de Sohtwyk, t. pat.
Hugh de Whytemor', t. pat.
Robert de Frodesham, t. pat.
Gregory Chaynel of 'Winwick', by special dim. dioc. Lincoln
Thomas de Wulfstanton, t. pat.
Simon de Langeton, pres. by the abbot of Owston, dim. dioc. Lincoln
William Cachet of Hinckley, [6]dim. dioc. Lincoln,[6] pres. by Sir John de Hardushull, kt.
William Knapet of Haughton, [dim.] dioc. Lincoln, pres. by the abbot of Merevale
Hugh de Chernock, pres. by Adam, lord of Charnock
Richard Edward of Elton, dioc. Lincoln, t. the hospital [of St. John] of Jerusalem

[Fo. 129v] *Priests*

Walter de Magna Lullington, dim. dioc. Lincoln, t. house of Luffield
Thomas de Mapelton, t. pat.
Henry Coleman of Longdon, pres. by Philip de Somervill'
Walker de Asshmeresbrok', t. pat.
Richard de Chebeseye, t. pat.
John de Chebeseye, t. pat.
Robert de Alrewych, pres. by John, lord of 'Bentley'
Richard de Sondford, pres. by Richard, lord of Sandford
William de Addingburg', [dim.] dioc. York, pres. by William Tokatt
William Whytecok' of 'Willoughby', dim. dioc. York, t. pat.
Peter Hervu of Tutbury, pres. by Philip de Barynton
Geoffrey de Balishal', Robert de Stakeston, Roger de Coventr', [canons] of Kenilworth
Robert de London, OSA
John de Stokton, monk of Canwell
Fr. Henry de Repindon
Fr. Nicholas de Weston
Fr. Richard de Aston
Fr. John de Chesterfeld
Fr. John de Coleshull
Fr. Peter de Asteleye
Fr. Henry de Brynkelowe
    [The rest of the col. is blank.
    [1-1] In col. 1. See **1313**.
    [2-2] Over an erasure.
    [3] Interlined.
    [4] Entry marked by a cross within a circle at the left-hand side.
    [5] *Reg. Greenfield*, v, no. 2874.
    [6-6] Interlined.]

1317 [Col. 2] NOMINA ORDINATORUM IN ECCLESIA CATHEDRALI LICH' DIE SABBATI IN VIGILIA PASCHE ANNO DOMINI .MILLESIMO .CCC[mo].XVII. PER .W[ALTERUM]. COVENTR' ET LICH' EPISCOPUM UBI FUIT SENTENCIA QUE EST IN ORDINIBUS DE RONTON COMMINATA[1] [2 April 1317].

Subdeacons

John de Ambryghton of Lichfield, pres. by r. 'Chelgrave'
John, r. Clent,[2] dim. dioc. Worcester
Robert Abel, John Russel, OFM

Deacons

Robert [de Egilton], r. Glooston, dim. dioc. Lincoln
Peter de Walton, t. pat.
Henry de Filungleye, t. pat.
Hugh Paganus, t. pat.
M. Robert Bernard, t. [St. Peter's] chantry, Lichfield cath.
John le Mercer of Ashbourne, pres. by the lord of Norbury
Robert de Clifton, pres. by Robert le Bek of Upper Tean
Henry Wareyn of Mayfield, pres. by Sir William Trussel
John de Houton, William de Leycestr', [monks] of Merevale
William de Merston, Geoffrey de Belegrave, monks of Coventry

Priests

Robert de Clipston, canon of Lichfield
Roger de Lodbrok', v. Offchurch
Richard de Craven, canon of Penkridge
Thomas, son of Sibyl le Kyng of Lichfield, t. pat.
William de Norton, pres. by the bishop
Thomas le Wallere of Coventry, t. pat.
William Parent of Eccleshall, pres. by John de Kynardeseye
Henry de Merston, pres. by the prior and conv. of Tutbury
Richard called Mochet of 'Marston', pres. by the prior and conv. of Tutbury
John de Wyseworth, Simon de Leycestr', John de Leycestr', Stephen de Bracebrugg', John de Bredon, William de Macstok, Thomas de Greseleye, [monks] of Merevale

[[1] See **1313**.
[2] *Reg. Cobham*, 264. Listed as John de Honesworth.]

1318 [Fo. 130] [1]NOMINA ORDINATORUM IN ECCLESIA CONVENTUALI SANCTI THOME JUXTA STAFFORD' DIE SABBATI QUATUOR TEMPORUM IN VIGILIA TRINITATIS :ANNO DOMINI :MILLESIMO :CCC^{mo}: XVII: PER W[ALTERUM] COVENTR' ET LICH' EPISCOPUM IN QUIBUS SENTENCIA QUE EST SUPRA IN ORDINIBUS DE RONTON FUIT LATA[1] [28 May 1317].

[Col. 1] *Subdeacons*

William de Wirkesworth, r. of moiety of Mugginton
Roger Foucher, pres. by the prior of St. James' [hospital], Derby
Geoffrey de Farneworth, pres. by John de Honford
William le Mercer of 'Newcastle', t. pat.
William de Marketon, pres. by Roger de Somervill', kt.
Ralph de Moldesworth, t. pat.

Robert le Taillour of Mackworth, pres. by Philip de Somervill' to all [orders]

Henry de Marketon, t. pat.

William de Oselaston, pres. by the prior of St. James' [hospital], Derby

Henry de Caldelowe, pres. by Thomas de Rolleston

Vivian de Daviport, t. pat.

Thomas de Assheburn, pres. by Roger de Okovere, kt.

Matthew de Bromle, pres. by the prior and brethren of Holy Trinity hospital, Bridgnorth to all [orders]

Reginald de Erthington, pres. by Thomas de Overton

William de Schepebrug', t. abbot and conv. of Combermere

Richard de Paylinton, pres. by Nicholas de Herdeberwe

Roger de Staunton, pres. by William Folejambe

Geoffrey de Wolveye, pres. by John de Schireford

John de Paddeleye, t. pat.

Augustine de Coppenhal', pres. by Richard de Preers

William le Porter of 'Newcastle', t. pat.

John Lycoris, pres. by William, son of Thomas Burges of 'Newcastle'

Richard de Longesdon, pres. by Thomas Folejambe, kt.

Richard del Hull', pres. by John de Hulton

Roger de Schardelowe, pres. by Adam de Amandesham

Alan de Salop', pres. by Hugh de Byriton

Thomas de Cesteford, pres. by John de Cotes

Richard Reynaud of Audley, t. pat.

Richard de Fernyleye, pres. by the abbot and conv. of Lilleshall

William Cordy of Repton, t. pat.

Robert the clerk of 'Tirlington', t. house of Owston, dim. dioc. Lincoln, to all [orders]

John de Leycestr', pres. by the house of Ulverscroft, dim. dioc. Lincoln

William de Swerkeston, pres. by John Bek

John de Assho, t. pat.

Roger de Prestecote, t. pat.

Henry de Burton, t. pat.

[Col. 2]

Robert, son of Nicholas de Makworth, t. pat.

John de Staunton, pres. by William de Colewych

William de Walton, t. pat.

Henry de Wodeford, pres. by Nicholas Fitzherbert

Richard, son of Ralph Frost, t. pat.

Peter called the malnourished of St. Albans, dim. to all [orders], pres. by Sir Thomas de Garsal'

Henry de Pyri, pres. by William, lord of Perry Barr

Robert Torald, t. pat.

Robert de Barton, t. pat.

William de Merston, pres. by the prior of Tutbury

John Lye, pres. by Nicholas de Hongerford

William de Irton, pres. by Richard de Roubeth

William de Ibol', pres. by Sir Robert de Ibol'

William le Hunt, pres. by John le Hunte
Adam de Ormeskirk, t. pat.
Hugh de Athelastr', pres. by Sir Hugh de Olgelthorp
Ralph le Tyntour of Ashbourne, pres. by John de Mapelton
Stephen de Hohwyn, t. pat.
Robert de Assheburn, pres. by Serlonus de Montereye
Thomas de Schoresworth, pres. by Thomas de Hoppewod'
Simon de Depdal', t. pat.
Henry Merus of 'Haywood', pres. by Geoffrey de Wasteneys
William de Weston, pres. by Richard de Smalris
William de Breydeston, pres. by Thomas in le Grove
Simon Sprot, dim. dioc. Lincoln, t. house of Godstow
William de Picheworth, t. pat.
Walter de Hykeling, pres. by the prior of St. James' [hospital], Derby
William Broun of Meonstoke [dim. dioc. Winchester], pres. by the dean of Lichfield
John de Hamelton
William de Milers, t. pat.
Peter de Grenebrgh, t. pat.
William de Cavereswell, t. pat.
Richard de Cavereswell, pres. by Richard de Cavereswell, kt.
Richard Mossok, pres. by Sir Ralph de Vernoun
Thomas de Aula, t. pat.
Nicholas de Fouleshurst, pres. by Richard de Fouleshurst

[Fo. 130v col. 1]

Fr.[2] Adam de Bradeschawe
Fr. Robert de Neuton
Fr. Adam de Ormeston
Henry Gerard, Henry de Stardechf, OP Shrewsbury
William de Wynton', Nicholas de Staunton, John de Schipton, Walter de Stodeleye, Thomas de Rompton, OSA Shrewsbury

Deacons

Walter de Perton, r. Stirchley
Amaury le Botiler, r. Wem
Simon de Scirford, r. Kinwarton,[3] dim. of the prior of Worcester, dioc. Worcester, *sede vacante*
[4]William de Wyrkesworth, r. moiety of Mugginton[4]
John de Calwych, pres. by Sir Roger de Okovere, kt.
Geoffrey de Ketleston, pres. by Philip de Somervill'
Richard de Morton, t. pat.
William de Brokhurst, pres. by John Wautrum of Pailton
Roger de Mallesovere, pres. by Philip de Somervill'
Adam de Rodich, pres. by Adam Keyne
Thomas the marshal of Derby, pres. by the prior of St. James' [hospital], Derby
Henry de Trentham, t. pat.
Robert de Brakeneg', pres. by Henry de Morinton

Richard de Assheburn, pres. by Sir Richard de Herchull
Henry de Beyvill, pres. by Thomas de Wassinglegh
Nicholas de Crast, t. pat.
John de Hulton called Wildegos, pres. by the abbot of Dale
Robert Barset, t. pat.
John de Athelastre, pres. by Philip de Stradele
Walter de Bilinton, t. pat.
Robert de Spenne, pres. by Walter de Verdon
Thomas Basset, pres. by Richard Corsoun
Hugh de Yoxhal', pres. by Roger de Bradeburn
Richard de Wyleby, pres. by Thomas de Garsal', kt.
Thomas de Herdewyk Prioris, t. pat.
William de Brokton, pres. by the prior and conv. of Tutbury
Geoffrey de Salford, pres. by Roger del Oldefelde
William de Aula of Priors Marston, t. pat.
William de Merston, pres. by William de Stokiford

[Col. 2]

John Pounfreyt of 'Harborough', t. pat.
Philip de Bretford, pres. by John le Palmere
Ralph le Fyscher, t. pat.
John le Parlour, t. pat.
Hugh de Toucestr', t. pat.
Hugh de Walcote, t. pat.
Simon Hongres of Melbourne, t. pat.
John de Everesle of Banbury, dim. dioc. Lincoln, pres. by the abbot and conv. of Eynsham to all orders
William de Stretton, pres. by Richard de Stretton
Richard de Olugton, t. pat.
Richard le Broun of 'Belne', dim. of prior of Worcester, dioc. Worcester, *sede vacante*, pres. by Simon Brun
William de Marchinton, pres. by Ralph de Vernoun, kt.
William, son of Dye de Tamworth, t. pat.
Henry de Brumle, pres. by John Bagot
Alan Snel, t. pat.
John de Ambrigton of Lichfield, t. pat.
Edmund Fytoun, r. Gawsworth
Edmund de Muttrom, t. pat.
Walter de Billinton, pres. by the prior of the Holy Sepulchre, Warwick
William de Herdewyk, t. pat.
John de Gnoushal, pres. by William de Burg'
William de Cranford, pres. by the abbot and conv. of Croxden
John de Sondon, t. pat.
William Aldeyn of 'Houghton', pres. by the Holy Sepulchre, Warwick, dim. [dioc. Lincoln]
Thomas de Durandesthorp, pres. by the prior of Tutbury
John de Tresel', pres. by John de Perton
Richard, son of Thomas de Derlaston, t. pat.

Thomas called the marshal of Lichfield, t. pat.
Roger de Acton, t. pat.
John le Gardyner of Rodsley, pres. by Henry de Bentele
Fr. Thomas de Rouclif
[Fr.] Arnold de Emesey
[Fr.] Richard de Wyco
Richard de Touk'
[Fr.] Roger de Breiles
John de Coventr', canon of the Holy Sepulchre, Warwick
Fr. Robert de Eynesham
   [The rest of the fo. is blank.]

[Fo. 131 col. 1] *Priests*

Robert de Egilton, r. Glooston, dim. dioc. Lincoln
William de Praers, r. Barthomley
M. John de Walecote, r. Wolverley,[5] dim. of prior of Worcester, dioc. Worcester,
sede vacante
M. Robert Bernard, t. St. Peter's chantry, Lichfield [cath.]
John de Etewell, pres. by M. John de Schoteswell
Thomas de Cristelton, t. pat.
John de Matherfeld, pres. by Roger de Okovere, kt.
John le Mercer of Ashbourne, pres. by John Herbert, lord of Norbury
Robert de Clifton, pres. by John de Ipston
John de Hornecastel, pres. by Edmund de Aston super Trentam
Adam de Wythibrok', pres. by John de Bromle, lord of Hapsford
William de Wolveye, pres. by John de Schireford
Nicholas de Baxterle, pres. by the abbot and conv. of Merevale to all [orders]
Thomas de Faston, pres. by William de Faston
William de Bruggeston, t. pat.
Robert de Barton, pres. by John Bakepuz, lord of Barton Blount
John de Bromlegh, t. pat.
William le Maceoun of Repton, t. pat.
Roger de Aston, t. pat.
William Nesse, t. pat.
Henry de Sticheford, pres. by Henry de Erdynton
William de Leye of Pailton, pres. by John Rivel of Newbold Revel
Richard de Stretton, t. pat.
William de Hethull', t. pat.
Alexander de Worth, pres. by Robert, son of Thomas de Worth
William Waleys, pres. by Robert Waleys of 'Eyton'
Thomas de Merston, t. pat.
Robert de Steyveston, pres. by the abbot and conv. of Rocester and John Gery of
Derby
M. Roger de Appelby, dim. dioc. Lincoln, pres. by Sir Richard de Herthull', kt.
Robert de le Graunges, pres. by the abbot of Dale
Thomas de Burton, t. pat.
Henry de Otherton, t. pat.
William Fox of Lichfield, t. pat.

William de Ewode, t. pat.
Richard de Alkemonton, pres. by Ralph de Bakepuz, lord of Alkmonton

[Col. 2]

Peter de Kelm of Melbourne, t. pat.
Hugh Payn of Derby, t. pat.
William Hereward, pres. by Sir John de Swynnerton
Robert le Latouner of Northampton, dim. dioc. Lincoln
John Donvalet of Cubbington, pres. by Nicholas Wy3ring of Austrey
William Cosyn of Rugby, t. pat.
John de Childwell, t. pat.
William de Tideswell, pres. by John Martyn of Tideswell
John de Bertumle, pres. by William de Bruer'
Richard de Sondbach, t. pat.
Nicholas del Welde, pres. by the prior and conv. of Tutbury
Walter Grym of 'Haywood', t. pat.
Richard Martyn, pres. by Adam, lord of Barford
Thomas, son of John the goldsmith of Stafford, pres. by Sir Roger de Swynnerton
William de Duston, pres. by the prior and conv. of the Holy Sepulchre, Warwick
Adam Wyldi of 'Aston', pres. by John de Perton
Alan de Thurmonton, pres. by the dean of Lichfield
John Mervyn, pres. by Thomas de Garsal', kt.
Richard Nel, dim. dioc. Lincoln, pres. by v. High Ercall
William de Neunam, t. pat.
Adam, son of William the cook of Lichfield, pres. by William Sparham
Ralph de Rode, t. pat.
Richard de Pekham, pres. by Richard de Wolsele
Richard Moubon of Maxstoke, pres. by I[da] de Clinton
Philip de Wyginton, dim. dioc. Lincoln
[6]Fr. Richard de Eton
Fr. John de Pipa
Fr. Henry de Audeleye[6]
 [The rest of the recto is blank.
 [1-1] Across the full width of the fo. above the heading of col. 1. See **1313**.
 [2] Bracketed at the left-hand side to the first three names.
 [3] *Worcester Sede Vacante Reg.*, 185; *Reg. Cobham*, 237, n. 14.
 [4-4] Deleted.
 [5] *Worcester Sede Vacante Reg.*, 184–5; *Reg. Cobham*, 257.
 [6-6] The names are bracketed together at the right-hand side.]

1319 [Fo. 131v] [1]NOMINA ORDINATORUM IN ECCLESIA PAROCHIALI DE HULL' MORTON' DIE SABBATI QUATUOR TEMPORUM MENSIS DECEMBRIS ANNO DOMINI .MILLESIMO. CCC.XVII. PER .W[ALTERUM]. COVENTR' ET LICH' EPISCOPUM IN QUIBUS SENTENCIA QUE EST SUPRA IN ORDINIBUS DE RONTON FUIT LATA[1] [17 December 1317].

[Col. 1] *Subdeacons*

Robert May, r. moiety of Mugginton

Robert de Freford, t. with which he considers himself satisfied
M. William de Stretton, r. of the same
Henry Hamond of Grandborough, t. pat.
Alan de Stretton of Stretton on Dunsmore, t. pat.
John de Cubbelegh, William, son of Andrew de Weston, pres. by R[obert] le Verdon, kt.
John le Couper of 'Aston', pres. by J[ohn] de Dalby
Ralph de Kyrkeby, pres. by Henry Pake
Stephen de Slymdon, t. pat.
Simon de Grendon, pres. by Roger Potelag'
John le Maceon, t. pat.
William Warde of 'Rothwell', [dim.] dioc. Lincoln, t. house of Osney
Roger Eunok of Avon Dassett, t. pat.
William de Stretton super Donnysmor', pres. by Robert le Norreys
William de Toft, pres. by Thomas de Garsal'
John de la Cloude, t. pat.
William de Brokhurst, pres. by William Boydin
John de Caldecote, t. pat.
William de Lynton' of West Hallam, t. pat.
Thomas, son of Ralph de Stanton, pres. by the abbot of Dale
Richard le Taverner of Castleton, t. pat.
Robert de Gloucestr', pres. by Robert de Stok'
John le Swen of Kenilworth, t. pat.
John de Cobynton, t. pat.
Robert de Sekindon, pres. by Lady Alice de Caumpvill'
William Persey, pres. by the abbot of Dale
Robert Kyde, pres. by the prior of Burscough
John de Franketon, pres. by John Palmer'
Richard Balle of Polesworth, pres. by Sir Richard de Herchull'
Geoffrey Coleman of Brinklow, t. pat.

[Col. 2] *Subdeacons*

John de Litelhay, t. pat.
Hugh de Blatherwyk, dim. dioc. Lincoln, t. house of Fineshade
Robert Mille of Thurlaston, pres. by Thomas de Chevuton
Ralph de Wychford, pres. by the prior of Canwell
Alexander de Langeton, dim. dioc. Lincoln, t. abbot of Owston
Robert de Wotton, t. pat.
John de Napton, pres. by Sir Robert de Napton
Adam de Hulton, t. pat.
Richard de Hope, t. St. Oswald's [hospital] near Worcester
John de Haddon, t. pat.
Richard de Hillary, r. Wymondham, dim. dioc. Lincoln
Fr. John de Grendon
Fr. William de Schepeleye
Fr. Thomas de Rodburn
Fr. Nicholas de Farndon
Fr. John de Martel

Fr. Norman de Castoft
Fr. John de Snayth
Fr. Edmund de Grafton
Henry de Estwell, canon of Leicester
Fr. Thomas the hermit of 'Ryton', t. pat.
   [The rest of the fo. is blank.]

[Fo. 132 col. 1] *Deacons*

Robert de Perham, r. Solihull
William de Lodelowe, r. Harvington[2], dim. dioc. Worcester
Robert de Alverston, r. Staunton in the Forest[3], dim. dioc. Hereford
Richard de Palynton, pres. by Nicholas de Wylie
Roger de Cosford, t. pat.
Richard de Crakinthorp', t. pat. and pres. by Thomas Maucheleg', dim. dioc. Carlisle
William le Porter of 'Newcastle'
William le Mercer of 'Newcastle', t. pat.
Ralph de Moldesworth, t. pat.
John Lycoris of 'Newcastle', t. pat.
Robert de Assheburn, pres. by Thomas de Peverwych
William de Ibol', pres. by Robert de Ibol', v. Ashbourne
William Broun of Meonstoke, pres. by the dean of Lichfield, dim. dioc. Winchester
Thomas de Assheburn, pres. by Sir Nicholas de Marchinton
Richard de Longedon, pres. by the dean of Lichfield
William Kemp of Southam, t. pat.
Geoffrey de Farneworth, pres. by John de Honford
William de Marketon, pres. by the prior of St. James [Derby]
Simon de Knyghtkot', t. pat.
Richard de Ichinton Longa, pres. by Sir Walter de Beauchamp
John de Paddel', t. pat.
William de Irton, pres. by Sir Roger de Bradeburn
Alan de Wyginton, pres. by the abbot of Merevale
Roger de Schardelowe, pres. by Adam de Aymundesham
William Cordi of Repton, t. pat.
John de Asschoo, t. pat.
Walter de Hikeling, pres. by the prior of St. James' [hospital], Derby
William de Merston, pres. by the prior of Tutbury

[Col. 2] *Deacons*

Reginald de Erdinton, pres. by Thomas de Overton
Henry, son of William de Lavenden, dim. dioc. Lincoln, pres. by the prior and conv. of St. James outside Northampton
Peter Oliver of Grandborough, t. pat.
Robert le Taillour of Mackworth, pres. by Philip de Somervill'
John Lye, pres. by Nicholas de Hungerford
Henry de Welham, pres. by the house of Owston, dim. dioc. Lincoln
Richard de Borughton, pres. by John de Schirford

Henry de Coventr', pres. by John de Cornera of Derby
Henry de Eccles, pres. by the abbot and conv. of Combermere
Richard Mussok, t. pat.
Robert, son of Nicholas de Makworth, t. pat.
Robert de Dodinton, t. pat.
John de Stanton, pres. by William de Colwych
William de Oslaston, t. pat.
John de Grenbregh, pres. by Sir Thomas Garshal'
Richard de Overa, pres. by Robert de Alsop
Henry de Marketon, t. pat.
William Redmon of Long Lawford, t. pat.
Ralph le Teyntour of Ashbourne, pres. by John, son of Thomas de Mapelton
Adam de la Sale, pres. by John de Radford
John Horn of Rugby, t. pat.
Roger de Stanton, pres. by William Folegambe of Gratton
Thomas de Morton, pres. by the lord of the same [Morton]
John Hughe of 'Norton', pres. by the abbot and conv. of Winchcombe, dim. dioc.
Worcester
William de Weston, t. pat.
William de Derlaston, t. pat.
Henry de Burton, t. pat.
Adam de Drayton, t. house of Selby, dim. dioc. York

[Fo. 132v col. 1] *Deacons*

Thomas Abel of Leicester, t. the house of Newnham by Bedford, dim. dioc. Lincoln
Richard de Fermlegh, t. pat.
Matthew de Bromleye, pres. by the prior of Holy Trinity, Bridgnorth
John Caly of Potton, pres. by the house of Newnham [by Bedford], dim. dioc. Lincoln
Thomas de Twyford, t. pat.
Thomas Marwe of Leicester, dim. dioc. Lincoln
    [Followed by one blank line.]

Brethren[4]

John de Hatherne
William de Wode Eton
Robert de Pechelton
Ralph Corteys
John de Lincoln'
William de Derlington
John Russel [OFM]
John Sutton
John Hotoft
Roger de Clifton
John de Burton
    [Followed by four blank lines.]

Priests

Walter de Perton, r. Stirchley
William de Wirkesworth, r. Slaidburn, dim. dioc. York
M. Richard de Glene, r. Broadwas,[5] dim. dioc. Worcester
Henry de Caldelowe, t. pat.
Walter de Beulton, t. pat.
Roger de Bobenhull, pres. by William de Wilughby
William Ernald of Brockhurst, pres. by John Wauter of Pailton
John de Herdeburgh, t. pat.
Richard de Stretton, t. pat.
Simon le Warde of 'Staunton', dim. dioc. Lincoln, t. pat.

[Col. 2] *Priests*

John Besele of Shackerstone, [dim.] dioc. Lincoln, t. pat.
Robert de la Spenne, pres. by Sir Walter de Verdon
Walter de Lillington, t. pat.
Richard de Toucestr', dioc. Lincoln, pres. by the house of St. John of Jerusalem
Richard de Yorton, t. pat.
William de Brokton, pres. by the prior of Tutbury
Peter de Magna Houghton, dim. dioc. Lincoln mentioning t.
Nicholas de Crast, t. pat.
Ralph le Fysshere of Newbold on Avon, t. pat.
John de Tresel', pres. by John de Tresel'
Thomas de Herdewyk, t. pat.
John de Calwych, pres. by William de Keythorp'
William de Merston, pres. by William de Stokford
William de Aula of Priors Marston, t. pat.
Hugh Toucestr' of Coventry, t. pat.
Roger Malleshovere of 'Weston', t. pat. and pres. by Sir Robert de Verdon
Richard de Wyleby, pres. by Sir Thomas de Garsal'
Thomas the marshal of Derby, pres. by the prior of St. James' [hospital], Derby
John de Alastr', pres. by Thomas de Beufey
William Halden of 'Houghton', dim. dioc. Lincoln containing t.
Robert de Weston, pres. by Robert de Napton, kt.
Thomas Bernard of Thornby, dim. dioc. Lincoln, pres. by the house of Launde
John de Dunstapel, dim. dioc. Lincoln, pres. by the master of Coventry hospital
John Pek of 'Newton', t. pat.
Roger de Kyrkeby, t. pat.
Thomas de Durandesthorp, pres. by the prior of Tutbury
Thomas de Kel, t. pat.
Richard de Derlaston, pres. by William, lord of 'Darlaston'
John Parlour of Coventry, t. pat.
William de Marchinton, pres. by Sir Ralph de Barinton

[Fo. 133 col. 1]

Peter de St. Albans, v. Wolston
William de Craunford, pres. by Sir Robert de Verdon

Henry de Trentham, t. pat.
Alan Snel of Prees, t. pat.
Richard de Erdbury, t. pat.
Walter de Wrokwardin, pres. by Sir Fulk le Strange
Henry de Horseley, t. pat.
Henry Waryn of Mayfield, pres. by Sir William Trussel
Henry, son of William de Hegham Ferers, dim. dioc. Lincoln, t. house of St. John[6] [the Baptist], Northampton
Richard de Asshburn, pres. by Sir Richard de Herchull
Richard Baillif of Wolverton, t. house of Luffield, dim. dioc. Lincoln
Geoffrey de Ketelaston, pres. by Philip de Somervill'
John de Bretford, t. Sir Robert de Verdon, kt.
Robert Wyer of Eckington, pres. by Robert Toke
Thomas de Aula, t. pat.
William de Walton, t. pat.
William de Dene, John de Knyghtecote, William de Lughteburgh, canons of Arbury
Roger, canon of Kenilworth
Fr. Simon de Coventr'
Fr. William de Coventr'
Fr. Richard de Neuton
Fr. Robert Lye
Fr. Edmund de Insula
Fr. Robert de Preston

> [The rest of the col. is blank.
> [1-1] Across the full width of the fo. above the col. headings. See **1313**.
> [2] *Reg. Cobham*, 251, 264. Listed as M. William de Hyntes called de Lodelowe.
> [3] *Registrum Ade de Orleton episcopi Herefordensis, A.D. MCCCXVII–MCCCXXVII*, ed. A.T. Bannister (CYS, 5, 1908), 367, 392.
> [4] Marginated.
> [5] *Reg. Cobham*, 259, 264.
> [6] Followed by *Jerosolom* deleted.]

1320   [Col. 2] NOMINA ORDINATORUM IN ECCLESIA PAROCHIALI DE PENNE DIE SABBATI IN VIGILIA SANCTE TRINITATIS ANNO DOMINI MILLESIMO .CCC^mo.XVIII°. PER W[ALTERUM] COVENTR' ET LICH' EPISCOPUM IN QUIBUS SENTENCIA FUIT LATA SUB EO QUI SEQUITUR TENORE [17 June 1318].
In the name of God, Amen. Walter [etc.] bishop of Coventry and Lichfield, celebrating holy orders in Penn parish church on Saturday, the eve of Holy Trinity [17 June] 1318, warns and enjoins each and every person present, assembled because of the orders to be received [etc.].[1]

Subdeacons

Thomas le Sympile of Birmingham, t. pat.
Henry de Newport, pres. by Roger, lord of Leamington Hastings
Gilbert de Horselegh, pres. by Sir William Rosel, kt.

[Fo. 133v col. 1] *Subdeacons*

Walter de Dewbury, pres. by Sir Walter Beauchamp, kt.
Henry Antelote of Wilnecote, t. pat.
Thomas de Wikeford, pres. by the prior of the hospital of St. John of Jerusalem to all [orders]
William de Longenore, t. pat.
William le Mason, pres. by Ralph de Brailesford to all [orders]
Richard de Patyngham, pres. by the prior and conv. of Launde
Peter called Brasour of Northgate, dim. dioc. Canterbury, pres. by the prior of St. Gregory, Canterbury
William de Baskervyle, pres. by Sir Thomas de Hastang', kt.
[2]John de Seysendon, t. pat.[2]
Henry le Gardouner of Wolston, pres. by Sir Thomas de Garsale, kt.
Roger de Normanton, pres. by the prior of St. James' [hospital], Derby
William de Wolveya, pres. by Lady Alice de Wolveya
William, son of Roger de Brocton, pres. by Sir John de Langeford
Robert Hyllar', r. Sutton Coldfield
John de Assheby, r. Baddesley Clinton
Thomas de Baddisleye, r. Westonbirt,[3] dim. dioc. Worcester
Thomas, r. Sheldon
John de Ideshale, pres. by John de Styminton
Geoffrey de Schelful, t. pat.
Roger de Mokeleye, dim. dioc. Hereford, pres. by the abbot of Shrewsbury
William de Stoke, pres. by the abbot and conv. of St. Mary, Lilleshall
William de Overa, pres. by the abbot and conv. of Croxden to all [orders]
John, son of Roger, son of Robert de Novo Castro, t. pat.
John de Wakebruge, pres. by the abbot of Dale
Simon de Reppyndon, t. pat.
Thomas Wykok of 'Over', pres. by John de la Cornere of Derby
Henry de St[4]one, r. Swarkeston
Fr. Thomas de Roucestr'
John de Newenton, Simon de Poywik, canons of Haughmond

[Col. 2]

Henry de Werinton, William de Billebury, OSA
John de Walton, pres. by Peter Giffard
James le Porter of Edgbaston, pres. by Thomas de Morton, lord of Ipsley
Richard de Fulschawe, t. pat.
William Dakenyl of Bridgnorth, t. pat.
[5]Richard de Bermingham, pres. by Sir William de Bermingham[5]

Deacons

John de Cubbeleye, pres. by Walter de Montgomery, adequate [t.]
Richard Balle of Polesworth, t. Sir Richard de Herchull, adequate [t.]
Robert de Chersale, pres. by the prior and conv. of Wombridge, adequate [t.]
William de Swerkeston, pres. by John de Beck

Geoffrey de Wolseleye, pres. by John de Cherford
John de Copere of 'Aston', pres. by John de Daleby
Stephen de Silimdon, pres. by John de Haston
Ralph, son of William de Grendon, pres. by Ralph [de Grendon], kt.
Alan de Salop', t. Hugh de Biriton
Robert de Barton, t. pat.
Henry de Hamond of Grandborough, t. pat.
Robert de Thurlaston, t. pat.
John de la Cloude, t. pat.
John de Burthyngbur', pres. by John Paynel
John de Letuleye, t. pat.
Hugh de Alaster, pres. by Hugh de Hulgathorpe
William de Tofft, pres. by Thomas Garsouht'
Richard de Hull', pres. by John de Holton'
Henry de Pyri, pres. by William, lord of Perry Barr
Augustine de Copenale, pres. by Roger de Preez of Barthomley
Richard Rainald of Audley, t. pat.
Richard le Taverner of 'Newcastle', t. pat.
Richard de Caveresvell, pres. by Richard, son of Richard of the same [Caverswall)
Robert de Sutton, dim., pres. by the prior of Daventry
William de Braynston, t. William of the same
Vivian de Danpord, t. pat.
Simon de Grendon, pres. by the prior of Charley

[Fo. 134 col. 1]

Philip de Dene, pres. by John de la Lee, kt.
William de Westone, pres. by Edmund de Aston
William de Haukeserd, pres. by Robert de Sheldon
William le Hunte, pres. by John le Hunte
John de Napton, pres. by John de Somervyl'
Adam de Hulton, pres. by Robert de Schepheye
John de Cobynton, pres. by Robert Symond
John le Mason of Coventry, t. pat.
John de Caldecote, t. pat.
Thomas de[6] Scheuterford, pres. by John de Cotes
Peter, son of William Novere of Chillington, pres. by Sir John Giffard
Robert, son of Adam de Walseken of Norwich dioc., t. pat.
Robert, son of Henry Kyde of 'Donnington', pres. by the prior and conv. of Burscough
Alexander de Langeton, dim. dioc. Lincoln

Beneficed clerks

M. Roger, r. Stoke on the Wirral
Alexander, r. Upper Langwith
Edmund, r. Mackworth
M. Ellis, port. Darley
Ralph, r. Brereton

Fr. John de Sneyth
Fr. John Martel
Fr. Nicholas de Torpe
Fr. Thomas de Rodbourn
Fr. Nicholas de Faryngdon
Fr. Edmund de Grafton
Fr. William de Wintonia
Fr. Nicholas de Staunton
Fr. John de Schipton
   [The rest of the col. is blank.]

[Col. 2] *Priests*

[7]Walter de Sauney of Stretton, r. Shangton, dim. dioc. Lincoln[7]
M. Robert de Preston, r. Fitz
Richard Hillari, r. Wymondham, dim. dioc. Lincoln
Robert le Taillour of Mackworth, pres. by Sir John de Beufoy
William le Mercer of 'Newcastle', t. pat.
Geoffrey de Farnworth, pres. by John de Honforth
Robert, son of Nicholas de Macworth, t. pat.
Roger de Acton Burnel, t. pat.
William de Irton, pres. by Henry de Bradbourn
William le Porter of 'Newcastle', t. pat.
Ralph de Moldworth, t. pat.
William de Oselaston, pres. by the prior and brethren of St. James' [hospital], Derby
Thomas Abel of Leicester, dim. dioc. Lincoln, containing his t.
Richard de Pailynton, pres. by Nicholas de Herdeburth'
Richard Fermlegh of Warmingham, t. pat. and pres. by John de Moston
William de Sutham, t. pat.
Thomas de Esshebourne, pres. by Nicholas de Marchenton
Hugh de Blatherwik, dim. Lincoln dioc., containing his t.
John de Cailly of Potton, dim. dioc. Lincoln, containing his t.
Geoffrey de Salteford, pres. by Roger de Oldfeld
Reginald de Erdington, pres. by Thomas de Overton, lord of Overton and Wombourn
Matthew de Bromlegh of the parish of Worfield, pres. by the prior and brethren of Holy Trinity [hospital], Bridgnorth
Adam de Rowedich, pres. by Adam Ceyny of 'Wolebrug'
Thomas Basset, pres. by Sir Richard de Herchull, kt.
Robert de Alderleie of St. Neots, dim. dioc. Lincoln, containing his t.
John, son of Robert de Staunton, pres. by William de Colewik' of 'Staunton'
Henry de Bourton super Trentam, t. pat.
Thomas de Hull' Morton, pres. by Thomas de Asteley
William de Marketon, pres. by the prior of St. James' [hospital], Derby
Roger de Prestecote, t. pat.
Adam de Ormeschirche, t. pat.
William de Bentelegh, pres. by the prior and brethren of Canwell

[Fo. 134v col. 1] *Priests*

John Licoris of 'Newcastle', t. pat.
John de Hamelton, dim. dioc. York, t. pat. and pres. by the dean of Lichfield
William Broun of Meonstoke, dim. dioc. Winchester, pres. by John de Dene, kt.
Roger de Cosford of the parish of Newbold on Avon, t. pat.
M. William de Stretton, r. 'Stretton'
Roger, son of John de Bromlegh of Tamworth, t. pat.
William de Herdewik Prioris, t. pat.
Peter Oliver of Grandborough, t. pat.
William de Ybole of Ashbourne, pres. by Robert de Ibole, v. Ashbourne
William de Stretton, pres. by Richard de Stretton
John de Gnawsale, pres. by William de Burgo
Adam Bagod of Fulready, pres. by Richard Bagod
Roger de Daggeshoo of 'Newbold', t. pat.
Adam de Findren, pres. by Robert de Findren
Henry de Chetewynde, pres. by John de Chetewynde
Robert de Eton, pres. by Sir Thomas de Carshale, kt.
John de Asshoe, t. pat.
Richard de Longesdone, pres. by Thomas Folejaumbe
John, son of Henry de Padeslee, t. pat.
Robert de Overa, pres. by John Gery of Derby
William de Merston, pres. by the prior and conv. of Tutbury
John le Gardiner of Rodsley, pres. by Nicholas Solveyn
William de Braidesale of Horsley, pres. by the abbot of Dale
Adam de Leye, pres. by Adam de Moccleston
Henry de Bromleye, pres. by John Bagod
Roger de la Dale, t. pat.
[Richard]⁸ Mossok, t. pat.
Robert de Cotyn, t. pat.

Religious

William de Wode Eton, [monk] of Combermere
Fr. John de Tetenhale
Fr. William de Novo Castro
Fr. Simon de Norhampton
John Herle, [monk] of Croxden

[Col. 2]

Fr. William de Derlington, Fr. Roger Martyn, of Derby
Robert de Pehktelton, canon of Repton
  [¹ See **1313**.
  ²⁻² Added by a second contemporary hand. Followed by one blank line.
  ³ *Reg. Cobham*, 133, 159, 228, 250, 253, 258, 260, 264.
  ⁴ MS. *k* changed to *t*
  ⁵⁻⁵ Added by the same second hand.
  ⁶ Interlined.

7–7 Added later at the right-hand side of the col. heading.
8 MS. *Rogerus*]

1321 [1]NOMINA ORDINATORUM IN ECCLESIA PAROCHIALI DE CHEBESEYE
DIE SABBATI QUATUOR TEMPORUM MENSIS DECEMBRIS ANNO DOMINI .M°
.CCC^mo.XVIII°. PER .W[ALTERUM]. COVENTR' ET LYCH' EPISCOPUM IN QUIBUS
SENTENCIA FUIT LATA SUB EO QUI SEQUITUR TENORE [23 December 1318].
In the name of God, Amen. Walter [etc.] bishop of Coventry and Lichfield, celebrating holy orders in Chebsey parish church on Saturday *quatuor temporum* [23]
December 1318, warns and enjoins each and every person present, assembled
because of the orders to be received [etc.], that no one shall enter such orders
unless he is examined and admitted by the examiners appointed for this; also no
one from another diocese without letters dimissory of his bishop; no one who is
bigamous or married to a widow; [or] married; by omission of a degree of ordination and simony; of illegitimate birth without having dispensation; of servile status;
no one shall receive two holy orders or a single holy order and another minor order
this day; [or be] a murderer; ordained to holy orders unless he has adequate title
with which he considers himself satisfied for [the bishop's] discharge and that of
[his] successors; from a royal chapel or prebend [in the bishop's] diocese without
[his] special licence; [and] if anyone happens or audaciously ventures to contravene the foregoing [the bishop] wishes the same to incur the aforesaid sentence of
excommunication etc.[1]

Subdeacons

John de Beurepeir, r. Wolverton,[2] dim. dioc. Worcester
Nicholas, r. Mucklestone
Robert de Langeton, r. Trimley St. Martin, dim. dioc. Norwich
Robert Takel, dim. dioc. Lincoln, t. pat.
Robert le Mayler, pres. by Robert le Mayler
Nicholas de Buckestanes, t. pat.
John de Hoby, dim. [dioc. York], t. the bishop
Roger Jory of Birmingham, t. pat.
John Wodecok' of Birmingham, t. pat.
William Brian of 'Haughton', pres. by Ralph de Halutona
John Caune, pres. by the prior and brethren of Holy Trinity hospital, Bridgnorth

[Fo. 135 col. 1] *Subdeacons*

John de Romesote, pres. by the abbot of Vale Royal
Thomas de Wodecot', t. pat.
William Aleyn of Shilton, pres. by r. Baginton
Hugh de Typschelf, pres. by Geoffrey de Dethek
William de Dersthull, t. pat.
Henry de Hull', pres. by John de Scheldon
William Husse of 'Eyton', pres. by William Pouger
William de Ylkyston, pres. by the abbot of Dale
William de Fouwolle, pres. by Adam de Micleston
William de Tomworth, pres. by Richard de Smethewyk

Stephen de Ronton, pres. by William del Burg'
William de Audelegh, t. pat.
William Poydras, pres. by the abbot of Combermere
Roger Dobyn, pres. by M. Alexander de Verdon
Robert de Derby', pres. by Robert de Henor'
William Kerdyf of Egginton, pres. by William de Egington
William de Boulton, pres. by Ralph de Gournay
Nicholas de Assburn, pres. by Sir Roger de Acover', kt.
Ralph de Strongeshull', pres. by the abbot and conv. of Croxden
William de Capella, pres. by Sir Nicholas de Marchenton, kt.[3]
John le Barber of Newport, t. pat.
Walter de Marchynton, pres. by Sir Walter de Mon[t]gomery
Robert de Bolton, dim. dioc. Lincoln, to all [orders]
William de Langeton, dim. dioc. Lincoln, to all [orders]
William de Salford, pres. by Henry de Pylkynton

Deacons

William Dagenel of Bridgnorth, t. pension of 5 marks, authorised by the lord [bishop]
Henry Antelot', t. pat.
Thomas de Stotham, r. Sheldon
Thomas le Simple of Birmingham, t. pat.
Robert de Alastr', pres. by the abbot of Dale
John de Codeshale, t. John de Stivyngton
Henry de Wodeford, t. lord of Somersall Herbert
John de Wakbrygg', t. pat.
Thomas de Schoresworth, t. Thomas de Hopwod'
William de Caverwell, t. pat.
William de Stok, t. abbot and conv. of Lilleshall
Gilbert de Horsleg', t. Sir W[illiam] Rosel
William Mazon, t. Ralph de Braillesford
William Baskervill', t. Sir T[homas] Hasting'
William de Lynton', t. pat.
Richard de Fulschawa, t. pat. and pres. by Richard de Squetenham
William de Longenor', t. pat.

[4]*Subdeacons*

John de Stone, OCarm.
Richard de Bristoll, Hugh Charite, OSA
William de Roucestr', canon [?of Rocester]
Andrew de Assburn, OFM[4]

[Col. 2 *Deacons*]

John, son of Roger de Novo Castro, t. William de Overa
Robert Hillar', r. Sutton Coldfield
Robert de Assheby, r. 'Waddesby'[5]
Richard de Patyngham, pres. by the house of Launde

Roger de Mokeleye, [dim. dioc. Hereford] t. abbot of Shrewsbury
John de Seysdon, t. pat.

Religious[6]

Fr. William de Dytheseworth
Fr. Robert Montfichet
Fr. Hugh de Lich'
Fr. William de Wemlok'
Fr. William de Lich'[7]

Priests

Alexander, son of Richard de Thorp' Langeton, dim. dioc. Lincoln, t. Owston
Hugh de 3oxhale, pres. by Roger de Bradbourn, kt.
John de Okam in Leicestr', dim. [dioc. Lincoln], t. house of Canons Ashby
John de Fourneys, dim. dioc. York, t. pat.
Roger de Blida in Wytham, dim., t. house of Owston
Laurence Borey, t. an annual pension
Richard de Coterstok', dim. dioc. Lincoln, t. house of Newnham by Bedford
M. Roger de Soterley, r. Stoke on the Wirral
Robert May, r. Mugginton
William le Hunte, t. John de Hunton
Richard Balle of Polesworth, pres. by Sir Richard de Herchull, kt.
Richard Reynald of Audley, t. pat.
Henry Skone, r. Swarkeston
John de Cobynton, t. pat.
Henry Hamond of Grandborough, t. pat.
Henry de Becclus, pres. by the abbot and conv. of Combermere
Hugh de Walecot', t. pat.
John de Cobbeley, pres. by Sir Walter de Montgomery
Vivian de Daniport, t. pat.
Ralph, son of William de Grendon, t. Sir Ralph de Grendon[8]
John de Littelhey, t. pat.
William, son of Andrew de Weston, pres. by Philip de Somervill', lord of Tatenhill
Henry de Welham, dim. dioc. Lincoln, t. house of Owston
Thomas de Godleston, pres. by r. Shustoke
William de Haukeserd, t. Robert de Scheldon
William de Repyndon, t. pat.
Augustine de Copenhale, t. Richard de Prares of Barthomley
John de Caldecot', t. pat.
John Horn of Rugby, t. pat.
John de Herlaston, r. Eastwood, dim. dioc. London

[Fo. 135v col. 1]

John de Estnorton, dim. dioc. Lincoln, t. house of Owston
Roger de Schardelowe, pres. by Adam de Amondesham
Richard de Merston, t. pat.

M. Adam Menill', r. Stoke Talmage [dim. dioc. Lincoln]
John de Napton, pres. by Philip de Somervile
Robert Kyde, pres. by the prior of Burscough
Richard de Schelton, r. Stretton on Fosse chapel,[9] dim. dioc. Worcester

Religious[10]

Fr. John de Offenham
Fr. William de Wynton'
Fr. Nicholas de Staunton
Fr. John de Schypton'
Fr. William de Hatern
Fr. William de Schepey
Fr. Thomas de Ruuton, hermit
  [1–1 In col. 2.
  2 *Reg. Cobham*, 229, 252, 253, 266, 269.
  3 Interlined.
  4–4 Added at the foot of col. 1 with a line drawn in the left-hand margin linking it to the previous subdeacon section in the same col.
  5 ?*Recte* Gaddesby, Leics.
  6 At the right-hand side of the following five names and linked by a wavy line.
  7 Interlined.
  8 Interlined.
  9 *Reg. Cobham*, 229, 258, 268. Listed as Richard de Schulton.
  10 At the right-hand side of the following seven names and linked by a wavy line.]

1322 [1]NOMINA ORDINATORUM IN ECCLESIA CATHEDRALI LICH' DIE SABBATI IN VIGILIA PASCHE ANNO DOMINI .M° .CCC^mo.XIX°. PER .W[ALTERUM]. COVENTR' ET LICH' EPISCOPUM[1] [7 April 1319].

Subdeacons[2]

Jordan de Marchal', r. St. Olaf, Chester
John le Waleys, r. Acton
John Hurne, t. pat.
John, son of Adam de Ormechurch, t. pat.
Henry de Uttoxhathre, t. pat.
Edmund, r. Draycott in the Moors
William Cursoun, r. Kedleston
Reginald de Chetewynde, r. Chetwynd
Henry de Wychenovere, pres. by Philip de Somervile
[3]Thomas de London, John Herveis, John Deyvile, Henry de Berton, John de Hodenet, canons of Kenilworth
Sir[4] Robert de Brikkhull, John de Derby, religious of Burton upon Trent[3]

Deacons[5]

Nicholas Mawveysyn, r. Ridware Mavesyn
Robert de Langeton, r. Trimley St. Martin, dim. dioc. Norwich
William de Audele, t. pat.

[Col. 2]

Robert Takel, t. pat., dim. dioc. Lincoln
John Wodecok' of Birmingham, t. pat.
John le Barber of Newport, t. pat.
Walter de Cokton', dim. dioc. Worcester, pres. by John de Morton, v. High Ercall,
and because the title was considered inadequate Sir Richard de Norton undertook
[it] for greater reliability

Religious[6]

Fr. Thomas de Cressewall
Fr. Adam de Mynsterton
Fr. Gilbert le Wastonays
Fr. William de Holand

Priests[7]

William Beaufoy, r. Whiston, dim. dioc. York
Robert de Athelastr', pres. by the abbot of Dale
John Hoby, dim. dioc. York, t. the bishop
Thomas de Cestford, pres. by John de Cotys
William de Swerkyston', pres. by John le Bek
Thomas le Symple of Birmingham, t. pat.
John de Wakebrugg', t. pat.
Walter de Castirton, dim. dioc. Lincoln, t. prior of Luffield
Henry de Pyrie, pres. by William, his brother, lord of Perry Barr
Fr. John de Karleton
   [The rest of the fo. is blank.
   [1-1] In col. 1.
   [2] Underlined.
   [3-3] Separated from the names above by a line drawn across a third of the col.
   [4] *Sic*
   [5] Underlined.
   [6] At the right-hand side of the following four names and linked by a wavy line.
   [7] Underlined.]

1323 [Fo. 136] [1]ORDINES CELEBRATI [2]PER DOMINUM WALTERUM
COVENTR' ET LICH' EPISCOPUM[2] IN ECCLESIA PREBENDALI DE ECCLESHAL'
DIE SABBATI IN VIGILIA SANCTE TRINITATIS .ANNO DOMINI .M^o .CCC^{mo}.
DECIMO NONO IN QUIBUS FUIT SENTENCIA LATA SUB HAC FORMA [2 June
1319].
In the name of God, Amen. Walter [etc.] bishop of Coventry and Lichfield, cele-
brating holy orders in Eccleshall prebendal church on Saturday, the eve of Holy
Trinity [2 June] 1319, warns and enjoins each and every person present, assem-
bled because of the orders to be received [etc.].[1, 3]

[Col. 1] *Subdeacons*

M. John Waleweyn, r. Hawarden
Thomas de Vernoun, r. Davenham
Richard, son of William de Alby of Derby, t. pat.
Robert le Spencer, pres. by Sir John de Twyford
Peter de Lymme, pres. by Sir Peter de Werbyrton to all [orders]
William de Yolretoft, dim. [dioc. Lincoln] to all [orders], pres. by Sir Walter de Danyver'
William de Coleshull, t. pat.
Richard, son of Hugh de Bostok, t. pat.
Philip de Multon, t. William de Multon
Thomas de Preston, t. Roger Banastr'
Richard, son of Nicholas de Westhalum, t. house of Dale
Richard de Novo Burgo, t. John le Strange of Cheswardine
Adam de Stretton super Donesmor', pres. by John le Palmer' of Frankton
John, son of Robert de Bosco of 'Haughton', t. prior and conv. of Felley
Robert de Tybeschelf, t. pat.
Robert de Ardern, r. Albrighton
Roger, son of Stephen Bonde of Audley, t. pat.
Adam de Wylmesowe, pres. by Thomas Fyton, lord of Gawsworth
Richard de Radeford, t. pat.
John de Olton, t. pat.
William, son of Simon Ster of Repton, t. pat.
John de Mouselowe, Simon de Poywyk, [canons] of Haughmond
Fr. William de Mukleston
Fr. Roger de Wolreton
Fr. John de Tyrleye
Fr. Henry Box

[Col. 2]

Walter, [monk] of Vale Royal
Fr. Robert de Craunton
Fr. Simon de Smeyton
Fr. William de Cotes

Deacons[4]

Henry le Gardyner, pres. by Sir Thomas de Garsale
William de Salford, pres. by Henry de Pilkylton
Robert Mailler, pres. by Robert Mailer, senior
Peter le Brasour of Canterbury, dim., t. prior [5]and conv.[5] of Tutbury
Hugh, son of Alan de Dukemanton, pres. by Geoffrey Dethek
John Caune of Bridgnorth, pres. by the prior and brethren of Holy Trinity [hospital], Bridgnorth
John Balraven, t. pat.
Nicholas de Buxstones, t. pat.
Robert de Woyton, t. pat.

Richard de Weston, t. pat.
William, son of Adam de Wyco Malbano, t. house of Combermere
William de Stretton, t. Robert le Norreys
Ralph de Strongeshull', pres. by the abbot and conv. of Croxden to all [orders]
Simon de Beldyng, t. pat.
William de Capella, pres. by Sir Nicholas de Marchynton
Jordan de Marchale, r. St. Olaf, Chester
John de Bromley, t. pat.
John de Waldeschef, r. Ilston, dim. dioc. St. David's
Adam de Bassecot', pres. by John de Somervyle
Stephen de Ronton, pres. by William de Bures
Nicholas de Asshborn, pres. by Thomas M...[6]
Simon de Repyndon, t. pat.

[Fo. 136v col. 1]

John le Parker, pres. by the abbot and conv. of Croxden
Fr. John Hodynet
Fr. John de Mouselowe
Fr. Simon de Poywyk
Fr. William de Dunstaple
Walter, [monk] of Vale Royal
Fr. Adam de Bradechahg'
Fr. Robert de Neuton
Fr. Adam de Urmeston

Priests[7]

Nicholas Mauveysine, r. Ridware Mavesyn
Ellis de Essinhurst, t. pat.
Richard del Hul, pres. by John de Hulton
Richard de Borowoton, pres. by John de Scirford
Walter the smith of Welwyn, dim. dioc. Lincoln, t. house of Bradwell
Roger de Mokeleye, dim. dioc. Hereford, pres. by Hugh de Beuvis
John le Couiper of 'Aston', pres. by Edmund de Aston
John de la Cloude, t. pat.
William de Longemor', t. pat.
Henry de Filungley, t. pat.
Richard Taverner of 'Newcastle', t. pat.
Richard de Patingham, t. house of Launde
Henry de Restewret, t. house of Dale
Roger de Stanton, pres. by William Folejaumbe, kt.
Gilbert de Horseley, pres. by Hugh le Meynell
Adam de Aula, t. Sir John de Radeford
William de Lauton, t. pat.
Henry de Beyvill', pres. by Thomas de Wassinglee

[Col. 2]

William de Overe, pres. by the abbot and conv. of Croxden
William de Careswell, t. pat.
Alan de Salop', t. pat.
Thomas de Schorisworth, pres. by Thomas de Hopewode
Hugh de Wibbinburi, t. pat.
John, son of Roger de Novo Castro, t. pat.
Richard de Careswell, pres. by Richard de Cariswell
Richard de Crich, pres. by the abbot and conv. of Dale
Hugh de Athelaster, pres. by Hugh de Ulgerthorp
Robert Fige, pres. by Thomas Wather
John Sersden, t. pat.
William Cordi, t. pat.
Richard Takel, dim. dioc. Lincoln, t. pat.
Robert de Langeton, r. Trimley St. Martin, dim. dioc. Norwich
William de Pull', pres. by Richard de Aston
William d'Audeley, t. pat.
Henry de Waleford of Uttoxeter, pres. by Nicholas Fitzherbert, lord of Somersall
Herbert

Religious priests

Fr. Thomas de Rouclyf'
Fr. Arnold de Emsey
Fr. Richard de Wyco
Thomas de Stafford, OFM
Roger, [monk] of Vale Royal
William, [monk] of the same [Vale Royal]
[Fr.] Adam de Mistirton
     [1–1 Across the full width of the fo.
     2–2 Interlined.
     3 See **1321**.
     4 At the right-hand side of the name above with a line drawn to separate it from the
     names below.
     5–5 Interlined.
     6 Abraded.
     7 Underlined.]

1324 [1]ORDINES CELEBRATI IN ECCLESIA COLLEGIATI DE GNOUSALE DIE SABBATI QUATUOR TEMPORUM MENSIS DECEMBRIS ANNO DOMINI .M⁰ .CCCᵐ⁰. DECIMONONO. PER .W[ALTERUM]. PERMISSIONE DIVINA COVENTR' ET LICH' EPISCOPUM IN QUIBUS FUIT SENTENCIA LATA SUB HAC FORMA [22 December 1319].
In the name of God, Amen. Walter [etc.] bishop of Coventry and Lichfield, celebrating holy orders in Gnosall collegiate church on Saturday *quatuor temporum* [22 December] 1319,[1] [fo. 137][2] warns and inhibits each and every person present, assembled because of the holy[3] orders to be received, firstly, secondly and thirdly and by calling God to witness that no one shall enter the said orders unless he is of legitimate birth or has been legitimised by the Apostolic See; also unless he is

examined and duly[4] admitted by the examiners, or any of them, appointed for this; no one who is a murderer or bigamous or married to a widow; by omission of a degree of ordination, or secretly or by simony; of illegitimate birth without having dispensation; of servile status; no one shall receive minor orders and a single holy order or two holy orders this day; no one from another diocese without the licence of his diocesan; from a royal chapel [in the bishop's] diocese without [his] special licence; without title with which he considers himself satisfied for [the bishop's] discharge and that of [his] successors; [and] if anyone happens or audaciously ventures to contravene the foregoing [the bishop wishes him] to fear the sentence of greater excommunication etc., not without cause.

[Col. 1] *Subdeacons*[5]

Thomas de Turvill', r. moiety of Malpas
Robert, son of Hugh de Uttokeshather, pres. by Sir William de Stafford
Robert March' of Newbold, pres. by Sir Philip de Somervill'
John de Knythlegh', pres. by Roger de Knythlegh'
Richard de Hatton, t. pat.
Henry de Tunstall, pres. by Roger de Bedulf'
Richard de Spounlegh', t. pat.
Alan de Rodham, pres. by the prior of Ipswich, dim. dioc. Norwich
Thomas le Heyr, pres. by the prior of Wombridge
Thomas Horn of Rugby, t. pat.
Henry de Wyrleg', pres. by John de Cotes
William the baker of Newport, pres. by John Randulf of Sheriffhales
Roger Thurkyl' of Sudbury, pres. by Sir Walter de Montgomery
John de Denston', pres. by the abbot of Croxden
John the baker of Wyken, t. pat.
John de Cruce Lapidea, dim. dioc. London, pres. by Thomas de Wassinglegh'
Thomas de Barton, pres. by John de Bakepuis
Henry de Thurleston, pres. by the abbot of Dale
John Swayn of 'Wigston', dim. dioc. Lincoln, t. pat.
Hugh de Novo Burgo, pres. by Adam de Morton
John de Croulesmer', t. pat.
Richard de Mamcestr', pres. by Sir Roger de Pylkynton
John de Roucestr', pres. by the abbot of Rocester
Henry de Wytemor', t. pat.
Hugh de Baynton, dim. dioc. York, t. pat.
Nigel de Aston, t. pat.
Roger de Bonhay, t. pat.
Richard de Mockeslowe, pres. by Sir William de Byrmyngham
Peter Scot, pres. by Roger del Wodhall
Peter de Braudeston, pres. by Simon Pouger
John de Stodfold, t. pat.
Walter de Thorp' Constantyn, t. pat.
Robert de Bylney, t. pat.
John de Overton, t. pat.

[Col. 2] *Subdeacons*[6]

John de Somervyle, r. Longbenton, dim. dioc. Durham
Robert, son of Robert the goldsmith of Bridgnorth, t. house of Holy Trinity of the same
Henry de Okebrok', pres. by the abbot of Dale

Religious subdeacons[7]

Thomas de Valle Regali, John de Bosworth, [monks] of Vale Royal
Fr. William de Barnesby, of Derby
Robert de Pakynton, Henry de Kyrkeby, [monks] of Burton upon Trent
Fr. Walter de Wynnesbur', Fr. Roger de Hounfreyston, Fr. Thomas de Opton, Fr. Henry de Alston, of Shrewsbury
Fr. William de Clyfton, of Derby
Robert de Stolynton, [canon] of Trentham
Fr. Roger de Rode
Fr. Roger de Lodelowe

Deacons

Richard Arkel of Darfield, dim. dioc. York, t. pat.
Roger, son of Stephen Bonde of Audley, t. pat.
M. Philip Aubyn, r. Drayton Bassett chapel
Robert de Ardern, r. Albrighton
Reginald, r. Chetwynd
William de Schulton, v. Lichfield [cath.]
John Waleys, r. Acton
William le Parker of Coleshill, t. pat.
William, son of Roger Capenter of 'Broughton', t. r. Longford
Robert le Spenser of Uttoxeter, pres. by John de Twyford
Roger Dobyn of 'Darlaston', t. M. Alexander de Verdon
William de Tameworth, t. Richard de Smethewych
William de Pychford, t. pat.
William de Beulton, t. Ralph le Gournay

[Fo. 137v Col. 1] *Deacons*[8]

William de Dersthull, t. pat.
William de Wolvey, t. Lady Alice of the same
William Kerdy of Egginton, t. pat.
William de Yolvertoft, dim. dioc. Lincoln, t. pat.
William de Rokeby, t. pat.
Robert de Belton, dim. dioc. Lincoln, t. house of Launde
Roger Eunok of Avon Dassett, t. pat.
John de Olton, t. pat.
Alan de Stretton, pres. by Sir Robert de Verdon, kt.
Robert Torald, t. pat.
William de Iwiston, pres. by the abbot of Dale

Henry de Neuport, [canon] of Trentham
Fr. Andrew de Assborn'
Roger de Assborn', OFM
Walter, [monk] of Vale Royal
Fr. Thomas de Leye
Fr. John de Insula
Fr. Robert de Bromhal'
Fr. Andrew de Assborn'
Fr. Roger de Wolverton
Fr. John de Tyrleye
Fr. William de Okebrok'
Fr. Robert de Over'
Roger de Patyngton, Robert de Knythleye, Robert de Mewes, John de Bruges, John de Morcote, Giles de Meignyl, [monks] of Much Wenlock

Priests[9]

Alan de Wygyngton, pres. by the abbot and conv. of Merevale
William de Thorp' juxta Langeton, dim. dioc. Lincoln, t. house of Owston
Ralph de Strongeshull', pres. by the abbot and conv. of Croxden
William de Salford, pres. by Henry de Salford
John Wodecok' of Birmingham, t. pat.
Richard de Overa, pres. by St. James' [hospital], Derby
Richard Marcle of Long Itchington, pres. by Sir John de Oddyngeseles, kt.
William de Schutyngton, t. pat.
John Waldeschef, r. Ilston, dim. dioc. St. David's, which we have had previously and a sealed copy remains in his possession
Jordan de Maxfeld, r. St. Olaf, Chester
Henry le Gardiner of Wolston, t. Sir Thomas de Kersale

[Col. 2]

John Bayn of Haughton, dim.[10] dioc. Lincoln, t. house of Shelford
William Bayn of Haughton, dim. dioc. Lincoln, t. house of Owston
William Redman, t. pat.
John Baleran of Southam, t. pat.
John de Tresyl', pres. by John de Perton
Nicholas de Buxstanes, t. pat.
Simon Boldyng, t. pat.
John Blund, t. pat.
William de Tonge, dioc. Lincoln, pres. by the prioress of Langley
Robert de Therleston, pres. by Thomas de Cheveteyn
Stephen de Ronton, pres. by William de Burgo
William de Stok', t. pat.
John le Barber of Newport, t. pat.
Simon de Grendon, t. pat.
Fr. Thomas de Craswell
John de Hodenet, [canon] of Trentham
William de Deseworth, OCist.

Fr. Thomas de Ronton
Fr. John de Ronton
Hugh de Asshborn, [canon] of Darley
John de Lodelowe, [monk] of Much Wenlock
> [1-1 In col. 2.
> 2 The admonition continues across the full width of fo. 137 above the col. headings.
> 3 Deleted.
> 4 Interlined.
> 5 Underlined.
> 6 Underlined.
> 7 Underlined.
> 8 Underlined.
> 9 Underlined.
> 10 Interlined.]

1325 [1]ORDINES CELEBRATI IN ECCLESIA NOSTRA CATHEDRALI LICH' DIE SABBATI IN VIGILIA PASCHE[2] ANNO DOMINI MILLESIMO TRECENTESIMO VICESIMO PER .W[ALTERUM]. PERMISSIONE DIVINA COVENTR' ET LICH' EPISCOPUM IN QUIBUS FUIT SENTENCIA LATA SUB FORMA PREDICTA[1] [29 March 1320].

Subdeacons[3]

John, son of Walter de Askeby, dim. of the official of Lincoln dioc., *sede vacante*
Thomas Someryld of Corsham, dim. dioc. Salisbury, pres. by the house of Tickford Hugh de Greseley, pres. by the prior and conv. of Church Gresley
Thomas de Orme of Peatling Magna, dim. dioc. Lincoln, t. house of Ulvescroft
William de Benteley, t. pat.
John de Alrschawe, pres. by Adam de Ruggele
Thomas de Norton, v. Lichfield [cath.]

Religious subdeacons[4]

Fr. Roger de Haydour
Fr. William de Weston

[Fo. 138 col. 1]

Fr. Thomas de Coventr'
Fr. William de Lougtheburgh'

Deacons

Robert, son of Hugh de Uttokeshathere, pres. by Sir William de Stafford
Roger Bongwhay, t. pat.
Richard de Hatton of Swynnerton, t. pat.
Thomas, r. moiety of Malpas
Henry de Wyrleye, t. John de Cotes
John le Masoun, t. pat.
Henry de Wychenovere, pres. by Philip de Somervill'

John de Wykynchull, t. pat.
Hugh de Baynton, dim. dioc. York, t. pat.

Religious deacons

Fr. William de Barnesby
Fr. Robert de Pakynton
Fr. Henry de Kyrkeby

Priests

John le Waleys, r. Acton
M. William de Clopton, r. Tydd St. Mary, dim. dioc. Lincoln
M. Philip Aubyn, r. Drayton Bassett
Reginald, r. Chetwynd
Roger, son of Stephen de Audeley, t. pat.
Alan de Rudham, t. house of Ipswich
Richard de Haselbech', r. Fenny Bentley
John de Olton, t. pat.
William de Shulton, v. Lichfield [cath.]
William de Holond, canon of Stone
John Kaune of Bridgnorth, pres. by the prior and brethren of Holy Trinity
hospital, Bridgnorth
Richard de Derford, dim. dioc. York, t. pat.
Guy, monk of Tutbury

> [Followed by a line drawn across half the col.
> ¹⁻¹ In col. 2. See **1324**.
> ² Followed by an erased word, now illegible, through which a line has been drawn.
> ³ Underlined.
> ⁴ Underlined.]

1326 ¹ORDINES CELEBRATI IN ECCLESIA PAROCHIALI DE SUTHAM DIE
SABBATI QUATUOR TEMPORUM IN VIGILIA SANCTE TRINITATIS ANNO
DOMINI .Mº .CCCᵐº. VICESIMO PER .W[ALTERUM]. COVENTR' ET LICH'
EPISCOPUM¹ [24 May 1320].

[Col. 2] *Subdeacons*²

Thomas de Ockebrok', pres. by the master of St. Helen's [hospital], Derby
William Toverey, r. Stone, dim. dioc. Lincoln
William de Burwes, pres. by Richard Meignyll'
John de Ichynton, pres. by Sir John de Somervill', kt.
William de Bassecot', pres. by Sir John de Somervill', kt.
Roger de Wolescot', pres. by Sir Thomas de Garsal', kt.
Roger de Hynestok', pres. by Thomas de Overton'
William de Costantine, t. pat.
John the miller of Tamworth, t. pat.
Thomas de Norment', pres. by the prior of St. James [Derby]
Thomas de Hethull', pres. by Roger de Lemyngton

John de Longedon, t. pat.
Thomas de Draycot, pres. by Sir Thomas de Garsale
Robert de Alrespath, pres. by Walter de Morcot'
Thomas de Lappeleye, t. pat.
Thomas de Schepeye, pres. by Fr. Richard de Pavele of the hospital of St. John of Jerusalem
Roger de Mees, pres. by Vivian de Staundon
Thomas de Whytemor', t. pat.
Richard Brayn, t. pat.
John de Wappynbur', pres. by Sir Robert Napton
John de Caldecot', pres. by Peter de Tewe
Philip de Lemynton, pres. by Nicholas de Dunchirch
John de Crofton, t. pat.
William de Selburn, t. pat.
Robert Horn, t. pat.
William Telle, pres. by Andrew de Braundon
Robert Couper of Uttoxeter, pres. by the abbot of Rocester
William de Sapyrton, t. pat.
Roger de Sapyrton, pres. by John de Kyngesley
Geoffrey de Denston', pres. by Robert de Bekden'
John Fraunceys of Rolleston, pres. by the prior of Wombridge
Geoffrey de Merston, pres. by John le Palmere, patron of Frankton ch.
Robert Dawe, t. pat.
Adam Gunne of Eccleshall, pres. by Ellis de Burgton'
Thomas de Omkyrdon', t. pat.
Hugh de Allesleye, pres. by John of the same [Allesley]
John Bernard of 'Clifton', pres. by John Rivel
William de Geydon', t. pat.
Simon de Kyrkalom, pres. by the abbot of Dale
William de Woford, pres. by William de Wyrley
Nicholas de Teynton, pres. by Roger de Pacwode
Osbert de Wythybrok', pres. by the abbot of St. Mary de Pratis, Leicester

[Fo. 138v] *Subdeacons*[3]

John de Clenefeld, t. pat., dim. dioc. Worcester
Henry de Astebur', pres. by William de Astebur'
John called Coterel, pres. by the prior of Kenilworth
Stephen de Egebaston, t. pat.
Richard de Derset, t. pat.
John le Warner of 'Morton', pres. by Thomas de Morton
William de Lalleford, pres. by Robert, lord of Church Lawford
John, son of Warin, pres. by the abbot and conv. of Combermere
Thomas de Derset, t. pat.
William de Pountfrayt, pres. by Walter Charnel'
Thomas de Wyleby, t. pat.
John de Ichynton, t. pat.
Henry de Vescy, pres. by William de Sutton
Richard de Roddesleye, pres. by Nicholas de Marchynton

John de Parva Overa, pres. by the prior and conv. of Launde
Ralph de Wengham, pres. by Sir Simon de Mancestr'
M. John de Bradelegh', t. pat.
John Folk' of 'Stretton', pres. by Sir Thomas de Garsale
Henry de Camera, pres. by Robert de Cotes
John de Bylneye, pres. by Robert de Duston
Hugh de Querndon, pres. by Sir Philip de Somervyll'
John de Brochurst, pres. by John Gautrou of Packington

Religious subdeacons[4]

John de Sutham, Richard de Dymesdale, [monks] of Coventry
William de Brokebur', OSA Warrington
Thomas de Blaby, Osbert de Leycestr', Nicholas de Dunstapul, OFM

Deacons[5]

Nicholas de Swynnerton, r. Mucklestone
John de Denston', t. pat.
John de Roucestr', pres. by the abbot of Rocester
Geoffrey Coleman, t. pat.
Ralph de Kyrkeby, pres. by John le Chalener of Co[6]ventry[6]
Richard de Longenolre, r. Little Ness
Henry ad Crucem of Coventry, t. pat.
Adam de Stretton, pres. by John Palmer' of Frank[7]ton[7]
John de Cruce Lapidea of London, pres. by Thomas de Wappynber', dim.
Thomas de Barton, pres. by Sir Walter Mont[8]gomery[8]
John Haddon of Morton, pres. by Thomas, lord of Morton
Roger de Normenton, pres. by the prior of St. James' [hospital], Derby
John de Croulesmere, pres. by the community of Ellesmere
Robert, son of Robert the goldsmith of Bridgnorth, pres. by brethren of Holy Trinity hospital [Bridgnorth] by the bishop's licence
Thomas Horn of Rugby, t. pat.
Robert March' of Newbold, pres. by Sir Philip de Somervill'
Henry de Tunstall, t. 4 marks
Peter de Braunston, pres. by Simon Poger
William called Ster of Repton, pres. by the prior and canons of Church Gresley
Stephen de Stocton, dim. of the official of Lincoln mentioning t. of house of Owston

[Col. 2]

William, son of Henry the baker of Newport, pres. by John Randulf
Henry de Hull' of Sheldon, t. pat.
Richard de Westhalum, pres. by Sir John de Somervill'
Richard, son of William de Aleby, t. pat.
Robert de Byleneye, t. pat.
John le Swen of Kenilworth, pres. by John Bonhome
John, son of Robert de Bosco, pres. by the prior and conv. of Selby

Richard de Stretton, t. pat.
Thomas de Wykeford, pres. by the hospital [of St. John] of Jerusalem
Richard de Radeford, pres. by Hugh de Copston
Ralph de Wygeford, pres. by the prior and conv. of Canwell
Adam de Wermynton, dim. of the official of Lincoln, t. Desford ch. dioc. Lincoln
Richard de Byrmyngham, pres. by William de Neuport
Philip de Multon, t. pat.
William de Wotton, pres. by Geoffrey, master of St. John's hospital, Warwick
Thomas le Heyr of 'Morton', t. pat.
Walter de Marchynton, pres. by Sir Walter de Montgomery
Ellis de Wotton, pres. by John de Wusthun
Robert de Tybeschulf, t. pat.
Thomas de Preston, t. pat.
Richard de Mokeslowe, t. pat.
William de Breideston, pres. by William de Breideston
Richard le fitz Huwe of Bostock, t. pat.
Henry de Thurleston' of Derby, pres. by the abbot and conv. of Dale
Thomas Someryld of Corsham, dim. dioc. Salisbury, pres. by the house of Tickford, dioc. Lincoln
Henry de Wytemor', t. pat.
John, son of Roger Swan of 'Wigston', dim. dioc. Lincoln, t. pat.
Richard de Merston, pres. by Sir Robert de Napton
Robert de Gloucestr' of Coventry, pres. by Robert de Stok'

Religious deacons[9]

Fr. Walter de Wynnesbur'
Fr. Roger de Homfreiston
Fr. Henry de Aston
Fr. Thomas de Opton
Fr. John de Sutham
Fr. John de Knithcot'
Fr. Henry de Murivall
Henry, monk of Coventry
Fr. Robert de Notyngham
Fr. Bartholomew de Lude
Fr. John de Longebrug'

Priests[10]

Thomas de Turvill', r. moiety of Malpas
John de Derb', r. 'Whittington'
Robert, r. Albrighton
John le Parker of Runcorn, pres. by the abbot and conv. of Croxden

[Fo. 139[11]] *Priests*

William de Capella of Ashbourne, pres. by Sir Nicholas de Marchynton
Henry Antolot, t. pat.

Robert Mayler of Manchester, pres. by Robert de Asshton
William Toft, pres. by Sir Thomas de Garsale
Roger Eunok of Avon Dassett, t. pat.
Stephen de Slymdon, pres. by John, lord of Bromley Bagot
John de Burtynbur', pres. by Robert de Verdon
Richard de Weston of Rugby, t. pat.
William de Derlaston, t. pat.
Roger Dobyn[12] of 'Darlaston', t. annual pension
Geoffrey de Wolveye, pres. by John de Schirford
Richard Fulchawe, t. pat. and pres. by John de Moston
William Andr' of Stretton on Dunsmore, pres. by John Palmer'
Richard Frost, t. pat.
Nicholas de Asshburn, pres. by Roger de Acovere
William de Picheford, pres. by Thurstan of the same [Pitchford]
John de Ideshal', pres. by John de Styvinton
William Dagenel of Bridgnorth, t. pat. by the lord bishop's special grace
Thomas de Wilmeslowe, t. pat.
William de Tameworth, pres. by Richard de Smethewyk
Hugh de Dyngele, r. Farndon, dim. of the official of Lincoln, *sede vacante*
William le Machon of Chesterfield, pres. by Sir Ralph de Brayleford
Simon de Repyndon, t. pat.
Roger Bonhay, t. pat.
Adam de Hulton, pres. by Robert Schepeye
William de Weston, t. pat.
Hugh, son of Alan de Dukemanton, pres. by Geoffrey de Dethek
Geoffrey de Maperley, pres. by the abbot and conv. of Dale
Simon de Knystcote, t. pat.[13]
Richard de Hatton, t. pat.
William de Ilkeston, pres. by the abbot and conv. of Dale
Robert atte Stile, pres. by Geoffrey de Hullewotton
Geoffrey de Lucy, r. High Bickington, dim. dioc. Exeter
William de Wolveye, pres. by Lady Alice de Wolveye
William le Parker, t. pat.
William Curtoys of Repton, t. pat.
William, son of Roger the carpenter of 'Broughton', pres. by r. Longford
Peter, son of William atte Nore of Chillington, pres. by Peter Giffard
William de Baskervile, t. pat.
John de Grenebergh, pres. by Thomas de Garsale

[Fo. 139v] *Priests*

Alan de Stretton, pres. by Sir Robert de Verdon
Robert de Dodyngton, t. pat.
Adam de Bascot', pres. by Simon de Mamcestr'
Alexander de Bradeleye, pres. by Richard de Bylynton
Henry de Uttokeshather, t. pat.
Walter de Hykelyng, pres. by John de la Corner'
John de Wykyngschul', t. pat.
William de Rokeby, t. pat.

John le Matheu, t. pat.

Religious priests[14]

John de Insula, Robert de Bromhale, OSA
Nicholas de Ferndon, [monk] of Combermere
William de Dunstaple, monk of Coventry
John de Ayleston, OFM
Fr. Roger de Wolverton, of Shrewsbury
John de Deivile, [canon] of Kenilworth

　[1-1] At the foot of col. 1.
　[2] Underlined.
　[3] Underlined.
　[4] Underlined and at the right-hand side of the next name.
　[5] Underlined.
　[6-6] Interlined.
　[7-7] Interlined.
　[8-8] Interlined.
　[9] At the right-hand side of the following names and linked by a wavy line.
　[10] Underlined.
　[11] This fo. is 8cm. wide.
　[12] *n* interlined.
　[13] Marked by a cross within a circle at the right-hand side.
　[14] Underlined and marginated.]

1327 ORDINES CELEBRATI DIE SABBATI QUATUOR TEMPORUM MENSIS SEPTEMBRIS ANNO DOMINI .M°. CCC^mo.XX°. IN ECCLESIA CONVENTUALI DE DERLEY A DOMINO .W[ALTERO]. DEI GRACIA COVENTR' ET LICH' EPISCOPO IN QUIBUS ERAT SENTENCIA LATA SUB FORMA SUPERIUS CONTENTA[1] [20 September 1320].

Subdeacons

Richard, son of William de Staveley, pres. by the abbot and conv. of Dale
Richard Truttok', t. pat.
Roger de Berley, t. annual pension from M. Adam de Berley
Richard de Braydeston, t. 40 shillings from William de Braydeston
William, son of William Michel 'de Wyco', t. pat.
John de Hurleye, pres. by Matthew de Hurleye
Roger Fitzherbert, r. Norbury
Simon de Blyth of Shustoke, pres. by M. Richard de Coleshull
John de Grendon, pres. by Thomas Meverel
Robert de Kersyngton, pres. by the abbot of Dale
Richard de Audeleye, pres. by Walter Wyther
Nicholas de Vescy, t. pat.
John, r. Heanor
William de Asshburn, pres. by Henry de Hambur'
William de Repyndon, pres. by the prior of Church Gresley
Richard Bygge of Stamford Bridge, dim. dioc. York, pres. by the prior and conv. of Ulverscroft

Thomas de Stanl', pres. by John de Somervill'
William de Statton, pres. by Sir Thomas Pleyaumbe
William de Aylvaston, pres. by Robert de Broml'
William de Astleye, pres. by Robert de Bromley'
Peter de Ambaston, t. pat.

[Fo. 140 col. 1]

Robert de Barewe, pres. by the prior of the hospital of St. John
William, son of William le Barkere, pres. by John de la Cornere
Robert ad Fontem, t. pat.
Richard de Lyllyngton, pres. by Sir Walter de Montgomery
Richard Fremon, pres. by Richard de Herchull
[2]Henry de Okebrok', pres. by Thomas Cheveteyn[2]
Thomas de Mora, t. pat.
John de Holbel', t. pat.
William de Barleburgh, t. pat.
Stephen en le Lene [3]of Bishops Tachbrook,[3] t. pat.
Simon de Westhalum, pres. by the abbot of Dale
Adam de Weston,[4] t. pat.
Robert de Alferton, pres. by the religious of Beauchief
Henry le Yepe of Ashbourne, pres. by Sir Henry de Bradeburn, kt.
Richard de Kembriston, pres. by Roger Careles
William de Housyndon, t. pat.
Michael Tyvel, t. pat.
Robert ad Fontem of Mackworth

Deacons[5]

Stephen de Egebaston, t. pat.
William Burwes, t. Richard Meignel of Derby
William de Sapurton, pres. by John de Sapurton
Thomas Wilcok of 'Over', pres. by John de la Corner' of Derby
Thomas de Coten, t. pat.
Roger de Sapurton, pres. by John de Kyngesl'
John de Parva Overa, pres. by the prior of St. James' [hospital], Derby
William de Benteley, t. pat.
Simon de Kyrkhalum, pres. by the abbot of Dale
Hugh de Griseley, pres. by the prior of Church Gresley
John de Clenefeld, t. pat., dim. dioc. Winchester
Peter Scot of Risley, pres. by Roger de Wodehall
William de Geydon, t. pat.
John called Coterel, pres. by the prior of Coventry
Thomas de Okebrok', pres. by the master of St. Helen's [hospital], Derby
Roger Turkel, pres. by Sir Walter de Montgomery
Roger de Hynestok', pres. by Sir John de Chetewynde
John de Knistelegh, pres. by Sir Fulk de Penebrig'
Robert le Couper of[6] Uttoxeter, pres. by Sir Thomas de[6] Furneval
Stephen de Overa,[6] pres. by the prior of St. John of Jerusalem

[Col. 2]

William, son of William de Barkeye, pres. by John del Corner'
William Persey of Morley, pres. by the abbot and conv. of Dale
John de Hyrna, t. pat.
William Pountfrett of 'Harborough', t. pat.
Walter de Thorp' Constant', t. pat.
Nicholas de Teynton, pres. by Roger de Pacworth
Geoffrey de Denston', pres. by Adam de Wetenhale
Henry le Vescy of Arbury, t. pat.
Adam de Eyton, pres. by John de Brynton, lord of 'Eyton'
William de Constantyn, t. pat.
Robert de Derb', pres. by the prior of St. James' [hospital], Derby
Thomas de Lappeley, t. pat.
Simon de Kyrkalum, t. pat.
Thomas de Wyliby, pres. by the prior of Thelsford
Henry de Astebur', t. pat.
Thomas de Staunton, t. pat.
Thomas de Emkerdon', pres. by Sir Robert de Knistele
[Roger][7] de Mees, pres. by Robert de Cotes
John de Crofton, t. pat.
John de Bradelegh', t. pension of 4½ marks from Sir Walter de Hugford
Henry de Okebrok', pres. by Thomas Cheveteyn
Adam Gunne, pres. by Ellis de Burhton'
Henry de Camera, pres. by Robert de Cotes
William de Wyford, t. pat.
Henry Merewys, t. pat.
Peter de Erbaston, t. pat.
William de Aston, Robert de Stalynton, canons of Darley
Robert de Stalynton, monk of Coventry
Fr. John de Boseworth, of Lilleshall
Fr. William de Aston

Priests[8]

Richard de Mocleslowe of Birmingham, t. pat.
John de Overton Madok', t. pat.
Henry, son of Nicholas de Wyrley, pres. by John de Cotys
Thomas de Barton, t. pat.
John Swon of Kenilworth, t. John Comyn
Ralph le Teyntor of Ashbourne, t. pat.
William de Breydeston, pres. by William de Breydeston
William de Boulton, t. pat.
William de Repyndon, pres. by the prior and conv. of Church Gresley
John de Roucestr', pres. by Walter de Montgomery
John de Croulesmere, t. pat.
John Swan of 'Wigston', dim. [9]dioc. Lincoln,[9] t. pat.
William de Wodeburgh of Derby, pres. by the master of St. Helen's [hospital], Derby

Robert de Chersale, t. the provision of the abbot of Haughmond
Nicholas, r. Mucklestone
Robert de Tybeschulf, t. pat.

[Fo. 140v col. 1]

Walter de Cougton', pres. by v. High Ercall
Robert, son of the goldsmith of Bridgnorth, t. pat.
John Lye, pres. by Nicholas de Hungerford
Robert Thorald, t. pat.
Richard de Westhalum, pres. by Philip de Somervill'
Robert Thorald of Melbourne, t. pat.
Henry de Tunstal, pres. by Roger de Bedulf'
Robert de Uttokeshather, pres. by Sir William de Stafford
Thomas le Heyr of 'Morton', pres. by the prior of Wombridge
John de Bosco, t. pat.
Henry de Swypston, dim. dioc. Lincoln, t. house of Berden
William de Langel', t. pat.
Peter Pecok of Tutbury, pres. by William de Neuton
Richard de Aleby, t. pat.
Henry Wych', t. pat.
Hugh de Irton, OFM
Henry de Neuport, canon of Trentham
Henry de Neuport
   [[1] See **1313**, **1321**, **1324**.
   2–2 Deleted and re-registered below under deacons.
   3–3 Interlined.
   4 Over an erasure.
   5 Underlined.
   6–6 These names have been written around a 1.5cm. hole at these points.
   7 MS. *Robert*
   8 Underlined.
   9–9 Interlined.]

1328 [1]ORDINES CELEBRATI IN ECCLESIA COLLEGIALI DE GNOUSALE PER .W[ALTERUM]. COVENTR' ET LYCH' EPISCOPUM DIE SABBATI QUATUOR TEMPORUM MENSIS DECEMBRIS ANNO DOMINI MILLESIMO TRECENTESIMO VICESIMO IN QUIBUS FUIT SENTENCIA LATA MODO QUO PATET IN ORDINIBUS SUPRASCRIPTIS [20 December 1320].
In Dei nomine, Amen, etc.[1]

Subdeacons

Robert de Wednesleye, r. Norton in Hales
Robert, son of Gervase de Codynton, t. pat.
William de Kyrkeby, pres. by Alan de Neunham
John de Baxterle, pres. by the abbot and conv. of Merevale
William Husse of 'Eyton', pres. by William Pouger
Hugh le Myr', t. pat.
Henry de la Scholle of Edgbaston, pres. by Sir William de Byrmyngham

Richard de Lemynton, pres. by John de Barre
Osbert de Tameworth, pres. by William de Stafford, kt.
William Crey of 'Cumton', t. pat.
Adam de Penberton, t. pat.
William de Allispath, pres. by Thomas Boydyn
Ralph de Essex of Leominster, dim. dioc. Hereford to all [orders], t. pat.

[Col. 2]

Robert le Bowyare of Lichfield, pres. by Sir William de Staf'
Henry de Mamcestr', pres. by John de Hulton
William, r. Stockton
Thomas Reyner of Shrewsbury, t. pat.
John Muriel of 'Norton', pres. by Sir William de Soneford
William de Ketevesden, t. pat.
Ralph, r. Mobberley
Henry de Merston, t. pat.
Thomas Deu of Gaydon, t. pat.
Richard, s. Henry the smith of 'Newbold', t. pat.
Henry de Drayton, pres. by the abbot ²and conv.² of Combermere
Robert de Marchomley, t. pat.
Hamond, son of Roger de Ercalewe, pres. by William de Prayers
Henry de Neuton, pres. by Sir Richard Herchull, kt.
John Gilbert of Audlem, t. pat.
Robert de Ansti, pres. by Robert, lord of Church Lawford
Thomas de Trentham, t. pat.
Thomas, s. the carpenter of Middlewich, t. pat.
Ralph de Wynwesleye, pres. by Nicholas de Hynwordeby
Robert de Louȝteborgh of 'Denton', pres. by Thomas de Louhteburgh
John the clerk of Stone, pres. by Vivian le Verdon
William de Cherlton, pres. by Vivian de Standon
Adam de Borouton, pres. by Philip, lord of 'Lutton'
Richard de Handesacr', t. pat.
William, s. William the apparitor of Sedgley, t. pat.
Philip de Brocton, t. John de Maveysyn
Gilbert le Faukener, pres. by Robert de Asshton
John de Daliley, pres. by William Hamund of Sedgley
John de Mere, t. pat.

*Religious subdeacons*³

Fr. John de Mortimer
Fr. Peter Blound
Fr. Simon de Sybbesdon
Fr. Thomas de Clive
Fr. Thomas de Hyde
Fr. Richard de Accindona
Fr. William de Ichynton

Deacons

Roger, r. Norbury
John Fraunceys of Rolleston, pres. by Sir William de Ercalewe
Richard de Breideston,[4] pres. by Sir William de Breideston

[Fo. 141 col. 1] *Deacons*

John Bernard, pres. by John Rivel
John de Longedon, t. pat.
John de Allerschawe, pres. by Adam de Rugele
Richard de Dersett, t. pat.
William de Bachekewell of Chester, t. pat.
William Brian of 'Haughton', t. pat.
Thomas de Draycot, pres. by Thomas de Garsale
Hugh de Allesley, pres. by Robert de Stoke
John le Wariner of Hillmorton, pres. by Thomas de Asteleye
William de Asshele, pres. by Roger de Levynton
John de Hurley, t. pat.
Robert de Barewe, t. pat.
Richard de Mamcestr', pres. by Sir Roger de Pilkynton, kt.
John de Walton, t. pat.
Thomas de Mere, pres. by William de Mere, kt.
John de Hethull', pres. by John Strange
Nicholas Vescy of Arbury, pres. by Walter Chaynel
Robert de Sekyndon, t. pat.
Hugh Lumbard of Newport, pres. by Adam de Neuport
Robert de Allespathes, pres. by Walter de Morcotes
William Telle of 'Kyrkeby', pres. by Roger Bulur of Brockhurst
Walter de Wareton, pres. by Richard de Herchull, kt.
Richard de Neuport, pres. by John Strange of Cheswardine
Richard Bygge of Stamford Bridge [dim. dioc. York], pres. by the prior of Ulverscroft
Richard Brayn, t. pat.
John Folk', pres. by Robert de Garsale
Stephen in le Lene of Bishops Tachbrook, t. pat.
Simon de Blye, pres. by M. Richard de Coleshull
Richard de Roddesleye, pres. by Sir Henry de Bradeburn
William de Housedon, pres. by Thomas de Perewych
Roger de Berley, pres. by Richard de Blythefeld
Hugh de Cornhull, pres. by Henry de Eyton
Richard de Kemberton, pres. by Roger Karles
Thomas de Whytemor', t. pat.

[Col. 2]

William de Repyndon, pres. by the prior and conv. of Repton

Religious[5]

Fr. John de Stone
Fr. Robert de Hugford
Fr. Henry de Wych'
Fr. William Syu
Fr. Ankerus de Woveye
Fr. John de Acr'
[6]Fr. John de Tydesworth[6]
John de Grendon, pres. by Thomas Meverel

Priests

Thomas de Preston, pres. by Roger Banastr'
William de Geydon, t. pat.
Roger de Hynestok', pres. by Sir John de Chetewynde
Robert Bylneye of Rugby, t. pat.
William Pountfrett of 'Harborough', pres. by Walter Chaynel, lord of 'Thorpe'
Thomas de Emkerdon', pres. by Robert, lord of Knightley
Thomas de Wyleby, pres. by the house of Thelsford
John de Knistelegh, pres. by Roger de Knistelegh
Thomas de Coten, t. pat.
William the baker of Newport, t. pat.
Adam Gunne of Eccleshall, pres. by Ellis, lord of 'Broughton'
Robert le Coupere of Uttoxeter, pres. by Sir Thomas de Furnival
John Hyrne, t. pat.
Thomas Horn of Rugby, t. pat.
John de Crofton, t. pat.
William, r. Stone, dim. of M. John de Harynton,[7] dioc. Lincoln *sede vacante*
John de Parva Overa, pres. by the prior of St. James' [hospital], Derby
William de Sapurton, pres. by John de Sapurton
Hugh de Greselegh, pres. by the prior and conv. of Church Gresley
Peter de Braunston, pres. by Simon Pouger
John called Coterel, t. a pension which he has against the house of Kenilworth
John de Clenefeld, v. Hampton in Arden
John Haddon of Morton, pres. by Thomas de Astele, lord of Morton
Henry ad Crucem of Coventry, t. pat.
John de Denston', pres. by Robert le Verney
Roger de Sapurton, pres. by John de Kyngesle

[Fo. 141v col. 1]

M. John de Bradelegh', t. a pension of 4 marks from Sir Walter de Hugeford to be
taken from the manor of Lapley
William de Weford, t. pat.
Henry de Scheldon, pres. by Lady Ida de Clynton, lady of Maxstoke
Walter de Thorp', pres. by John de Notyngham
Roger de Kynewaston, t. pat.
Adam de Eyton, t. pat.

Robert de Belton, dim. dioc. Lincoln, t. house of Launde
Thomas de Lappeleye, t. pat.
Fr. Nicholas de Thorp'
Edmund de Grafton, Robert Abel, Thomas de Stonley, Andrew de Assheburn, William de Ashton, OFM
John Erveys, [canon] of Kenilworth
John de Mouselowe, Simon de Poywyk, [canons] of Haughmond
William de Gresele, [canon] of Rocester

[1–1 In col. 1. Unfinished, see **1313**, **1321**, **1324**.
2–2 Interlined.
3 At the right-hand side of the following seven names and linked by a wavy line.
4 This name has been written around a hole at this point, see **1327** n. 6–6.
5 At the right-hand side of the following seven names and linked by a wavy line. The last deacon listed, John de Grendon, is a secular clerk.
6–6 Over an erasure.
7 Official of Lincoln dioc. *sede vacante*: Lincoln Cathedral Archives Dij.64.1.16–17, 19–20. For his career see K. Edwards, *The English secular cathedrals in the Middle Ages* (Manchester, 1949), 332–40. I wish to thank Dr Nicholas Bennett for this reference.]

1329 [1]ORDINES CELEBRATI IN ECCLESIA CATHEDRALI LICH' DIE SABBATI IN VIGILIA PASCHE ANNO DOMINI .M°.CCC° .VICESIMO PRIMO. PER .W[ALTERUM]. DEI GRACIA EPISCOPUM COVENTR' ET LICH'[1] [18 April 1321].

Subdeacons[2]

William de Aston, r. Ridware Mavesyn
John de Pyrie, r. Aylestone, dim. dioc. Lincoln
Roger de Scheffeld, r. Ruyton
Ralph de Wappenbur' t. Thomas, lord of Wappenbury
William Bataille, pres. by the abbot and conv. of Merevale
Henry de Barton, t. pat.
Adam de Heywod', pres. by John de Werleye
Henry de Russyngton, t. pat.
Fr. Nicholas de Bromleye, religious

Deacons[3]

[4]John Gilbert of 'Ectlesch'', t. pat.[4]

[The rest of the fo. is blank and the ordination list is unfinished.
1–1 In col. 1.
2 Underlined.
3 Underlined.
4–4 Added by the same hand that wrote list **1328**.]

[Fo. 142 measures approximately 19cm. wide and 8.5cm. long. Fo. 142r blank.]

1330 [Fo. 142v] [1]Boniface VIII to the master, priors and all the friars of the Dominican order.[1] Because the friars of the same order are frequently sent from place to place of the same order, because of which there is no specified and permanent house from houses of the same order, also because you cause good, suitable and worthy friars among you to be promoted to holy orders, it shall be lawful for you to present the friars of the same order to be ordained by any Catholic bishops you shall choose who have the communion and grace of the Apostolic See, and to promote to holy orders the friars presented by you to the same bishops without any examination to be made by those bishops, and without any promise or pledge of the friars to be ordained.

[The rest of the fo. is blank.

A hand drawn in the left-hand margin, with nota written at the finger tip, points to this entry. Printed in *Bullarium ordinis FF. praedicatorum sub auspiciis SS.D.N.D. Benedicti XIII, pontificis maximi, ejusdem ordinis, opera reverendissimi patris F. Thomae Ripoll, magistri generalis, editum, et ad autographam fidem recognitum, variis appendicibus, notis, differationibus, ac tractatu de consensu bullarum, illustratum a P.F. Antonino Bremond, S.T.M., provinciae Tolosanae ordinis memorati alumno. Tomus primus ab anno 1215 ad 1280* (Rome, 1729), 349. I wish to thank Professor Bernard Hamilton for this reference.

1–1 Underlined.]

APPENDIX A

Full original texts of entries marked with asterisks in Volume I

Additional information supplied in notes is not repeated here, where any notes concern textual issues.

63

[Fo. 3] LITTERA DIRECTA ARCHIDIACONO CANT'. Viro provido et discreto domino .. Cantuar' archidiacono aut ipsius locum tenenti .W[alterus]. divina permissione Coventr' et Lich' episcopus salutem et sincere dilectionis amplexum. Quia die dominica proxima post festum circumcisionis Domini proximo jam venturum apud Coventr' ac die dominica proxima postea tunc sequente apud Lich' intronicari disponimus domino concedente, vos premuniendo requirimus et rogamus quatinus prefate intronicacioni nostre ad dies et loca predicta intersitis officium vestrum quod in hac parte ad vos pertinet impleturi et facturi prout hactenus consuevit fieri circa ista. Et ne de negligencia nuncii presencium portitoris hesitare possimus de die recepcionis istarum nobis si placeat rescribatis. Dat' Ebor' .xv. kalendas Decembris consecracionis nostre anno .ij°.

68

[Fo. 3v] OBLIGACIO FACTA ADE DE AILLESBUR'. [1]...[2] MESSUAGIO IN WIRKESWORTH ET ALIBI IN COMITATU DERBIE[1]. Omnibus Christi fidelibus ad quos presentes littere pervenerint .W[alterus]. permissione divina Coventren' et Lych' episcopus ac Robertus Peverel miles germanus suus salutem in Domino. Noveritis nos ambos et alterum nostrum per se teneri Ade Baldewyne de Aillesbur' in ducentis et viginti libris pro quodam mesuagio quod idem Adam nobis dedit in Wirkesworth in Pecco et pro quibusdam terris quas idem Adam nobis dedit in eadem villa et alibi in comitatu Derbeye prout carta ipsius Ade nobis inde confecta purportat, et tenemur solvere dicto Ade predictas ducentas et viginti libras citra festum Pentecostes proximo venturum ad voluntatem ejusdem Ade ubi et quando eidem Ade placuerit, ita tamen quod non ad puros sterlingos sed ad ordinariam monetam que jam currit eidem volumus obligari quocumque tempore sive ante Pentecosten sive post peccuniam[3] predictam solvi contigat. Tenemur eciam dare predicto Ade annis singulis dum vixerit unam robam in festo natalis Domini de secta armigerorum nostrorum, ad quam quidem solucionem et predicte robe annuam presentacionem nos et heredes nostros obligamus et omnia bona nostra habita pariter et habenda, renunciantes in hac parte omni juris presidio per quod predictarum ducentarum et viginti librarum solucio aut predicte robe annua donacio impediri valeat seu differri. In cujus rei testimonium sigilla nostra presentibus sunt appensa. Dat' Ebor' die jovis proxima[4] ante festum Sancti Petri in cathedra [5]anno regni regis Edwardi vicesimo septimo[5].

[1-1] In a later hand.
[2] One word illegible.
[3] Recte *pecuniam*
[4] Recte *proximo*
5-5 Underlined.]

69

[Fo. 3v]   ECCLESIA DE CONEDOVERE PRO MEDIETATE. W[alterus] permissione etc. officiali suo salutem, graciam et benedictionem. Cum Thomas de Charnes subdiaconus ad porcionem ecclesie de Conedovere nuper vacantem per .. abbatem et conventum Salop' veros ejusdem patronos nobis dudum fuerit presentatus nichilque canonicum admissionem ejusdem comperimus obviare, nisi quod Johannes de Shelton' occasione cujusdam provisionis sedis apostolice sibi per nos faciende eidem presentato nuper opponere se curavit; vobis mandamus quatinus cum de meritis ejusdem provisionis vobis constat ad plenum, si vobis constiterit oppositionem dicti Johannis virtute seu veritate carere, dictum Thomam ad porcionem dicte ecclesie admittatis et in corporalem possessionem ejusdem inducatis, salva nobis institucione in posterum sibi facienda, ad quas admissionem simplicem et inductionem si ipsam de jure videritis faciendam vices nostras vobis committimus cum canonice cohercionis potestate. Dat' Ebor' pridie kalendas Marcii consecracionis nostre anno tercio. Dictante R[adulpho] de Leyc'.

73

[Fo. 4]   PILAT. Religioso viro domino .. priori de Witeham Cartusien' ordinis amico nostro karissimo .W[alterus]. permissione divina Coventren' et Lich' episcopus salutem et in sinceris affectibus graciam salvatoris. Cum Jaconimus Pilat de Doaco mercator in quadam parte peccunie[1] pro lana quam de vobis habet vobis teneatur solvenda, atque dominus noster rex eidem Jaconimo in magna peccunie[2] quantitate astrictus quam eidem solvere pro domino nostro rege ad presens nequimus, vestram amiciciam requirimus et rogamus quatinus ob domini nostri regis reverenciam ac nostram pro eodem Jaconimo intervenientem instanciam eidem Jaconimo in solucione quam vobis facere debet, id favoris et gracie faciendi quod vobis exinde ad graciam astricti reddamur repensivam temporibus op[p]ortunis. In Christo feliciter valeatis. Dat' Ebor' .vj[to.] nonas Julii consecracionis nostre anno tercio.

Consimilis littera mittebatur abbati de Cleve pro eodem Jaconimo. Consimilis littera abbati de Boxlee pro eodem. Consimilis littera priori de Hemton' pro eodem. Consimilis littera abbati de Dunkewell pro Bernardo Pilat, et consimilis littera abbati de Bucfast pro eodem Bernardo.

[1] Recte *pecunie*
[2] Recte *pecunie*]

77

[Fo. 4]   Memorandum quod dominus scripsit per litteram suam clausam Thome de Charneles qui se gerit pro rectore medietatis ecclesie de Conedovere quod sit Ebor' ad eum in octaba Trinitatis super quibusdam negociis ipsum et statum suum contingentibus cum domino tractaturus. Et debet esse finis negocii quod provideatur Johanni de Shelton' cui de eodem die provideri debebat de annua pensione .xl. vel .xx.s. ad minus per abbatem Salop' conferenda [1]... et quod per eundem abbatem de illa alia exili ecclesia de qua jam dicto Johanni providetur Ricardo de ... per predictum abbatem provideatur ...[1]

[[1-1] Abraded.]

177

[Fo. 9] THORNTON'. Item anno Domini .M.°CCC.° primo die jovis in vigilia concepcionis Beate Marie Virginis apud Cestrefeld admissus fuit dominus Robertus de Askeby ad ecclesiam de Thornton' super Moram et institutus in eadem, presentatus ad ipsam per dominum regem ratione custodie[1] Petri filii et heredis Ranulphi le Ruter defuncti, qui de rege tenuit in capite, infra etatem et in custodia predicti domini regis tunc temporis existentis, per magistrum Thomam de Abberbur' tunc vicarium episcopi. Et sciendum quod dominus J[ohannes] de Drokenesford, habito consilio justiciariorum utriusque banci et baronum de scaccario, similiter J[ohannes] de Langeton' cancellarius, scripserunt per litteras suas in manu Johannis de Lang[eton] existentes dicto vicario quod pro vitando contemptu regis et filii regis, qui pro eo quod est comes Cestr' partem illam fovebat, et pro vitando dampno domini episcopi, absque omni difficultate admitteretur clericus antedictus. Et insuper habuit vicarius litteram domini regis clausam super eodem.

[[1] Underlined.]

183

[Fo. 9v]   ECCLESIA DE GROPPENHALE. Memorandum quod .vij. idus Octobris anno Domini .M°.CCC primo et consecracionis domini .. episcopi anno .v°. apud Acum institutus fuit magister Willelmus de Rodyerd in ecclesia de Groppenhale ad presentacionem prioris et conventus de Northon' archidiaconatus Cestr'. Et sciendum est quod idem Willelmus veniens personaliter apud Stepelaston' .xvj°. kalendas Januarii anno Domini .M°.CCC°. secundo et petiit de magistro Thoma de Abberbur' litteras dimissorias ad ordines presbiteratus, et qui pro eo quod annus fuit lapsus infra quem ordinari debuerat in presbiteratum litteram dimissoriam negavit eidem, et pro eo quod college sui non erant presentes, quorum presenciam pluries habere potuisset. Et ab ista denegacione idem magister Willelmus appellavit.

364

[Fo. 20]   Memorandum quod T[homas] de Eadburbur' de precepto episcopi liberavit Galhardo de Pursato et Johanni de Corbino nunciis pape de creacione ipsius de sigillo decem marcas, et postea domine Lucie ...[1] Devorcis .xl.s.

[[1] One word erased and illegible.]

408

[Fo. 22] [1]ECCLESIA DE PRESCOTT.[1] W[alterus] etc. dilecto filio magistro .A[lano]. de Britonii thesaurario ecclesie nostre Lich' salutem graciam et benedictionem. Litteram felicis recordacionis .R[ogeri]. quondam predecessoris nostri de commenda ecclesie de Prestecote nostre diocesis tibi facta non viciatam in aliqua sui parte inspeximus continencie infrascripte. R[ogerus] Dei gracia Coventr' et Lich' episcopus dilecto in Christo filio magistro Alano dicto Britoni rectori ecclesie de Codinton' salutem graciam et benedictionem. Labores pensantes multiplices quos non absque corporis gravi periculo subiisti pro nobis et ecclesia antedictis, utilitatem necnon attendentes ecclesie de Prestecote si tua sub defensione consisteret, cujus ordinacio collacioque nos hac vice contingere dinoscuntur, eandem ecclesiam de Prestecote tibi auctoritate presencium tuo perpetuo commendamus. In cujus rei testimonium ac eciam fidem plenam impressio sigilli nostri presentibus est appensa. Dat' Brewodie .ij. idus Aprilis anno gratie .M°.CC°.lx°vi°. Attendentes siquidem jura ac libertates ipsius ecclesie per quorumdam forsan predecessorum tuorum negligenciam in plerisque collapsa, bona ejusdem ecclesie indebite alienata ac statum ejusdem ecclesie reformacionis presidio in pluribus indigere, prefatam commendam de prefata ecclesia tibi factam ita demum ratificamus, continuantes eandam dumtamen collapsa reducere alienata revocare ac statum ipsius ecclesie in hiis in quibus lesa [fo. 22v] noscitur reformari studiose procures, ita quod in concessa tibi gracia ipsius ecclesie utilitas evidenter clarescatur et ejusdem necessitas in liberalitate respiret graciam concendentis. In cujus rei testimonium sigillum nostrum fecimus hiis appendi.[2] Dat' Lich' .v. kalendas Marcii anno Domini .M°.CC°. nonagesimo nono.

[[1–1] In a later hand.
[2] Recte *appendum*]

470

[Fo. 24v] [1]ABSOLUCIO ARCHIEPISCOPI CANT' AB EXCOMMUNICACIONE CONTRACTA IN JUDICIO ROMANO[1] In nomine Domini amen. Hoc est exemplum cujusdam rescripti apostolici bulla plumbea et filo canabi more curia Romane bullati non in aliqua sui parte viciati cujus tenor talis est. Bonifacius episcopus servus servorum Dei venerabilibus fratribus Sar' et Lond' ac Linc' episcopis salutem et apostolicam benedictionem. In causa appellacionis et negocii principalis que inter venerabilem fratrem nostrum .R[obertum]. archiepiscopum Cant' et magistrum Rodulphum de Mallingges, qui se dicit rectorem ecclesie de Pageham Cicestren' diocesis, ex parte una et Theobaldum de Barroducis thesaurarium Ebor' ex altera, occasione dicte ecclesie de qua idem Theobaldus sibi auctoritate apostolica provisum fuisse proponit et quorumdam processuum per abbatem monasterii de Sancto Michaele Virdunen' diocesis asserentem se executorem ipsi Theobaldo super provisione hujusmodi deputatum contra ipsos archiepiscopum et Rodulphum habitorum vertitur, dilectum filium magistrum Onufrium de Trebis decanum Melden' capellanum nostrum nostrique palacii auditorem causarum concessimus partibus auditorem coram quo ex parte archiepiscopi et magistri predictorum, oblatis sub certa forma libellis et per magistrum Andream de Piperno procuratorem dicti Theobaldi nonnullis propositis excepcionibus, demum magistro Georgio de Interampne procuratore archiepiscopi et Rodulphi predictorum petente prefatos archiepiscopum et Rodulphum dominos suos et se pro eis prout super hoc habebat mandatum sufficiens ab eisdem, ad cautelam absolvi a quibusdam excommunicacionum, suspensionum et interdicti sentenciis, quas in eosdem archiepiscopum et Rodulphum dicebat per prefatum abbatem et quosdam subdelegatos ipsius post et contra appellaciones eorum ad sedem apostolicam interpositas promulgatas. Nos auditori commisimus memorato ut archiepiscopo et Rodulpho predictis de hujusmodi absolucionis beneficio ad cautelam prout suaderet justicia provideret, sic quod prefatus auditor visis appellacionibus et sentenciis supradictis consideratis omnibus que procuratores partium predictarum coram eo producere, exhibere, allegare et proponere voluerint facta, quod super hiis coauditoribus suis dicti pallacii relacione fideli de ipsorum consilio prefatis partium procuratoribus in ejus presencia constitutis hujusmodi peticioni dicti magistri Georgii tanquam juri consone annuens, eundem magistrum Georgium procuratorio nomine dictorum archiepiscopi et Rodulphi et per eum archiepiscopum et Rodolphum predictos juxta formam ecclesie ab eisdem sentenciis latis post et contra appellaciones coram eo exhibitas ad cautelam absolvit justicia exigente, prout in instrumento publico inde confecto dicti auditoris sigillo minuto plenius dicitur contineri. Nos itaque ipsorum archiepiscopi et Rodulphi supplicacionibus inclinati [2]fraternitati vestre[2] per apostolica scripta mandamus quatinus hujusmodi absolucionem ubi expedire videritis solempniter publicare curetis, quod si non omnes hiis exequendis potueritis interesse duo vestrum ea nichilominus exequantur. Dat' Lateran' .v. idus Februarii pontificati nostri anno octavo.

Et ego Hugo Hugonis de Musele clericus Linc' diocesis sacrosancte Romane ecclesie publicus auctoritate notarius ipsum rescriptum fideliter exemplavi, nichil addendo vel minuendo quod sensum mutet vel viciet intellectum presensque exemplum ad suum originale astultum et concors inventum meo signo et nomine roboravi rogatus.

[1–1] In a later hand.
[2–2] Recte *fraternitatibus vestris*]

471

[Fo. 24v]   [1]INSTRUMENTO ETC. PENDENTE[1]. In nomine Domini amen. Hoc est exemplum cujusdam rescripti apostolici vera bulla plumbea et filio canabi more curia Romane bullati non aboliti non cancellati nec in aliqua sui parte viciati cujus tenore talis est. Bonifacius episcopus servus servorum Dei venerabilibus fratribus Sar' et Linc' ac Lond' episcopis salutem et apostolicam benedictionem. In causa appellacionis et negocii principalis que inter venerabilem fratrem nostrum archiepiscopum Cant' et magistrum Radulphum de Mallingges clericum Cant' diocesis ex parte una et Theobaldum de Barroducis clericum ex altera super ecclesia de Pageham Cicestr' diocesis vertitur, dilectum filium magister Onufrium de Trebis decanum ecclesie de Melden' capellanum nostrum nostrique pallacii auditorem causarum concessimus partibus auditorem coram quo super libellis ex parte archiepiscopi et Radulphi predictorum oblatis inter magistrum Georgium de Interampne archiepiscopi et Radulphi ac magistrum Andream de Piperno Theobaldi predictorum procuratores lite legittime contestata de calumpnia ac de veritate dicenda prestitis juramentis, prefatus magister Georgius procuratorio nomine dictorum archiepiscopi et Radulphi auditore predicto cum instancia petiit parti alteri inhiberi ne causa hujusmodi coram eo pendente quicquid in eorum aut ipsius cause prejudicium attemptaret. Memoratus vero auditor attendens peticionem hujusmodi consonam esse juri volensque super hoc equalitatem servare, prefatis partium procuratoribus in ejus presencia constitutis et per eos dominos eorum predictis duxit [Fo. 25] districtius inhibendos, ne aliqua parcium predictarum quicquam in alterius aut cause predicte prejudicium vel ipsius auditoris jurisdictionis contemptum, causa sic pendente predicta innovent vel attemptent, prout in instrumento publico inde confecto dicti auditoris sigillo minuto plenius dicitur contineri. Quocirca ²fraternitati vestre² per apostolica scripta mandamus quatinus vos vel duo aut unus vestrum per vos vel alium seu alios inhibicionem hujusmodi ubi et quando expedire videritis solempniter publicetis. Dat' Lateran' .v. idus Februarii pontificati nostri anno octavo [as in **470**].

[¹⁻¹ In a later hand.
²⁻² Recte *fraternitatibus vestris*]

473

[Fo. 25]   .W[alterus]. permissione divina Coventr' et Lych' episcopus dilectis filiis magistris .G[alfrido]. de Blaston' commissario nostro generali ac .R[icardo]. archidiacono Salop' salutem, graciam et benedictionem. Cum per visitaciones diversas tam per nos quam per alios tam apostolica quam nostra auctoritate fungentes ¹in monasterio de Haumond'¹ nostre diocesis dudum factas studiose invenerimus quod licet fratres Johannes de Sar', Petrus de Sumerford, Ricardus de Peppelawe, Willelmus de Leghton', et Thomas de Bruges canonici monasterii memorati de Haumond' regularem habitum deferant, irregulariter tamen et inordinate viventes et in suis maliciis obstinati incorrigibiles penitus multipliciter se ostendunt. Quod quidem non sine amarissima cordis anxietate graviter perferentes, nec inordinatam eorum condicionem ulterius per connivenciam absque grandi periculo sustinere valentes, discrecioni vestre committimus et mandamus quatinus visis presentibus aliis singulis negociis intermissis ad prefatum monasterium de Haumond' personaliter accedentes, predictos fratres indisciplinatos et inordinatos videlicet fratrem Johannem de Sar' apud monasterium de Kenelword', Petrum de Sumerford apud Repyndon', Ricardum de Peppelawe apud Derle, Willelmum de Leghton' apud Stanes, et Thomam de Bruges apud Noghton' auctoritate nostra destinare curetis, eademque auctoritate locorum presidentibus vestra littera nomine nostro arcius injungatis ut fratres predictos obedienter admittant tamdiu in monasteriis suis secum tenendos donec de eisdem fratribus aliud duxerimus ordinando. Volumus quoque et idem locorum ipsorum presidentibus vestra littera designetis quod predictos fratres tractent sub tradicione et modo subscriptis. Nam volumus quod intersint horis debitis tam de die quam de nocte obsequiis divinis in ecclesia cum ceteris fratribus, sint ultimi tam in choro quam in refectorio pane cervisia debili et legumine dumtaxat contenti, singulis quartis et sextis feriis in pane et aqua tantummodo jejunantes, ecclesiam claustrum dormitorium ac refectorium horis debitis exerceant locis aliis eis interdictis omnimo. Quod si forsan per assuetam inobediencie et rebellionis notam contra ista vel aliquid de istis eorum aliquis venire presumpserit, volumus sic rebellem in loco securo in monasterio ad quod mittitur sub custodia arta reponi, et pane cum aqua duntaxat vesci, donec super hoc aliud per nos extiterit ordinatum.

Hec siquidem vobis committimus tam discrete quam eciam celeriter cum solicitudinis studio exequenda. In Christo feliciter valeatis rescripturi nobis quam cito commode[2] poteritis vestra patenti littera harum seriem continente id quod feceritis super istis. Dat' Lond' .x. kalendas Februarii consecracionis nostre anno nono.

[[1-1] Underlined.

[2] Interlined.]

476

[Fo. 25v] ECCLESIA CASTRI ALTI PECCI [1]DOTACIO ET ORDINACIO VICARIUS[2] DE CASTELTON' IN PECCO. CASTELTON'.[1] Universis sancte matris ecclesie filiis ad quos littere presentes pervenerint Thomas de Abberbur' canonicus Lich', venerabilis patris domini W[alteri] Dei gracia Coventr' et Lich' [3]ipso extra regnum in remotis agente[3] vicarius, salutem in auctore salutis. Cum religiosi viri abbas et conventus de Valle Regali ecclesiam parochialem Castri de Alto Pecco se in usus habere proprios pretendentes dominum Willelmum Notekyn presbiterum ad vicariam ipsius ecclesie per dominum nostrum episcopum canonice ordinandam eidem domino episcopo dudum duxerint presentandum, nos prefatus vicarius premissa inquisicione fideli super vero valore quarumcumque porcionum et obvencionum sigillatim et particulariter ipsius ecclesie tam per rectores et vicarios vicinos quam per viros fidedigniores per quos rei veritas melius sciri poterat et debebat, ejusdem ecclesie parochianios studiose ac diligenter facta, vocatis ut dicte inquisicioni interessent tam dictis religiosis quam omnibus aliis quorum interesse poterat. Et demum inquisicione ipsa sub sigillis eorum per quos facta fuit nobis reportata et relata et super ipsa plena deliberatione prehabita, vocatisque tam dictis religiosis quam prefato presbitero ad vicariam ipsius ecclesie per dominum nostrum episcopum canonice ordinandam per prefatos religiosos eidem domino presentato ut pronunciacioni diffinicioni ac ordinacioni nostre super dicta vicaria faciende certis die et loco interessent, pronunciacionem diffinicionem ac ordinacionem nostram audituri ac eciam recepturi. Considerato cujuscumque porcionis ipsius ecclesie si[n]gillatim valore, consideratis eciam oneribus que vicario et vicarie sue continue et semper incumbunt omnibusque aliis que in hac parte attendenda consistunt omni studio recensitis, vice et auctoritate prefati domini nostri episcopi ad ordinacionem dicte vicarie taliter duximus procedendum.

Pertinebit namque ad prefatos religiosos et eorum successores jure appropriacionis quod se habere pretendunt medietas mansi quod esse consueverat ipsius ecclesie rectoris, videlicet medietas mansi pro parte illa in qua orreum situatur cum utilitatibus et proficuis ejusdem medietatis. Percipient eciam iidem religiosos et eorum successores decimam bladi tocius parochie de terris nunc cultis, et decimam feni omnium parochianorum sine diminucione. Habebunt eciam mortuaria viva et decimam minere ac decimam pullanorum de haracio domini regis, una cum decima molendini aquatici domini regis.

Ordinamus quidem statuimus et diffinimus quod alia medietas mansi rectoris a predicta ad vicarium ecclesie parochialis Castri de Alto Pecco et ad omnes successores suos vicarios qui pro tempore erunt, pro eo quod in loco personaliter residere tenentur, imperpetuum pertinebit, una cum terra dominica et parco dominico ecclesie antedicte, decime vero agnorum, lane, lactis, alieque minute decime et obvenciones oblaciones[4] ac proventus quicumque predicte ecclesie, preter decimas et obvenciones predictis religiosis superius assignata, ad vicarium predictum et successores suos imperpetuum pertinebunt. Predictus vero vicarius et successores sui preter onus hospitalitatis excercende quam vicariorum residencia personalis requirit, quod quod[5] precipue in illis partibus in quibus ecclesia Castri situatur sumptuosum dinoscitur, cum licentes partes ille tenues et exiles vaste et silvestres fore noscaritur frequentes tamen ex consuetudine patrie residentibus occurrit hospitium confluencia onerosa; in primis prefate ecclesie Castri per se ipsos et per alios ministros idoneos honeste deservient et deserviri facient et nichilominus sinodalia archidiaconalia ac librorum vestimentorum et ornamentorum quorumcumque ipsius ecclesie ac universa quecumque onera ordinaria; salvo dumtaxat onere cancelli de novo construendi si forsan i[m]mineret necessitas quod onus ad predictos religiosos et eorum successores imperpetuum pertinebit subibunt et perpetuis temporibus sustinebunt. Extraordinaria vero onera ad dictos religiosos et eorum successores pro duabus partibus onerum hujusmodi extraordinariorum et ad vicarios pro tercia parte eorumdem extraordinariorum imperpetuum pertinebunt.

Reservamus quidem domino nostro episcopo ac successoribus suis episcopis[6] plenam potestatem augmentandi, minuendi, mutandi, corrigendi, declarandi, ac omnia alia faciendi que ad episcopalem[7] nostri pertinent et in[8] omnibus et singulis premissis et circa singula premissorum prout eis videbitur o[p]portunum, jure dignitate statu ac honere Coventr' et Lich' ecclesiarum ac domini nostri episcopi et successorum suorum in omnibus semper salvis. In cujus rei testimonium sigillum officii nostri presentibus est appensum. Dat' Lich' .viij. idus Aprilis anno Domini .M°.CCC^mo. secundo. Quibus die anno et loco supradicto institutus fuit predictus Willelmus Notekyn in dicta vicaria per dominum vicarium episcopi.

[1-1 In a later hand.]
2 Recte *vicarie*
3-3 Underlined.
4 Interlined.
5 Interlined.
6 Interlined.
7 Recte *episcopatum*
8 Interlined.]

519

[Fo. 28v]   SALOP[1], LILLESHULL. Item .ij. kalendas Marcii dominus Johannes de Chetewynd canonicus ecclesie de Lilleshull, per cessionem fratris Willelmi de Brugges pastoris solacio destitute vacantis, concorditer est electus. Et quamvis propter multiplices defectus et intolerabiles cassata erat electio de eo facta, volens tamen dominus domui prospicere ne per escaetores seu alios ruat vel detrimentum paciatur aliqualiter in hac parte, de eodem electo providit ecclesie memorate et ipsum prefecit in abbatem ex officio et pastorem. Actum Lich'.

[1 In a later hand.]

604

[Fo. 34] LICENCIA STUDENDI PRO RECTORE DE FILONGLE IN FORMA CONSTITUCIONIS NOVE. W[alterus] permissione divina Coventr' et Lich' episcopus dilecto filio Conrado Howeschilt de Alemannia rectori ecclesie de Filongelegh nostre diocesis salutem, graciam et benedictionem. Cum animum ad studendum habeas ut fructum o[p]portunum in Dei ecclesia afferas ut proponis et ratione florentis in te etatis ac alias ad studendum habilis videaris, nos tuis devotis supplicacionibus inclinati ut per unum annum a data presencium numerandum in loco solempni ubi studium viget generale litterarum studio insistere, et nichilominus fructus ecclesie tue predicte interim cum integritate percipere valeas, ac hujusmodi studio sit insistens ad ordines ulteriores preterquam ad subdiaconatus ordinem ad quem infra annum a tempore tibi commissi regiminis suscipiendum astringeris durante predicto termino percipiendos minime tenearis, tecum auctoritate constitucionis domini Bonifacii pape octavi super hoc edite dispensamus, ita tamen quod in ecclesia tua predicta medio tempore bonum et sufficientem vicarium pro animarum cura diligenter exerceatur in ea et eidem in divinis laudabiliter deserviatur juxta constitucionis ipsius tenorem habeas, cui quidem vicario de ipsius ecclesie proventibus necessaria ministrari volumus prout constitucio ipsa requirit. Salvis tam[en] nostro quam successoribus nostrorum ac Coventr' et Lich' ecclesiarum nostrarum juribus et consuetudinibus quibus non intendimus aliqualiter derogare. In cujus rei testimonium sigillum nostrum presentibus est appensum. Dat' London' .xvj. kalendas Novembris anno Domini .M°.CCC^{mo}. quinto et consecracionis nostre nono.

609

[Fo. 34v] ...[1] W[alterus] permissione divina Coventr' et Lich' episcopus dilectis filiis dominis .. archidiacono Coventr' vel ejus .. officiali salutem, graciam et benedictionem. Presentarunt nobis religiosi viri frater Thomas prior de Ordbury et ejusdem loci conventus dominum Willelmum de Knyghtecote clericum ad vicariam de Chelvercot' vacantem ad presentacionem suam spectantem ut dicunt. Quocirca vobis mandamus quatinus de statu ipsius vicarie au[t] vacet necne, et si vacet a quo tempore vacare incipit et qualiter, quis sit verus patronus ejusdem et quis ultimo presentavit ad eamdem, et ad cujus presentacionem admissus fuit ille qui ultimo vicarius tenebat eamdem, au[t] sit litigiosa necne, pensionaria necne et si sit pensionaria cui aut quibus et in quantum et cujus estimacionis existat; de meritis quoque presentati utpote de moribus, sciencia, etate pariter, et de[2] ordinibus ejusdem, au[t] sit liber et legitimus, alias ve beneficiatus existat necne ac de aliis articulis consuetis in pleno loci capitulo per rectores ac vicarios ejusdem capituli vocatis omnibus de jure vocandis sollicite inquiratis. Et id quod per inquisicionem hujusmodi factam inveneritis nobis sub sigillo vestro et sigillis eorum per quos facta fuerit inquisicio fideliter rescribatis. Dat' London' kalendas Decembris anno Domini .M°.CCC^{mo}. octavo.

[[1] An illegible later marginal note is erased or abraded.
[2] Interlined.]

622

[Fos. 35v–36] HYNWODE. Memorandum quod post cessionem domine Katerine Boydin quondam priorisse de Hynwode quam ipsa fecit de prioratu predicto sponte, pure apud Lich' coram domino Waltero Coventr' et Lich' episcopo eciam in manus ipsius episcopi in majori camera pallacii sui[1] Lich' .vj. idus Aprilis anno Domini .M°.CCC^mo.x°. dictus dominus episcopus recepta ex causis legittimis cessione predicta scripsit .. suppriorisse et conventui ut procederent ad electionem nove priorisse et dedit eis ad hoc licenciam quantum in ipso fuit per litteras suas sub data ejusdem diei, et fecit litteras suas .. abbatisse et conventui de Pollesworth ut dictam Katerinam reciperent ac morandum ibidem per aliquod tempus sub eadem data.[2] Postmodum dicta suppriorissa et conventus petita a Radulpho de Perham tenente locum abbatis Westm' ipsarum patroni eligendi licencia. Elegerunt concorditer seu pocius nominarunt dominam Margaretam le Corzon in priorissam suam, et ipsam electionem seu nominacionem presentarunt dicto .. episcopo per suas litteras sigillo commmuni signatas et per Milisentam de Fokerham suppriorissam, Margeriam atte Barre et Agnetem de Wyveleston' moniales domus, que similiter porrexerunt patentem litteram patroni sui de assensu apud Lich' .xvij. kalendas Maii anno predicto; [Fo. 36] quibus litteris receptis et examinatis per dictum episcopum et consilium suum assidentibus ei magistro Roberto de Radeswelle archidiacono Cestr' et magistro Luca de Ely cancellario ecclesie Lich' ac magistro G[alfrido] de Blaston' canonico ejusdem ecclesie, quia predicta suppriorissa et conventus nullam in eligendo seu nominando priorissam formam observaverant a canone traditam [3]dictus episcopus[3] ipsam electionem justicia exigente cassavit et invalidim pronunciavit. Et postmodum de officio suo et gracia speciali providit predicto prioratui de predicta domina Margareta ipsam que fecit in priorissam, [4]et cantato Te Deum ipsam bene dicabat,[4] mandans litteras suas suppriorisse et conventui ut eam reciperent et ei ut priorisse obedirent, et rectori ecclesie de Macstok' per alias litteras ut eam installaret sub data ejusdem diei.

[[1] Interlined.
[2] Followed by a 2cm. blank space.
[3–3] Interlined.
[4–4] Marginated with a line indicating it should be placed here.]

628

[Fo. 36v] NOMINA. COMMISSIO PRO CURATORE PREFICIENDO. W[alterus] permissione, etc. dilecto nobis in Christo domini Willelmo de Bulkenior presbitero salutem, graciam et benedictionem. Ex incumbente nostris humeris pastorali officio facti secundum apostolum sapientibus et insipientibus debitores, illis perpensius adesse tenemur op[p]ortunis suffragiis, qui scriptis deesse videntur et quibus propria potencia minus debito suffragatur. Cum igitur dominus Petrus rector ecclesie de Mackstok nostre diocesis adeo gravi infirmitate laborare noscatur quod cura indigeat aliena prout per inquisicionem per .. officialem archidiaconi Coventr' inde captam concepimus evidenter ei debito compacientes affectum, te de cujus industria et circumspectione fiduciam optinemus predicti rectoris et ecclesie sue predicte ac rerum suarum custodem preficimus et eciam curatorem, proviso quod de bonis ipsius rectoris nunc exstantibus fidele facias inventarium et de hiis et aliis in futuris pronuncientibus nobis seu alteri quem ad hoc deputaverimus racionem reddas cum fueris[1] requisitus. In cujus rei testimonium litteras nostras tibi fieri fecimus has patentes. Datum[2] Lich'[3] anno [4]Domini Millesimo .CCC^{mo}.[4]

[[1] Interlined.
[2] Interlined
[3] Followed by a 2.5cm. blank space.
[4]-[4] Underlined.]

630

[Fo. 36v]   VICARIA DE ETON. NIHIL. Item apud Eccleshale .xiiij. kalendas Aprilis anno predicto Galfridus de Vylers admissus fuit ad vicariam de Eton' nostre diocesis vacantem, ad presentacionem fratris Petri de Criketot procuratoris religiosorum virorum abbatis et conventus de Lyra in Angl' et Wall' generaliter constituti[1] verorum ejusdem vicarie patronorum, et vicarius perpetuus cum onere personalis residencie juxta formam constitucionis legati super hoc edite, canonice institutus in eadem. Et incipit dicta vicaria vacare die martis proximo ante festum Sancti Martini ultimo preterito per mortem magistri Johanni de Hinkele ultimi vicarii ejusdem. Et mandabatur .. archidiacano vel ejus officiali quod inducerent eum in corporalem possessionem sub eadem data.

[[1] MS. *constuti*]

633

[Fo. 36v]   PRO VICARIO DE ETON'. Universis ad quos presentes littere pervenerint .W[alterus]., etc. salutem in salutis auctore. Cum in singulis artacionibus a jure statutis legittimum semper impedimentum excusat pastorali convenit sollicitudini excusaciones subditorum legittimas favorabiliter admittere et super hiis testimonium perhibere, cum igitur Galfridus de Vilers diaconus ad vicariam de Eton' a veris patronis ejusdem nobis presentatus et per nos postmodum in ea observato in omnibus jure ordine canonice institutus ad nos usque Ebor' ad prefixum sibi per nos proximum terminum ad ordines conferendos statutum ad suscipiendum ordinem sacerdotalem secundum exigenciam sacrorum canonum personaliter accessisset. Nos tunc temporis tanta fuimus corporis infirmitate detenti quod absque periculo corporali ipsum nequivimus ad sacerdotalem ordinem promovere; ne igitur predictus vicarius in periculum canonis super hoc editi aliqualiter incidat seu per hoc aliquod discrimen incurrat, ipsius diligencie quam potuit et de jure debuit adhibite in hac parte ac impedimento predicto nobis tunc casu aliter occurrenti, tamquam rei geste veritati testimonium perhibemus, ipsum vicarium a suscepcione ordinis predicti ad prefatum terminum rationabiliter fuisse prepeditum tenore presencium declarantes ac sufficienter excusatum habentes, dum tamen in proximis ordinibus post datam presencium celebrandis ad gradum sacerdocii ordinari se faciat ut tenetur. In cujus rei, etc. Dat' Ebor' in vigilia Trinitatis anno predicto.

708

[Fo. 43v]   Walterus permissione etc., dilecto nobis in Christo Johanni dicto Wille de Ottokeshather nostre diocesis acolito salutem, graciam et benedictionem. Peticionem tuam recepimus continentem quod, cum tu olim canonicarum sanctionum ignarus ac simplicitate animi levitateque ductus predictus acolitatus ordinem furtive recepisses, tecum ut in suscepto ordine ministrare et ad superiores ordines posses ascendere dispensare misericorditer curaremus. Nos devocionis tue precibus favorabiliter annuentes impositaque tibi porro commisso hujus penitencia salutari, ut in eodem ordine sic furtive suscepto, dum tamen per nos seu per aliquem archidiaconum aut alium ministrum nostrum non fueris super hoc sub anathematis interminacione prohibitus licite ministrare et ad ordines superiores ascendere possis, dum tamen aliud tibi canonicum non obsistat, tecum auctoritate nostra misericorditer dispensamus; proviso quod penitenciam per nos tibi inflictam fideliter peragas et in suscepcione ordinum superiorum si ad eos ascendere te contingat iterato similiter non delinquas. In cujus rei testimonium litteras nostras tibi fieri fecimus has patentes. Dat' Lich' kalendas Aprilis anno Domini .M°.CCC^{mo}. decimo et consecracionis nostre quartodecimo.

719

[Fo. 44] COMMISSIO PRO PROBACIONE TESTAMENTORUM FACIENDA. Walterus etc. dilecto filio magistro Galfrido de Balston' commissario nostro generali salutem, graciam et benedictionem. De tue circumspectionis industria plenam in Domino fiduciam optinentes, ad recipiendum probaciones testamentorum quorumcumque defunctorum dicte nostre diocesis quorum bona summam triginta librorum non excedunt et ad concedendum executoribus defunctorum liberam administracionem bonorum hujusmodi defunctorum in forma juris, necnon ad audiendum raciocinium administracionis executorum defunctorum de bonis eorumdem et ad concedendum et faciendum executoribus litteras de acquietancia de raciocinio reddito cum venerint easdem petituri et ad omnia et singula facienda [fo. 44v] que in premisses de jure requiruntur tibi committimus vices nostras cum canonice cohercionis licencia potestate, jure et consuetudine ecclesie nostre Lych' in omnibus semper salvis. In cujus rei, etc. Dat' Lych' .iij. nonas Februarii anno Domini .M°.CCC^{mo}. decimo et consecracionis nostre quintodecimo.

Et consimilem commissionem habet magister Ricardus de Norht' sub eadem data. Et committitur singulis decanis archidiaconatuum Coventr', Staff', Derb', et Salop' quod ipsi possint recipere probaciones testamentorum quorumcumque in suis jurisdictionibus decedencium infra summam centum solidorum et conceditur executoribus eorumdem liberam administracionem bonorum hujusmodi defunctorum in forma. Et consimilis potestas conceditur domino Roberto de Donechirch vicario in ecclesia nostra Lich' usque ad summam quadraginta solidorum, cum adjectione illius clausule quod potest audire raciocinium administracionis executorum defunctorum de bonis eorumdem, sub data predicta.

726

[Fo. 44v] COMMISSIO PRO PERMUTACIONE FACIENDA. .W[alterus]. permissione etc. dilectis filiis domino .. priori de Repyndon' et magistro Ade Byrom officiali Staff' salutem, graciam et benedictionem. Cum ex certis et urgentibus causis simus ad presens agentes in remotis extra nostram diocesam, de vestris et utriusque vestrum circumspectione et industria plenius confidentes ad conferendum quamcumque prebendam vacaturam infra quindenim a tempore recepcionis presencium in ecclesia nostra Lich' per viam permutacionis dilecto filio domino Johanni de Kynardesleye nunc rectori ecclesie de Tatenhull ejusdem nostre diocesis, necnon ad admittendum resignaciones hincinde faciendas, ac eciam ad concedendum inquisicionis litteras persone ydonee ad dictam ecclesiam de Tatenhull presentande et ad instituendum et inducendum in corporalem possessionem ejusdem, ac eciam ad exequendum exercendum et expediendum omnia et singula que negocium permutacionis hujus exigit et requirit, vobis et utrique vestrum committimus vices nostras et plenarie in premissis et ea contingentibus ac specialem hac vice tenore presencium cum cohercione canonica concedimus potestatem. Non intendentes per hac provisionibus apostolicis in ecclesia nostra Lich' predicta dependentibus aliqualiter derogare. In cujus rei testimonium. Dat' Ebor' .iij. nonas Julii anno predicto.

754

[Fo. 47] LICENCIA PRO CAPELLA HABENDA. [1]LANGLEY INFRA SUTTON COLEFIELD.[1] .W[alterus]. permissione divina Coventr' et Lich' episcopus dilecto nobis in Christo domino Willelmo Bereford militi, domini regis Anglie justiciario, salutem in Domino. Attendentes devocionis fervorem quem ad cultum divinum ingerit habere dinosceris et qui nonnunquam propter difficultatem timeris eundi ad parochialem ecclesiam tuam de Sutton' in Colfeld inevitabiliter impeditur, ut in manerio tuo de Langele infra parochiam predictam honestum oratorium cingere valeas et habere in quo possis pro beneplacito tuo divina facere celebrare[2] et tibi quoad vixeris specialem concedimus licenciam per presentes sigilli nostri appensione munitas, ita tamen quod per hoc juribus et obvencionibus parochialis ecclesie nullatenus derogetur. Dat' London' .ix. die Julii anno Domini Millesimo.CCC^{mo}.xiiij. consecracionis nostre .xviij.

[1–1] In a later hand.
[2] Recte *celebrari*]

757

[Fo. 47] [1]COMMISSIO OFFICIALITATIS[1]. Walterus permissione divina Coventr' et Lich' episcopus dilecto filio magistro Philipo de Turvill' canonico nostre ecclesie Lich' predicte salutem, graciam et benedictionem. De vestre fidei integritate consciencie puritate ac circumspecta industria confidentes vos nostrum .. officialem facimus et constituimus per presentes, et ad audiendum omnes et singulas causas et negocia ad jurisdictionem nostram sive ex officio sive ad instanciam partis qualitercumque spectantes, interloquendum pronunciandum diffiniendum et cum canonice cohercionis potestate quociens et quando opus fuerit exequendum, et ad faciendum et complendum in eisdem omnia et singula que pro expedicione earumdem incumbunt vobis committimus plenariam potestatem. Ad hec quoque de subditorum nostrorum quorumcumque excessibus et criminibus inquirendi, excessus et crimina et corrigendi excedentes et criminosos puniendi, et contradictores et rebelles si qui fuerint per censuram ecclesiasticam compescendi vobis tenore presencium plenam concedimus potestatem, sentencias quidem quas rite tuleritis in rebelles favente Domino faciemus inviolabiliter observari. In cujus rei testimonium sigillum nostrum presentibus est appensum. Dat' London' .x. kalendas Decembris anno Domini .Mᵒ.CCC. tertiodecimo.

[¹⁻¹ In a later hand.]

788

[Fo. 49v]   DISPENSACIO SUPER PLURALITATE AUCTORITATE APOSTOLICA. Walterus permissione divina Coventr' et Lich' episcopus domino Ricardo de Bello Monte rectori ecclesie de Wytelesham Norwycen' diocesis, salutem in auctore salutis. Litteras graciosas sanctissimi patris domini Clementis divina providencia pape quinti recepimus et habemus sub verborum continencia infrascripta.

Clemens episcopus servus servorum Dei venerabili fratri Waltero Coventr' et Lich' episcopo, salutem et apostolicam benedictionem. Libenter tibi illam concedimus graciam per quam gratificari valeas clericis in tuis obsequiis constitutis. Tuis igitur supplicacionibus inclinati fraternitati tue dispensandi hac vice cum sex ex clericis tuis quos duxeris eligendos ut quilibet eorum duo beneficia ecclesiastica curam animarum habencia, si eis canonice offerantur, licite recipere ac ea simul libere retinere valeant, constitucione generale concilii et alia qualibet in contrarium edita non obstante, plenam et liberam auctoritate presencium concedimus facultatem; proviso quod hujusmodi beneficia debitis obsequiis non fraudentur et animarum cura in eis nullatenus negligatur. Nulli ergo omnino hominum liceat hanc paginam nostre concessionis infringere vel ei ausu temerario contraire. Si quis autem hoc attemptare presumpserit indignacionem omnipotentis Dei et Beatorum Petri et Pauli apostolorum ejus se noverit incursurum. Dat' apud Sanctum Siricum .viij. kalendas Marcii pontificatus nostri anno primo.

Sane dum tue merita probitatis attendimus non immerito amimamur¹ ut sicut dono virtutum et gracia meritorum haberis conspicuus sic ad tui promocionem honoris graciosis favoribus intendamus, ipsa namque probitas sibi premium vendicat et quasi debitum exigit ut amplis favoribus et gratis muneribus attollaris. Ut itaque a prefata ecclesia tua de Wyttlesham curam animarum habente beneficium aliud ecclesiasticum consimilem curam habens si tibi canonice offeratur, recipere et cum ea simul retinere licite valeas, constitucione generale concilii et alia qualibet in contrarium edita nonobstante, tecum auctoritate premissa tenore presencium dispensamus, ita tamen quod hujusmodi beneficia debitis obsequiis non fraudentur et animarum cura in eisdem nullatenus negligatur, te infra numerum sex clericorum de quibus supra sit mencio includentes, super quo tibi fieri fecimus hanc nostram patentem litteram in testimonium veritatis. Dat' London' .x. kalendas Julii anno Domini .Mᵒ.CCCᵐᵒ. septimo.

[¹ Recte *animamur*]

789

[Fo. 49v] PROCURATORES AD CONTRAHENDUM MUTUUM IN ROMANA CURIA. Universis presentes litteras inspecturis Walterus permissione etc., salutem in Domino. Noveritis nos ordinasse, fecisse et constituisse dilectos nobis in Christo magistros R. de P. et S. de S. procuratores nostros conjunctim et divisim ad contrahendum mutuum in Romana curia pro negotiis nostris ibidem expediendis usque ad summam quam iidem procuratores nostri decreverint mutuandam secundum qualitatem negotiorum et nostrarum exigenciam facultatum; et ad obligandum nos, ecclesiam nostram et successores nostros, et bona nostra et ecclesie nostre mobilia et inmobilia presencia et futura ecclesiastica et mundana illi vel illis a quo vel a quibus iidem procuratores nostri mutuum reciperint antedictum; et ad jurandum in animam nostram de dicta peccunia[1] certo tempore creditoribus persolvenda sub quibuscumque condicionibus et penis que de jure vel consuetudine curie in tali requiruntur contractu, ac eciam ad submittendum nos jurisdictioni cujuscumque capellani domini pape quem dicti creditores elegerunt in quem tamquam in judicem nostrum consentimus et ut ipse tamquam judex noster possit de dicta peccunie[2] summa vel ejus parte nos et procuratores nostros predictos nostro nomine condempnare et in nos et eosdem procuratores nostros excommunicacionis sentenciam ferre si peccuniam[3] de qua nos aut procuratores nostri fuerimus condempnati non solverimus in termino ab eodem auditore provide statuendo; renunciantes constitucioni de duabus dietis edite in concilio generali ceterisque constitucionibus, probacionibus et excepcionibus quibus nos contra creditores ipsos qualitercumque tueri possemus et per quas posset eis super eodem mutuo prejudicium aliquod generari, promittentes nos ratum et gratum perpetuo habituros quicquid per ipsos procuratores seu eorum alterum actum procuratum seu promissum fuerit in premissis aut aliquo premissorum. In cujus rei testimonium, etc. Dat' ...[4]

[[1] Recte *pecunia*
[2] Recte *pecunie*
[3] Recte *pecuniam*
[4] Unfinished.]

797

[Fo. 51] [1]DISPENSACIO CLERICI IN DEFECTUM ETATIS.[1] Walterus permissione divina Coventr' et Lych' episcopus dilecto nobis in Christo Willelmo de Draco clerico, salutem in salutis auctore. Litteras graciosas sanctissimi patris domini Clementis divina providencia pape quinti recepimus et habemus sub verborum continencia infrascripta.

Clemens episcopus servus servorum Dei venerabili fratri Waltero Coventr' et Lych' episcopo salutem et apostolicam benedictionem. Devocionis tue probata sinceritas apud nos et sedem apostolicam mereri dinoscitur ut personam tuam speciali gracia prosequamur. Hinc est quod nos tuis devotis precibus annuentes fraternitati tuo dispensandi hac vice cum quatuor clericis secularibus patientibus in ordinibus et etate defectum dum tamen fuit in quintodecimo etatis sue anno constituti, ut qualibet eorum unicum beneficium ecclesiasticum cum cura vel sine cura possit licite recipere ac libere retinere si ei canonice offeratur, defectu etatis et ordinis ac qualibet constitucione in contrarium editis non obstantibus, plenam et liberam auctoritate presencium concedimus facultatem. Nulli ergo omnino hominum liceat hanc paginam nostre concessionis infringere vel ei ausu temerario contraire. Si quis autem hoc attemptare presumpserit indignacionem omnipotentis Dei et Beatorum Petri et Pauli apostolorum ejus se noverit incursurum. Dat' apud Sanctum Siricum .viij. kalendas Marcii pontificatus nostri anno primo.

Attendentes itaque quod licet in ordinibus et etatis paciaris defectum morum cum fecunditas generis prefulendi[2] nobilis ac studii litteralis assiduitas quibus laudabiliter prepollere dinosceris vite suplent quod etatis condicio non matura diminuit, ac volentes ob id et consideracione nobilis viri nobis in Christo karissimi domini Willelmi de Dacre militis cujus filius esse dinosceris, personam tuam prosequi gracia speciali te in quintodecimo etatis tue anno et ultra absque cujuscumque scripulo dubii constituto tecum et unicum beneficium ecclesiasticum cum cura vel sine cura si tibi canonice offeratur licite recipere ac libere retinere valeas defectu etatis et ordinum ac qualibet constitucione in contrarium edita non obstantibus auctoritate predicta tenore presencium dispensamus, te infra numerum quatuor clericorum de quibus in litteris apostolicis habentur mencio ut premittitur secundum videlicet includentes. In cujus rei testimonium hanc nostram patentem litteram tibi fieri fecimus sigilli nostri munimine roboratam. Dat' London' .iiij. idus Maii anno Domini .M°.CCC^mo.ix° et consecracionis nostre .xiij°.

[1–1] In a later hand.
[2] Recte *prefulgendi*]

801

[Fo. 51v]   Universis ad quos presens scriptum pervenerint Walterus permissione etc., salutem in Domino. Noveritis nos teneri et per presens scriptum nostrum obligatos esse domino Radulpho de Hengham et ejus executoribus in ducentis et decem libras sterlingas quas ab eodem mutuo recepimus, solvendas eidem vel suo certo attornato ad terminos subscriptos, videlicet in quindena Pasche a confectione presencium proximo futuro centum et quinque marcas, et in quindena Sancti Johannis Baptiste proximo sequenti centum et quinque marcas, et in quindena Sancti Michaelis proximo tunc sequenti centum et quinque marcas, sine ulteriori dilacione. Ad quarum solucionem terminis predictis fideliter faciendam obligamus nos heredes et executores nostros, et omnia bona nostra mobilia et inmobilia[1] ubicumque et ad quorumcumque manus devenerint. In cujus rei testimonium sigillum nostrum presentibus apposuimus. Dat' London' die mercurii proxima post festum Sancte Fidei Virginis anno regni regis E[dwardi] filii regis E[dwardi] quarto.

[1] Recte *immobilia*]

803

[Fo. 51v]   COLLACIO DOMUUM IN CLAUSO LICH'. Pateat universis quod nos W[alterus] permissione divina Coventr' et Lich' episcopus dedimus et concessimus dilecto nobis in Christo magistro Galfrido de Blaston' canonico ecclesie nostre Lich' ad totam vitam suam aulam illam infra clausum nostrum Lich' quam quondam fuit magistri Walteri de Clipston' nepotis nostri, una cum solario et celario inferiori capite illius aule situatis quibus nuper de novo edificare incepimus, ac eciam solarium et celarium ad capud inferius dicte aule, necnon coquina et pistrina infra idem mansum existentes, ita tamen quod idem magister Galfridus predictas domos suis sumptibus infra quadriennium vel quinquennium ad ultimum a tempore date presencium reparari faciat sicut decet. Si autem infra idem tempus hoc facere neglexerit, volumus quod ex tunc habeat nostra concessio seu donacio nullius existat roboris seu vigoris. In cujus rei testimonium etc. Dat' Ebor' .ix. kalendas Septembris anno Domini Millesimo.[1]CCC[mo]. xi.[1] et consecracionis nostre xv.

[[1-1] Underlined.]

805

[Fo. 52]   [1]LIB'[2] EXEMPTIO DE ONERE COMPOTI DE BALLIVA[1]. Universis ad quos pervenerint[3] hec scriptura W[alterus]. permissione divina Coventr' et Lich' episcopus salutem in Domino sempiternam. Stabilitatem et fidei puritatem dilecti filii Rogeri de Schulton' rectoris ecclesie de Henover' nostre diocesis quas ab omni tempore mutue noticie nostre de ipso multipliciter sumus experti testantes, eundem Rogerum ab omni onere compoti sive calculi pro quacumque balliva seu officio nos qualitercumque tangente in qua vel in quo hucusque ministerium prebuit qualecumque pro nobis successoribus quibuscumque et executoribus nostris absolvimus, ac liberum et solutum ab omni actione, impeticione vel demanda quibus idem Rogerus heredes, successores vel executores sui in futurum hac occasione quovismodo calumpniari possent, acquietamus finaliter et imperpetuum per presentes quibus sigillum nostrum apponi fecimus in fidem et testimonium premissorum. Dat' Lich' primo die mensis Aprilis anno Domini Millesimo.CCC[mo].xvij[mo].

[[1-1] In a later hand.
[2] Deleted.
[3] MS. *pervenerit*]

806

[Fo. 52]   W[alterus] etc. dilecto filio magistro Simoni rectori ecclesie de Kirkaby in Wyrhale nostre diocesis salutem, graciam et benedictionem. Licet ad nostram noticiam pervenisset quod tu non fecisses ab anno Domini M°.CCC[mo] decimo in ecclesia tua predicta prout ipsius cura requirit residenciam personalem, ex causis tamen per te nobis expositis quas justas et legitimas reputamus; volentes facere graciam et favorem, te quoad non residenciam predictam ab officio nostro dimittimus et volumus quod per nos seu ministros nostros ea occasione contra te nullatenus procedatur nec tibi gravamen aliquod inferatur. Dat' apud Lich' .iij. nonas Aprilis anno Domini .M°.CCC[mo].septimodecimo.

809

[Fo. 53]   DECRETUM VISITACIONIS ABBATHIE CESTR'. Walterus permissione divina Coventr' et Lich' episcopus dilectis filiis abbati et conventui monasterii Sancte Werburge Cestr' nostre diocesis salutem, graciam et benedictionem. Nuper kalendis Decembris anno Domini Millesimo.CCC.xv. ad monasterium vestrum causa visitacionis inibi excercende ex nostri officii debito declinantes, peracta visitatione nostra ibidem aliqua tam circa personas quam statum monasterii vestri predicti luculenter invenimus que correctione et reformacione egebant super illis presenti decreto taliter duximus ordinandum.

In primis cum domus vestra ere alieno in presenti graviter oneretur et multo amplius ante finem anni inevitabiliter debeat onerari, statuimus et ordinavimus quod in singulis officiis dicte domus familia inutili sive non necessaria totaliter resecata; abbas sex clericis dumtaxat robas ministret, quinque armigeris seu vallettis; ad robas suas in monasterio sit contentus; extra monasterium vero non necessaria robe non dentur.

Item quod nec abbas nec monachi neque seculares quicumque leporarios aut alios canes habeant infra septa monasterii vel extra sumptibus domus.

Item volumus et ordinamus quod decetero dominus abbas in magnis et arduis negociis majorum et seniorum fratrum suorum et non unius vel duorum dumtaxat consilio utatur.

Item quod nec corrodia nec pensiones amodo de doma[1] vestra vendantur vel concedantur nisi ex urgenti causa et necessaria, et tunc non nisi de consilio communi et singulorum de capitulo vestro et consilio nostro.

Item quod abbas non faciat communia nisi in solempnibus festis vel nisi ad adventus magnatum vel alia evidens causa hoc exposcat; nec tamen expendat in vino [2]et specibus[2] sicut solebat; et de decem doleis vini annuatim reputet se contentum. Item quod abbas confratres suos in camera sua vel alibi secum comedentes in esculentis et potulentis uniformiter absque personarum accepcione[3] faciat procurari, nec contra fratres suos sit sine causa suspiciosus[4] nec statim credat privatis denunciationibus contra fratres suos nisi prehabita cause cognicione. Item quod fratres suos nunc hos nunc alios tam diebus carnium quam piscium ad cameram suam vocet ad prandium absque accepcione[5] personarum.

Item insistat abbas diligenter quod redditus domus et homagia colligantur integraliter et petantur.

Item quod in caritate et mansuetudine debitis fratres corrigat seu corrigi faciat delinquentes.

Item quod monachi officiarii secundum antiquam consuetudinem in capitulo preficiantur.

Item quod abbas quicquid perceperit de peccunia fabrice ecclesie ordinata restituat quam cicius poterit et decetero mutuum de pecunia fabrice vel elemosine non recipiat.

Item quod monachi de maneriis revocentur ad conventum et ponantur in eis alii custodes fideles et sufficientes qui diligenter volunt et possunt insistere circa culturas. Item juxta composicionem in monasterio editam ab antiquo abbas ministret seu faciat ministrari coquine .iiij. libras et .x. solidos pro monachis commorantibus aut moraturis apud Hildeboruneygh' et Salougton'.

Item ordinamus et statuimus quod prior qui nunc est et alii qui pro tempore erunt moram faciant in conventu juxta tenorem regule.
Item prior qui nunc est ad foresta pro feris capiendis decetero non accedat. Item ne decetero dictus prior utatur arcu et sagittis contra regulam set religioni intendat prout decet.

Item ne decetero dictus prior vel alii commonachi sui utantur vestibus alterius coloris vel forme quam regula concedit seu permittit set uniformiter vestiantur et secundum eorum indigenciam prout constituciones ordinis et regula exigunt et requirunt.

Item quod dictus prior inter fratres suos in refectorio comedat tam diebus carnium quam piscium ut tenetur.

Item injungimus quod silencium decetero observetur a vobis secundum regule vestre tenorem et constituciones ordinis.

Item precipimus et injungimus ne decetero fratres mittant exeunia in esculentis et potulentis extra refectorium vel alium locum ubi comedant; set ea que supersunt de cibariis eorumdem post refectionem in elemosinam que jam fere prout convertantur.

Item quod libri legales quoddam[6] empti per abbatem de peccunia[7] domus restituantur monasterio vel estimacio eorumdem.

Item fratres post collacionem commessacionibus secretis et potacionibus non insistant set ad completorium vadant.

Item ad succidendum et tollendum palmites pestiferos et nocivos monasterii vestri videlicet fratres Matheum de Pentyn, Galfridum de Bosdoun, et Johannem de Gilbesmeire, per quorum insolenciam et maliciam pax et tranquilitas fratrum vestrorum fuerat conturbata, ad loca infrascripta determinus transmittendos, videlicet fratrem Matheum de Pentyn apud Coventr', fratrem Galfridum de Bosdoun apud Salop', fratrem Johannem de Gilbesmere apud Hildeborneigh', et non revocentur quousque aliter de eisdem duxerimus ordinandum. Ordinamus eciam quod frater Robertus de Markynton' revocetur domi et staret amodo in conventu.

Et quia illi qui se dominico obsequio devoverunt a forincetis artificum ministeriis esse debeant alieni, statuimus et ordinamus quod frater Robertus Mareschall qui de cirurgia aliquociens intromisit vel aliquis monachus monasterii vestri operibus illius artis decetero non intendant, nisi quatenus ex mera caritate alicui languenti paupere per modicam unctionem valeat subvenire et tunc quoad aliquam wlnerum incisionem ipsius opere[8] vel consilio nullatenus pro[9] concedatur.

Vobis igitur omnibus et singulis precipimus et in virtute obediencie sub pena excommunicacionis majoris injungimus et mandamus quatinus presenti decreto nostro et singulis articulis in eodem contentis humiliter pareatis et illa studeatis inviolabiliter observari. Scituri quod si vos vel aliquis vestrum contra idem decretum seu aliquam illius partem quicquam presumpseritis vel presumpserit attemptare, vel ea ausu temerario contraire sive ipsis scienter non pareatur, contra vos et quemlibet temeratorem hujusmodi quantum de jure poterimus procedemus. Volumus nichilominus et districte precipimus ut hoc decretum nostrum frequenter in vestro capitulo coram omnibus fratribus recitetur, nequis circa ipsius observanciam in posterum se per ignoranciam valeat excusare. [10]Datum apud Astbur' die mercurii[11] martis proximo post festum Sancte Lucie virginis anno Domini supradicto.[10]

[[1] Recte *domo*
[2-2] Interlined. Recte *specis*
[3] Recte *exceptione*
[4] Recte *suspicionis*
[5] Recte *exceptione*
[6] Recte *quidam*
[7] Recte *pecunia*
[8] MS. *ope*, no contraction.
[9] Interlined.

10-10 In another hand.
11 Deleted.]

815

[Fo. 55] Universis Christi fidelibus ad quos presentes littere pervenerint Walterus permissione divina Coventr' et Lich' episcopus, salutem in omnium salvatorem. Suscepti regiminis cura nos excitat et inducit ut religiosos viros et providos nostre jurisdictioni subjectos, quos imensa[1] merita probitatis et in religione fructuosi[2] labores apud Dominum et homines reddunt, premaxime commendandos ampliori gracia prosequamur, ita quod cum viribus corporalibus destitui ceperint ex nostra provisione presidium senciant opportunum. Cum igitur religiosus vir frater .W[illelmus]. de Alsop abbas monasterii de Derlegh nostre diocesis nobis cum instancia supplicasset quod, cum ipse senio et prolixis in religione, laboribus sit confractus timeatque quod propter debilitatem corporis ingruentem ad regimen domus sue processu temporis fiet mutilatus, pro statu suo futuris temporibus providere dignaremur. Nos attendentes dicti fratris Willelmi inmensa[3] merita, videlicet in religione pium et laudabile regimen gratos labores et que bona temporalia domus sue ipsius diligencia et industria sunt in quantitate non modica augmentata ipseque urgente condicione corporea in visu aliis que corporis habitudinibus multo debilior solito sit effectus, suis supplicacionibus inclinatu[4], tractatu in conventu suo habito primitus de premissis, de expresso et unamini concensu omnium fratrum suorum circa statum ipsius taliter duximus ordinandum.

Videlicet quod si ipse successu temporis propter inpotenciam[5] corporis dignitati sue vel officio gratis cedat sive aliquo casu amotus fuerit, ex tunc habeat suo perpetuo intra monasterium de Derlegh predictum unam cameram sibi competentem, videlicet solarium camere quondam domini Rogeri de Draycote cum capella et garderoba cum foco et candela sibi in eadem camera necessaria secundum quod tempori fuerit o[p]portunum.

Habeat eciam ecclesiam de Schirley cum domibus rectorie et omnibus aliis ad dictam ecclesiam pertinentibus ita quod teneatur agnoscere et sustinere onera ordinaria [ad] dictam ecclesiam qualitercumque contigencia[6] et que ad dictam rectoriam rite noscuntur et jure[7] ordinario pertinere.

Volumus eciam et concedimus quod habeat singulis diebus vite sue de celario de Derlegh duos panes conventuales et duas lagenas cervisie melioris et de coquina de singulis estis[8] ad opos[9] conventus preparatum unum ferculum integrum cum caseo et buturo, sicut ei qui preest ordini et tenet locum abbatis in refectorio ministratur.

Concedimus eciam eidem quod habeat per assignacionem abbatis qui pro tempore fuerit unum concanonicum sibi loco capellani ministratur qui capellanus habeat singulis diebus de dicto celario unum panem conventualem et unam lagenam melioris cervisie cum cibo suo consueto de coquina, sicut uni de canonicis in refectorio contigerit ministrari.

Concedimus similiter eidem quod habeat pro suo libito unum valletum sive camerarium ad sibi sedule serviendum, qui quidem valletus sive camerarius habeat singulis diebus de celario unum parvum album panem et unum panem secundum[10] cum una lagena melioris cervisie et de coquina singulis horis diei sicut valleto domini abbatis contigerit ministrari.

Ordinamus eciam quod totum panem predictum cum tota cervisia predicta possit in camera sua antedicta expenderi vel extra septum dicti monasterii cariari sive quocumque sibi placuerit transmitteri prout sibi melius viderit expedire. De coquina vero nichil percipiat quamdiu cum suis ministris moram traxerit extra monasterium antedictum, si autem aliquando predictos dominus Willelmus habere voluerit in predicta camera sua[11] aliquos confratres suos de conventu secum in mensa, volumus et concedimus quod iidem fratres habeant ibi victualia sua consueta tam de celario quam de coquina sicut in refectorio habere debuerunt.

Similiter concedimus eidem Willelmo quod habeat quolibet die unum panem secundum et duos panes servientum pro scissoriis sive trenchoriis ad suam mensam sive intra monasterium sive extra fuerit antedictum quocienscumque apud predictam ecclesiam de Schirley sive ad alia maneria nostra causa consolacionis seu mutacionis a eris voluerit declinare.[12]

Volumus quod habeat tam in eundo quam redeundo conviviam sive familiam sibi competentem tam in equis quam in garcionibus de stabule domini abbatis qui pro tempore fuerit secundum quod status suus requirit et sibi videbitur convenire.[13]

Per hanc autem ordinacionem sive provisionem nostram cessionem vel renunciacionem quam idem frater Willelmus commissa sibi dignitate vel officio quovis spiritu ductus forsitan duxerit faciendam non intendimus admittere vel approbare quia tucius credimus esse ut co[m]missa sibi ecclesia sub umbra sui nominis gubernetur quam si parsone nove et forsan incognite commitatur. In quorum omnium testimonium et fidem sigillum nostrum presentes duximus apponendum. Dat' apud Dokemanton' in festo apostolorum Petri et Pauli anno Domini .M°.CCC.xvj.

[1 Recte *immensa*
2 Recte *fructuosos*
3 Recte *immensa*
4 Recte *inclinati*
5 Recte *impotenciam*
6 Over an erasure.
7 Interlined.
8 Recte *festis*; *es* over an erasure.
9 Recte *opes*
10 Interlined over *secundum* deleted and underdotted.
11 Interlined.
12 *declinare* repeated and deleted.
13 Recte *conveniri*]

839

[Fo. 57v] PROFESSIO ABBATIS DE WHALLEYE. Item. Ego frater Elias de Workesle abbas de Walley subjectionem reverenciam et obedienciam a sacris patribus constitutam secundum regulam Sancti Benedicti tibi domine pater episcope tuisque successoribus canonice substituendis et [ecclesie] sancti sedi Coventr' et Lich' salvo ordine nostro perpetuo me exhibiturus promitto. Ista professio fuit facta in ecclesia cathedrali Lich' die dominica in Ramispalmarum videlicet .ij. idus Aprilis anno Domini .Millesimo.CCC^mo. decimo.

840

[Fo. 57v]   ACQUIETANCIA .XII. LIBRAS DE PRESTECOTE DE ARRERAGIO
DECIME BONIFACI PAPE VII^{ti}.[1] Pateat universis per presentes quod nos
.W[alterus]. etc. recepimus de domino Willelmo de Dacre rectore ecclesie de
Prestecote nostre diocesis .xij. libras sterlingas de arreragio decime in subsidium
racione ecclesie per dominum Bonifacium papam .viij.^{tum} clero Anglie dudum
imposite, quas quidem .xij. libras ad opus domini nostri regis qui tunc est virtute
cujusdam brevis regis nobis nuper inde directi de ecclesia de Prestecote levari
fecimus antedicta, de quibus eciam .xij. libris predictum rectorem erga dominum
nostrum regem predictum tenemur acquietare per presentes. In cujus etc. Dat'
apud Heywode .xxix. die Aprilis anno Domini M^o.CCC^{mo}.decimo. Et memorandum quod solute fuerunt dicte .xij. libre magistro Ricardo de Norhampton'
Lich' primo die Maii anno predicto [2]per manus J[ohannis] de Langeton'[2] ad
solvendum ad scaccarium domini nostri regis pro domino.

   [[1] Recte *VIII^{ti}*
2–2 Interlined.]

841

[Fo. 58]   CONCESSIO DE PRIMIS FRUCTIBUS ECCLESIE DE BERTUMLE FACTA
RECTORI EJUSDEM. Pateat universis per presentes quod nos Walterus etc. in
crastino ascensionis Domini anno Domini MillesimoCCC^{mo}.iiij^{to}. apud Westm'
omnes fructus et proventus ecclesie de Bertumle nostre diocesis ad nos eodem anno
virtute concessionis per dominum Bonifacium papam .viij. super primis fructibus
et proventibus beneficiorum in dicta nostra diocese vacantium per certum tempus
optinendis nobis concesse racione vacacionis ejusdem ecclesie spectantes Roberto
de Chishull rectori in dicta ecclesia instituto vendidimus concessimus et dimisimus
ad instanciam dilecti nobis in Christo domini Willelmi de Blibrug' clerici per .xx.
libras sterlingas, de quibus assignavimus eidem domino Willelmo ad operaciones
cujusdam camere sue in clauso ecclesie nostre Lich' decem libras et de residuis .x.
libris plenarie nobis satisfecit. Et quia dictus Robertus asseruit se litteram super
vendicione concessione et dimissione hujus hactenus nullatenus habuisse, nos
super hoc testimonium litteras sigillo nostro signatas eidem fieri fecimus patentes.
Dat' Lych' .viij. kalendas Maii anno Domini M^o.CCC^{mo}.x^o. et consecracionis
nostre quartodecimo.

853

[Fo. 58v]   COMMISSIO PRO PENITENTIARIO. W[alterus]. permissione etc.
dilecto filio magistro Galfrido de Moeles rectori ecclesie de Codynton' nostre
diocesis salutem, graciam et benedictionem. Ne populum archidiaconatus Cestr'
pro absolucionis beneficio optinendo et penitencia injungenda in casibus nobis a
jure reservatis per frequentes ad nos accessus gravari contingat, parochianis nostris
dicti archidiaconatus parcere in hac parte volentes de tua circumspecta industria
confisi officium penitentiarii in archidiaconatu predicto salubriter exercendi tibi
committimus per presentes. [In] testimonio earumdem quas nostro fecimus sigillo
muniri. Dat' Lich' .xix. kalendas Februarii anno Domini predicto. Et consimilem
commissionem habet frater Johannes de Notyngham monachus monasterii Sancte
Werburge Cestr' sub eadem data.

883

[Fo. 61]   EXCUSACIO RECTORIS DE ECCLESTON' NON ORDINATI INFRA TEMPUS SUUM. Universis ad quos presentes littere pervenerint W[alterus] permissione etc., salutem in Domino. Cum in singulis artacionibus juris impedimentum legitimum excusare debeat impeditos pastorali convenit sollicitudini excusaciones subditorum benivole exaudire et super hiis remedium quatenus sibi possibile est apponere opportunum. Cum igitur [Robertus][1] de Dotton' acolitus quem nuper in ecclesia de Eccleston' nostre diocesis instituimus post ipsam institucionem in proximis temporibus pro ordinibus celebrandis statutis ad subdiaconatus et diaconatus ordines se fecerit rite sicut debuit promoveri, volens infra annum a tempore sibi commissi regiminis secundum formam canonis in presbiterum ordinari post predicti diaconatus ordinis suscepcionem, adeo gravi et adversa valitudine vexabatur quod nullo modo potuit ad ordinem ascendere sacerdotalem infra spacium dicti anni absque magno[2] periculo corporali, et sicut hucusque in ordinem diaconatus perseverans ad ulteriores nullatenus ascendebat, super quo petiit quod nos secum misericorditer agere dignaremur; nos vero probato impedimento predicto coram nobis testimonio fidedignorum omni [absque] excepcione majorum ipsum rectorem justa et racionabili de causa fuisse prepeditum quare presbiteratus ordinem hactenus non admisit sufficienter[3] excusatum tenore presencium declarimus ac sufficienter excusatum habentes, dum tamen in proximis ordinibus post datam presencium celebrandis ad gradum sacerdotii ordinari se faciat ut tenetur. In cujus rei testimonium etc. Dat' London' .viij. die Decembris anno Domini etc.

[[1] MS. *Thomas*
[2] Interlined.
[3] Deleted.]

901

[Fo. 62]   MOTTRUM IN LONGEDENDAL'. Item .ij. nonas Februarii anno Domini supradicto apud Bracebrugg' juxta Lincoln' Thomas de Cressacr' Ebor' diocesis admissus fuit ad ecclesiam de Mottroun in Longedendal', vacantem, ad presentacionem Thome de Burg' veri ecclesie ejusdem patroni, et canonice institutus fuit canonice[1] in eadem. Et mandabatur archidiacono Cestr' vel ejus officiali quod induceret eum in orporalem possessionem illius ecclesie vel procuratorem suum sub eadem data. Et vacavit dicta ecclesia per resignacionem magistri Jordani de Maclesfeld qui ultimo tenebat eandem de facto et processus fuit ordinatus contra eum [2]et inchoatus[2] per episcopum in visitacione sua eodem anno facta in archidiaconatum Cestr' ad privacionem ipsius, sed ipse preveniens pronunciacionem sponte resignavit illud beneficium.

[[1] *Sic*
[2]–[2] Interlined.]

935

[Fo. 65]   ABSOLUCIO DOMINI RICARDI DE LEGHTON'. Memorandum quod die lune proximo post festum epiphanie Domini anno Domini Millesimo.CCC[mo]. nono apud Ranton' a domino .. episcopo dominus Ricardus de Leghton' miles a

sentencia excommunicacionis quam propter multiplicatas contumacias suas in
consistorio ejusdem .. episcopi Lich' coram commissario ejusdem episcopi
contractas incurrit in forma juris extitit absolutus. Et injunxit sibi dominus .. quod
citra festum Beati Michaelis archangeli proximo futurum in Romam adeat et
ibidem in ecclesia Beati Petri offerat .xij. libras cere in ceriis et in ecclesia Beati
Pauli consimilem oblacionem faciat sub pena quadraginta marcarum.

945

[Fo. 65v]   INCLUSIO ANNACORITE. Walterus etc. dilecte filie Emme Sprenghose
nostre diocesis salutem, graciam et benedictionem. Tue devocionis pium
propositum attendentes quod tu divino spiritu inspirata Deo omnipotenti in vita
solitaria annacorite a pueritia tua jugiter famulari affectasti et adhuc affectas in
presenti, nos tamen ex habundanti scire vellemus de premissis quatenus possemus
veritatem de vita et conversacione tua, ac ydoneitate per viros ydoneos qui tuam
conversacionem per tempora preterita et presencia cognoverunt diligentem
fecimus inquisicionem, per quam comperimus te ad hujus vitam solitariam quoad
mores et alia predictam vitam tangencia ydoneam, propter quod te ad
annacoritam in domibus cimiterii capelle Sancti Georgii Salop' Deo deservituram
admittimus per[1] presentes. In cujus rei etc. Dat' apud Eccleshale .xvj. kalendas
Februarii anno Domini predicto. Et mandatur .. archidiacono Salop' vel decano
ecclesie Sancti Cedde Salop' [2]aut ejus procuratori[2] quod induceret eam sub eadem
data.

[[1] Interlined.
[2–2] Interlined.]

1170

[Fo. 82v]   APPROPRIACIO ECCLESIE DE TYBSCHULF. Universis sancte matris
ecclesie filiis presens scriptum visuris vel audituris Walterus permissione divina
Coventr' et Lich' episcopus salutem in omnium salvatore. Cum secundum
apostolum operari debeamus bonum ad omnes et maxime ad eos qui per devota
pietatis opera domesticos fidei se esse demonstrant ac relictis vagis mundi
discursibus sub arte religionis observancia muro se muniunt honestatis per
variosque virtutum gradus scandere satagunt ad artem beatitudinis ex qua
dependet omnis materia fortium et bonorum omnium magnitudo; ac dilecte filie
priorissa et conventus albarum monialium ecclesie Sancti Leonardi de Brewode
nostre diocesis ordinis Sancti Augustini et comitatus Salop' ecclesiam parochialem
bonorum apostolorum Petri et Pauli de Tybschulf dicte nostre diocesis nunc de
jure et de facto vacantem, in qua eedem religiose jus optinet patronatus et in
possessione juris vel quasi presentandi ad eandem existunt, disposicioni et
ordinacioni nostre simpliciter et absolute duxerint supponendam ut nobis
secundum voluntatis nostre arbitrium liceret disponere de eadem prout in
instrumento ipsarum religiosarum super hoc confecto continetur sub tenore qui
sequitur.
    Universis sancti matris ecclesie filiis ad quos presens scriptum pervenerint
priorissa albarum monialum ecclesie Sancti Leonardi de Brewode Coventr' et[1]
Lich' diocesis et ejusdem loci conventus ordinis Sancti Augustini eternam in
Domino salutem. Noveritis nos unanimi consensu et communi omnium nostrum

voluntate ecclesiam parochialem de Tybbischulf Coventr' et Lich' diocesis de jure et de facto vacantem, in qua jus patronatus habemus, dispositioni et ordinacioni venerabilis in Christo patris domini Walteri Dei gracia Coventr' et Lich' episcopi supposuisse simpliciter et absolute, volentes quatenus in nobis est ut de ipsa ecclesia secundum sue disponat arbitrium voluntatis ratum habiture et gratum quicquid prefatus dominus episcopus circa predictam ecclesiam sub quacumque forma duxerit ordinandum. In cujus rei testimonium sigillum capituli nostri presentibus est appensum. Dat' apud Brewode in capitulo nostro .ij. idus Januarii anno Domini M°.CCC^mo.xviij.

Attendentes quod dicte religiose adeo manifeste paupertatis onere oppresse quod sepe intimtates[2] plurimas patiantur et defectus, considerantes insuper devocionem quam habent ad Deum et ad proximum utpote pietatem et hospitalitatem sectantes pauperes ac debiles benigne suscipiant et eisdem impendunt subsidia caritatis ut hec devocius ac melius in futurum facere valeant ne pro defectu temporalium ab hujusmodi desistant, habita super hiis diligenti inquisicione et tractatu, vocatis eciam omnibus in hac parte vocandis ceterisque solempniis qui in hujusmodi negociis requiruntur de jure servandis legitime observatur, nos invocata Spiritus Sancti gracia ipsam ecclesiam de Tybbyschulf sic ut premittitur vacantem de consensu capitulorum nostrorum Coventr' et Lich' ac consensu et assensu illustris regis Anglie domini Edwardi filii regis Edwardi, prout in carta ejusdem super hoc confecta et eisdem data evidenter, vidimus contineri dictis religiosis dominabus et eorum successoribus suoque monasterio concedimus et appropriamus cum omni integritate et pertinenciis suis perpetuis possidendam temporibus et habendam. Verum quia divinis preceptis et apostolicis mandatis excitamur ut divinum cultum prout nobis fuit possibilem augeamus et maxime in nostra Lich' ecclesia cui licet immerito presidemus ipsi pre ceteris tenemur obnoxii, ordinamus et ordinando statuimus ut dicte religiose et earum successores ad augmentacionem commune vicariorum dicte nostre ecclesie Lich' qui pro tempore fuerunt et qui in ipsa ecclesia nostra laborem sustinent diurnum et nocturnum viginti solidos sterlingorum in festo Sancti Michaelis archangeli Lich' imperpetuum solvent singulis annis libere et absque diminutione aliqualiter communariis ecclesie nostre memorate. Reservata nobis et successoribus nostris potestate taxandi vicariam competentem in ecclesia de Tybeschulf antedicta, ad quam dicte religiose domina priorissa et conventus et ipsarum successores nunc et quotienscumque vacaverit nobis et successoribus nostris ac sede Lich' vacante illi vel illis ad quem vel ad quos de jure vel consuetudine institucio vel destitucio personarum hujusmodi pertinebit, prout in ordinacione in hac parte facienda plenius continetur personam ydoneam qui onus procuracionum et alia onera ordinaria ad nos et ad successores nostros seu locorum archidiacanos qualitercumque pertinencia imperpetuum sustinebit libere presentabunt. Salvis in omnibus jure et auctoritate pontificali nostra et successorum nostrorum ac ecclesiarum nostrarum Coventr' et Lich' dignitate. In cujus rei testimonium ad fidem et evidenciam pleniorem sigillum nostrum huic scripto apposuimus. Dat' Lich' .xix^us. kalendas Februarii anno Domini M°.CCC^mo.xviij.

[1 Over an erasure.
2 Recte *intimantes*]

APPENDIX B

Table of known ordination services held in the diocese

** denotes Bishop Langton officiated.

YEAR	Lent	Sitientes	Easter	Trinity	September	December
1297						*
1300				**		**
1301						*
1302					*	
1303					*	
1304			**			**
1305						*
1306		*				*
1307						*
1308				*	*	
1309					*	**
1310	**			**	**	**
1311	**					
1312						*
1313						
1314	**					**
1315				**		**
1316	**			**		**
1317			**	**		**
1318				**		**
1319			**	**		**
1320			**	**	**	**
1321			**			

APPENDIX C

List of ordination services, showing the date, where they were held, and the celebrant

SERIAL NUMBER	DATE	PLACE	CELEBRANT
	21 Dec. 1297	Shrewsbury	St. Asaph[1]
1285	4 June 1300	Eckington	Langton
1286	17 Dec. 1300	Burton upon Trent	Langton
1287	23 Dec. 1301	Derby	Carlisle
1288	22 Sept. 1302	Derby	Carlisle
1289	21 Sept. 1303	Lichfield	Langton
1290	28 Mar. 1304	Lilleshall	Langton
1294	19 Dec. 1304	Kenilworth	Langton
1295	18 Dec. 1305	Colwich	Whithorn
1296	19 Mar. 1306	Derby	Whithorn
1297	17 Dec. 1306	Stafford	Whithorn
1298	23 Dec. 1307	Derby	Carlisle
1299	8 June 1308	Berkswell	Annaghdown
1300	21 Sept. 1308	Chester	Annaghdown
1301	20 Sept. 1309	Colwich	Annaghdown
1302	20 Dec. 1309	Ranton	Langton
1303	14 Mar. 1310	Tamworth	Langton
1304	13 June 1310	Coventry	Langton
1305	19 Sept. 1310	Bishops Itchington	Langton
1306	19 Dec. 1310	Colwich	Langton
1307	6 Mar. 1311	Eccleshall	Langton
1309	23 Dec. 1312	Tamworth	Annaghdown
1310	2 Mar. 1314	Lichfield	Langton
1311	21 Dec. 1314	Eccleshall	Langton
1312	17 May 1315	Colwich	Langton
1313	20 Dec. 1315	Ranton	Langton
1314	6 Mar. 1316	Sandwell	Langton
1315	5 June 1316	Abbots Bromley	Langton
1316	18 Dec. 1316	Bishops Itchington	Langton
1317	2 Apr. 1317	Lichfield	Langton
1318	28 May 1317	Stafford	Langton
1319	17 Dec. 1317	Hillmorton	Langton
1320	17 June 1318	Penn	Langton
1321	23 Dec. 1318	Chebsey	Langton

[1] *Reg. Sutton*, vii.111.

SERIAL NUMBER	DATE	PLACE	CELEBRANT
1322	7 Apr. 1319	Lichfield	Langton
1323	2 June 1319	Eccleshall	Langton
1324	22 Dec. 1319	Gnosall	Langton
1325	29 Mar. 1320	Lichfield	Langton
1326	24 May 1320	Southam	Langton
1327	20 Sept. 1320	Darley	Langton
1328	20 Dec. 1320	Gnosall	Langton
1329	18 Apr. 1321	Lichfield	Langton

APPENDIX D

Bishop Langton's Itinerary

Numbers in bold type in the right-hand column indicate the serial number of entries in the calendar. Other sources for the bishop's movements are detailed in footnotes.

1296

22–28 Dec.	Cambrai, France[1]	
31 Dec.	Thérouanne	

1297

1 Jan.	Wissant	
7 Jan.	Ipswich, Suff.[2]	
11 Jan.	Chelmsford, Essex	
14 Jan.	London	
3–6 Feb.	Walsingham, Norf.[3]	**375**
19 Feb.	London	
27 Feb.	England	
4–15 Mar.	Bruges, Belgium	
16 Mar.	Cambrai, France	
23 Mar.	Antwerp, Belgium	
	Brussels	
25 Mar.	Brussels	
27 Mar.	Bruges	
	Brussels	
28–31 Mar.	Brussels	
6–7 Apr.	Lille, France	
8 Apr.	Courtrai, Belgium	
	Brussels	
1, 5, 7 May	Antwerp	
10, 12 May	Brussels	
15, 17 May	Antwerp	
18 May	Ghent	
21 May	Bruges	
8–10 June	Bruges	
11 June	?Ghent	

---

[1] BL Cotton MS. Cleopatra .D.ix, fo. 74v. Unless stated otherwise, the source for the itinerary to 19 Nov. 1297 is G.P. Cuttino, 'Bishop Langton's Mission for Edward I 1296–1297', *Studies in British History* (University of Iowa, 11, 2, 1941), 180–1.

[2] NA, C53, 83/19; Denton, *Winchelsey*, 104, n.14.

[3] *Foedera*, I, ii.857–9.

12, 25–28 June	Bruges	
28 June	Antwerp	
15, 30 July	Bruges	
1 Aug.	Bruges	
17 Sept	?Cambrai	
8 Nov.	Ghent	
Nov.	Louvain, Brabant	
	Malines	
	Lierre	
	Hoogstraeten, Netherlands	
	Breda	
	Geertruidenberg	
	Dordrecht	
19 Nov.	England	
23 Nov.	Westminster[4]	
1298		
3 Jan.	Langley, Herts.[5]	
27 Feb.	London	**87**
15 Mar.	Sandwich, Kent[6]	
5 Apr.	London	**89**
19 Apr.	Ely, Cambs.	**222**
23 Apr.	St. Albans, Herts.	**90**
19 May	Ashley, Np.	**323**
15 June	York[7]	
16 June	Lead Grange, Yorks.	**4, 382**
18 June	Littleborough, Notts.	**221**
24 Sept.–1 Oct.	York	**1, 3, 223, 383**
4 Oct.	Acomb, Yorks.	**6, 224**
4 Oct.–17 Dec.	York	**5, 7–9, 11–18, 62, 63, 94, 153, 154, 225, 226, 324, 384**
28 Dec.	Cottingham, Np.[8]	
1299		
2 Jan.	Sibson, Leics.	**19, 95**
4–6 Jan.	Coventry	**20–2, 70, 155, 156, 279**
8–12 Jan.	Lichfield	**23–6, 28, 29, 70, 96, 157, 227, 277, 280, 281, 325**
23 Jan.	Acomb	**65**
23 Jan.	York	**30, 282**

4   M.C. Prestwich, *Documents illustrating the crisis of 1297–98 in England* (Camden, 4th ser., 24, 1980), 172.
5   *CPR 1292–1301*, 327.
6   *CPR 1292–1301*, 335.
7   *Records of Antony Bek, bishop and patriarch, 1283–1311* (Surtees Society, 162, 1947), nos. 58, 59.
8   *CPR 1292–1301*, 393.

15–16 Feb.	York	**31, 32, 97, 385**
19 Feb.	Acomb & York	**67, 68**
22 Feb.	York	**48**
23 Feb.	Acomb	**27**
28 Feb.	York	**69**
20 Mar.–21 Apr.	London	**24, 33–7, 40, 43, 44, 49,**
		67, 71, 79, 98, 99, 158,
		228–31
17 May	Acomb	**236**
18 May–2 June	York	**46, 47, 50, 51, 61, 72,**
		159, 232
27–28 June	Acomb	**52, 54, 161**
30 June–18 July	York	**53, 55, 56, 100, 326**
6 Oct.	Acomb	**57, 101**
18 Oct.	London	**58, 59, 78, 386**
23–28 Oct.	London	**76, 80**
3 Nov.	St. Albans[9]	
5 Nov.	London	**363**
13 Nov.	York	**361**
14 Nov.	Acomb	**60, 387**
18–19 Nov.	York	**82, 83, 162**
21 Dec.	York	**84**
26 Dec.	Acomb	**399**
31 Dec.	York	**400**
1300		
7 Jan.–18 Feb.	York[10]	**84, 102, 327, 401, 402**
25–26 Feb.	Lichfield	**234, 328, 404, 408**
28 Feb.	Eccleshall, Staffs.	**388**
1 Mar.	Kenilworth, Warw.	**405**
15 Mar.–14 Apr.	London (parliament)	**163, 235, 237, 403, 407**
5 May	Worksop, Notts.	**409**
13 May	Lichfield	**164, 329**
17 May	Brewood, Staffs.	**165**
18–21 May	Eccleshall	**166, 167, 410, 411**
24 May	Great Haywood, Staffs.	**412**
27–30 May	Lichfield[11]	**103, 168**
4 June	Eckington, Derb.	**104, 331, 1285**
7–8 June	Pontefract, Yorks.[12]	
14–20 June	York[13]	
6–11 July	York[14]	
24 Aug.	York[15]	

9   NA, E 159, 73, m. 34.
10   NA, E 159, 73, mm. 49, 49d.
11   LJRO MS. D30 XIII, fo. 6.
12   *CCR 1296–1302*, 354, 401.
13   NA, E 159, 73, mm. 31, 61, 50d; *CChW 1244–1326*, 110.
14   NA, E 159, 73, mm. 61, 51, 61d.
15   NA, E 159, 73, m. 31d.

11–27 Sept.	?overseas[16]	
6 Oct.–9 Nov.	York[17]	**110, 111, 171, 172, 332, 413, 414**
20 Nov.	York[18]	
1 Dec.	Acomb	**173**
3–4 Dec.	York[19]	
13 Dec.	Marr, Yorks.	**240**
17 Dec.	Burton upon Trent, Staffs.	**174, 415–17, 1286**
18 Dec.	Lichfield	**241**
20 Dec.	Leicester	**418**
24–26 Dec.	Northampton	**112, 419**
1301		
16 Jan.	Coventry	**287**
27 Jan.	York[20]	
28 Jan.	Nettleham, Lincs.[21]	
29 Jan.–14 Feb.	Reepham, Lincs. (parliament)	**113, 175, 242–3, 333, 420–30, 474**
14 Feb.–2 Mar.	Lincoln (parliament)[22]	**244, 245**
6 Mar.	Rickling, Essex	**431**
23 Mar.	Hailes, Glos.	**114**
24 Mar.	Evesham, Worcs.	**334, 432**
c.25 Mar.	Offenham, Worcs.	**436**
31 Mar.	Evesham	**433**
2 Apr.	Stock Wood, Worcs.	**246, 288**
4–7 Apr.	Feckenham, Worcs.[23]	**434, 435**
18–21 Apr.	Acomb	**389, 437, 438**
22–26 Apr.	York	**439, 441, 442**
4 May	Acomb	**289, 443**
19–25 May	London	**176, 448**
31 May–1 June	Kenilworth	**335, 336, 449**
21 June	Thorpe Waterville, Np.	**290**
29 June	York	**444**
30 June–2 July	Acomb	**115, 390, 445, 446**
9 July	Woodstock, Oxon.	**247**
10 July	Hinton Waldrist, Oxon.	**450**
18 July	Woodstock	**447**
5 Aug.	Woodstock	**248**
23–31 Aug.	York	**116, 451–3**
9 Oct.	Acomb	**183**
28 Oct.	London	**291, 455**

[16] NA, E 159, 73, m. 51; Beardwood, 'Trial', 22, 23.
[17] *CChW 1244–1326*, 116, 117.
[18] *CChW 1244–1326*, 123.
[19] *CChW 1244–1326*, 124.
[20] *MRA*, no. 265.
[21] *CPR 1292–1301*, 564.
[22] *CPR 1292–1301*, 571–3, 575, 576, 578, 625.
[23] *CPR 1292–1301*, 586, 626.

15 Nov.	York[24]	
30 Nov.–Dec.	France[25]	
25 Dec.	Asnières[26]	
1302		
Jan.–May	Papal curia[27]	
6 May	Montreuil[28]	
1 July–30 Aug.	London (parliament)[29]	
Sept.–Dec.	England[30]	
14–21 Oct.	Westminster (parliament)[31]	
20 Dec.	Filton, Nb. (council)[32]	
1303		
1 Jan.–16 Feb.	England[33]	
Feb.–17 June	Papal curia[34]	
1 Sept.	London	**392**
21–22 Sept.	Lichfield	**184, 253, 338, 1289**
12–22 Oct.	York	**293, 392–4**
25–31 Oct.	Acomb	**128, 129, 294, 462**
1304		
15–30 Jan.	Acomb	**130, 185, 254, 255, 339, 340, 395–8**
6 Feb.	York	**256**
21 Feb.	York[35]	
24 Feb.	Muskham, Notts.	**187**
24 Mar.	Shrewsbury	**188, 340, 341**
28–31 Mar.	Lilleshall, Salop.	**189, 343, 477, 478, 1291**
3 Apr.	Lenton, Notts.	**190**
28 Apr.	Stirling, Scotland	**131**
8 May	Westminster	**841**
28 June	York	**344**
28 June	Acomb	**257, 258, 295**
8 July	Acomb	**296**
21 Aug.	Steeple Aston, Oxon.	**191**
23 Sept.	York	**133, 259**

[24] *CChW 1244–1326*, 146.
[25] *Treaty Rolls, i. 1234–1325*, ed. P. Chaplais (London, 1955), no. 377.
[26] *Ibid.*, no. 376; M.C. Prestwich, *Edward I* (London, 1988), 496; *CDRS*, ii.323.
[27] Langton was suspended from episcopal office from 30 Mar. 1302 to 8 June 1303: *CChW 1244–1326*, 154, 158, 160; *CPR 1301–7*, 24, 59; *CPL*, i.601; *MRA*, no. 5.
[28] *CPR 1301–7*, 59; *CChW 1244–1326*, 154; *CDRS*, ii.326.
[29] *CFR 1272–1307*, 457; *CPR 1301–7*, 43–8, 50, 53.
[30] *CPR 1301–7*, 61, 63, 71–5, 94.
[31] *Parl. Writs*, i.114, 116.
[32] *Parl. Writs*, i.369; *CPR 1301–7*, 101.
[33] *Reg. Winchelsey*, ii.652; *CPR 1301–7*, 103–16.
[34] *CCR 1302–7*, 81–2; *CPL*, i.610, 611; *MRA*, no. 305.
[35] *The Register of Thomas Corbridge, Lord Archbishop of York, 1300–1304*, vol. i, ed. W. Brown, vol. ii, ed. W. Brown, A. Hamilton Thompson (Surtees Society, 138, 141, 1925–8), ii.154.

3 Oct.	Acomb	**260**
24 Oct.	Acomb	**134**
1 Nov.	Acomb	**192**
8 Nov.	York	**479**
11 Nov.	Acomb	**262, 263**
1 Dec.	York	**374**
11 Dec.	Lichfield	**193, 480**
17 Dec.	Packington, Warw.	**140**
8–19 Dec.	Kenilworth	**303, 1295**
20 Dec.	Monks Kirby, Warw.	**139**
1305		
16 Jan.	Little Exchequer, Westminster[36]	
19 Jan.–11 Feb.	London	**194–6, 198, 199, 264, 298, 345, 473**
8–23 Mar.	London	**135, 197, 346, 481**
26 Mar.	Brewood	**306**
30 Mar.–8 Apr.	London	**136, 137, 265, 299, 300, 347**
18 Apr.	Coventry	**300**
11 May–26 July	London	**138, 141, 142, 200, 201, 266, 305, 349, 350, 354, 482, 483**
4 Aug.	Fulbrook, Oxon.	**202**
12 Aug.	Coventry	**143, 144**
14–15 Aug.	Brewood[37]	**487**
20 Aug.	Burton upon Trent	**351**
16 Sept.–24 Oct.	London (parliament)	**145, 203, 261, 267–9, 307, 352, 484, 485, 605**
24 Oct.	Newington, Kent[38]	
25 Oct.	Dover	
26 Oct.	France: Wissant	
27 Oct.	Boulogne	
28 Oct.	Crécy, Saint-Riquier	
29 Oct.	Amiens	
30–31 Oct.	Saint-Just	
1 Nov.	Paris	
2 Nov.	Saint-Maur, Fontenay	
3 Nov.	Provins	
4 Nov.	Pavillon, north west Troyes	
5 Nov.	Bar-sur-Seine	
6 Nov.	Montbard	
7 Nov.	Flavigny	

---

36 *CPR 1301–7*, 309.
37 *MRA*, no. 599.
38 The source for the itinerary to 12 Nov. 1305 is C.L. Kingsford, 'John de Benstede and his missions for Edward I' in *Essays in History Presented to R.L. Poole*, ed. H.W.C. Davis (Oxford, 1927), 355.

8 Nov.	Beaune	
9–10 Nov.	Chalon-sur-Saône	
11 Nov.	Belleville	
12–14 Nov.	Lyon[39]	
Nov.–Dec.	France	
1306		
2 Jan.	Lyon[40]	
Jan.–Mar.	France	
4 Mar.	Lyon[41]	
5 Mar.	Villefranche-sur-Saône	
6 Mar.	Belleville	
7–9 Mar.	Mâcon	
10 Mar.	Dijon	
11 Mar.	Autun	
12 Mar.	Saulieu	
13 Mar.	Avallon	
14 Mar.	Auxerre	
15 Mar.	Villeneuve-sur-Yonne	
16 Mar.	Villeneuve-la-Guyard	
17 Mar.	Melun	
18–20 Mar.	Paris	
20 Mar.	Luzarches	
21 Mar.	Saint-Just	
22 Mar.	Amiens	
23 Mar.	Saint-Riquier	
24 Mar.	Montreuil	
25 Mar.	Wissant	
26 Mar.	Dover	
27 Mar.	Canterbury, Newington	
28 Mar.	London	
2 Apr.	?London[42]	
12–16 Apr.	London	**208, 315**
21 Apr.	Westminster[43]	
13 May	London[44]	
30 May	London	**270**
7 June	London	**271**
17 June	London	**606**
23 June	Exchequer (council)[45]	
3 July	Northampton	**272**
11 July	London	**357**

[39] *Reg. Winchelsey*, i.xxiii; *Councils and synods*, II, ii.1230; Beardwood, 'Trial', 10.
[40] Beardwood, *Records*, 173.
[41] Kingsford, *op. cit.*, 339, 355–6 is the source for the itinerary to 28 Mar. 1306.
[42] *Reg. Halton*, i.250.
[43] *Reg. Halton*, i.261.
[44] *Reg. Gandavo*, i.211.
[45] *Parl. Writs*, ii.280.

23 Oct.	Lanercost, Cumb., (council)[46]	
7–29 Nov.	London	**273, 274, 316, 317, 359, 454, 464, 605, 689, 690**
15 Dec.	London	**209**
30 Dec.	London	**210, 318**
1307		
9 Jan.	London	**148**
16 Jan.	Beningbrough, Yorks.	**212**
8–9 Feb.	Carlisle (parliament)[47]	**214, 360**
9 Apr.	Carlisle	**319**
19 May	Bowes	**603**
29 May	Ongar, Essex	**1019**
3–22 June	London	**686, 687, 788, 922**
24 June	Theydon Mount, Essex	**818**
30 June	London	**607**
5 July	London	**688**
31 July	Ripon, Yorks.	**691**
1 Aug.	Selby, Yorks.	**785**
4 Aug.	Selby *or* Lichfield	**786, 787**[48]
7 Aug.	Loughborough, Leics.[49]	**1020**
Aug.	Leicester, Northampton Waltham Abbey, Essex[50]	
27 Aug.	Wallingford, Oxon.	**819**
Aug.–Sept.	Wallingford	
Nov.–Dec.	Windsor, Berks.[51]	
1308		
Jan–23 Feb.	Windsor	
Mar.	Tower of London[52]	
17 July	London	**1027**
9 Nov.	London, released from prison	headings preceding **608, 820, 923, 1021**
1–12 Dec.	London	**609, 820, 923**
20 Dec.	Theydon Mount	**608**
29 Dec.	London	**692**
1309		
2 Feb.	London	**924**
6–7 Feb.	Theydon Mount	**821, 1021**

[46] *Parl. Writs*, i.180.

[47] *MRA*, no. 473.

[48] Both letters are dated Friday after the feast of St. Peter *ad vincula*, **786** at Selby and **787** at Lichfield.

[49] Langton was arrested after 7 Aug. 1307 and imprisoned until 9 Nov. 1308.

[50] Beardwood, *Records*, 33, 243; Beardwood, 'Trial', 25; *Flores Historiarum*, ed. H.R. Luard, 3 vols. (Rolls ser., 1890), iii.138; *Chronicles of the Reigns of Edward I and Edward II*, ed. W. Stubbs, 2 vols. (Rolls ser., 1882–3), i.257.

[51] Beardwood, 'Trial', 11–12; Beardwood, *Records*, 1, 5.

[52] *CCR 1307–13*, 57; Beardwood, *Records*, 1.

23 Feb.–6 Mar.	London (parliament)	**693–5, 822–4, 925, 926, 1022, 1023, 1025**
12–20 Mar.	Greenford, Middx.	**696, 825, 826, 1028**
22 Mar.	Theydon Mount	**610**
27 Apr.	Westminster (parliament)[53]	
30 Apr.–14 May	London	**611–16, 697–700, 792–5, 827–33, 927, 928, 1029**
18 July–7 Aug.	Papal curia[54]	
7 Sept.	Pentlow, Essex	**1030**
29 Oct.–20 Dec.	Ranton, Staffs.	**703–5, 835–7, 929, 931, 932, 1032, 1302**
1310		
6 Jan.–3 Feb.	Ranton	**933–8**
8 Feb.	Westminster (parliament)[55]	
19–28 Feb.	London	**620, 799, 838, 939, 940, 1033**
6 Mar.	Merevale, Warw.	**621**
14–15 Mar.	Tamworth, Staffs.	**706, 1035, 1303**
17–19 Mar.	Lichfield	**941, 942**
27 Mar.	Solihull, Warw.	**617**
28 Mar.–24 Apr.	Lichfield	**622, 707, 708, 839, 841, 1036**
28 Apr.	Eccleshall	**623**
29 Apr.	Great Haywood	**840**
1–16 May	Lichfield	**709, 800, 842, 1037, 1038**
3 June	Lichfield	**943**
13–14 June	Coventry	**843, 1304**
21 June	Lichfield	**706, 710, 718**
21 July	Lichfield	**844**
23 Aug.	Lichfield	**1039**
4–12 Sept.	Lichfield	**855, 1040**
19 Sept.	Bishops Itchington, Staffs.	**1305**
26 Sept.	London	**711**
7 Oct.	London	**801**
16 Oct.	London	**845**
1 Nov.	London	**846, 847**
15 Nov.	Lichfield	**713**
16 Nov.	Bishops Itchington	**624**
8–16 Dec.	Lichfield	**718, 849, 850**
19 Dec.	Colwich, Staffs.	**1306**
1311		
14–16 Jan.	Lichfield	**626, 853**
17 Jan.	Eccleshall	**945, 1042, 1043**

[53] *Parl. Writs*, ii.24.
[54] *CPL*, ii.49, 57, 58.
[55] *Parl. Writs*, ii.40.

23 Jan.–3 Feb.	Lichfield[56]	**627, 714–17, 719, 851, 852**
18 Feb.	London	**629**
6–27 Mar.	Eccleshall	**630, 802, 856, 857, 947, 948, 958, 1307**
29 Mar.	Lichfield	**1284**
30 Mar.	Melbourne, Derb.[57]	
4 Apr.	Beauchief, Derb.	**859**
13 Apr.–24 Aug.	York[58]	**631–4, 720, 721, 723, 725, 726, 730, 803, 860–4, 951, 1046**
31 Aug.	Gainsborough, Lincs.	**1047**
10 Sept.–18 Dec.	London (parliament, Nov.)	**635–41, 727, 729, 731, 732, 865–8, 952–5, 1048–9**
19 Dec.	St. Albans	**1050**
22 Dec.	Daventry, Np.	**642**
29 Dec.	Lichfield	**734**
1312		
1–7 Jan.	Lichfield	**643, 735, 956**
10 Feb.	Lichfield	**870**
21–26 Feb.	York (parliament)	**736, 957**
24 Mar.	Lichfield	**644**
30 Mar.	Brington, Np.	**737, 738, 959**
3 Apr.	Westminster[59]	
1 May	England	
3 July	France: papal curia[60]	
19 Sept.	Pont-de-Sorgue	**739**
1313		
17 Jan.	Pont-de-Sorgue	**740**
31 Jan.	Avignon[61]	
3 Mar.	Avignon	**741**
30 Apr.	papal curia	
16 June	overseas[62]	
10 July	Hackington, Kent	**742**
20 Aug.	Northampton	**743**
23 Sept.	Westminster (parliament)[63]	

56 *MRA*, no. 757.
57 *MRA*, no. 373.
58 (?Apr.,- 1–5 July, ?Aug.) York, in prison: *Reg. Greenfield*, v. nos. 2549, 2551; *Foedera*, II, ii.138; *Registrum Palatinum Dunelmense, the Register of Richard Kellawe, Lord Palatine and Bishop of Durham, 1311–1316*, ed. T. Hardy, 4 vols. (Rolls ser., 1873–8), i.38–9.
59 J.C. Davies, *The Baronial Opposition to Edward II, its character and policy: a study in administrative history* (Cambridge, 1918), 390.
60 *CPR 1307–13*, 458; *CCR 1307–13*, 459; *Foedera*, II, ii.171.
61 *MRA*, no. 485.
62 *CPR 1307–13*, 566; *CCR 1307–13*, 538.
63 *Parl. Writs*, ii.100.

4 Oct.–26 Dec.	London	**645–7, 649, 654, 744–7, 757, 873–5, 883, 961–4, 1052**
1314		
3 Jan.	Grove, nr. Stevenage, Herts.	**650**
15 Jan.	Kirkstead, Lincs.	**877**
24 Jan.–8 Feb.	London	**651, 652, 748, 749, 876, 878, 879, 969, 1053**
2–3 Mar.	Lichfield	**882, 1310**
5–6 Mar.	Eccleshall	**653, 880, 881**
16 Mar.	Westminster[64]	
29 Apr.	London	**885**
17 May	Westminster[65]	
5 June	Bishops Itchington	**750**
9 June	Brewood	**1055**
12 June	Prees, Salop.	**970, 971**
14 June	Great Haywood	**752**
15–18 June	Lichfield	**751, 753**
24 June	Bishops Itchington	**1056**
8 July	Grove	**655**
8–15 July	London	**656, 754, 755, 886, 1057, 1058**
10–25 Sept.	York (parliament)	**657–60, 887, 888**
27 Oct.–1 Nov.	London	**756, 973**
7 Dec.	Prees	**974**
11 Dec.	Wybunbury, Ches.	**889**
20–21 Dec.	Eccleshall	**890, 1311**
23 Dec.	Lichfield	**761**
29 Dec.	Eccleshall	**891**
30 Dec.	Lichfield	
1315		
6 Jan.	Lichfield[66]	
17 Jan.	Grove	**892**
20 Jan.	Westminster (parliament)[67]	
22 Jan.–7 Feb.	London	**661–4, 977, 978, 1060**
17–23 Feb.	Coldham, Middx.	**893, 1061**
25 Feb.	Peterborough, Np.	**665**
2 Mar.	Castle Ashby, Np.	**666**
12 Mar.	Bishops Itchington	**1062, 1063**
17–26 Mar.	Lichfield[68]	**758, 759, 894, 895, 1065**
27 Mar.	Brewood	**667, 760**
10 Apr.	London	**1066, 1067**

---

[64] *Records of the Borough of Nottingham, 1155–1399*, ed. W.H. Stevenson (London, 1882), i.80–1.
[65] *Parl. Writs*, ii.122.
[66] *MRA*, nos. 94, 226.
[67] *Parl. Writs*, ii.137.
[68] *MRA*, no. 675.

14 Apr.	Greenford	**1068**
17 May	Colwich	**1312**
23–30 May	Eccleshall	**897, 979, 1069**
5 June	Prees	**981**
10 June	Haughmond, Salop.	**949, 950**
2–3 July	Lichfield	**763, 984**
5 July	Merevale	**1070**
2 Aug.	Castle Ashby	**668**
21 Aug.	Coldham	**897**
5 Sept.	Coldham	**670**
29 Sept.–4 Oct.	Weston, nr. Stamford, Np.	**766, 982**
6 Oct.	Everton, Beds.	**983**
9–13 Oct.	London	**1071–5**
16–17 Oct.	Grove	**671, 1076**
23 Oct.	Coleshill, Warw.	**768**
25 Oct.	Stone, Staffs.	**898**
27 Oct.	Wolstanton, Staffs.	**1077**
28 Oct.	Vale Royal, Ches.	**767**
2–7 Nov.	Eccleshall	**769, 899**
?8 Nov.	Penwortham, Lancs.	**672**[69]
10 Nov.	Eccleshall	**770**
17 Nov.	Cheadle, Ches.	**900**
1 Dec.	St. Werburgh's abbey, Chester	**809**
13 Dec.	Wybunbury	**673**
14 Dec.	Astbury, Ches.	**809**
20 Dec.	Ranton	**1313**
22 Dec.	Eccleshall	**771**
29 Dec.	Lichfield	**804**
1316		
19 Jan.	London[70]	
29 Jan.	Tarvin, Ches.	**807**
2–4 Feb.	Bracebridge, Lincs.	**901, 902, 1078, 1079**
4 Feb.	Lincoln	**1083**
11 Feb.	Bracebridge	**1080, 1081**
20–21 Feb.	Bracebridge	**674, 1084**
6 Mar.	Lichfield	**808**
6–7 Mar.	Sandwell, Staffs.	**772, 1087, 1314**
15 Mar.	Packington, Staffs. *or* Warw.	**1088**
27 Mar.	Packington	**773**
20 May	Arlesey, ?Beds.	**774**
28 May	Bishops Itchington	**675**
5 June	Abbots Bromley, Staffs.	**1315**
9 Jun	Church Gresley priory, Derb.	**812**
10 June	Repton priory, Derb.	**811**

---

[69] This letter has been erroneously entered in a Coventry archdeaconry section of the register with the date *vi Idus Novembris anno Domini supradicto*, that is 1315. Langton could not have travelled from Eccleshall to Penwortham and back again in such a short time.

[70] NA, SC 10, 7/222.

17 June	Darley, Derb.	**811**
29 June	Duckmanton, Derb.	**815**
1 July	Dronfield, Derb.	**777**
7 July	Tutbury, Staffs.	**905**
17 July	Offord Cluny, Hunts.,	**676**
5–7 Aug.	Sheepwash; Kirkstead, Lincs.,	**777, 907**
7 Aug.	Lincoln	**778, 779, 908**
25 Aug.–12 Sept.	London	**677, 775, 776**
20 Sept.	Southwark[71]	
4 Oct.	Hackington	**909**
6 Oct.	London	**780**
20 Oct.	London	**678**
19 Nov.	Lichfield[72]	
25 Nov.	Haughmond	**988**
28 Nov.–5 Dec.	Eccleshall[73]	**911, 1097–9**
12 Dec.	Sawley, Derb.	**912**
18 Dec.	Bishops Itchington	**1316**
1317		
7 Jan.	Coldham	**1104**
22 Jan.–5 Feb.	London	**784, 913, 914, 989, 1106, 1246**
14–16 Feb.	Coldham	**680, 990**
1–3 Apr.	Lichfield	**805, 806, 991, 1317**
9 Apr.	Brington	**918**
18 Apr.	London	**682**
16–19 May	London	**683, 685**
28 May	Stafford	**1318**
29–30 May	Eccleshall	**919, 1247**
5 June	Abbots Bromley	**1188**
20 June	Prescot, Lancs.[74]	
3 July	Prees	**992**
4 July	Pitchford, Salop.	**993, 994**
12 July	Fulbrook	**1191**
13 July	Brington	**995**
7 Oct.	Ashley	**1111**
16 Nov.	Wolston, Warw.	**1121**
27 Nov.	Aston, Warw.	**1248**
17 Dec.	Hillmorton, Warw.	**1319**
1318		
11 Feb.	Lincoln	**1202**
3 Mar.	London	**1125**
20 Apr.	Lichfield[75]	

---

[71] *The Registers of John de Sandale and Rigaud de Asserio, bishops of Winchester (A.D. 1316–1323)*, ed. F.J. Baigent (London and Winchester, 1897), 347.
[72] *MRA*, no. 96.
[73] *MRA*, no. 95.
[74] *The Coucher Book of Whalley Abbey* (Chetham Soc., 1st ser., 10, 1847), 307–10.
[75] *MRA*, no. 245.

2–11 June	Westminster[76]	
17 June	Penn, Staffs.	**1320**
9 July	Eccleshall	**1199**
8 Aug.	Sawley	**1254**
9 Aug.	Leake, Notts.[77]	
23 Aug.–7 Sept.	Coldham	**1200–2, 1259**
27 Sept.	Fulbrook	**1255**
20 Oct.	York (parliament)[78]	
16 Dec.	Eccleshall[79]	
23 Dec.	Chebsey, Staffs.	**1321**
1319		
7 Jan.	Pattingham, Staffs.	**1258**
9 Jan.	Sandwell[80]	
10 Jan.	Walsall	
11 Jan.	Canwell	
	Shenstone	
12 Jan.	Farewell	
	Lichfield	
13 Jan.	Tamworth	
14 Jan.	Tamworth	**1205**
	Lichfield	**1170**
	Harlaston	
	Clifton Campville	
15 Jan.	Burton upon Trent	
16 Jan.	Barton under Needwood	
	Tatenhill	
17 Jan.	Tutbury	
12 Feb.	Coldham	**1260**
7–12 Apr.	Lichfield[81]	**1322**
27 Apr.	London	**1131**
6 May	York (parliament)[82]	
2 June	Eccleshall	**1323**
10 June	Lichfield	**1132**
11 June	Great Haywood	**1168**
9 July	Eccleshal	**1169**
29 Oct.	Lichfield[83]	
22 Dec.	Gnosall, Staffs.	**1324**
1320		
8 Jan.	Eccleshall	**1174**
12 Jan.	Edlaston, Derb.	**1220**

[76] J.R.S. Phillips, *Aymer de Valence, Earl of Pembroke 1307–1324* (Oxford, 1972), 320–2

[77] *Foedera*, II, i.370.

[78] *Parl. Writs*, ii.182; Davies, *op. cit.*, 450.

[79] *MRA*, no. 328.

[80] For the itinerary from 9 to 17 Jan. see Hughes, 'Clergy list', 2–4, 14–20.

[81] *MRA*, nos. 369, 392, 393, 728.

[82] *Parl. Writs*, ii.197.

[83] *MRA*, no. 571.

14 Jan.	Butterley, Derb.	**1138**
20 Jan.	York (parliament)[84]	
2 Mar.	Coldham	**1180**
24 Mar.	?Balsall, Warw.[85]	**1238**
29 Mar.	Lichfield	**1325**
26 Apr.	Pitchford[86]	
24 May	Southam, Warw.	**1326**
7 July	Bishops Itchington	**1269**
22 July	Westhall, ?Oxon.	**1228**
1 Aug.	Lichfield	**1231**
7–29 Aug.	Westhall	**1144, 1179, 1231, 1232**
20 Sept.	Darley	**1327**
21 Sept.	Sawley	**1145**
26 Oct.–5 Nov.	London	**1146, 1148, 1271**
29 Nov.	Bishops Itchington	**1016**
11 Dec.	Brewood	**1233**
17 Dec.	Brewood	**1274, 1280**
20 Dec.	Gnosall	**1328**
29 Dec.	Eccleshall	**1235**
1321		
5–6 Jan.	Great Haywood	**1275, 1276**
1 Feb.	London	**1017**
10–11 Feb.	Coldham	**1018, 1282**
16–19 Apr.	Lichfield	**1154, 1155, 1277, 1329**
15 May	London	**1156**
23 May	Blyth, Notts.	**1150**
25 May	Pontefract	**1183**
28 May	Belgrave, Leics.	**1239, 1278**
3 June	London	**1184**
13–14 June	Walton on Thames	**1151, 1240**
29 June	Walton on Thames	**1279**
15 July	Westminster (parliament)[87]	
21 July–2 Aug.	London	**1157, 1158**
8 Sept.	Everton	**1186**
21 Sept.	Bishops Itchington	**1241**
30 Sept.–9 Nov.	London	**1161, 1242, 1244**
(died 9 Nov.)[88]		

[84] *Parl. Writs*, ii.215.
[85] *MRA*, no. 645, quoting Langton's register, gives Walsall, Staffs., but **1238** has Balsall.
[86] *The Cartulary of Haughmond Abbey*, ed. U. Rees (Shropshire Archaeological Society and University of Wales, Cardiff, 1985), no. 233.
[87] *Parl. Writs*, ii.234.
[88] BL Cotton MS. Cleopatra .D. ix, fo. 75; BL Cotton MS. Vespavian .E. xvi, fo. 33v.

INDEX OF PERSONS AND PLACES

A

Abberbury, Abberbur', Abberburi,
  Abburburia, Adberbury,
  Eadberbur', Eadburbur',
  Eadburbury, M. Thomas de, 67,
  70, 80; bp.'s chancellor, xxxiv; bp.'s
  clerk, 384; canon of Lichfield, 476;
  chancellor of Lichfield cath. [and
  preb. Alrewas], xxvii, 38, 46, 85,
  109, 170, 364*, 366, 368, 370, 463;
  holds manor of Steeple Aston, xxxi,
  183*; papal administrator of
  Coventry and Lichfield dioc.,
  xxx–xxxii, xxxiv, 183*; preb.
  Wellington, 31, 385; preb.
  Whittington and Berkswich, 18,
  384, 397; precentor of Lichfield
  cath., 392, 397, 688; vicar-general,
  xxvii, xxx, xxxiv, 105–8, 117, 119,
  120, 122, 124, 146, 147, 169, 170,
  177*–181, 204–8, 238, 250, 283–6,
  308, 309, 311–14, 330, 353, 355,
  356, 456–9, 475, 476*, 486, 1287
  Richard s. John de, granted custody of
  sequestration on Rodington ch.,
  399; r. Rodington, 330; alias
  Richard de Abberbury, r.
  Rodington, 417; alias Richard de
  Abberbur', 1286S; alias Richard de
  Abberburi, 1295D; alias Richard, r.
  Rodington, 1298P
Abbot, Richard, of Coventry, 1305S,
  1307D
Abbots Bromley (Bromleg', Bromleg' Abb',
  Bromlegh' Abbatis, Bromleye,
  Bromleye Abbatis), Staffs., 1289S(2),
  1294D, 1300S, 1301D, 1310S
  letter dated at, 1188
  parish ch., ordinations in, 1315
  vicarage, 1257; v., see Bromcote, Ralph
  de; Wetote, Nicholas de
Abel, Richard, preb. St. Chad's coll. ch.,
  Shrewsbury, 391; alias Richard s.
  John Abel, kt., 734; preb.
  Bishopshull, 734

Robert, OFM, 1317S, 1328P
Thomas, of Leicester, 1319D, 1320P
Walter, of Tamworth, 1301S; alias
  Walter Abel, 1303D; alias Walter
  Abel, of Amington, 1307P
Abendon, Abindon, M. Richard de, preb.
  Wellington, 480; proctor of Robert
  de Clipston, 885
Abingdon (Abindon), Oxon., letter dated
  at, xxxi, 127
  papal administrators of Coventry and
  Lichfield dioc. at, xxxi
Abington, Martin de, v. Weaverham, 172
Abonethewey. See Abovethewey
Abovethewey, Aboveþewe, Aboveþewey,
  John, brother of Robert, 808
  Richard, 1298S, 1300D, 1306P
  Robert s. William, 808
  William s. Richard, of Bishopstone,
  808
Absolon, Adam, citizen of London, 369
Abyndon, M. William de, preb. Gnosall,
  380
Accindona, Fr. Richard de, 1328S
Achard, Robert, r. Honily, 144
  Thomas, of 'Hampton', 1303D
Acomb (Acum, Acum prope Ebor', Akum),
  Yorks., 57, 67, 183*
  letters dated at, 6, 27, 45, 52, 54, 60, 65,
  101, 115, 118, 129, 130, 134, 161,
  173, 185, 192, 224, 236, 254, 255,
  257, 258, 260, 262, 263, 289,
  294–6, 339, 340, 370, 387, 389,
  390, 395–9, 437, 438, 440, 443,
  445, 446, 462
Acover', Acovere, Roger de, kt., 1321S,
  1326P
Acr', Fr. John de, 1328D
Acton (Acton Bloundel, Acton Blundel),
  Ches., ch., 186, 373, 1188, 1206; r.,
  1190, 1210, 1290D, 1322S, 1324D,
  1325P, and see Waleys, Gilbert le;
  Waleys, John le; Waleys Thomas
  called le
Acton, Ches., vicarage, 171; v., 891, 1286P,
  and see Prestecote, Thomas de

Alstonfield (*cont.*)
      William de Astebury, 762; v., *see*
         Astebury, William de; Caumpeden,
         M. Robert de; Codeshal', John de
Alton (Alveton), Staffs., dean of, 1264
   vicarage, 736, 772; v., *see* Boyfeld,
         Henry de; Dalby Paynel, James de;
         Kemesey, John de
Alvane, John, 1311P
Alvaston (Aylwaston), Derb., vicarage, 26,
      227, 1044; v., 515, *and see* Godman;
      Suwelle, Hugh de
Alvecote (Avecote), Warw., Ben. priory;
      prior of, 308, 1296D, *and see* Beulu,
      William de
Alvereston, Roger de. *See* Albriston
   Roger de, 1300P
   William de, r. Kingswinford, 753
Alverston, Robert de, r. Staunton in the
      Forest, 1319D
Alveton, Andrew de, 1303D, 1307P
   William de. See Avletton, William de
Alvreston, Alexander de, 1313P
Alwaston, Aylwaston, William de [patron],
      1301S, 1303D
Amandesham, Amondesham,
         Aymundesham, Adam de [patron],
         1318S, 1319D, 1321P
Ambaldeston, Richard de, 1303P
   Roger de, 1303D; *alias* Roger de
         Ambaston, 1307P
   William de, 1300S, 1301D, 1303P
Ambaston, Ambeldeston, John de, 1286P
   Peter de, 1327S
   Richard de, 1288S, 1289D, 1295P
   Roger de, 1286P
   Thomas de, 1286D, 1288P
   Thomas de, 1301S, 1303D, 1307P
Ambrighton, Adam de, 1289D, 1294P
   Roger de, 1289P
Ambriton, Ambrighton, Nicholas de, bp.'s
      clerk, 785–7, 1314D
Ambryghton, Ambrigton, John de, of
      Lichfield, 1317S, 1318D
Amerton (Ambrighton), Staffs., 1289S
Amiens, France, Appendix D
Amington (Amynton), Warw., 1307P
Amite, Richard, of Tutbury, 1310S
Amynton, Geoffrey de, 1298D, 1300D,
      1301P
   John de, 1310S
Amyot, John, of 'Sutton' [patron], 1312S
Amyz, William, of Tunstall, 1289S; *alias*
      William Amys of Tamworth,

1296D; *alias* William Amys of
      Tunstall, 1298P
Andr', William, of Stretton on Dunsmore.
      See Stretton super Donnysmor',
      William de
Andreu, Henry, of Tideswell, 1294S,
      1312D, 1316P
Andrew de ..., [patron] 1309S
Andrew, William s., 1315P
Angers (Andegaven'), France, Ben. abbey
      of St. Nicholas; Abbot William and
      conv. of, 663
Anibaldis, Richard de, archd. of Coventry,
      xxiii, xxiv, 1144; preb. Reims, xxiv,
      1144
Annabel, prioress of Farewell, 743
Annaghdown (Enagdunens'), Ireland, bp.
      of, celebrates ordinations in dioc.,
      xxi, 1299, 1300, 1301, 1309, *and see*
      O'Tigernaig, Gilbert
Ansedeleye, Annesdeleye, Richard de,
      1296D, 1297P
Ansley (Ansteleye), Warw., vicarage, 674;
      v., *see* Eton, Roger de; Pollesworth,
      John s. Richard de
Ansteleg', Richard de, 1294S
Ansti, Anesti, Ansty, Robert de, 1294S,
      1296D, 1298P
   Robert de, 1328S
Ansty, Warw., 1310S; lord of, 1315P, *and
      see* Irreys, Henry
Antwerp, Belgium, Appendix D
Apeston, Nicholas de, 1286A
Apparitor, William s. William the, of
      Sedgley, 1328S
Appeford, Henry de [patron], 1310S
Appelby, Roger de, 1313D
   Thomas de, 1285D
   William de, 1289S, 1294D, 1295P
   William de, of Repton, 1286A
Appilby, Appelby, M. Roger de, 1309A,
      1313D, 1318P; *alias* Roger de
      Appelby, 1312S
Aquitaine, France, duke of, *see* Edward,
      king of England
Aran (Aranen'), archd. of, 1040, *and see*
      Testa, M. William de
Arbury (Erdbur', Erdbury, Erdebur',
      Horbur', Hurdeburgh, Ordbur',
      Ordbury, Ordebur'), Warw.,
      1289D, 1327D, 1328D
   Aug. priory; canons of, 1285S(3),
      1286P(3), 1319P(3), *and see*
      Burbache, John de; Dene, William

Simon de, v. Eastham, 912
Thomas de, monk of Buildwas, 1289D, 1290P
Thomas de, r. Handley, 1220, 1236
Walter de, canon of Rocester, v. St. Michael's ch., Rocester, 592
William de, canon of Darley, 1327D
William de, monk of Shrewsbury, 1286S; *alias* William de Wlston, [monk] of Shrewsbury, 1289P
William de, r. Mavesyn Ridware, 1275, 1329S
William de, v. Backford, 203
Aston upon Trent (Aston, Aston super Trent', Aston super Trentam, Aston super Trentham), Derb., 1288S, 1289D
ch., xvii, 261, 557, 1041, 1172; custody of, 261; r., *see* Derby, Henry de; Frodesham, M. Robert de; Sandale, John de; Walton, Henry de
Astonesfeld, Alstanesfeld, Astenefeld, Henry de, 1310S, 1312D, 1313P
Asty, Robert, of 'Eyton', 1286A
Roger, of 'Eyton', 1310S
Astyn, Thomas, of 'Dassett', 1312D
Athelard, John, of Withybrook, 1289S, 1294D, 1295P
Athelastr', Athelaster, Hugh de, 1318S, 1323P; *alias* Hugh de Alaster, 1320D
Peter de, 1287D
Athelaxtre, Ralph de, 1289S
Atherston, John de, of Lichfield, 1312P
John de, 1313D, 1315P
Atherstone (Atherston), Warw., 1301S, 1303D, 1306P, 1310S
r., 1301S
Atherton, Alexander de, OFM Chester, 1295S
Attelberge, John de, subprior of Stone, 693–5; elected prior of Stone, 693–4; prior of Stone, 694–5
Attelberug', Attelberge, Robert de, 1301S, 1303D, 1305P
Atterlegh, Robert de, r. Tong, 928
Atthelastre, Athelastre, Alastr', John de, 1316S, 1318D, 1319P
Attingham, Salop., vicarage, 351; v., *see* Lilleshull, Richard de
Aubyn, M. Philip, r. Drayton Bassett chapel, 1254, 1259, 1273, 1324D, 1325P
Aucel, Robert, 808

Audeford, John de, 1313S
Audele, Aldeleye, Hugh de, r. Blore, 492, 1300D, 1301P
Audelee, Hugh de, justice of Chester, 807
Audelegh, Audele, Audeleye, Alan de [patron], 312, 492, 691
William de, 1321S, 1322D; *alias* William d'Audeley, 1323P
Audeley, Sir Nicholas de, 1312D
Roger s. Stephen de. *See* Bonde, Roger s. Stephen de, of Audley
Audeleye, Fr. Henry de, 1318P
Richard de, 1327S
Audelym, William de, canon of Hulton, 1295S
Audlem (Aldelyme), Ches., 1328S
Audley (Audele, Audeley, d'Audeley), Staffs., 1318S, 1320D, 1321P, 1323S, 1324D
Aula, Adam de, of Coventry, 1315S; *alias* Adam de Aula, 1323P
John de, of Bishton [patron], 1314D
John de, of Derby, 1311S, 1312D
Richard s. William de, in Derby, 1310S; *alias* Richard s. William de, of Derby, 1311P
Robert de, v. Weaverham, 585
Thomas de, 1318S, 1319P
Thomas de, of 'Walton', 1312D, 1313P
Thomas de, v. Leek, 314, 763
William de, of Derby, 1311P
William de, of 'Marston' [patron], 1303S; ?*alias* William de Aula, of Derby, 1312D
William de, of Priors Marston, 1318D, 1319P
Ault Hucknall (Alto Hokenhale, Hauthokenal), Derb., vicarage, 221, 1077; v., *see* Torkard, John; Kirkeby, Nicholas de
Aumesbur', John de, canon of Ranton, 1285S
Aumundestham, M. Adam de [patron], 1303D
Auneys, John, 1301S
Austanefeld, Alstansfeld, Henry de, 1296D, 1300P
Austrey (Aldelvestr', Aldestr', Aldovestre), Warw., 1313D
ch., 130; r., *see* Warde, William de la
Austyn, Austin, Roger, of Leamington Spa, 1310S; *alias* Roger Austin, 1312D; *alias* Roger de Lemynton, 1313P

Ralph the, of Nantwich, 1310S, 1312D, 1315P

Richard the, of Nantwich, 1311S, 1313D

Richard the, 1300S; *alias* Richard the baker, of Lichfield, 1301D, 1307P

Richard the, of Lichfield, 1299D, 1306P

Robert the, of Coventry [patron], 1296D, 1307P, 1312D, 1313P

Thomas s. William the, of Southam. See Sutham, Thomas de

William the, of Coventry, 1294S, 1296D; *alias* William the baker, 1300P

William the, of Newport, 1324S, 1328P; *alias* William s. Henry the baker, of Newport, 1326D

Bakewell (Bachwell, Baquell, Baquelle, Baukquelle, Bauquell, Bauquelle), Derb., 1289S(2), 1296D(2), 1298P, 1301S, 1303D, 1310S

parson of, 1298P, *and see* Roger

Bakewelle, Baukwell, Ralph de, 1312S, 1313D, 1315P

Baldewyn, Fr. Thomas, 1315S

Thomas, 1312S; *alias* Thomas Baldwyne, of 'Chesterton', 1313D, 1315P

Baldewyne, Adam, of Aylesbury. *See* Aillesbur', Adam de

Robert [patron], 1298D, 1300P

Baledeyn, Baliiden, Balyden, John de, 1296S, 1309D; v. Bolsover, 562

Balehevede, William, of Rolleston, 1303S

Balishal', Geoffrey de, canon of Kenilworth, 1316P

Ball, Robert, of Coventry [patron], 1301S

Balle, Richard, of Polesworth, 1319S, 1320D, 1321P

Walter. *See* Neuport, Walter de

Ballecot, Hugh de, r. Great Ness, 922

Balraven, John, 1316D

John, of Southam, 1316S; *alias* John Balraven, 1323D; *alias* John Baleran, of Southam, 1324P

Balsall (Baleshale), Warw., letter dated at, 1238

Balyden, Baliden', William de, 1309S; v. Crich (deacon), 1052

Bambourg', John de, v. Winwick, 214

Bampton, Hugh de, r. Gratwich, 313

Banastr', Roger [patron], 1323S, 1328P

Banastre, Thomas, OFM, 1289D

Banbur', Thomas de, monk of Dieulacres, 1286A

Banbury (Bannebur'), Oxon., 1316S, 1318D

letters dated at, xxxi, 182, 292

papal administrators of Coventry and Lichfield dioc. at, xxxi

Bangor, Wales, ch., 441

Bannebury, Nicholas de, monk of Croxden, 1288D

Thomas de, 1301S

Bannok, William, 1288S, 1289D, 1295P

Baquell, Baquelle, Robert s. Roger de, 1300S, 1301D, 1303P

Barber, John le, of Lichfield, 1286S

John le, of Newport, 1321S, 1322D, 1324P

Bardingmor', Gilbert de, 1285D

Barewe, Henry de, v. Harbury, 1143

Hugh de, 1303S, 1307D

John de, 1289D, 1298P

Robert de, 1327S, 1328D

Thomas de, 1303S, 1307D

Barford (Beresford), Warw., lord of, 1318P(2), *and see* Bereford, Adam de

Barholm (Berham), Lincs., 1286S

Barinton, Sir Ralph de, 1319P

Barkere, William s. William le, 1327S

Barkesford, William de, 1312D

Barkeye, William s. William de, 1327D

Barkols, Robert, 1309P

Barlborough (Barlbrugh', Barleburgh), Derb., ch., 11, 225, 1051; r., *see* Berchelmen, Henry; Longeford, Adam de

Barleburgh, William de, 1327S

Barling, Ellis de, canon of Dale, 1286S

Barneby, John de, 1239

Barnesby, Fr. William de, of Derby, 1324S; *alias* Fr. William de Barnesby, 1325D

Barnevill', Philip de, 1312P

'Barnwell' (Bernewell), Np. *or* Cambs., 889

Baroun, Baron, William, 1298S, 1301D, 1303P

Barowe, Richard s. Henry de, 1310S; *alias* Richard de Barewe, 1312D, 1313P

Barr', Barre, Hugh de, 813

William de, 1298S, 1299D, 1300P

Barre, John de [patron], 1307D, 1309P, 1328S

Robert de. *See* Parva Barre

William de, 1298D; *alias* William de Ware, 1300P

Chester (*cont.*)
St. John's coll. ch. (*cont.*)
chantry of B.V.M. in, 545; *alias* St.
Mary's chantry, 831, 910; chantry
priest of, *see* Aston, Andrew de;
Briddebrok', Nicholas de;
Donecastr', Adam s. William de
dean of, 864, 866, 874, 910
dean and chapter of, 820, 831, 1187
letter dated at, 921
prebs., *see* Clipston, Robert de;
Conestable, M. William called le;
Eston, William de; Haselarton, M.
Roger de; Hengham, Ralph de;
Henovere, M. William de;
Hothum, John de; Lustrishull,
Richard de; Marcell, M. John;
Napton, M. Ellis de; Picard, John;
Pikerel, M. William; Scalariis,
William de; Style, William de;
Wesenham, William de
St. Mary's, Ben. nunnery; conv. of, 581
nuns of, 911
prioress of, 211, 581, 911, *and see*
Alderdelegh, Alice de; Dutton,
Agatha de; Vernoun, Emma de
prioress and conv. of, 586
St. Mary's ch., near Chester castle, 885;
r., *see* Clipston, Robert de
St. Olaf's ch., 1207; r., 1322S, 1323D,
1324P, *and see* Marchale, Jordan de
St. Peter's ch., 169, 865, 879, 1232; r.,
see Chyu, Roger de; Mackelesfeld,
Robert de; Marthale, Jordan de;
Neuton, Guy de
St. Werburgh's, Ben. abbey; abbot and
conv. of, 152, 165, 168, 169, 175,
180, 181, 187, 198, 200, 204, 206,
212, 500, 552, 557, 809*, 853*,
865, 871, 878, 879, 885, 905, 912,
1030, 1041, 1172, 1219–21, 1232,
1244, 1269, 1298P, 1300S(2)
monk of sent to Coventry cath.
priory, 809*, *and see* Pentyn,
Matthew de
monk of sent to Hilbre Island, 809*,
and see Gilbesmeire, John de
monk of sent to St. Peter's Abbey,
Shrewsbury, 809*, *and see* Bosdoun,
Geoffrey de
monks of, 809*, 822, 1289D(2),
1290S, 1290D, 1290P(2), 1295S,
1295D, 1295P, *and see* Asthull,
Alexander de; Binington, William

de; Bosdoun, Geoffrey de; Bugges,
Henry de; Burton, John de; Cestr',
Ranulph de; Cestr', Richard de;
Foxwist, John de; Gilbesmeire,
John de; Longerigg', Richard de;
Mamcestr', Jordan de; Mareschall,
Robert; Markynton, Robert de;
Notyngham, John de; Pennesby,
Robert de; Pentyn, Matthew de;
Penwne, Walter de; Wenlok, John
de; Werburgton, Henry de
religious of, 867
St. Oswald's altar in, 867; v., *see*
Falhes, John de
visitation of, 809*
Chesterfeld, Fr. John de, 1315D, 1316P
Fr. John de, 1315D
Chesterfield (Cesterfeld, Cestrefeld,
Cestrefeud), Derb., 177*, 1300S,
1301S, 1303S, 1303D, 1307P,
1310S, 1312D, 1312P, 1326P
ch., 268, 1083
letter dated at, 716
vicarage, 222, 242, 465, 1105; v., 1167,
and see Bauquell, Richard de;
Suthleyrton, Walter de; Welton,
Thomas de
'Chesterton' (Cesterton, Chasterton),
Staffs. *or* Warw., 1303S, 1305P,
1313D, 1315P
Chesterton (Cesterton, Cestreton), Warw.,
1303S, ch., 93; r., 1135, 1296P,
1301S, *and see* Guldeford, Nicholas
de
Cheswardine (Chesewardyn',
Cheseworthyn, Chestwarthyn,
Cheswardyn, Cheswode), Salop.,
1323S, 1328D
ch., 950, 984
vicarage, 780; v., *see* Dunston, John de;
Poyvour, Richard le
Chetewynd, Chetewynde, John de, canon
of Lilleshall, elected abbot, 519*
Philip de [patron], 283, 313, 1298P
Chetewynde, Henry de, 1313S, 1316D,
1320P
John de kt., 1313S, 1316D, 1320P,
1327D, 1328P
Reginald de, r. Chetwynd, 1000, 1005,
1322S, 1324D, 1325P
Chetuln', Margery, daughter of Thomas
de, 813
Chetwynd (Chedewynd, Chetewinde,
Schetewynde), Salop., ch., 1000; r.,

Fr. Thomas de, 1328S

Clone, Clune, John de, r. third part of
Wroxeter ch., 348

  M. Walter de, granted custody of
  sequestration on portion of
  Wroxeter ch., 444; r. third part of
  Wroxeter, 348

Clopton, M. William de, r. Tydd St. Mary,
1325P

Clopton, dioc. Ely, r., 1296D, *and see* Bray,
M. Richard le

Cloude, John de la, 1319S, 1320D, 1323P

Cloune, Giles de, 1300S, 1301D, 1303P

Clowne (Cloune, Clune), Derb., ch., 55,
234, 672, 1085, 1114; r., 403, 432,
1114, *and see* Leycester, John de,
called Mauclerk; Nassington, M.
John de; Novelton, William de

Clungunford, Clungeford, Clungenford,
Roger de, preb. Coton in
Tamworth coll. ch., 293; *alias* preb.
Tamworth, 1289S, 1289D; *alias*
Roger Klingesforde, canon of
Tamworth, 1309P

Clutton, Roger de, 807

Clydelowe, Cliderhou, Adam de, 1289D,
1290P

Clyderowe, Richard de, 1300D

Clyf, Clif, William de, granted custody of
sequestration on Acton Burnell ch.,
44; r. Acton Burnell, 44, 326, 356,
449

Clyfton, Fr. William de, of Derby, 1324S

Clynton, Clinton, Ida de, lady of
Maxstoke, 1149, 1313S, 1318P,
1328P

  Philip s. John de, of Coleshill, r. Ratley,
  136; *alias* Philip de Clynton, 621;
  alias Philip de Clinton, 1295S

Clypston, William de, 1303S

Clyve, Clive, Ralph de, 1312D, 1313P

  Robert de, 1311P

  Simon de, 1301S, 1303D; *alias* Simon
  de Clyve, of Kingsbury, 1307P

  Thomas de, 1301S, 1303D, 1307P

Cobbeleye, Cobeleye, Alexander de,
1300S, 1301D, 1303P

Cobeleye, Cobeleye, William de, 1300S,
1301D, 1303P

Cobinton, Peter de, 1286D

  William de [patron], 1307P

Cobynton, Cubynton, Henry de, 1301S,
1307P

  John de, 1285P

John de, 1319S, 1320D, 1321P

John de, 1310S, 1313D; *alias* John
Donvalet, of Cubbington, 1318P

Peter de, 1285D, 1289P

Cockeslene, Walter de. *See* Hubert, Walter

Coddington (Codinton, Codynton
Cotyndon), Ches., ch., 152, 206; r.,
853*, 878, 888, 1297D, 1298P,
1311P, *and see* Bretoun, M. Alan le;
Bruera, M. William de; Meules,
Geoffrey de; Neuton, Guy de

Codeshale, Codeshal', John de, 1321D

  John de, v. Dilhorne, 590, 1264; v.
  Alstonfield, 1264

Codeshalle, Codeshale, Robert de, 1298S,
1299D, 1300P

Codinton, Codynton, Roger de, 1285D,
1289P; *alias* Roger de Codyngton,
r. Pulford, 191

  W. de [patron], 1298S

Codnor (Codenovere), Derb., 1178

Codynton, John de, 775

  Robert s. Gervase de, 1328S

Cok', William, of Bednall, 1300S, 1301D,
1303P

  William, of Hinckley, 1315D

Cokenage, William de, 1298P

Coket, Henry, of Tamworth, 1289P

  Robert, of Astbury, 1286A, 1306P; *alias*
  Robert de Astebury, 1300S; *alias*
  Robert Coket, 1301D

Cokkeslene, Richard de, 1301S(2)

Cokton', Walter de, 1322D; *alias* Walter de
Cougton, 1327P

Colcestr', Robert, 1289D

Coldham, Middx., 669

  letters dated at, 670, 680, 893, 897, 990,
  1061, 1104, 1200–2, 1259, 1260,
  1282

Coldwyne, Ralph, of Bishops Itchington,
1297S; *alias* Ralph Coldwyne, of
Mollington, 1298D

Cole, William, of Rugby, 1313S, 1315D,
1316P

Colebeyn, John, 1296P

Coleman, Henry, 1310S; *alias* Henry
Colemon, of Longdon, 1312D,
1316P

  William, 1303S, 1306D, 1307P

Colemon, Geoffrey, of Brinklow, 1319S;
alias Geoffrey Colemon, 1326D

Coleshill (Coleshull), Warw., 136, 1286A,
1301S, 1303S, 1312P, 1324D

  letter dated at, 768

Coventry and Lichfield dioc. (*cont.*)
  dim. of. *See* Index of Subjects
  official, xxviii, xxxiv, 64, 66, 69*, 300,
      328, 363, 602, 653, 657, 757*, 759,
      760, 877, 880, 972, *and see* Thorp,
      M. Walter de; Turvill', M. Philip de
  papal administrators of, xxx–xxxii, 125,
      126, 127, 182, 183*, 186, 251, 252,
      292, 337, 391, 460, 461, 1288, *and
      see* Abberbury, M. Thomas de;
      Everdon, Philip de; Napton, M.
      Ellis de
  receiver, 86, *and see* Gilbert
  sequestrator-general, xxvii, xxix, 81, 86,
      207, 300, 342, 344, 463, 634, 668,
      750, 859, 956, 958, 963, 970, 1047,
      1050, 1055, 1056, *and see* Dolaby,
      Richard de; Northampton, M.
      Richard de; Pupard, M. John;
      Swepston, M. William de
  vicars-general, xvii, xxxiv–xxxv, 105–8,
      117, 119, 120, 122, 124, 146, 147,
      169, 170, 177*–81, 204–8, 233,
      238, 250, 283–6, 308, 309, 311–14,
      330, 353, 355, 356, 489–601,
      heading before 608, heading before
      645, 667, heading before 701, 702,
      834, 849, heading after 870, 1021,
      1027, 1028, 1299 heading, 1300
      heading, 1309 heading, *and see*
      Abberbury, M. Thomas de;
      Leicester, M. Ralph de; Redeswell,
      M. Robert de; Thorp, M. Walter
      de
Cox, Alan, 1300S, 1301D, 1303P
Coylter, William le, of Lichfield, 1311D,
      1312P
Crakinthorp', Richard de, 1319D
Crane, Thomas de la, 1289S
Cranfield (Craunfeld), Beds., r., 1311S,
      1312P, *and see* Hillar', John
Crast, Nicholas de, 1316S, 1318D, 1319P
  Richard, 1298P
  William de, of Wolston, 1288S, 1289D,
      1294P
Craster, Geoffrey de [patron], 1310S,
      1311D, 1312P
Craunage, Geoffrey, 1298S; *alias* Geoffrey
      de Craunage, 1300D, 1301P
Craunford, Cranford, William de, 1316S,
      1318D, 1319P
Craunton, Fr. Robert de, 1323S
Cravene, Craven, Richard de, canon of
      Penkridge, 1312D, 1317P

Crécy, France, Appendix D
Cressacr', Cresacr', Thomas de, r.
      Mottram in Longdendale, 901*,
      902, 1194
Cressewall, Fr. Thomas de, 1322D; *alias*
      Fr. Thomas de Craswell, 1324P
Cressi, M. John de, r. Longford, 257
Cressington, Nicholas de, 1286A
Cressy, Cressi, John de [patron], 1313P
  Ralph de, 2, 40; r. Thorp, 46, 232
Crey, William, of 'Compton', 1328S
Crich (Cruch, Crugh), Derb., vicarage,
      220, 1052; v., *see* Baliden', William
      de; Whalleye, John de
Criketot, Cryketot, Peter de,
      proctor-general of the abbot and
      conv. of Lire, 630*, 1128
Cripst, William, of Amerton, 1289S
Cristelton, Thomas de, 1315S, 1316D,
      1318P
Croft, Henry de, 1301S; *alias* Henry super
      Croftum, of 'Weston', 1303P
  William de le, 1311S
Crofton, John de, 1326S, 1327D, 1328P
Crok', Thomas, preb. St. Chad's ch.,
      Shrewsbury, 923
Crokedayk, Adam de, king's justice, 813
Crophull, Roger de, r. Lullington, 1281
Cros, Henry atte, of Coventry, 1316S
Crosseby, Ranulph de, 1303S, 1306D,
      1307P
Crosto, Henry s. Henry de, 1300S
Croston, Lancs., ch., 851, 1204; r., *see*
      Clipston, M. Walter de; Lancastr',
      William de; Tunstall, M. Ralph de
Croukhul, Croukhull, Thomas de, 1301S,
      1303D, 1306P
Croulesmer', Croulesmere, John de,
      1324S, 1326D, 1327P
Croxall (Croxh', Croxhale), Staffs., lord of,
      1296D; *alias* William, lord of
      Croxall, 1307D; *alias* Sir William
      [of Croxall], 1309P
Croxden (Crokesd', Crokesden',
      Crokesdene, Crokesdeyne,
      Croxton, Krakesdene, Krokesden),
      Staffs. Cist. abbey; abbot of, 1298S,
      1310S, 1313S, 1313P, 1316S,
      1324S
  abbot and conv. of, 736, 772, 1312D,
      1315D, 1316P, 1318D, 1320S,
      1321S, 1323D(2), 1323P, 1326P
  monks of, 1285S(2), 1286A, 1286S,
      1286D(2), 1287S, 1288S, 1288D(2),

Robert de, 1294S, 1298D

Dunchirche, Donchirch, John de, 1288D, 1289P

Peter de, 1289S, 1296D, 1298P

Dunchurch (Dunchirch), Warw., 1316D

Dunchurch, Roger de, 1285P

Dunchurche, Ralph de, 1285D, 1286P

Dunclent, Dunklent, John de, r. Berkswell, 510, 542, 613

Dunham, William de, clerk of the bp. of Whithorn, 1296S; *alias* William de Dunhod, 1300D

Dunkeswell (Dunkewell), Devon, Cist. abbey; abbot of, 73*

Dunklent, John de. *See* Dunclent

Dunneschurche, Nicholas de, v. Leamington, 102

Dunstable (Donestaple, Dunstaple), Beds., Aug. priory; canons of, 38, 229, 1048, *and see* Merston, Geoffrey de; Woderore, William de

Dunstapel, John de, v. Lichfield cath., 1286P

John de, 1319P

Dunstaple, Fr. William de, 1323D; *alias* William de Dunstaple, monk of Coventry, 1326P

John de, v. Lichfield cath., 1287P

Dunstapul, Nicholas de, OFM, 1326S

Dunston, John de, v. Cheswardine, 780

Duram, Ralph de, canon of Hulton, 1295S

Durandesthorp, Thomas de, 1316S, 1318D, 1319P

Durham (Dulniens', Dunelmensis), Co. Durham, bp. of, 484, *and see* Bek, Antony

dioc., dim. of. *See* Index of Subjects

Duston, Robert de, 1326S

William de, 1289D

William de, 1313D, 1318P

Dutton, Dotton, Geoffrey s. Adam de, 920

Hugh de, kt., 807, 921, 1303P

Hugh s. Hugh de, 920

Robert de, admitted to Eccleston ch., 494; r. Eccleston, xxxvi, 849, 883*, 1306S, 1307D

Robert de [patron], 1300S, 1303P, 1307P, 1312S, 1313D, 1315P

Thomas de, 1300S, 1301D, 1303P

William de [patron], 1300S, 1300P

William de, pres. to Tatsfield ch., 1302A; r. Tatsfield, 1307D; *alias* William de Dunton, r. Tatsfield, 1306S

Duttone, Thomas de, v. Over, 586

Duyn, William le, of Brickhill, r. moiety of Malpas, 35, 158; *alias* William Duyn, 1214

Dyer (tinctor, tingtor, tynctor), Thomas the, 1307D, 1309P

William the, 1309A

Dyffryn, Clwyd, Wales (Deffrencloyt, Deffreyncloyth), lord of, 553, 1176, *and see* Grey, John de

Dymesdale, Richard de, monk of Coventry, 1326S

Dymgeley, William de, canon of Newstead, 1286D

Dymnok, Dymmok, Reginald, 1298S, 1300D; *alias* Reginald Dymmok, of Shrewsbury, 1301P

Dymok, Robert [patron], 1303D

Dyngele, Hugh de, r. East Farndon, 1326P

Dyrkesworth, John de, canon of Darley, 1287P

Dyseworth, Adam de, canon of Norton, 855

Dytheseworth, Fr. William de, 1321D

E

East Farndon, Np., r., 1326P, *and see* Dyngele, Hugh de

East Lexham (Estlexham), Norf., ch., 1142; r., *see* Norton, John de

Eastham (Estham), Ches., vicarage, 912; v., *see* Aston, Simon de; Clif, Adam del

Eastwood (Estwode), Essex, r., 1321P, *and see* Herlaston, John de,

Eaton Constantine (Eton, Eton Constantin, Eton Constantyn), Salop., chapel of, 420; r., 1295S, 1296D, 1297P, *and see* Despenser, Richard s. William le

Eborum, William, v. Radway, 1152

Eccles, William de, 1310S

Eccles, Lancs., vicarage, 1227, v., *see* Blakeburn, Adam de

Ecclesale, Eccleshale, Hugh de, 1289S, 1300D; *alias* Hugh Gunne, of Eccleshall, 1301P

Robert de, 1289P

Roger de, 1289S

Eccleshal', William de, 1311D, 1312P

Eccleshale, Ecclesale, Hugh de, 1285P

Nicholas de, 1300S

Eccleshale (*cont.*)
  Robert de, canon of Ranton, 1286S,
    1287P
  Roger s. Richard de, 1301S, 1303D,
    1307P
  Thomas de, 1303D, 1306P
Eccleshall (Eccleshal', Eccleshale), Staffs.,
    897, 1301S(2), 1301P, 1307D,
    1310S, 1317P, 1326S, 1328P,
    Appendix D
  letters dated at, 166, 388, 410, 411, 623,
    630*, 653, 769–71, 802, 856–8,
    880, 881, 890, 891, 899, 919, 945*,
    947, 948, 979, 1042, 1043, 1069,
    1097–99, 1169, 1171, 1174, 1199,
    1235, 1247
  prebendal ch., 911; ordinations in, 1307,
    1311, 1323
  preb., 726* n.2, *and see* Kynardeseie,
    John de
  v. [patron], 1301S, *and see* W.
Eccleston (Eccleston ultra Dee, Ecleston),
    Ches., ch., 194, 494, 602, 849,
    883*; r., 602, 1306S, 1307D, *and see*
    Dutton, Robert de; Venables, John
    de; Vernun, M. Richard
Eccleston (Eccliston,), Lancs., ch., 5, 47,
    83, 159, 856, 1212, 1228, 1239,
    1278; custody of to William de
    Catun, 5
  r., xxxvi, 856, 886, 1228, 1285D, *and see*
    Ellerker, John de; Lancastr', M.
    William de; Schepeye, Nicholas de;
    Tunstal, M. Ralph de;
    Womberegh, Richard de
Eccleston, William de, monk of Whalley,
    1289D
Eckington (Eginton, Egynton, Ekinton,
    Ekynton), Derb., 1287P, 1303S,
    1309D, 1310S, 1312D, 1313P,
    1319P
  letters dated at, 104, 331
  moiety of ch., 1, 45, 223, 236, 252, 558,
    559, 1024; custody of moiety, 45,
    236
  r., *see* Beaumont, Theobald de;
    Cusaunce, Reginald de; Mar,
    Robert de; Pontefracto, Adam de;
    Pratellis, M. Peter de; Stotevyle,
    John de; Sutton, M. John de
  ordinations in, 1285
  patronage of, 1103
Ecles, Eccles, Henry de, 1313S, 1319D;
    alias Henry de Becclus, 1321P

Edalveston, Edeleston, Edleston, Henry
    de, 1301S, 1303D, 1306P
Edenesover, Edesovere, Ednesovere, John
    de, 1286A, 1289S, 1294D, 1295P
Ederinghale, Edeinghal', Etinghal', John
    de, 1312S, 1313D, 1315P
Edgbaston (Egbaston, Egebaston,
    Ethebaston), Warw., 1301D,
    1320S, 1328S
Edgmond (Egemundon, Egmondon,
    Egmundon), Salop., ch., 350, 1011,
    1014; r., 928, 953, 1011, 1159, *and
    see* Bolde, Ralph de la; Scheynton,
    John de
Edihale, Edyhale, William de, 1285D,
    1287P
Edingale (Elynhale), Staffs., 1312D
Edith, Henry s. John, of Featherstone,
    1310S
Edlaston (Edulston, Edulveston), Derb.,
    ch., 1082, 1095; r., *see* Brademere,
    William de; Stowa, Robert de
  letter dated at, 1220
Edleston, Edeleston, Roger de, 1303D,
    1306P
Edmund, baron of Stafford, 316
  earl of Lancaster, 43, 231
  r. Buildwas, 1157
Ednesovere, Stephen de, 1301S, 1307P;
    alias Stephen de Ednyngshore,
    1303D
Edrichesleye, William de, r. Grendon, 114,
    1287P
Edrych, John, of Melbourne, 1286A
Edulston, Reginald de, 1301S
Edward I, king (1272–1307), xxxx, xxxii,
    xxxiv, xxxvi, 1, 28, 45, 82, 93, 131,
    157, 162, 170, 177*, 223, 236, 243,
    252, 310, 315, 326, 348, 356, 360,
    362, 464, 488, 813, 814
  court of, 70
  household, xxxiii
Edward, prince of Wales, earl of Chester,
    177*, 188
  King Edward II (1307–27), xxvi, xxxiii,
    xxxix, 706, 814, 817, 1103, 1122,
    1124, 1196, 1252, 1256
Edward, earl of Chester, 1196, 1211
Edward, Richard, of Elton, 1316P
Edyngburgh, William de, 1315D
Egbaston, Adam de, 1300S, 1301D, 1303P
  Richard de, 1300S, 1301D, 1303P
  Walter de, 1300S, 1303P; *alias* Walter
    de Cubbele, of Edgbaston, 1301D

Egebaston, Stephen de, 1326S, 1327D

Egelton, Egliton, Robert de, 1300S; r. Moreton Corbet chapel, 574

Egerton, John de, 1285S

Egginton (Egington, Eginton, Egynton), Derb., 1289S, 1295P, 1298S, 1300D(2), 1301S, 1301P(2), 1303S, 1303D, 1307P, 1313D, 1324D

  ch., moiety of, 1108; r., *see* Sutton, M. John de

Egilton, Robert de, r. Glooston, 1317D, 1318P

Eginton, Egington, Ralph de, OP Derby, 1286A

  Robert de. *See* Ekynton

  Roger de, canon of Repton, 1287S, 1288D

  William de [patron], 1303S, 1321S

Egynton, Henry de, 1300S, 1301D, 1303P

  John de, 1296D, 1300P

Ekynton, Eginton, Egenton, John de, 1298S, 1300D, 1301P

  Richard de, 1306S, 1307D

  Robert de, 1289S, 1294D, 1301P

Elaston, John de, 1312D, 1313P

Eles, Robert, preb. St. Chad's coll. ch., Shrewsbury, 995

Elford (Elleford), Staffs., ch., 729, 775; r., 1277, 1298S, *and see* Caldecote, John de; Freford, Robert de; Freford, Thomas de; Pollesworth, John de

  manor, 775

Elie, Ralph, of Killingworth, 1316D

Ellastone (Athelaxton'), Staffs., vicarage, 21, 279; v., *see* Kenilleworth, Robert de

Elleford, Elueford, John de, 1298S, 1299D, 1300P

  Richard de, 1300S, 1301D, 1303P

  Thomas de, of Eccleshall, 1301S; *alias* Thomas de Eccleshale, 1303D

  William de, 1286A

Ellerker, John de, r. Eccleston, 1239; r. Rolleston, 1251, 1278

Ellesmere (Ellesmer'), Salop., community of [?Knights Hospitallers], 1326D

  vicarage, 575; v., *see* Wonbourne, John de

Ellisworth, William de, proctor of Robert de Beverlaco, 1134

Elmedon, Richard de, 1298P

  William de, xx, 1285P

Elmehirst, Robert de, 1288P

Elmhurst, John de, 1298S, 1301D, 1303P

Elmton (Elmeton), Derb., vicarage, 1099; v., *see* Batheley, Robert de; Otrington, Gilbert de

Elton (Elfeton), Hunts., 1316P

Elton, John de, monk of Whalley, 1289D

  Roger de, 1300S, 1301D, 1303P

Ely (Elien'), Cambs., dioc., 1312S; dim. of. *See* Index of Subjects

  letter dated at, 222

Ely, M. Luke de, chancellor of Lichfield cath. [and preb. Alrewas], 622*, 718; land of, 786; [patron] 1295P

Elynton, John de, of Coventry, 1289P

Elyot, Roger called, 1300S; *alias* Roger Elyot, 1303P

Elys, John, of Melbourne, 1298S, 1300D, 1301P

  Walter, of Melbourne, 1301D

  Walter, of Melbourne, 1303S, 1305D, 1307P

  William, of Melbourne, 1289S, 1290D, 1294P

Elyves, John de, 1298S

Emsey, Emesey, Fr. Arnold de, 1313S, 1318D, 1323P

Engelby, Richard de, 1287S, 1288D, 1289P

Engelby, Hengelbi, Peter de, 1286A, 1294S, 1296D; *alias* Peter s. Roger de Engelby, 1298P

Engelton, Thomas de, 804

Ensaunt, John le, r. Upton Magna, 936

Eppeley, Robert de, 1309S

Erbaston, Peter de, 1327D

Ercalewe, Hamond s. Roger de, 1328S

  Sir William de, 1328D

Erdbury, Richard de, 1319P

Erdeley, Erdele, William de, 1286D, 1288P

Erdington (Erdinton), Warw., 1299D

Erdynton, Roger de, 1298S, 1300P; *alias* Roger atte Grene, of Erdington, 1299D

Erdynton, Erdinton, Erdyngton, Henry de, kt., 1303D, 1310S, 1312D

  Robert de, 1310S, 1312D, 1313P, 1318P

Ergum, Ergoun, Ralph de, r. Matlock, 1076, 1080

Erleston, Geoffrey de, 1300D, 1301P

Ern, Thomas, 1312S; *alias* M. Thomas Ern, 1313D

Ernald, William, of Brockhurst, 1316S, 1319P; *alias* William de Brokhurst, 1318D

Ernesford, Thomas de, 1303S
Erthington, Erdington, Erdinton, Reginald
  de, 1318S, 1319D, 1320P
Ervefen, Adam de, 1300S, 1301D, 1303P
  William de, 1300S, 1301D; *alias* William
    de Ervefeld, 1303P
Erveys, John, canon of Kenilworth. *See*
  Herveis, John
Eschebourn, Walter de, 1296D
Esenyngton, Robert de, licence for
  oratory, 717
Eshebourn, Essheborn, Essheburn, M.
  Andrew de, preb. Gnosall, 539,
    1290S, 1294P
Espenser, John le, 1286A, *alias* John le
  Despenser, of Lichfield, 1289S;
    alias John s. William le Spenser,
    1294D; *alias* John le Spenser, of
    Lichfield, 1295P
Esquyer, Robert le, 1315D
Esseby, Robert de, canon of Lilleshall,
  1313P
Esseby la Souche, John de, r. Plemstall,
  889
Essex, Ralph de, of Leominster, 1328S
Essheborne, Thomas de, 1300S
Essheborn, Assheburn, Esshebourn,
  William de, xxxvi, 1289S, 1294D;
    v. Castleton in the Peak, 496
Essheburn, Esheborn, Richard de, monk
  of Dieulacres, 1290S, 1294D
Essington (Esenyngton), Staffs., 717
Essinhurst, Ellis de, 1323P
Estby, Fr. John de, 1313P
Estham, Richard de, 1300S, 1301D,
  1303P
Esthop, Roger de, r. Stirchley, 941
Estl..., William de, canon of Haughmond,
  1290D
Estlemynton, Henry de, 1300S, 1303P;
    alias Henry de Lemynton, 1301D
  Philip s. Richard de, 1294D; *alias* Philip
    de Estlemynton, 1295P
  Richard de, 1285P
  William de, 1312S; *alias* William le
    Gardener, of Leamington Hastings,
    1313D, 1316P
Estnorton, John de, 1321P
'Eston', lord of, 1310S, 1312D, *and see*
  Eston, William de
Eston, William de, Bp. Langton's clerk, 71,
  366, 368, 371, 372, 820; preb.
  Gnosall, 539; preb. St. John's,
  Chester, 820

William de, lord of 'Eston', 1310S; *alias*
  William, lord of 'Eston', 1312D
Estowe, John del, 1286D
Estryveyn, Richard le, of Stone, 1288P
Estwell, Henry de, canon of St. Mary de
  Pratis, Leicester, 1319S
Etewell, Ethewell, John de, 1313D, 1318P
  Nicholas de, 1286A, 1310S, 1312D,
    1313P
Etewelle, Etewell, Richard de, 1289S,
  1294D; *alias* Richard Foliot, of
  Etwall, 1296P
Ethorp, Henry de, 1316S
  Robert de, 1294S, 1295D, 1298P
'Eton', W., lord of, 1310S
Eton, Abel de, 1306S, 1307D, 1309P
  Fr. Richard de, 1318P
  John de, 1285P
  John de, 1303S
  Nicholas de, lord of Ratley, 1300S
  Nicholas de, lord of Stockport, 1313D
  Nicholas s. Nicholas de [patron], 209;
    alias Nicholas de Eton, 1315P
  Provincialus de, 1289P
  Reginald de, 1289S, 1294D, 1295P
  Richard de, 1290S, 1311D
  Robert de, 1289S, 1296D, 1298P
  Robert de, 1310S, 1315D, 1320P
  Roger de, v. Ansley, 674
Etwall (Etewell, Ettewell), Derb., 1296P,
  1303D, 1306P
  vicarage, 248, 1061, 1070, 1173; v., *see*
    Aslacton, William de; Bollesovere,
    William de; Kyrketon, Gilbert de;
    Sutton, Robert de
Etwell, Walter de, 1286A
Euledon, Eweldon, Adam de, 1294D,
  1295P
Eunok, Roger, of Avon Dassett, 1319S,
  1324D, 1326P
'Euovere', William de [patron], 1303S
Everdon, Philip de, cofferer of the
  Wardrobe, xxx; papal
  administrator of Coventry and
  Lichfield dioc., xxx–xxxii, 186;
  houses in Lichfield close, xxx, 412;
  preb. Wellington, xxx, 31, 385,
  480
  Robert de, 1287P
Evereslegh, Everesle, John de, of Banbury,
  1316S, 1318D
Eversholt (Tiveresholt), Beds., r., 1294S,
  and see Thornestoft, Stephen de
Everton, Beds., letters dated at, 983, 1186

Felde, William de, of Breaston, 1310S,
    1315P; *alias* William de Campo, of
    Breaston, 1312D
Felicia, William s., 814
Felley (de Felloya), Notts., Aug.; prior and
    conv. of, 1323S
Felonglegh, Henry de, 1309S
Felton, Hugh s. Philip de [patron], 944
    John de, 1310S, 1311D, 1315P
    Stephen s. Thomas de [patron], 345
Fenny Bentley (Benteley, Benteleye),
    Derb., ch., 1093, 1164; r., 1325P,
    and see Hale, M. John de;
    Hasilbech', Richard de; Malet,
    Robert
Fennycompton, Simon de, 1286P
Ferbraz, Feerbraz, Robert [patron],
    1312D(2), 1313P
Fermente, John le, of Ockbrook, 1301S
Fermlegh, Richard de, 1319D; *alias*
    Richard Fermlegh, of
    Warmingham, 1320P
Fermo, dioc. of, xxvi
Ferndon, Nicholas de, monk of
    Combermere, 1326P
Fernyleye, Richard de, 1318S
Ferour, Richard s. Alexander le, 1300S;
    alias Richard le Ferour, of Shipton,
    1301D; *alias* Richard le Ferour, of
    'Sutton', 1303P
Ferrar', Ferar', Ferariis, William de, kt.,
    1310S(2), 1312D, 1313P
Fetherston, Faþreston, Adam de, 1301S,
    1303D
Field (Falde), Staffs., 1285P
Fige, Robert, 1323P
Fillingleye, Fillangleye, M. Richard de, v.
    Offchurch, 32, 97
Fillongley (Filongelegh, Filongeleye,
    Filungelegh, Fylongele,
    Fylungeleye), Warw., 1298P,
    1303D, 1307P(3), 1312D, 1315P
    ch., 145; r., 659, *and see* Howeschilt,
    Conrad
Filongeleye, Fylongele, William de, 1306S,
    1307D
Filton, Northumberland, Appendix D
Filungle, Thomas de, 1294S
Filungley, Walter de, 1289D; *alias* Walter
    de la Slade, of Fillongley, 1298P
Filungley, Filungleye, Richard de, 1286A,
    1289S; *alias* Richard de Filongeleg',
    of Ryton, 1294D; *alias* Richard de
    Filongel', of Ryton, 1295P

Filungleye, Robert de, 1286D, 1288P
Findern (Fynderne), Derb., 1288P
Fineshade (Fynneshed), Np., Aug.; house
    of, t. to for ordinand, 1319S
Finmere (Fynmere), Oxon., r., 1285P, *and
    see* Langeton, John de
Fisherwick (Fisscherwyk, Fissherwyk,
    Fysherwyk'), Staffs., lord of,
    1307P
    waste land in, 794, 795
Fishmonger (piscarius), Richard the, of
    'Newcastle', 1289D; *alias* Richard
    le Fysher of 'Newcastle', 1301P
Fiskerton, John de, 1295S, 1296D, 1297P
Fitteleye, Thomas s. Richard de, 1310S;
    alias Thomas de Flittelegh, 1312D;
    alias Thomas de Flitteleye, 1313P
Fitz (Fittes, Fyttes), Salop., ch., 979; r.,
    985, 988, 1313S, 1320P, *and see*
    Preston, M. Robert de; Golden, M.
    Richard de
Fitzalan, Edmund, earl of Arundel, 538,
    991, 997, 998, 1018, 1156
    Richard, earl of Arundel, 335, 444; heir
    of, 348
Fitzherbert, Henry, 1301S; *alias* Henry
    Herbert, kt., 1303D
    John, kt., 1177
    John, 1316S; *alias* John Herbert, lord of
    Norbury, 1318P
    Nicholas, 1318S; *alias* lord of Somersall
    Herbert, 1321D; *alias* Nicholas
    Fitzherbert, lord of Somersall
    Herbert, 1323P
    Roger, of Parwich, r. Norbury, 1177;
    alias Roger Fitzherbert, r. Norbury,
    1327S; *alias* Roger, r. Norbury,
    1328D
    Roger, r. Norbury, 426, 1177
Flamstede, John de [patron], 1303D,
    1307P
Flaumvill', John de, 1294S; *alias* John de
    Flaumvill' of Willoughby, 1298P
Flavigny, France, Appendix D
Flecher, Robert le, of Melbourne. *See*
    Melbourn, Robert s. Henry de
Fleming, Robert, r. Harrington, 1315S
Flintshire, Wales, parishes in, xxii
Flixton (Flyxton), Lancs., prebend in
    Lichfield cath., 482, 486, 726* n.2,
    766, 782, 1217; prebs., *see* Burnel,
    M. William; Clipston, Robert de;
    Harewedon, Robert de; Hustwayt,
    John; Kynardeseie, John de;

Freford, Frefford, Robert de, 1319S
   Robert de, preb. Syerscote, 1266
   Robert de, r. Elford, 1277
   Sibyl, wife of William de, 794
   Thomas de, r. Elford, 775, 776
   William de [patron], 1301S(2), 1303S,
      1307D, 1311D
   William de, 775, 787, 792–6,
Frekelton, Freculton, Roger de, 1307D; r.
      Bury, 1205; r. Radcliffe, 1205
Freman, Thomas, of Coleshill, 1301S
   William, 1289S; *alias* William s. John
      Freman, of Ash, 1294D; *alias*
      William s. John Freman, 1296P
   William, of Ockbrook [patron], 1301S,
      1303D, 1307P
   William, of 'Willey', 1298P
Fremon, Richard, 1327S
Fremont, Nicholas, of Newport, 1300S;
      alias Nicholas Fremond, 1301D;
      alias Nicholas Fremond, of
      Newport, 1303P
Frere, Richard, of Burton, 1298S, 1300D,
      1301P
   Robert, 1301D, 1303P
Fretheuvill', Frefthevill', Ralph de, kt.,
      1034, 1087
Froddesham, Richard de, 1288P
   Walter de, 1307P
Froddesleye, Roger de, 1301P
Frodeley, William de, 1309P
Frodesham, Froddesham, John de, 1298S,
      1300D
   M. Robert de, r. Aston upon Trent, 557,
      1172
   Nicholas de, 1300S, 1301D, 1303P
   Nicholas s. Richard de, 834, 1300S,
      1301D, 1303P
   Robert de, 1313S, 1315D, 1316P
   Walter de, 1300S; *alias* Walter s.
      Richard de Frodesham, 1301D,
      1303P
Frodesley (Frodeslegh), Salop., chapel,
      359, 1015; chaplain of, *see*
      Aldenham, Hugh de; Honold,
      Thomas
   custody of to Thomas, r. Cound, 359
   lord of. *See* Honold, John
Frodeswell, John de. *See* Hore, John de
Frodsham (Frodesham, Froddesham,
      Froddisham), Ches., 1289P,
      1301S
   vicarage, 584; v., *see* Wodeford, Benedict
   de

Frollesworth, William de, 1307P
Frome Whitfield (Fromwysfeld, From
      Wystfeld), Dorset, r., 1306S,
      1307D, *and see* Bourton, M.
   William de
Frost, Richard s. Ralph, 1318S; *alias*
      Richard Frost, 1326P
Fryet, Alan, 814
Fryvyll, Frevill', Alexander de, kt., 309,
      713, 732, 1266, 1296D
Fuchun, Peter le. See Fomython, Peter de
Fulbrook (Folbrok, Fulbroc, Fulbrok),
      Oxon., letters dated at, 202, 1191,
      1255
Fulburn, Folbourn, William de, r. Heswall,
      167, 887
Fulcushull, John de, in Wolston, 1310S;
      alias John de Folkeshull, 1312D
Fuleburn, William de, custody of
      Tarporley ch., 13; r. Tarporley, 20,
      155
Fulford, Folford, Thomas de, 1310S,
      1311D, 1312P
Fulk, canon of Norton, 1286P
Fulkstan, John s. Henry de, 1313P
Fulready (Fulfreleye), Warw., 1320P
Fulschawe, Fulchawe, Fulschawa, Richard
      de, 1320S, 1321D, 1326P
Furnerlegh, Henry de, 1288S, 1289D
Furnivall, Furneval, Furnival, Thomas de,
      kt., 1110, 1327D, 1328P
Furnoys, Furneys, Robert de, 1300S,
      1303P
Fuyrbraz, Robert le, of Willington
      [patron], 1301S
Fychet, Robert, of Field, 1285P
Fylongele, William de, 1306D
Fylongeleg', Fylongeleye, John de, 1301S,
      1303D; *alias* John Agnes, of
      Fillongley, 1307P
Fylungeley, Fylungleye, John de, 1309A,
      1313D, 1315P; *alias* John s. Henry
      de Fylungleye, 1312S
Fylungley, Filungley, Filungleye,
      Fylungleye, Henry de, 1309A,
      1316S, 1317D, 1323P
Fynderne, Nicholas de [patron], 1306D
   Ralph de, 1295P
Fyndirne, Findern, Fyndren, Richard de,
      1289D
   Robert de, 1307P, 1313S, 1315D; *alias*
      Sir Robert de Findren, 1320P
Fyndron, Findren, Fyndirne, Adam de,
      1313S, 1315D, 1320P

Haralt, Gregory called, of Sutton
  Coldfield, 1286A; *alias* Gregory
  Harald, of Sutton Coldfield,
  1294D, 1295P
'Harborough', Magna *or* Parva,
  (Hardeborug', Herdebergh,
  Herdebur', Herdesborugh), Warw.,
  1303S, 1312P, 1316S, 1318D,
  1328P
Harbury (Herberburi, Herberbury,
  Herburbur'), Warw., 1294D,
  1296P
  vicarage, 527, 1143; v., *see* Barewe,
    Henry de; Libener', John
Harcourt, H. de, of Ludlow [patron],
  1310S
Harding, William, 814
Hardushull, John de, kt., 1316P
Hardwick (Herdewyk), Warw., 1154
Hare, Roger le, of Northwich, 1295D
Harecurt, Harecourt, John de, kt., 80,
  1296D, 1298P
Harenhale, Henry de, v. Holy Trinity,
  Coventry, 25, 96
Harewedon, Harwedon, Robert de, preb.
  Darnford, 758, 781; preb. Flixton,
  766
Hareweld, Nicholas de, r. Tarporley, 1218
Harewell, Thomas de, r. Cubbington, 610,
  650
Hareworth, John de, 1306D, 1307P
Harewy, Robert, of Church Lawford,
  1294S; *alias* Robert Hathewy, of
  Church Lawford, 1298D; *alias*
  Robert Hathewey, 1300P
Harlaston (Herlaston), Staffs., 1306D,
  Appendix D
Harle, Harleye, Philip de, granted custody
  of sequestration on Great Ness ch.,
  922; r. Great Ness, 504, 924, 937,
  1069
  Richard de, kt., 334, 349, 964, 1296D
Harlee, Thomas de, 1290S
Harley (Harle, Harlegh), Salop., ch., 334,
  349, 354, 964; r., 1310S, *and see*
  Kynredeleye, Richard de;
  Langeton, Thomas de; Leicestr',
  John de
Harleye, Fr. John de, 1315D
Harpelegh, Happelegh, Adam de, 1312D,
  1313P
Harpour, Robert le, of 'Chesterton'
  [patron], 1303S; *alias* Robert le
  Harpour, 1307D

Harrington (Harington), Lincs., r., 1315S,
  and see Fleming, Robert
Harrow (Harewe), Middx., r., 718, 720,
  and see Bosco, M. William de
Harthill (Herthull), Ches., chapel, 549,
  1216; r., *see* Pyctesleye, Thomas de;
  Stonlee, John de
Hartington (Hertingdon), Derb., vicarage,
  6, 224, 1091; v., *see* Wycumbe,
  Richard de; Wylghton, Alexander
  de
Hartshorne (Herteshorn', Herteshorne,
  Hertishorn'), Derb., ch., 255, 1183;
  r., 404, 518, 1063, 1183, 1185,
  1231, 1290D, 1294P, *and see*
  Melbourn', John de; Riston, John
  de; Sauvage, Henry; Warde,
  William de la
Harvington (Herforton), Worcs., r.,
  1319D, *and see* Lodelowe, William
  de
Harwood (Horwode), dioc. Lincoln,
  1313S, 1315D
Harynton, M. John de, Official dioc.
  Lincoln, *sede vacante*, dim. of, 1325S,
  1326D(2), 1326P, 1328P
Hasbury (Hassebury), Warw., 1310S
Haselarton, M. Roger de, preb. St. John's
  coll. ch., Chester, 864
Haselovere, William de, 1307P
Haselovre, Haselovere, William de, 1303S,
  1306D, 1307P
Haselwell, Ralph s. David de [patron], 887
Hasilbech', Haselbech', Richard de, r.
  Fenny Bentley, 1164, 1231, 1325P
Haslington (Haselington, Heselurton),
  Ches., chapel, 182, 1195, 1201;
  chaplain of, *see* Kanneleye, M.
  Henry de; Vernoun, Thomas de;
  Vernoun, William de
Hassop, Gervase de, 1303D, 1307P
  William, 1311D; *alias* William de
    Hassop, 1312P
Hastang', Henry [patron], 1307P
Hasting', Hastang', Thomas de, kt.,
  1307P, 1310S, 1312P, 1320S,
  1321D
Hastinges, John de, kt., 145; *alias* Sir John
  de Hastang', 1311P, 1312D,
  1313D, 1316P; *alias* John de
  Hastang', 1313S
Hastings (Hastingges), Sussex, king's
  chapel of St. Mary, 1141
Haston, John de [patron], 1320D

Richard de, monk of Dieulacres, 1295P
William de, 1295D, 1296P
Hordewyk, Robert de, v. Chilvers Coton,
    642
Hordley (Hordel', Hordelegh', Hordeleye,
    Hordyleg'), Salop., chapel, 577,
    999; ch. *or* chapel, 873; chaplain of,
    see London, John de
  custody of sequestration on to Robert de
    Marchumle, 577, 873
  r., 933, *and see* Deryngton, Richard de
Hore, John de, of Fradswell, 1301S; *alias*
    John de Frodeswell, 1303D, 1306P
Horlegh, Horleye, Hurleye, Hugh de,
    1289S, 1294D
  Ralph de, 1289S, 1294D, 1295P
  Walter de, 1285P
Horleye, Hurleg', Roger de, 1298S,
    1300D, 1301P
Hormingwod, Marmaduke de, port.
    Darley ch., 1094
Horn, John, of Rugby, 1313S, 1319D,
    1321P
  Robert, 1326S
  Thomas, of Rugby, 1324S, 1326D,
    1328P
Horncastr', Horncastel, John de, 1315S,
    1316D, 1318P
Horseleg', Horseleye, Roger de, 1301S,
    1303D, 1306P
  Thomas de [patron], 1301D
Horselegh, Horseley, Horslcg', Gilbert de,
    1320S, 1321D, 1323P
Horseleye, Horseley, Henry de, 1313S,
    1316D, 1319P
  Robert de, v. Marston on Dove, 1100
  William s. Henry de, 1313P
Horsington, Lincs., r., 1315S, *and see*
    Stapilton, Ellis de
Horsknave, Thomas le, of Tideswell. *See*
    Tydeswelle, Thomas de
Horsle, Robert de, 1290A
Horslegh, John de, 1312P
Horsley (Horsele, Horseleg', Horseleye,
    Horsle), Derb., 1313D
  vicarage, 258, 568, 1035, 1079, 1109,
    1302D; v., 1303P, *and see* Halum,
    Henry de; Palmere, William le, of
    Nottingham; Poucher, Herbert;
    Pouger, Henry
Horsley, William de, 1286P
Horton, John de, 1290D, 1294P
Horwod', Horwode, Sir Richard de,
    1310S, 1313S, 1315D

Hosse, Roger, of 'Eyton' [patron], 1310S;
    alias Roger Husse, 1313D
Hotcumbe, Hocumbe, Hotcombe,
    Thomas de, 1289S, 1296D, 1298P
Hothum, John de, preb. St. John's,
    Chester, 779, 866, 908
Hotoft, Fr. John, 1319D
  Hugh de. *See* Hotot, Hugh de
Hoton, Thomas de, OCarm., 1315S
Hotot, Hotoft, Hottot, Hugh de, r.
    Berrington, 446, 1287S; r. Church
    Eaton, 299, 716
  John de, 792, 796, [patron] 1301S
Hotton, John de, 1289S
'Houghton' (Hoghton, Houghton), dioc.
    Lincoln, 1318D, 1319P
Houghton, M. Ralph de, proctor, 774
Hounfreyston, Fr. Roger de, of
    Shrewsbury, 1324S; *alias* Fr. Roger
    de Homfreiston, 1326D
Houre, Thomas de, 1303D
Housyndon, Housedon, William de,
    1327S, 1328D
Houton, John de, monk of Merevale,
    1317D
  John de, r. moiety of Staveley, 1087
Houve, William de, 1285P
Hovygham, John de, v. Marton, 683,
    1310S
Howel, M. Rhys ab, preb. St. Chad's ch.,
    Shrewsbury, 481
Howeschilt, Conrad, of Germany, r.
    Fillongley, 145, 604*, 605, 606;
    alias Conrad de Almania, 659
Hoyland, Sir R. de, 1301S
Hubert, parson of Donington, 920
  Walter, of Cook's Lane, 1300S; *alias*
    Walter de Cockeslene, 1301D; *alias*
    Walter de Cokeslene, 1303P; *alias*
    Walter Hubert, r. Sedgley, 755
Hug', John, of Chadshunt [patron],
    1296P
Hugeford, William de [patron], 1301S
  William de, r. Stockton, 1161
Hugford, Hugeford, Fr. Robert de, 1328D
  Sir Walter de, 1327D, 1328P
Hugh, lord of Baslow, 1312D
  John, s., 1287S
  monk of Birkenhead, 1295S
  Robert s. John s. 1298S
  s. Sir John de Lodbrok', 1132
  William s., 1309P
Hughe, John, of 'Norton', 1319D
  William, of Melbourne, 1286A

Lowne (Lound, Lund'), Derb., vicarage,
1020, 1175; v., *see* Hykelinge, John
de; Scharneford, Robert de
Luceby, John de, canon of St. Mary's,
Shrewsbury, 1295D
John de, 1301D, 1303P
Lucius, pope, 1061
Luco, Francis de, canon of York, 1135
Luçon (Lexen'), France, dioc., 499
Lucy, Geoffrey de, r. High Bickington,
1326P
Richard de, 1286A, 1301S, 1303D,
1306P; presented to Hartshorne
ch., 1183
Luda, M. Harvey de, granted custody of
Kirk Ireton chapel, 555
Lude, Fr. Bartholomew de, 1326D
Ludlow (Luttolw), Salop., 1310S
Luffe, William, of Wellesbourne, 1286P
Luffield (Loffeld, Luffeld), Np., Ben.
priory; prior of, 1310S, 1312S,
1312D, 1319P
t. to for ordinand, 1312S, 1312D,
1313D, 1316P, 1322P;
Lughteburgh, William de, canon of
Arbury, 1319P
Lullington (Lollington, Lullynton), Derb.,
r., 773, 1281, *and see* Crophull,
Roger de
Lullington, Henry de, 1286P
Robert de, 1286A, 1300S, 1301D,
1303P
Lullinton, Ranulph de, 1309A
Lumbard, Hugh, of Newport, 1328D
Lungassh, Longassh, John de, 1286A, 1296D
Lusseby, John de, 1289S
Lustrishull, Richard de, preb. St. John's,
Chester, 779, 908
Lutemay, John, of Stone, 1286A; *alias* John
Lotemay, 1294S; *alias* John
Lytemay, 1295D; *alias* John
Lutebmay, 1297P
Luton, Thomas de, 1285P
Luttele, William de, 1309S
Lutterworth, Walter de, monk of Combe,
1288S
Lutton, William de, v. Ormskirk, 17, 154
'Lutton', lord of, 1328S, *and see* Philip
Luzarches, France, Appendix D
Lych', Lich', Ingram de, 1286A, 1294D,
1295P
Lycoris, John, 1318S; *alias* John Lycoris, of
'Newcastle', 1319D; *alias* John
Licoris, of 'Newcastle', 1320P

Lye, Fr. Robert, 1319P
John, 1318S, 1319D, 1327P
William de la, of Pemberton, 1310S
Lyle, William de, 1309D
Lyllyngton, Richard de, 1327S
Lymbergh, Adam de, granted Berkswell
ch. *in commendam*, 682
Lyme, Lime, John, of Coleshill, 1303S,
1312P
Lymm (Lymme), Ches., moiety of ch., 913,
1223; r., *see* Lymme, Jordan de;
Lymme, Peter de; Mascy, Adam s.
Robert de
Lymme, Lyme, Gilbert de, 920
Jordan de, 1303S, 1307D; r. moiety of
Lymm, 1223
Peter de, 1323S
Peter de, r. moiety of Lymm, 913
Lymmerse, Lemiseye, Lymese, Lymeseye,
Lymesy, Sir Peter de, 1301S,
1303S, 1303D, 1306D, 1307P,
1311P
Lympodeshei, Lympodeseye, Richard de,
85, 301
Lyndraper, William le, of Derby, 1288S,
1295P; *alias* William le Lyndraper,
1289D
Lynet, Simon, 1300S, 1303P; *alias* Simon
Lynet, of Lichfield, 1301D
'Lynhull', 1313S
Lynton', William de, of West Hallam,
1319S; *alias* William de Lynton',
1321D
Lynton', Linton', William de, 1310S,
1312D
Lyon (Lugdun'), France, 486, Appendix D

M

M..., Thomas [patron], 1323D
'Mablethorpe' [St. Mary *or* St. Peter]
(Malberthorp), Lincs., r., 1300D,
and see Gerard, Roger
Macclesfield (Machesfeld, Maclesfeld,
Makesfeld), Ches., 1310S(2),
1312P(2)
dean of, 1240
Maceon, Maceoun, Mazon, Gilbert le,
1313S; *alias* Gilbert le Maceon, of
'Sutton', 1315D
Simon le, of Chesterfield, 1312P
John le, 1319S; *alias* John le Mason, of
Coventry, 1320D

John le, of 'Weston', 1298S, 1301P

William le, of Repton, 1313S, 1315D, 1318P

Machoun, William, of Breaston. *See* Breydeston, William de

Mackelesfeld, Maklesfeld, Robert de, r. St. Peter's, Chester, 169, 865

Mackeworth, William de, v. Weaverham, 51, 160

Mackworth (Macworth, Mackeworth, Makworth), Derb., 1296D, 1318S, 1319D, 1320P, 1327S

    ch., 1163; r., 429, 1165, 1320D, *and see* Touschet, Edmund; Tuchet, Simon

Mackworth, Mackeworth, Makworth, Robert de, 1289S, 1295D, 1298P

Maclesfeld, Maklesfeld, Andrew de, 1298P

    M. Jordan de, r. Mottram in Longdendale, xxxvii, 174, 901*

    Peter de, 1301S, 1307P; *alias* Peter de Maxfeld, 1303D

    William de, 1303S, 1306D, 1307P

    William de, 1312S, 1313D

Mâcon, France, Appendix D

Macstok', William de, monk of Merevale, 1317P

Mactlisfeld, Maklesfeld, Ralph de, 1289S, 1294D, 1295P

Macwode, William, of Birmingham, 1298P

Macworth, Mackeworth, Hugh de, prior of Breadsall, 271, 1032

Macy, Richard de. *See* Massi

Madburleye, William de, [patron], 54, 161

Madeley (Madeleye, Maddele), Staffs., 1303D

    ch., 294; r., 1290D, *and see* Hunte, Thomas le

'Madewell', 1154

Madleye, William de, 1301S; *alias* William Ludkyn, of Madeley, 1303D; *alias* William de Madeley, warden of Holy Sepulchre hosp., Radford, 1305P

Magna Cuve, Ellis de, 1310S, 1312P

Magna Derset, Simon de, 1312S, 1313D; *alias* Simon de Derset, 1315P

Magna Houghton, Peter de, 1319P

Magote, Walter s. William s., 1300S; *alias* Walter Maggot, 1301D; *alias* Walter Magot, 1303P

Makeney, Makeneye, Nicholas de, 1303S, 1307D, 1309P

Makeneye, William de, 1285P

Makestoke, Sir John de, 1298P

Maklesfeld, John de, 1289P

    Roger de, 1300S

Makstok', Maxstok', Richard de, 1313S, 1315D; *alias* Richard Moubon, of Maxstoke, 1318P

Makworth, Macworth, Robert s. Nicholas de, 1318S, 1319D, 1320P

Malberthorp, Roger de, r. Whittington, 251

Malet, Robert, r. Fenny Bentley, 1093

Maleton, Robert s. John de, 1301P

Malines, Belgium, Appendix D

Mallingges, M. Ralph de, r. Pagham, 470*, 471*

Mallisor', Roger s. Robert de, 1316S; *alias* Roger de Mallesovere, 1318D; *alias* Roger de Malleshovere, of 'Weston', 1319P

Mallori, Peter, v. Wolston, 1121

Malnourished (male nutritus), Peter called the, of St. Albans, 1318S

Malo passu, Hugh de, 1313D, 1315P

Malocellus, Lazarinus s. George, preb. Freeford, 1270

    Theodosius, preb. Freeford, 1270

Malopassu, Richard de, 1294D

Malpas (de Malo passu, Maupas), Ches., moiety of ch., 35, 158, 1214; r., 1214, 1215, 1324S, 1325D, 1326P, *and see* Duyn, William le; Turvill', Thomas de

Malpas, Roger de, 1290S

Mamcestr', Fr. Henry de, 1286P

    Henry de, 1328S

    John de, 1300S, 1301D, 1307P

    Jordan de, monk of St. Werburgh's, Chester, 822

    Richard de, 1324S, 1328D

Mammesfeld, Henry de, dean of Lincoln, 1083

Mancestr', Mamcestr', Mauncestr', Alexander [patron], 1307D

    Hugh de [patron], 1310S, 1312D, 1315P

    Simon de [patron], 1326S, 1326P

    William de, 1301S

    William de, 1310S, 1312D, 1315P

Mancetter (Manecestr', Manecestre), Warw., ch., 33, 98; r., 1306P, *and see* Herle, John de

Manchester (Mamcestr', Mamecestr', Mammecestr'), Lancs., 1326P

Manchester (*cont.*)
  ch., 75, 82, 162, 208, 876; custody of
    sequestration on to Geoffrey de
    Stokes, 208
  r., *see* Deverdon, M. John de;
    Grandisson, Otto de; Langton,
    Walter; Stokes, Geoffrey de; Sygyn,
    William
  dean of, 75
Mandut, Richard, 1294D
Manduth, Manduyt, William, 1310S,
  1312D, 1313P
Manecestr', John de, 1285D
Manecestr', Mamcestr', Thomas de,
  1296S, 1301D, 1303P
Mangepayn, William s. William, 1310S;
  alias William Mangepayn, of
  Repton, 1312D
Mapelton, Henry de [patron], 1315D
  John de [patron], 1313S, 1318S; *alias*
    John s. Thomas de, 1319D
  Thomas de, 1313S, 1315D, 1316P
Maperlegh, Henry de, 1286A
Maperleye, Maperlegh, Richard de,
  1303S, 1312P
Mapledurham (Mapeldoreham), Hants.,
  ch., 1252; r., *see* Bruera, M. Gilbert
  de; Longavilla, Isumbert de
Mapurleye, Maperley, Geoffrey de, 1310S,
  1313D, 1326P
Mar, Ma, Robert de, r. moiety of
  Eckington, 1, 223, 559
Marcell, M. John, preb. St. John's,
  Chester, 820
March', Hugh, of 'Newbold', 1310S,
  1311D, 1312P
  Robert, of Newbold, 1324S, 1326D
Marchal', Thomas le, of Derby, 1316S;
  alias Thomas the marshal, of
  Derby, 1318D
Marchale, Marchal', Marthale, Jordan de,
  r. St. Olaf's, Chester, 1207, 1322S,
  1323D; *alias* Jordan de Maxfeld, r.
  St. Olaf's, Chester, 1324P; r. St.
  Peter's, Chester, 1232
Marchan, Richard de, canon of Norton,
  1295P
Marchet, March', Maresch', John, of
  Newbold, 1294S, 1298D, 1300P
Marchington (Marchinton), Staffs.,
  1312D(2)
Marchinton, Henry de, r. Cubley, 1023
  William de, 1310S, 1313P
  William de, 1318D, 1319P

Marchomley, Robert de, 1328S
Marchumle, Marchumlee, Marchumleye,
  Robert de, 1286A; granted custody
  of sequestration on Hordley chapel,
  577, 873
Marchynton, Marchenton, Marchinton,
  Nicholas de, kt., 1300D, 1316S,
  1319D, 1320P, 1321S, 1323D,
  1326S, 1326P
  Walter de, 1321S, 1326D
Mardewell, Philip de, v. Milwich, 769
Mare, John de la [patron], 346
Mareschal, Henry le, of Coventry, 1294S,
  1301P
  Jordan le, of Farnborough, 1301S
  Nicholas, called le, preb. St. Chad's coll.
    ch., Shrewsbury, 377, 381; preb.
    Gnosall, 380
  Nicholas le, of Nantwich, 1289S,
    1296D; *alias* Nicholas le Mareschal,
    1298P
  Richard le, 1314S
  Roger le, 814
Mareschale, Hawise la, 340; *alias* Hawise le
  Mareschall, 687
Mareschall, Robert, monk of St.
  Werbergh's, Chester, 809*
  Roger called, preb. Darnford, 1258
Margaret, baroness of Stafford, 1300S(2)
Markeaton (Marketon), Derb., 1310S,
  1312D
Marketon, Henry de, 1318S, 1319D
  Richard de, 1310S, 1311D, 1315P
  Walter de, 1296D
  William de, 1318S, 1319D, 1320P
Markeuton, John de, 1286A
Marklau, Markelawe, Markislau, M.
  William de, granted Prestwich ch.
  in commendam, 443; custody of
  Prestwich ch., 461; r. Prestwich,
  907
Markyate, Herts., Ben. nunnery of Holy
  Trinity of the Wood; prioress and
  conv. of, 105, 624, 652, 1289S,
  1295P
  prioress and nuns of, 103, 1294D
  religious of, 1298P
Markynton, Robert de, monk of St.
  Werbergh's, Chester, 809*
Marmeon, Sir Robert, 1303S
Marmyon, Geoffrey, v. Kenilworth, 595; v.
  Packington, 599
Marnham, Notts., r., 75, *and see* Gringelee,
  William de

Nore, Peter s. William atte, of Chillington,
1312S, 1326P; *alias* Peter s.
William Novere, of Chillington,
1320D
Noreys, Richard, 1285P
Norhampton, Fr. Simon de, 1320P
Roger de, v. Lichfield cath., 1297S,
1298D, 1299P
Norman, William, 1288S
Normanton (Normunton), Derb., ch., 501;
r., *see* Wyne, Roger
Normanton, Normenton, Roger de,
1320S, 1326D
William de, canon of Dale, 1286P
Norment', Thomas de, 1326S
Normonesleye, Normoneslegh, Hugh de,
1303D, 1306P
Norreys, Robert le [patron], 1319S, 1323D
Norrton, William de, 1313S
North Meols (North Moeles), Ches., ch.,
84, 163, 164, 890; r., *see* Hampton,
M. Henry de; Herty, Nicholas de;
Preston, Robert de
North Wingfield (Hallewynefeld,
Hallewynefeud, Wynefeld), Derb.,
ch., 249; r., 433, 1311S, 1312D,
and see Deyncurt, Roger;
Wermington, M. Richard de
Northampton (Northt'), Np., 1318P,
Appendix D
Aug. abbey of St. James; prior and conv.
of, 1319D
Cluniac priory; monk of, 1289S, *and see*
Morthwayt, Hugh de
letters dated at, 112, 272, 419, 743
St. John the Baptist's hosp., t. to for
ordinand, 1319P
Northampton, Norhampt', Norhampton,
Norht', M. Richard de, 511,
[patron] 1295P, 1301S; r.
Adderley, 346, 1008;
sequestrator-general, xxix, 634,
668, 715, 719*, 750, 840*, 859,
955, 963, 1047, 1050, 1055, 1056
Northburgh, Roger, bp. of Coventry and
Lichfield (1322–58), xiii, xviii, xxvi,
xxviii
register of, xiii
Northenden (Norworthyn), Ches., ch., 198;
r., *see* Blechelegh, Henry de
Northerene, John de, of Coventry, 1310S;
alias John called le Northerne, of
Coventry, 1312D
Northkyte, Roger de, 1297P

Northmondesleg', Hugh de, 1301S
Northwell, Norwell, Henry de, canon of
Thurgarton, v. Blackwell, 560,
1043
Northwich (de Norwyco), Ches., 1295D
Northwych, Norwyco, Robert de, 1289S,
1290D, 1295P
'Norton', 814, 1312S, 1313D
'Norton', dioc. Worcester, 1319D
Norton (Noghton', Northon), Ches., Aug.
priory; canon of Haughmond sent
to, 473*, *and see* Bruges, Thomas de
canons of, 530, 855, 1286P, 1294D,
1295P *and see* Bruges, Thomas de;
Dyseworth, Adam de; Fulk;
Marchan, Richard de; Neuton,
Hugh de; Putok', Gilbert called;
Wyco, William de
letter dated at, 530
prior of, 855, 920, 921, 1300S, *and see*
Andrew; Buddeworth, Roger de;
Colton, John de; Putok', Gilbert
called
coadjutors to prior, 855, 859
election of, 530, 877
prior and conv. of, 183*, 870, 916, 920,
921, 1225
religious of, 1300S, 1303D
obliged to provide chaplain for
Poolsey chapel, 921
visitation of, 855, 859, 921
Norton, John de, r. Brinklow, 1142; r. East
Lexham, 1142
John de, 1300D, 1301P
John de, 1285P
Nicholas de, r. Stretton, 1090
Richard de, granted custody of
sequestration on Prees vicarage,
974; v. Prees, 981, [patron] 1316S
Richard de, proctor of Richard de
Touecestr', 647; notary public, 756
Richard de, t. for ordinand, 1322D
Richard s. William de, 1301S, 1307P
Robert de, 1298S, 1299D, 1300P
Thomas de, v. Lichfield cath., 1325S
Walter de, 1310S, 1311D, 1312P
Walter de, v. Prestbury, 168
William de, 814, and Elizabeth, his wife,
814
William de, 1298P
William de, 1313S; *alias* William s.
Robert de Norton, 1315D
William de, clerk [patron], 1296S
William, s. Reginald de, 1294S

Thurstan, of Pitchford [patron], 1326P

Thurstaston (Thurstanston, Thurstanton), Ches., ch., 204, 1244; r., 1244, 1289S, 1290D, 1295P, *and see* Brynynton, William de; Hurel, M. John; Moeles, Simon de

Thyrneby, Geoffrey de, r. Stoke upon Tern, 578

Tibbot, Nicholas, of Tamworth, 1288S, 1289P

Tibesale, Tixhale, William de, 1289S, 1296D

Tibshelf (Tibbeshulf, Tibbeshulf in E, Tippeshulf, Tybbeshulfe, Tybeschulf, Typpeshulf), Derb., ch., 247, 256, 401, 413, 1169, 1170*; r., xxiii, 1089, 1294P, *and see* Bradeleig', John de; Brawode, Stephen de; Stafford, M. Robert de; Weston, William de

   rectory, xxiii

   vicarage, 1169, 1170*, 1171; v., *see* Gonaltston, William de

Tickford (Tikeford, Tygeford, Tykford), Bucks., Ben.; religious of, 1307D

   t. to for ordinand, 1325S, 1326D

Ticknall (Tykenhal', Tykenhale), Derb., 1300D, 1316S

Tideswel, Tideswell, William de, 1315D, 1318P

Tideswell (Tideswell, Tideswelle, Tyddeswell, Tydeswell), Derb., 1294S, 1312D, 1315D, 1315P, 1316P, 1318P

   v., 1309P, *and see* Folejambe, John

Tideswell, Clement *or* William de [*sic*], of York, 1315D

Tideswelle, John de, 1289D

Tifford, James de, port. Wroxeter, 538

Tigeswell, Henry de, 1286A

Tillot, Thomas, of 'Newton', 1289S; *alias* Thomas Tyllot, of Melbourne, 1290D; *alias* Thomas Tillot, 1294P

Tilston (Tilstan, Tylstam, Tylstan), Ches., ch., 179, 199, 450; r., 1289D, *and see* Bletcheleye, Henry de; Bletcheley, Richard de

'Tirlington'. *See* Thrussington

Tirvill', Robert [patron], 1312D; *alias* Robert Turvill', 1313P, 1315D; *alias* Robert de Turvyll', 1315D

Titteleye, Thomas de [patron], 1297S

Tixhale, Tyxhale, Geoffrey de, 1303S, 1305D, 1306P

William de. *See* Tibesale

Tochet, Richard [patron], 1313P

Toft, Tofft, John de, 1313S, 1315D, 1316P

   John de, 1313S, 1315D; *alias* John s. Henry de Toft, 1316P

   John s. John de, of Egginton, 1300D; *alias* John de Toft, of Egginton, 1301P

   Richard de, 808

   William de, 1319S, 1320D; *alias* William Toft, 1326P

Togod, Adam, 814

Tok', Ermintrude, wife of Robert de, 1037

   John de, r. Grindon, 691

   Richard, 1315S; *alias* Richard Touk, 1318D

   Robert de, kt., 1037, 1303D; *alias* Sir Robert Toke, 1301S; *alias* Sir Robert Tok', 1307P; *alias* Sir Robert Tookey, 1312D; *alias* Robert Toke, 1319P

Tok, Touk, John, r. Blore, 312, 1297P; *alias* John de Stok', r. Blore, 1296S

Tokatt, William, 1316P

Tolone, Ralph, 1300S, 1301D, 1303P

Toly, Nicholas, of Tamworth, 1288D

Tomworth, Tameworth, William de, 1321S, 1324D, 1326P

Tong (Tonge), Salop., r., 928, *and see* Atterlegh, Robert de

Tonge, Alan de, 1298D; *alias* Alan Tonge, 1300P

   William de, 1324P

Torald, Ranulph called, v. Bowdon, 845; *alias* Ranulph Thorald, 1305D, 1306P

   Robert, 1318S, 1324D; *alias* Robert Thorald, 1327P

Torkard, John, v. Ault Hucknall, 221; *alias* John de Hokenhal, v. Ault Hucknall, 1077

Torleston, Robert de, 1285D

Torold, Ranulph, of Birkenhead, 1301S

Torpe, Thorp, Fr. Nicholas de, 1320D, 1328P

Torporleg', Torpurle, Bertram de, 1300S, 1301D, 1306P

Torrynton, Torrynge, John de, r. Acton Burnell, 356, 1010; r. Tarring, 1010

Tothale, William de, prior of hosp. of St. John of Jerusalem in England, 576

'Torvenhorn', William, lord of, 1306S

Totnesovere, Roger de [patron], 1312S

Ulkel, John, 1289S, 1295P; *alias* John de
  Ulkel, 1294D
Ulkeyl, Andrew, 1285P
Ulsby, Richard de, papal notary, 1144
Ulverscroft (Hullescroft, Olvescroft,
  Ovescroft, Ulvescrofte), Leics.,
  Aug.; prior of, 1328D
  prior and conv. of, 1327S
  t. to for ordinand, 1318S, 1325S
Underwod', Henry, 1167
Underwode, Nicholas de, v. Doveridge, 1174
Unkeswrth, Henry de, 1298D
Uphavene, M. John de, r. Chetwynd, 1000
Upholland (Holand', Holande juxta
  Wygan, Houland), Lancs., coll. ch.
  of St. Thomas the Martyr; dean of,
  850, 857, 862, 881, *and see* Gede,
  William le; Sondbache, Ralph de
  prebs., 583, 881, *and see* Acton, Robert
  de; Berghton, Nicholas de;
  Castello, William de; Derb', Walter
  de; Donstaple, John de; Fossebrok',
  William de; Hereward, William;
  Snayth, William de; Spenser, Hugh
  le, of Norwich; Sutton, Thomas de;
  Walton, William de; Wyco,
  William de
Upinton, Opinton, John de, 1310S,
  1311D, 1312P
Upper Langwith (Languath), Derb., ch.,
  1098; r., 1098, 1102, 1320D, *and see*
  Henovere, Nicholas de;
  Thurgarton, M. Alexander de
Upper Tean (Tene), Staffs., 763, 1310S,
  1317D
Upton (Opton), Ches., lord of, 1307P, *and
  see* Opton, John de
Upton Magna (Opton), Salop., ch., 936; r.,
  see Bruneshope, M. John de;
  Ensaunt, John le
Upton Waters (Upton Parva), Salop.,
  chapel, 1001; chaplain of, *see*
  Hatton, John de; Ridel, Robert
Upwell, Uppewell, Uppewelle, Hugh de,
  granted custody of sequestration on
  Brinklow ch., 52, 57; r. Brinklow,
  57, 101, 411
  Thomas de, 1285P
Urbe, John Gaetani de, cardinal deacon of
  St. Theodore, archd. of Coventry,
  xxiii, xxiv, 1144; preb. Reims, xxiv,
  1144
Urmston (Urmeston), Lancs., lady of. *See*
  Citharede

Uttokeshather, Uttokeshathere, Robert s.
  Hugh de, 1324S, 1325D; *alias*
  Robert de Uttokeshather, 1327P
Uttokeshatr', Ottekeshather, Uttoxhather,
  Richard de, 1310S, 1312D, 1313P
Uttoxeter (Huttokshare, Ottokeshare,
  Ottokeshather, Uttokasher,
  Uttokeshather, Uttoxhather),
  Staffs., 708*, 1323P, 1324D,
  1326S, 1327D, 1328P
  ch., 317; r., 712, *and see* Hungeford, John
  de
  vicarage, 712; v., 1307P, *and see*
  Hungerford, Stephen de;
  Longedon, William de
Uttoxhather, Adam de, monk of
  Dieulacres, 1290S
Uttoxhathre, Uttokeshather, Henry de,
  1322S, 1326P

V

Vacc', William, of Wales, preb. St. Chad's
  coll. ch., Shrewsbury, 1003
Vale Royal (de Valle Regali, Vall' Regal',
  Vall' Sancte Marie), Ches., Cist.
  abbey; abbot of, 1321S
  abbot and conv. of, 51, 160, 172, 201,
  476*, 496, 584, 585
  letter dated at, 767
  monks of, 1313D(3), 1323S, 1323D,
  1323P(2), 1324S(2), 1324D, *and see*
  Bosworth, John de; Peter; Roger;
  Valle Regali, Thomas de; Walter;
  William
Valeys, John de, 1287S, 1288D
  John le, 1300S, 1303D; *alias* John le
  Valeys, of Lichfield, 1304P
  Robert le [patron], 1303D; *alias* Robert
  le Valeys, v. Longdon, 1300S
Valk, Robert de, v. Grandborough, 137
Valle Regali, Thomas de, monk of Vale
  Royal, 1324S
Venables, Hugh de, kt., 194, 494, 849
  Roger de, 1300S, 1301D
  Roger de, r. Rostherne, 1211
Verdon, Robert de, kt., 1296D, 1296P,
  1298P(3), 1301S, 1303D, 1307P,
  1310S, 1313S, 1319P(3), 1324D,
  1326P(2); *alias* Sir Robert de
  Verdeyn, 1316S; *alias* Robert
  Verdoyn, 1316S; *alias* Robert le
  Verdon, kt., 1319S(2)

Wappenbur', Wappenbury, Wappinbur',
    Bartholomew de, 1301S
  John de, 1286A
  Ralph de, 1329S
  Richard de, 1286D, 1288P
  Thomas de [patron], 1307P
  William, 1286A, 1294S, 1298D, 1300P
Wappenbury (Wappenbur', Wappingbur',
    Wappingbury), Warw., 675
  ch., 673; custody of sequestration on to
    Robert de Halughton, 457
      r., 673, 1313S, 1314D, 1315P, *and see*
      Halughton, Robert de; Kirkeby,
      M. Henry de
  lord of, 1329S, *and see* Thomas
Wappynbur', John de, 1326S
Wappyngbury, Wappenbur', William de,
    1303S, 1307D
Warde, John de la, r. Newton Regis,
    1140
  Robert de la, kt., 255, 311; *alias* Robert
    le Warde, of Mackworth, 1296D
  Simon le, of 'Staunton', 1319P
  Sir William de la, 1301S, 1303D
  William de la, r. Austrey, 130; r.
    Hartshorne, 404; custody of fruits
    of sequestration on Kingsley ch.,
    404
  William, of 'Rothwell', 1319S
Ware, Herts., Ben. priory; prior of, 328,
    1268, *and see* Ralph; William
Ware, John la, kt., 973
  Peter de, r. St. Dunstan's, London, 947;
    v. Prees, 947, 981
  William de, 1300P
  William de. *See* Barre
Waresio, Tydo de, preb. Whittington and
    Berkswich, 705
Wareton, Walter de, 1328D
Warewyke, Henry de, 1299P
Wareyn, Waryn, Henry, of Mayfield,
    1316S, 1317D, 1319P
Warin, John s., 1326S; *alias* John le
    Wariner, of Hillmorton, 1328D
Warkenhamby, M. Hugh de, r.
    Carsington, 1049
Warle, Philip de, preb. St. Chad's,
    Shrewsbury, 939
Warleye, Warle, Ingelard de, granted
    Albrighton ch. *in commendam*, 505; r.
    Albrighton, 526; granted
    Mucklestone ch. *in commendam*, 529;
    r. Mucklestone, 544; preb. St.
    Chad's, Shrewsbury, 939

Warmeyte, Warmet, Warmete, Richard,
    1301S, 1303D, 1307P
Warmingham (Wermingham,
    Wermyngham), Ches., 1320P
  ch., 9, 28, 157, 170, 1202; r., 512, 837,
    847, 884, *and see* Havering, M. John
    de; Longespeye, Richard; Sitouns,
    Richard de; Trussel, Thomas
Warmington (Warmyncton, Warmynton,
    Wermynton), Warw., Ben. abbey,
    211
  abbot and conv. of, 635
  prior of, 499, 619, *and see*
    Canpyngnio, Nicholas de
  ch., 635; r., *see* Bokstanes, M. William
    de; Napton, M Ellis de
Warminton, John de, 1306P
Warmynton, Fr. Thomas de, 1286S
  John de, 1311S, 1312D, 1313P
  M. Richard de [patron], 1313P
  Philip de, 1301S, 1303D, 1306P
  Richard de, 1301S, 1303D, 1306P
  William de, 1289S
Warner, Adam le, 1301S
  Adam, of Long Itchington, 1301S; *alias*
    Adam le Warner, of Long
    Itchington, 1303D; *alias* Adam
    called le Warner, 1306P
  John le, of 'Morton', 1326S
Warr', Hugh de, 1296D
  John de, 1311S
Warre, John de la, kt., 505; *alias* John la
    Ware, kt., 876; *alias* John la Warr',
    kt., 1016
Warrington (Werington, Werinton,
    Wermington, Weryngton), Ches.,
    Aug. friary; friars of, 1286A,
    1286P, 1326S, *and see* Bovey,
    Geoffrey de; Brokebur', William
    de; Staunford, Ralph de
  dean of, 7, 153
  r., 48, *and see* William
Wartling and Hooe (Writlinggerhoo),
    Sussex, prebend, 1141; preb., *see*
    Stratford, M. John de
Warwick (Warr', Warwyk), Warw., Aug.
    priory of the Holy Sepulchre;
    canon of, 1318D, *and see* Coventr',
    John de
  prior of, 1303S, 1310S, 1312D, 1313D,
    1318D
  prior and brethren of, 1312S
  prior and conv. of, 1294D, 1318P
  religious of, 1307P

William (*cont.*)
    monk of Merevale, 1315S
    monk of Merevale, 1315D
    monk of Vale Royal, 1313D, 1323P
    prior of Ware, 1268
    r. Ilkeston, 1065
    r. Warrington, 48
    the clerk, 920
    v. Sawley, 1064
Willington (Wylyngton), Derb., 1301S
'Willoughby' (Wilughby, Wylugby), Notts.,
    1314S, 1315D, 1316P
Willoughby (Wyleby, Wylugby), Warw.,
    1298P
    vicarage, 597, 644; v., *see* Allespath,
        William s. Gerard de; Benet,
        Nicholas called; Trunket, Henry
        called, of Wolston
Willugby, Willughby, Wyloby, Wyluby,
    Wylugby, Hugh de, OP Derby,
    1285S, 1286D
    John de, 1285P
    Philip de, dean of Lincoln, 46, 222, 232,
        239–42, 251, 262, 263, 409; preb.
        Bubbenhall, 388, 477; preb. Ryton,
        398, 484
Wilmend, Adam de, 814
Wilmeslowe, Thomas de, 1326P
Wilmslow (Wylmeslowe), Ches., r.,
    1285P
Wilnecote (Wilmyndecote, Wylmondecote,
    Wylmundecote), Staffs., 1312D,
    1320S
    prebend in Tamworth coll. ch., 10, 278;
        preb., *see* Wykeford, Simon de
Wilsthorpe (Wilesthorp, Willesthorp,
    Wylesthorp, Wyllesthorp), Derb.,
    1312S(2), 1313P, 1316P(2)
Wilugby, William de [patron], 1315D
Winchcombe (Wynchecumb), Glos., Ben.
    abbey; abbot and conv. of, 1319D
Winchelsey, Robert, abp. of Canterbury,
    xxii, xxx, xxxii, xxxvi, 470*, 790;
    manor of, xxxii, *and see* Teynham
Winchester (Winton', Wynton'), Hants.,
    bp. of, 1252, *and see* Sandale,
    John
    dioc., 1252
    dim. of. *See* Index of Subjects
    see of, xxi
Windsor (Wyndesore), Berks., Appendix D
    letter dated at, 817
Wine, William de, r. Eyam, 1110
Wintringham, John de, 1285D

Winwick (Wynnequik, Wynquik), Lancs.,
    vicarage, 214, 215; v., *see*
    Bambourg', John de
'Winwick' (Wynewyk), Np., 1316P
Wippenbury, Hugh de, 1310S
Wirkesworth, William de, r. Slaidburn,
    1319P
Wirksworth (Wirkesworth in Pecco,
    Workeswode, Wyrkesworth),
    Derb., 555
    ch., 268, 1083
    land in, 68*
    vicarage, 572; v., 402, *and see* Bredbur',
        Robert de; Leicester, Miles de
Wirral (Wyrhal), Ches., dean of, 905
Wishaw (Wishawe, Wyshawe), Warw., ch.,
    148, 503, 626, 627; r., 1298S, *and
    see* Castello, Nicholas de; Laberton,
    William de
Wissant, France, Appendix D
Wisshaghe, John de, 1286A
Wisshawe, Thomas de, 1286D
Witham (Witeham), Som., Carthusian
    priory; prior of, 73*
Wiþer, Wyther, Walter [patron], 1310S,
    1312D, 1313P, 1327S
Withybrook (Wythebrok', Wythibrok',
    Wythybrok'), Warw., 1289S,
    1294D(2), 1295P, 1301S
    ch., 646; r., 406, *and see* Leone, William
        de; Tankard, M. Robert
    lady of, 1312D, 1313P, *and see* Alice
Wlston, William de, monk of Shrewsbury.
    See Aston, William
Wode, Henry del, of Ranton, 1313P
    Robert del, of Longdon, 1298S
Wode Eton, Fr. William de, 1319D; *alias*
    William de Wode Eton, monk of
    Combermere, 1320P
Wodecok', John, of Birmingham, 1321S,
    1322D, 1324P
    William, of Birmingham, 1311P
Wodecot', Thomas de, 1321S
Wodecote, William de, monk of
    Combermere, 1286S, 1289P
Wodecroft, Thomas de, canon of
    Newstead, 1286S
Wodeford, Benedict de, v. Frodsham,
    584
    Henry de, 1310S
    Henry de, 1318S, 1321D
Wodehall, Roger de [patron], 1298D,
    1327D; *alias* Roger del Wodehalle,
    1300P

Wolvey, Wolveye, Richard de, 1286A
    Thomas de [patron], 1300S; *alias* Sir
        Thomas, lord of Wolvey, 1303S;
        alias Sir Thomas de Wolvey, 1307P
    William de, 1315D, 1318P
Wolveya, Wolvey, Lady Alice de, 1320S,
    1324D, 1326P
    William de, 1320S, 1324D, 1326P
Wolveye, Wolvey, Geoffrey de, 1318S,
    1326P; *alias* Geoffrey de Wolseleye,
    1320D
    Ralph de, 1285P
    Thomas de, 1300S, 1301D, 1303P
    Thomas de, 1303S, 1307P
Wolvy, Richard de, 76
Wolwardinton, Roger de, v. Leamington
    Priors, 670
Womberegh, Wamberge, Richard de, r.
    Eccleston, 1212, 1228
Womborn, Wombourn, Simon de, v.
    Lichfield, 1313S, 1314D, 1315P
Wombourn (Wombourne, Womburn),
    Staffs., lord of, 1320P, *and see*
    Overton, Thomas de
    vicarage, 29, 281; v., 1285P, *and see*
    Bowode, Roger de
Wombridge (Wombrigg', Wombrug',
    Wombrugg'), Salop., Aug. priory;
    canons of, 810, 1286P, 1315S, *and*
    see Broughton, Thomas de;
    Gnousale, Richard de; Watford,
    Walter de
    prior of, 1300P, 1301D, 1303S, 1324S,
    1326S, 1327P, *and see* Melton,
    Richard de; Philip
    election of prior, 1155
    prior and conv. of, 810, 1300S, 1310S,
    1311P, 1320D
    religious of, 1306P
    visitation of, 810
Womburn', Wombourn, Wombourne,
    Richard de, 1311D, 1312P
    William de, 1311D, 1312P
Wonbourne, John de, v. Ellesmere, 575
Woodchurch (Wodechurch), Ches., ch.,
    906; r., 74, *and see* Tuwe, John de;
    Wetenhal, Adam de
Woodford Halse (Wodeford), Norf., ch.,
    1150; r., *see* Blaby, Richard de
Woodstock (Wodestok), Oxon., letters
    dated at, 247, 248, 447
Wootton (Wotton), Warw., vicarage, 677;
    v., *see* Boyvill', Roger de; Coleshull,
    Thomas de

Worcester (Wygorn'), Worcs., bp. of, 659
    dioc., 1017, 1140
    dim. of. *See* Index of Subjects
    prior of, issues dim. *sede vacante*,
    1318D(2), 1318P
    vicar-general of, 1295S
    St. Oswald's hosp., t. to for ordinand,
    1319S
Worfeld, Roger de, 1301P
Worfield (Werefeld, Worfeld), Staffs., ch.,
    706, 784, 1279
    custody of fruits and revenues of to M.
    Gilbert de Bruera, 1237
    granted *in commendam* to M. Ralph de
    Salop', 1279
    parish of, 1320P
    r., 710, 733, 745, 761, 1237, 1279, *and*
    see Benstede, John de; Boterwyk,
    Thomas de; Longavilla, Isumbert
    de; Thorp, M. Walter de
Woriegoot, Pagan, 1301P
Workesle, Ellis de, abbot of Whalley, 839*
Workesleye, Workesley, John de, 1303S,
    1307D, 1309P
Worksop (Wirsop, Wyrcsop, Wyrsop),
    Notts., Aug. priory; prior and conv.
    of, 234, 672, 1085, 1114
    letter dated at, 409
Wormleighton (Willmeleyhgton), Warw.,
    vicarage, 140
Worrey, Laurence. *See* Borrey
Worth, Alexander de, 1318P
    Robert s. Thomas de Worth [patron],
    1318P
Worthfeld, Wortfeld, Roger de, 1298S,
    1300D
    Stephen de, 1285P
Wottenhull, Richard de, 802
Wotton, Ellis de, 1316S, 1326D
    Robert de, 1319S; *alias* Robert de
    Woyton, 1323D
    Thomas de, monk of Stoneleigh, 1289D
    William de, 1286D
    William de, 1289S, 1289P
    William de, 1316S, 1326D
Woveye, Fr. Ankerus de, 1328D
Woxcestr', Wroxcestr', John de, 1310S,
    1312D
Wratting, Gilbert de, r. 'Newton', 1301S
Wroctesleg', Richard de, 1300S
Wrocworthyn, Walter s. John de, 1311S;
    alias Walter de Wrocwardyn,
    1314D; *alias* Walter de
    Wrokwardin, 1319P

Wytemor', Whitemor', Henry de, 1324S, 1326D
 William de, 1289S, 1294D, 1298P
Wytenasch, Richard de, 1316D
Wythebrok', Fr. Thomas de, 1286S
Wyther, Wythier, Richard, 1300S, 1301D, 1303P
Wytherdele, Thomas de, monk of Merevale, 1287S
 Thomas de, monk of Merevale, 1289S(2)
Wytheresleye, Richard, 1303P
Wythergeyn, Thomas [patron], 1316P
Wythibrok', Wythybrok', Adam de, 1310S, 1316D, 1318P
 Geoffrey de, of Coventry, 1289S; *alias* Geoffrey Ceret, of Withybrook, 1294D
 George de, 1301S, 1303P
 Oliver de, 1294S, 1301D, 1303P
 Osbert de, 1310S, 1312D, 1313P
 Richard de, 1312D, 1313P
 Roger de, 1309S
Wythybrok', Wythibrok', Gilbert de, 1301S, 1303D, 1305P
 Osbert de, 1326S
Wytinton, Whytinton, Peter de, 1311D, 1312P
Wytonstal, Richard de, 1313S
Wytteney, Roger de, 1301D, 1303P
Wyverstone (Wyvereston'), Suff., Henry, lord of, 1310S; *alias* Henry de Wyverston, 1311D; *alias* lord of Wyverstone, 1312P

Y

Yeaveley (Yeveleye), Derb., hosp. of St. John of Jerusalem [Knights Hospitallers]; master and brethren of, 1306S, 1307D
 t. to for ordinand, 1301S, 1303D
Yelgreve, Yelegreve, Richard de, 1286P
 William de, 1289D, 1294P
Yepe, Henry le, of Ashbourne, 1327S
Yepstones, John de, 1309A
Yerdele, Ingram de, presented to Birdingbury ch., 451; r. Birdingbury, 116
Yevelegh, Walter de, 1286D; *alias* Walter s. Jordan de Yevele, 1295P
Yeveley, Yevele, ƷeveleyeJohn de, 1309A, 1312S, 1313D, 1316P

Yire, Richard, of Melbourne, 1289S
Ylkyston, William de, 1321S; *alias* William de Iwiston, 1324D
Ymmer, Richard. *See* Immere
Ynge, Robert, 1301S
Yol, William s. Richard, of Birmingham, 1310S; *alias* William Yol, of Birmingham, 1312D; *alias* William Yool, of Birmingham, 1313P
Yolegreve, Yolgrave, John de, 1303S, 1311P
Yolretoft, Yolvertoft, William de, 1323S, 1324D
York (Ebor'), Yorks., 1315D, Appendix D
 abp. of, xvi, 472, 1035, *and see* Romeyn, John le; Rotherham, Thomas; Wickwane, William
 Bp. Langton at, 72, 77*
 licenced to ordain in ch. of Friars Minor, xxi
 dean and chapter of, 1294D, 1295D(4), 1316D
 dioc., xxi, 901*, 1242
 dim. of. *See* Index of Subjects
 letters dated at, 1–3, 5, 7–18, 30–2, 41, 44, 46–8, 50, 51, 53, 55, 56, 61–63*, 68*, 69*, 73*, 74, 82–4, 94, 97, 100, 102, 110, 111, 116, 133, 153, 154, 159, 160, 162, 171, 172, 223, 225, 226, 232, 239, 251, 256, 259, 278, 282, 293, 324, 326, 327, 332, 344, 361, 374, 378, 383–5, 392–4, 400–2, 413, 414, 439, 441, 442, 444, 451–3, 461, 479, 631–4, 657–60, 720–6, 728, 730, 736, 803*, 860–4, 887, 888, 951, 957, 972, 1046
 mayor of, 361
 papal administrators of Coventry and Lichfield dioc. at, xxxi, 251, 461
 treasurer of, 470*, *and see* Barroducis, Theobald de
Yorton, Richard de, 1316S, 1319P
Youlgreave (Ʒelgreve, Ʒolgrave, Yolegreve, Yolgreve), Derb., 1303S, 1307D, 1309P, 1310S, 1312D, 1313P
 vicarage, 554, 565; v., *see* Billesdon, William de; Lekebourne, Hugh de
Yoxale, Fr. Henry de, 1287D
Yoxhale, Yoxhal', Henry de, monk of Burton upon Trent, 1286S, 1287D, 1288P
 Hugh de, 1313S, 1318D; *alias* Hugh de Ʒoxhale, 1321P

INDEX OF SUBJECTS

1252, 1258, 1269, 1274, 1279, 1280, 1282
by abp. of Canterbury, 779
by lapse of time, 22, 156, 339, 533, 607, 648, 654, 689, 721, 830, 943
Collegiate churches in dioc. *See* Chester, St. John's; Derby, St. Alkmund's; Gnosall; Shrewsbury, St. Chad's; Shrewsbury, St. Mary's; Stafford, St. Mary's; Tamworth, St. Edith's; Tettenhall; Upholland; Wolverhampton
Commissary-general, xxviii–xxix, *and see* Blaston, M. Geoffrey de; Shirleye, M. Simon de
Common Bench, justices of, 177*
Compurgators, 362
Corn, 1154
Council, of Lyon (1274), 8n., 788*
of Oxford, 118n.
Third Lateran (1179), 22n., 389, 607, 648, 654, 721, 789*, 830, 943
Court, consistory, xxix, 935*
lay, 810
of Canterbury, 363, 1276
Criminous clerk, 362
Cum ex eo, 45, 49, 604*-6, 681, 776, 818, 909, 914, 986, 1002, 1004–7, 1021, 1092, 1096, 1119, 1129, 1137, 1147, 1153, 1158, 1159, 1161, 1165, 1166, 1180–2, 1185, 1197, 1198, 1203, 1209, 1210, 1213, 1215, 1220, 1224, 1230, 1234, 1236, 1243, 1259, 1263, 1272, 1277, 1283
Curia, papal, Appendix D
auditor at, 987
bp.'s loan at, 789*
faculty to travel to, 66
licences to travel to, 402, 414, 861, 1036
Curtilage, tithes of, 1154

D

Deans, rural, 7, 36, 75, 153, 459, 515, 668, 669, 671, 719, 1045, 1240, 1264
Debt, of rector, 369
Deprivation of rector, 987
Drink, 809*, 815*, 950
Dues, marriage, 602
mortuary, 602

E

Election, of bp., xxxii
of heads of religious houses, 519*, 622*, 693–5, 816, 1155
Excesses of parishioners, 799
Exchange of benefices, 726, 947, 1134, 1141, 1142, 1144, 1146, 1151, 1205, 1217, 1219, 1231, 1239, 1252, 1264, 1269, 1274, 1278, 1280
Exchequer, 813, 814, 840*, Appendix D
barons of, 177*
Excommunication, absolution from, 470*, 935*
threatened, 708*, 789*, 809*, 810, 987

F

Farm of church, 75
licenced, 520, 700, 716, 844, 872, 931, 1039, 1157
Final concord, 80
Food, 809*–11, 815*, 950
Forest, 809*
Friaries in dioc.:
Augustinian. *See* Shrewsbury; Warrington
Dominican. *See* Derby; Newcastle under Lyme; Shrewsbury; Warwick
Franciscan. *See* Chester; Coventry; Stafford
Friars:
Augustinian (OSA). *See* Bovey, Geoffrey de; Bradeford, John de; Brokebur', William de; Rompton, Thomas de; Schipton, John de; Staunford, Ralph de; Staunton, Nicholas de; Stodeleye, Walter de; Wodestok', William de; Wynton', William de
Carmelite (OCarm.). *See* Hoton, Thomas de; Stone, John de
Dominican (OP). *See* Bedewas, Madoc de; Buterbon, Richard de; Cestr', William de; Castro, Robert de; Chedle, Richard de; Com, David de; Curcoun, William; Deping, Thomas de; Derb', Henry de; Eginton, Ralph de; Gerard, Henry; Hales, John de; Harald, Richard; John; Joorum, Roland; Leycestr', John de; Lodbrok', Richard de; Lodelowe, William de; Louseby, Roger de; Mether, Griffin de;

Procurations, 1154, 1170*, 1171
Profession, of abbot, 777, 839*
  of prior, 439, 816
Provisions, episcopal, 667, 1027, 1028, 1238
  papal, 69*, 470*, 688, 726*, 1282
  royal, 790
Purgation, of criminous clerk, 362

Q

Quitclaim, 1292

R

Religious houses of dioc.:
  Augustinian. *See* Arbury; Baswich by
      Stafford; Breadsall; Brewood White
      Ladies; Burscough; Calwich;
      Church Gresley; Dale; Darley;
      Haughmond; Kenilworth;
      Lilleshall; Norton; Ranton; Repton;
      Rocester; Stone; Trentham;
      Warwick; Wombridge
  Benedictine. *See* Alcester; Alvecote;
      Birkenhead; Brewood Black Ladies;
      Burton upon Trent; Canwell;
      Chester, St. Werburgh's; Coventry;
      Derby, King's Mead by; Farewell;
      Henwood; Hilbre Island;
      Lancaster; Lapley; Monks Kirby;
      Nuneaton; Polesworth; Sandwell;
      Shrewsbury, St. Peter's; Tutbury;
      Warmington; Wolston
  Cistercian. *See* Buildwas; Combe;
      Combermere; Croxden;
      Dieulacres; Hulton; Merevale;
      Stoneleigh; Vale Royal; Whalley
  Cluniac. *See* Much Wenlock
  Premonstratensian. *See* Beauchief
  Resignations of benefices, 194, 195, 264,
      273, 306, 356, 367, 379, 483, 560,
      565, 594, 610, 616, 618, 619, 622*,
      637, 642, 647, 652, 662, 669, 671,
      680, 687, 696, 702–4, 706, 713,
      716, 722, 746, 758, 764, 769, 771,
      778, 820, 828, 836, 856–8, 870,
      879, 887, 889, 890, 895, 991, 939,
      940, 941, 947, 964, 965, 975, 983,
      995, 997, 1001, 1012, 1013, 1015,
      1016, 1018, 1041, 1044, 1047,
      1052, 1060, 1066, 1067, 1069,
      1070, 1071, 1077, 1079, 1080,

1085, 1087, 1089, 1090, 1097,
  1104, 1109, 1114, 1128, 1131,
  1134, 1135, 1138, 1148, 1156,
  1164, 1167, 1176, 1183, 1186,
  1194, 1199, 1202, 1205, 1208,
  1216–19, 1223, 1228, 1231, 1233,
  1239, 1240, 1252, 1256, 1262,
  1269, 1271, 1274, 1278, 1280
  because of infirmity, 64
Retirement, of abbot, 519*, 815*, 950, *and
  see* Darley Abbey, Haughmond
      Abbey, Lilleshall Abbey
Ring, of bp., 689, 741, 756
Rural deans, xxvi–xxvii, 515, 719*

S

Sequestrations, of benefices, 9, 13, 15, 44,
  52, 53, 55, 57, 81, 84, 208, 297,
  298, 399, 400, 401, 404, 405, 409,
  413, 415, 418–20, 433, 437, 441,
  444, 447, 450, 451–3, 456–9, 463,
  523, 524, 528, 555, 577, 603, 614,
  615, 626, 634, 641, 645, 668, 709,
  714, 750, 826, 835, 842, 866, 873,
  875, 893, 896, 897, 922, 932, 955,
  958, 963, 970, 972, 974, 1034,
  1055, 1056, 1229, 1237
  of money, 1237
  relaxed, 268, 422
  revenues from, 86
Sequestrator-general, xxix, *and see* Dolaby,
      Richard de; Northampton, M.
      Richard de; Pupard, M. John;
      Swepston, M. William de
Sheaves, tithes of, 1154, 1171
Surgery, 809*
Synodalia, 1154

T

Taxation of clergy, papal, 840*
Tenants, 602, 813, 814
Tithes, 75, 218, 275, 476*, 509, 602, 1154,
      1171

V

Vestments, 476*
Vicarages, ordination of, 476*, 1154,
      1171, 1245, 1284

CORRIGENDA

Volume I

2, 46 (pp. 1, 7): *for* Thorp *read* Thorpe
217 (p. 28): *for* Bishop Nonant *read* Bishop William Cornhill
205 (p. 27): *for* Ashton *read* Ashton on Mersey
299, 716 (pp. 37, 90): *for* Water Eaton *read* Church Eaton
318 (p. 39): *for* Mucclestone *read* Mucklestone
328, 1268 (pp. 40, 172): *for* Saint-Evroul *read* Saint-Evroult-d'Ouche
400 (p. 48): *for* Biddulf *read* Biddulph
543 (p. 66): *for* abbot *read* prior
602 (pp. 72, 73): *for* Pulton *read* Poulton
613 (p. 75): *for* Henley *read* Henley in Arden
679 (p. 85): *for* Nonham *read* Nouham
701 (p. 88): *for* Bowden *read* Bowdon
766, 982 (pp. 98, 135): *for* Stanford *read* Stamford
808 (p. 106): *for* Bishopstone *read* Bishton
863, 1208 (pp. 119, 165): *for* Walton *read* Walton on the Hill
879 (p. 121): *for* Chyn *read* Chyu
880 (p. 121): *for* Wynbunbury *read* Wybunbury
966 (p. 965): *insert* church *after* (Ithtefeld)
1001 (p. 138): *for* Upton *read* Upton Waters
1090, 1113 (pp. 149, 152): *for* Stretton *read* Stretton en le Field
1105 (p. 151): *for* Baugnell *read* Bauquell
1108 (p. 151): *for* Eckington *read* Egginton
1126 (p. 153): *for* Shelden *read* Sheldon
1145 (p. 155): *for* Olenesel *read* Clenefel'
1191 (p. 163): *for* William de Osgodeby *read* Adam de Osgodeby. *Disregard* n. 4
1260, 1263 (p. 171): *for* Draycott *read* Draycott in the Moors
1261 (p. 171): *for* Stoke *read* Stoke upon Trent
1279 (p. 173): *for* Walton upon Trent *read* Walton on the Hill